Thomas Knieps-Port le Roi (Ed.)

A Point of No Return?

INTAMS Studies on Marriage and Family /
INTAMS-Studien zu Ehe und Familie

edited by / herausgegeben von

Thomas Knieps-Port le Roi
(KU Leuven)

Philippe Bordeyne
(Institut Catholique de Paris)

Jochen Sautermeister
(Universität Bonn)

Clare Watkins
(University of Roehampton)

Volume / Band 2

LIT

A Point of No Return?

Amoris Laetitia
on Marriage, Divorce and Remarriage

edited by

Thomas Knieps-Port le Roi

LIT

Cover illustration: Paul Harrington, *Minds Eye*
© Paul Harrington, www.paulharringtonart.com

This book is printed on acid-free paper.

Bibliografische Information der Deutschen Nationalbibliothek
Die Deutsche Nationalbibliothek verzeichnet diese Publikation in der Deutschen Nationalbibliografie; detaillierte bibliografische Daten sind im Internet über http://dnb.d-nb.de abrufbar.

ISBN 978-3-643-90925-1 (pb.)
ISBN 978-3-643-95925-6 (PDF)

Verlagskontakt:
Fresnostr. 2 D-48159 Münster
Tel. +49 (0) 2 51-62 03 20
E-Mail: lit@lit-verlag.de http://www.lit-verlag.de

Auslieferung:
Deutschland: LIT Verlag, Fresnostr. 2, D-48159 Münster
Tel. +49 (0) 2 51-620 32 22, E-Mail: vertrieb@lit-verlag.de

E-Books sind erhältlich unter www.litwebshop.de

Table of Contents

II. *AMORIS LAETITIA* – PERSPECTIVES ON AND FOR DIVORCED AND REMARRIED PERSONS

III. PASTORAL MINISTRY TO THE DIVORCED AND REMARRIED AFTER *AMORIS LAETITIA* – VOICES FROM THE PRACTICE

Introduction

Questions of personal life choices with regard to partnership and family continue to have high importance for most of our contemporaries. At the same time, however, decisions and positions in these domains have become highly contested issues. Does it make any difference whether you cohabit or get married? Are same-sex partnerships totally equivalent to the union between a man and a woman? Should divorce be an easy way out of a marriage in which love has faded away? Are all forms of family life equal if only appropriate care is taken for those who are a part of it? Has sexual difference any role to play in parenting? Or should gay or lesbian couples readily be granted the right to become parents via adoption and artificial reproduction?

Whether in private life or in public discussion, these and similar questions are not easy to answer. Only prevailing cultural trends and conservative strands which go against them seem to have ready-made answers available: while the first consequently opt for non-discrimination and maximizing individual freedom, the latter see in the present transformation of sexual and relational life an undue infringement upon the natural or God-given order and thus upon the foundations of human society. The case of the proposed legislation in France in 2012 to open up marriage to everybody (*Mariage pour tous*), and the fierce and still ongoing opposition to it expressed by many civil associations organized in the so-called *Manif pour tous*, is a good illustration of the polarization which our late-modern western societies are facing when it comes to issues of close relationships and their institutional framing.

The Christian churches are not ranged on one side of this divide in the public sphere. Instead, the polarization cuts right across their churches, splitting leaders and faithful alike. Fuelled by theological arguments, the controversy may at first sight lay bare legitimate tensions characteristic for any group of believers who, along with their non-believing neighbours, have to make personal and institutional choices amidst highly complex living conditions. However, one may wonder whether genuine differences of opinion are now increasingly making room for a fundamental controversy about how Christians should situate themselves vis-à-vis a secularized world that values autonomy of decision and a plurality of life choices above anything else.

The synodal process which Pope Francis inaugurated in 2013 and which has come to a provisional conclusion with the publication of the Post-Synodal Exhortation *Amoris laetitia* has revealed a Roman Catholic Church which seems seriously divided over questions of marriage and family life. The tensions are not new – they have continuously been smouldering under the surface ever since the Second Vatican Council initiated a major shift in the church's theological understanding of marriage and family and have erupted every time that post-conciliar magisterial teaching seemed to call into question the Council's new approach. The controversy flared up during the two recent Bishops' Synods and, thanks to a broad media coverage which both sides have astutely used for their purposes, has brought to full light the split between the two camps. What is new in the present situation, however, is that the dividing line is no longer between the pope and the bishops on the one side and a large portion of the faithful and the theological academia on the other side. The bishops themselves are divided, as became clear even before the synod started when the German Cardinal Walter Kasper suggested a penitential path for divorced and remarried Catholics, who after careful discernment of their respective situation should be readmitted to the sacraments of Reconciliation and Eucharist[1] – and was sharply criticized for that proposal by some influential colleagues.[2] The divide has continued after the publication of *Amoris laetitia* with individual bishops trying to cement the traditional non-admittance of remarried divorcees to the sacraments[3] while the mainstream of local bishops and bishops' conferences seeming to cautiously welcome a pastoral opening in this field.[4] More importantly, however, the pope himself has become the target of harsh criticism from the side of bishops, theologians, and faithful who fear that some of the positions adopted in the exhortation "pose a grave danger to the faith and morals of Catholics".[5]

---

1 See W. CARD. KASPER: *The Gospel of the Family*, Mahwah, NJ: Paulist Press, 2014.

2 See R. DODARO (ed.): *Remaining in the Truth of Christ: Marriage and Communion in the Catholic Church*, San Francisco: Ignatius Press, 2014.

3 See e.g. the "Pastoral Guidelines for Implementing *Amoris Laetitia*" in the Archdiocese of Philadelphia, issued on July 1, 2016; available from http://archphila.org/wp-content/uploads/2016/06/AOP_AL-guidelines.pdf; accessed 17.03.2017.

4 See e.g. the document published by the bishops of Malta: "Criteria for the Application of Chapter VIII of *Amoris laetitia*" in January 2017, available from http://ms.maltadiocese.org/WEBSITE/2017/PRESS%20RELEASES/Norms%20for%20the%20Application%20of%20Chapter%20VIII%20of%20AL.pdf; accessed 02.02.2017; and the Declaration of the German Bishops's Conference: "'Die Freude der Liebe, die in den Familien gelebt wird, ist auch die Freude der Kirche': Einladung zu einer erneuerten Ehe- und Familienpastoral im Licht von *Amoris laetitia*", February 2017, available from http://www.dbk.de/fileadmin/redaktion/diverse_downloads/presse_2017/2017-015a-Wortlaut-Wort-der-Bischoefe-Amoris-laetitia.pdf; accessed 17.03.2017.

5 See the critical analysis of *Amoris laetitia* by 45 theologians addressed to the College of Cardinals in June 2016, http://sspx.org/en/news-events/news/45-theologians-criticize-amoris-laetitia-17347; accessed 17.03.2017.

In the eyes of many, what has happened is that the pope and those bishops who support him have changed sides. While previously conservative positions could blindly rely on the backing from the hierarchy, they now seem to have fallen out of favor. Conversely, those who in the past felt repudiated and even silenced by Rome get the impression that after long years of vain efforts the pope has finally rehabilitated them. The majority of speakers and participants at the International Symposium on *Amoris laetitia*, organized by INTAMS from 25-27 October 2016 at the Faculty of Theology and Religious Studies of the Catholic University of Leuven, were undoubtedly to be ranged in the second category and believed that the "winds of change" were now blowing in their favor. The title chosen for the conference, "A Point of No Return? *Amoris Laetitia* on Discernment and Conscience for Divorced and Remarried Couples", seemed for many of them a rhetorical question to which they responded in the affirmative, thus urging that the fortuitous moment should be seized and pinned down before the clock could be turned back again. It became clear, however, that there were also those present who honestly feared that Pope Francis would forsake traditional church teaching on marriage, and that they were now the defeated party in this lingering debate. It was legitimate and good that they could make their voice heard, too, and articulate their concerns at a conference in which they remained in a minority position (which is also reflected in the collection of contributions in these conference proceedings). What they in particular had to learn from the conference was a double insight. First, that there is no escape from recognizing and accepting that Pope Francis had definitively answered a question which seemed still open in the first months after the publication of the exhortation. In his letter to the bishops of the Buenos Aires pastoral region in September 2016, he unambiguously confirmed that in particular cases, and after a process of careful discernment, the church now officially grants the possibility to divorced and remarried Catholic to have access to the sacraments of Reconciliation and Eucharist.[6] Everyone attending the conference had to realize that this was indeed a "point of no return" – whether one liked it or not! It will from now on become part of what future generations will call the "approved practice of the church".

Secondly, it was often heard that *Amoris laetitia* does not change doctrine but simply calls for a better pastoral care on the basis of that doctrine. The conference made clear that this is an overly scrupulous way of presenting things and is, in the end, not true. The pope's call for a renewed practice of pastoral and personal discernment does not, of course, abolish the church's teaching on the indissolubility of marriage, but it will necessarily have an impact on and ultimately

---

6 See https://cruxnow.com/global-church/2016/09/18/guidelines-buenos-aires-bishops-divorce dremarried/; accessed 17.03.2017.

modify Catholic understanding of that doctrine. It might therefore be more true to say that *Amoris laetitia* is less concerned about content than about procedure and methodology. Not so much *what* we pronounce as Christian doctrine on marriage and family but rather *how* we pronounce it is what preoccupies the pope. This is perfectly in tune with the Second Vatican Council's understanding of revelation to which human beings do not adequately respond by pronouncing propositional truths but only by accepting God's invitation to enter into a personal relationship with Him (see *Dei verbum*, 1). It implies that Christians risk offending God much more by distorted ways of talking about and to Him than by being mistaken in what they say about Him. Having reminded Catholics of this, Pope Francis's appeal goes much further than merely calling them to adapt their pastoral attitudes.

It is here also that Francis has a pertinent message for all of us, whether we agree or disagree with *Amoris laetitia*. And one hopes that the following three rules which the exhortation has *in petto* for our ways of expressing our belief, of doing theology, and of shaping pastoral practice will ultimately provide a new common basis across the current ideological split in the Catholic Church.

1. *Amoris laetitia* echoes the Synod Fathers' warning against an "extreme individualism" (AL 33) and cautions against what it calls a "culture of the ephemeral" which also affects today's relationships: "everything is disposable; everyone uses and throws away, takes and breaks, exploits and squeezes to the last drop. Then, goodbye" (AL 39). However, Francis clearly distances himself from the cultural pessimism that has been so characteristic of previous church teaching: "... there is no sense in simply decrying present-day evils, as if this could change things" (AL 35); and calls for a "healthy dose of self-criticism" (AL 36) within the church: "we have often been on the defensive, wasting pastoral energy on denouncing a decadent world without being proactive in proposing ways of finding true happiness" (AL 38). The pope invites us to leave behind the mentality of self-defense and lamentation in which the church has trapped itself, and to face the challenges as they occur. This approach is not less demanding nor does it give in to contemporary sensibilities or fashions. Rather, it calls for "new forms of missionary creativity" (AL 57), requiring an attitude of humbleness, generosity, and care which does not find itself too good to engage with the world, even if the latter does not seem to show much interest in the Christian message. No anxious and self-defensive mentality! – that is a first rule which should be taken seriously across diverging theological camps.

2. A second rule is: Do not reduce complexity! We had to learn again in recent times how demagogues of different colours succeeded in seducing people by offering one-size-fits-all solutions for complex problems. *Amoris laetitia* has a very clear message for those in church and theology who tend to simply apply a moral law to all situations, "as if they were stones to throw at people's lives" (AL

305): "We know that no 'easy recipes' exist" (AL 298), writes Francis, when it comes to dealing with the situation of divorced and remarried persons. In fact, the whole exhortation can be read as an "apology of complexity". It talks about the "complexity of the issues that arose" during the bishops' synods (AL 2); dedicates the whole second chapter to "the reality of the family today in all its complexity, with both its lights and shadows" (AL 32); points out that the synods have shown that "there is no stereotype of the ideal family, but rather a challenging mosaic made up of many different realities, with all their joys, hopes, and problems" (AL 57); redefines what previous church teaching had called "irregular situations" as "complex situations" (see AL 247-252); and insists on the pastoral principle of discernment in order "to avoid judgements which do not take into account the complexity of various situations" (AL 296). Do not reduce but face and discern complexity! – this is the pope's clear admonition for all those doing theology and pastoral work. Then, he promises, "our lives become wonderfully complicated" (AL 308).

3. A third rule that can be found in *Amoris laetitia* is: Do not obstruct the working of God's grace! Pope Francis reminds us that theologians and ministers may succumb to the temptation to set themselves up as guardians of a doctrinal or moral truth and thus to put themselves in the place where not they but God should be given room. We would probably all agree that it would be much better "to present marriage more as a dynamic path to personal development and fulfilment than as a lifelong burden" (AL 37). Why then would we wish to load people up with excessive and unrealistic demands which they will probably never comply with, instead of inviting them to a path that promises personal development and fulfilment? The pope writes: "Marital love is not defended primarily by presenting indissolubility as a duty, or by repeating doctrine, but by helping it to grow ever stronger under the impulse of grace" (AL 134). Trusting that God's grace may be at work everywhere frees us from the neurotic compulsion to play God ourselves. Instead of "arbiters of grace", theologians and ministers should regard themselves as "facilitators of grace" because "the Church is not a tollhouse; it is the house of the Father, where there is a place for everyone, with all their problems" (*Evangelii gaudium*, 47).

This volume contains the contributions, both keynote lectures and papers, delivered by senior and junior researchers and practitioners from the pastoral field at the International Symposium which was held from 25-27 October 2016 at the Faculty of Theology and Religious Studies of the Catholic University of Leuven, Belgium, under the title: "A Point of No Return? *Amoris Laetitia* on Discernment and Conscience for Divorced and Remarried Couples". The first part gathers articles that situate *Amoris laetitia* in a broader theological, ethical, and pastoral perspective. The Archbishop of Munich and President of the German Bishops'

Conference, *Cardinal Reinhard Marx* reviews the synodal process and welcomes *Amoris laetitia* as a document that revitalizes fundamental Catholic convictions but at the same time calls for a considerable reorientation in the pastoral work of the Catholic Church, both on the level of personal competences of the pastors and at the organizational level. For *George S. Worgul* the principles of synodality, dialogue, and decentralization endemic to the vision of *Amoris laetitia* reveal Pope Francis's inculturated theological approach, which is aware of and resists all forms of intellectual colonialism and provides a practical response to living in an era in which diversity and plurality are normative rather than exceptional. According to *Todd A. Salzman* and *Michael G. Lawler*, *Amoris laetitia* has reinstated the importance of three central elements in Catholic ethics: the role of an informed conscience in moral decision making of any sort, the gradualness of moral life, and the emphasis on the virtues of love, mercy, and non-judgment of other people and their situations. *Branislav Kuljovsky* also analyzes the ethical underpinnings of Pope Francis's pastoral proposal for people living in irregular situations and arrives at a different conclusion: he argues that the exhortation's elaboration of the "law of gradualness" ends up in endorsing the "gradualness of law" and thus finds itself in opposition to fundamental principles of Catholic moral teaching. *Timothy Radcliffe* asks how the church can "make room for the consciences of the faithful" and concludes that she can and should do so by raising individuals who live by a double rhythm, folding one inwards into the core of one's being, and propelling one outwards into the community of Christ's body. *Nadia Delicata* traces in *Amoris laetitia* a robust theology of sin in which the personal God-human relationship, rather than the description of individual acts, is central, and suggests reading the exhortation through the lens of a universal, and simultaneously deeply personal, human experience of sinfulness to which God responds with infinite mercy. *Peter Hünermann*'s lens is that of a dogmatic theologian who presents a meticulous reading of chapters 3 and 8 of *Amoris laetitia* against the backdrop of the church's tradition and shows that the exhortation does not only provide for the first time a holistic theological understanding of marriage but also corrects erroneous positions held in previous church teaching. Referring to a characteristic feature of intimate relationships today, i.e. the excessively high expectations that partners have toward each other, *Stephanie Höllinger* shows that *Amoris laetitia* not only shows a great awareness of the complexity of contemporary married life but also taps into the Christian tradition to critically discern its negative effects and offer helpful guidance.

The second part of this volume focuses more specifically on the issue of divorced and remarried spouses and explores what *Amoris laetitia* has to offer to them. *Martin M. Lintner* argues that offering divorced and remarried persons the help of the sacraments of Reconciliation and the Eucharist is not so much a case of pastoral leniency but rather a real requirement of mercy that belongs to the very core of the Gospel and, therefore, of the doctrine of the church. Asking what *Amoris laetitia* has to say about divorce and remarriage from a practical-theological perspective, *Arnaud Join-Lambert* observes that Pope Francis accords pastoral priority to the children of divorce which, he suggests, is one way of getting beyond the traditional articulation of the relation between the doctrinal and the pastoral so typical of the exhortation. According to *Paul Galea*, *Amoris laetitia*, with its strong emphasis on acknowledging and accompanying fragility, brings about a paradigm shift in the pastoral care of the divorced and remarried, away from the external forum and the confessional toward a pastoral counselling model that encourages personal discernment, autonomy, and responsibility and thus helps to develop problem-solving skills. *Christine Galea* explores the tension in the church's care for the remarried divorcees between insisting on the value of personal commitment and of indissoluble marriage on the one side and on accommodating human frailty on the other and concludes that *Amoris laetitia* finds a way in between truth and pastoral care. Recalling the canonical principle that the pastoral care of each and every one of the faithful is the supreme law in the church, *Vincent Mynem C. Sagandoy* argues that, with *Amoris laetitia*, perhaps the church is being led to a point where Catholics in irregular marriages are no longer an issue but an opportunity for the church to show that there is room for God's mercy to dwell in the hearts of every person. *Michaela C. Hastetter* compares the theological and pastoral approaches to the divorced and remarried in the three main Christian denominations and suggests that in *Amoris laetitia* a new supra-confessional synthesis may be emerging, embracing classical Protestant, Orthodox, and Catholic positions. *Corinne Bernhard-Bitaud* and *Thomas Knieps-Port le Roi* welcome the exceptional, yet regular, admission to communion of the divorced and remarried made possible by *Amoris laetitia*, but wonder whether a similar solution could not be offered to spouses and their families who live in interchurch families and are longing for Eucharistic sharing.

In the third and final part of this volume practitioners and responsible persons in marriage and family ministry from various European countries provide insights on how *Amoris laetitia* has been received by the official churches, whether or not it marks a break with previous pastoral practice, and what implications it might have in the future, particularly in pastoral care for divorced and remarried persons. *Elizabeth Davies* reports from England and Wales, *Monique Baujard* highlights the situation in France, *Hilde Pex* reviews the pastoral care of the divorced and remarried in the Flemish dioceses of Belgium, *Franz Harant* presents new pastoral paths in the diocese of Linz in Austria, and *Teresa Ventimiglia* and *Giordano Barioni* report about experiences of accompanying the divorced and remarried in Italy.

I would like to thank all those who have contributed to making this publication possible: INTAMS, with its Director Aldegonde Brenninkmeijer-Werhahn for her constant inspiration and manifold support; all the authors who have provided papers of excellent quality; Hans Storme for editing all articles; Dominique van Haelst who coordinated contact with the authors; the co-editors of the series *INTAMS Studies on Marriage and Family/INTAMS-Studien zu Ehe und Familie* for having agreed to include these conference proceedings in the series; and Michael J. Rainer from LIT Verlag for his willingness to publish this volume as the second one in the INTAMS series.

Thomas Knieps-Port le Roi

Part I

AMORIS LAETITIA – THEOLOGICAL, ETHICAL AND PASTORAL PERSPECTIVES

Reflections on the Synod Process and *Amoris Laetitia*

Reinhard Cardinal Marx

"We hope that the result of this work, now delivered into the hands of the Successor of Peter, might give hope and joy to many families in the world, guidance to pastors and pastoral workers, and a stimulus to the work of evangelization." These words appear at the end of the *Relatio Synodi* of the XIV Ordinary General Assembly of the Synod of Bishops in 2015 (no. 94).

The Synodal Journey

The synodal journey on which the church embarked in 2014 and 2015 "*cum Petro et sub Petro*" was a fascinating, encouraging occurrence in many ways. The very fact that believers in the local churches were integrated into the preliminary considerations to the synods through worldwide surveys was a courageous step towards a new communication within the church which dares to deal openly with the diversity of voices within the one church. The Synod Fathers themselves also contributed highly-diverging cultural backgrounds and brought in circumstances from the local churches. To this end, Pope Francis coined the image of "a multifaceted gem reflecting many legitimate concerns and honest questions" (AL 4). As was to be expected, contrary positions were put forward. There was an open, honest debate, but there were also always the guarantors of unity which made this journey possible at all: The joint concern of strengthening marriage and the family on the basis of the Christian faith, the efforts to bring about the inner and outer unity of the church, and not lastly of course the personality of the Pope himself. Francis stressed from the outset that he would bring the threads together and integrate the discussions, which may also run contrarily, into his service to unity, and thus bind diversity to unity.

Pope Francis fulfilled this pronouncement with the Post-Synodal Apostolic Exhortation *Amoris laetitia*. Its composition relies in considerable breadth both on the tradition of the church, as well as on the considerations of the synod. And it links this with the in some cases highly-personal reflections, thoughts, pieces of advice and references on unity by Pope Francis himself. This renders *Amoris laetitia*, as a doctrinal exhortation, at the same time an able and also a particularly skilful synthesis. It is a particularly sympathetic aspect of this Exhortation that the Pope does not at all enter the realm of changing the church's dogma or needing to formulate new principles. Instead, he puts it in a nutshell: It is about the love which is proclaimed in the Gospel, the love which is to be lived in marriage and in the family – every day anew and a whole life long. "For we cannot encourage a path of fidelity and mutual self-giving", says Pope Francis, "without encouraging the growth, strengthening and deepening of conjugal and family love." (AL 89) Where there is love, there is also God, and He calls on people to exercise such active love – regardless of the situation in which they find themselves. In all the discussions regarding the significance and the message of *Amoris laetitia*, it must therefore not be forgotten that it is the meaning of love and the stimulus to love which Pope Francis himself regards as constituting the indispensable core message of his Post-Synodal Exhortation. Particularly as a result of the considerations, references and pieces of advice regarding the realisation of love in the everyday lives of married couples and families, *Amoris laetitia* takes on a very personal, accessible note, whilst at the same time making something real of each ethos of accompanying, discerning and integrating for which Pope Francis calls in the same exhortation. It is in the significance of love for people's lives that *Amoris laetitia* has its inner core, and the conceptual threads extend from this starting point. Many things are rediscovered from this new, old perspective.

Accompanying, Discerning, Integrating

The first place is taken here by the significance of the individual life story which each person brings along. An abstract theology, and especially standardised pastoral work, which do not take account of the biographical context in which they are situated, becomes irrelevant. Pope Francis says: "This effort calls for missionary conversion by everyone in the Church, that is, one that is not content to proclaim a merely theoretical message without connection to people's real problems." Pastoral care for families "needs to make it clear that the Gospel of the family responds to the deepest expectations of the human person" (AL 201). Each individual is to be able to discover for themselves how God accompanies him on his own path through life, constantly "summoning him to love good and avoid evil, the voice of conscience when necessary speaks to his heart: do this, shun that" (*Gaudium et spes*, 16).

Against the background of this insight, *Amoris laetitia* develops the triad of "accompanying, discerning, integrating" (AL 8). This triad is the *cantus firmus* of pastoral work which wishes to really reach people and to open up to them the journey which God Himself takes with them in their life story. In *accompanying*, pastoral work must be a process of going along on a person's path through life. This can take place at individual times, over short or long sections of this journey. However, the biography must always be considered in order to understand the journey. *Discernment* is a particular concern for Pope Francis, as he stressed in his most recent letter to the bishops of the Buenos Aires Pastoral Region.[1] It particularly relates to the individuality of the biographies and of the biographical situations in which people find themselves. There is a need here to take a precise look and to distinguish between the intentions, abilities and acts of will, as well as the characterisations, constraints and needs of the respective individual, instead of reaching global judgments. Each person should be perceived and accepted in terms of their individuality as far as possible. Finally, *integration* means the openness of the church and of her pastoral care. She is to invite people, and where allowed by the respective situation and by the will of the respective individual, to permit them to be taken into God's pilgrim people, which itself is on the move.

This idea of action on the part of the church is not new, but is in fact the revitalisation of an original Catholic fundamental conviction. This is shown not lastly in the references to some important lessons of the Catholic dogmatic tradition, such as in particular the teaching of conscience and the doctrine of the need to adapt all norms to the reality of action. I would like to briefly explain these two central aspects.

Conscience

Pope Francis states: "Recognizing the influence of such concrete factors, we can add that individual conscience needs to be better incorporated into the Church's praxis in certain situations which do not objectively embody our understanding of marriage." (AL 303) There is not sufficient space here to explain the entire teaching of the church regarding conscience, which has been an explicit part of the canon of the dogma of the Christian faith at the latest since the Letter of the Apostle Paul to the Romans (Rom 2,12-16). Let me merely point out that the Second Vatican Council already gave a prominent place to the significance of conscience in *Gaudium et spes*: "Conscience is the most secret core and sanctuary of a man. There he is alone with God, Whose voice echoes in his depths." (GS 16) Therefore, the conscience of the individual should be adhered to just as they should be called and taught to be true to their conscience and to give it space in their

[1] Cf. *Letter of Pope Francis to Mons. Sergio Alfredo Fenoy, Delegate of the Bunos Aires Pastoral Region,* 5 September 2016, available from https://www.lifesitenews.com/images/pdfs/Letter_of_pope_to_Pastoral_Region_of_Buenos_Aires__September_5__2016.pdf; accessed 07.02.2017.

own lives. This is what we understand by the term formation of conscience. This also and particularly takes place when the individual who takes the teachings of the church seriously addresses them and endeavours to integrate this teaching into their own lives. The unmistakable appeal of Pope Francis: "We have been called to form consciences, not to replace them" (AL 37), is addressed to pastoral care. The statements contained in *Amoris laetitia* are, incidentally, to be understood completely in terms of this line of thought, which refer to the teachings on contraception in Pope Paul VI's encyclical *Humanae vitae*. Referring to *Gaudium et spes*, Pope Francis stresses parental responsibility for the number and time of children, and states: "Moreover, the use of methods based on the 'laws of nature and the incidence of fertility' are to be promoted." (AL 222) It would hardly be possible to underline even more explicitly the concept of a church doctrine which is submitted to the individual conscience for a responsible, independent decision.

Norms and the Reality of Action

The other aspect that was mentioned above is added to this, namely the need to apply and adapt all norms to the reality of action. Here Pope Francis explicitly quotes a thought of Saint Thomas Aquinas: "Although there is necessity in the general principles, the more we descend to matters of detail, the more frequently we encounter defects... In matters of action, truth or practical rectitude is not the same for all, as to matters of detail, but only as to the general principles; and where there is the same rectitude in matters of detail, it is not equally known to all... The principle will be found to fail, according as we descend further into detail." (AL 304, quoting *Summa Theologica*, I-II, 94,4) This somewhat complicated concept ultimately addresses the fact that general norms and rules are not always unambiguous when they are applied to concrete, specific action situations. Not everyone is always able to understand the precise meaning, and the situation can sometimes also not be correctly covered by a rule. Human prudence is then called upon in order to make the best of each situation. This can also mean that a rule is adapted, or preference given to a competing rule, because this would otherwise not lead to expedient action. Thomas Aquinas himself knows of an impressive example of this. The rule is clear and insightful; he states that it is necessary to give something back that was held in trust from the owner for a time. However, what happens if someone has entrusted his weapons to me and is now asking for them back for the purpose of fighting against my country? Can I still apply the rule regardless (cf. *Summa Theologica*, I-II, 94,4)? Thomas points out that a rule cannot cover the whole complexity of human life and of human circumstances. And the more it is necessary to take account of individual aspects, the less it is possible to apply a rule directly: "because the greater the number of conditions added, the greater the number of ways in which the principle may fail, so that it be not right to restore or not to restore" (*Summa Theologica*, I-II 94,4).

Pope Francis makes this sober theory of action fruitful for the church's pastoral work. It is made clear by this that prudent action is not a "fiddle", and is not "laxism", but that prudent action is indispensable if one wishes to reach sensible goals. For this reason, pastoral work should act prudently in line with the church's teaching, and at the same time in the light of mercy, which must determine the church's actions from inside.

Challenging Pastoral Work

These accents which have been set constitute a massive challenge for the specific pastoral work on the ground. Pastoral work was naturally always concerned with the individual, their belief, their hope, their love and their journey with God. We are however concerned less and less with "normal biographies", "standard situations" and "standard rites" today. The paths taken by the lives of the people who come to us are more and more clearly individual in their character. Hence, the requirement to first listen, take in, presume, and categorise without judging and then to look ahead together and find paths, is first of all becoming stronger and stronger. It is therefore more and more about the profile of *challenging pastoral work*. It is not intended here to claim that pastoral work has not had any quality in the past. However, the work involved in doing justice to the pastoral work of the person in question has increased. The idea is no longer realistic that, for instance, a couple comes for preparation for marriage to the responsible local pastor who has known both of them since they were small children, baptised them, administered their first communion, prepared them for confirmation and is now to marry them. The situations in which people find themselves – and even more so the situations in which couples find themselves – are frequently highly unconventional, often complicated and sometimes even confusing.

Amoris laetitia in particular, however, requires that we do not leave people to themselves in the presumption that they will do the right thing in the end. The pastoral work of the church may neither exercise rigorism which imposes equally high demands on all regardless of this, nor may it withdraw to a *laissez-faire* style which ultimately no longer has any message to impart to people. Accompanying, discerning and integrating means searching for a path which avoids these errors in particular. This is painstaking, but here also lies the chance of an encounter between individuals from which only belief can grow. The above-mentioned letter of Pope Francis is explained and quoted in *L'Osservatore Romano* of 23 September 2016: "It is pastoral work involving direct physical contact which may not be reduced to programmatic, organisational or legal mediatory activities, even though these are necessary."[2]

Necessary Competences

This requirement which Pope Francis formulates in *Amoris laetitia* must have both personal and structural consequences for us. At the level of personal consequences, it will be a matter here of a corresponding qualification of our staff in pastoral work. I cannot differentiate this here at detailed level. I would nonetheless like to mention a few main points as an overview which we should incorporate into basic and further training in future. This includes trained sensitivity for biographical contexts. Aspects of biographical work coming from the therapeutic field can certainly be helpful building blocks and tools here. The pastoral discussion is an indispensable element which we must refine and of which we must take greater care. Our workers must form a focus of expertise in this field: How do I start a pastoral conversation? How do I approach my counterpart? What signals do I need to look out for? How can I avoid misunderstandings? How can I tackle controversial topics? How do I express myself clearly? How do I end a discussion? How to bring the gospel in this encounter? – to name only a few aspects. The old Christian art of spiritual guidance also needs to find greater inclusion in basic and further training: How can I suitably guide an individual on his or her path with God? How can I support his or her search for meaning and reflection on his or her own life? It is however also highly significant to have solid basic training in moral theology which is sound and which can be called upon in practice, particularly in fundamental morals: What is conscience? What is a conflict of interests? How do I deal with a question where arguments require weighing up? On what values are the church's norms based? How can I distinguish between and evaluate the aspects of a situation, and how can I accompany responsible decision-making? The fact that pastoral workers are to be trained in the church's teaching on marriage and in the church's law on marriage is self-explanatory. Also in the area of the church's advice, above all in marriage, family and life counselling, we in Germany have skills at our disposal of which we should make greater use for pastoral work. There will be a need to consider which elements of this training should also be input more broadly into the basic and further training of pastoral workers.

Structures and Individuals

All these skills are naturally of little use if our priests and pastoral workers are occupied with administrative, managerial and organisational tasks to such an extent

2 Cf. "Discernment and Pastoral Care", in: *L'Osservatore Romano* (23.09.2016), 6.

that they simply do not have the time to engage in pastoral conversations and challenging pastoral work. This requires not only the time taken up by the discussion pure and simple, but also a suitable framework for reflection. There will therefore be a need to also shape the structures of pastoral work on the ground in such a way that people come to us with their questions and with their need for accompanying, discerning and integrating and that they can find an open ear and a tangible interest in their path with God. There can be a variety of different methods and concepts for this. It needs to be trialled in pastoral practice whether pastoral advice centres, clearly regulated consultation times, specially-trained contacts, firmer invitations to engage in discussion, or other forms of service, need to be developed. There will be a need to see what proves to be successful. But anyone who would like to take *Amoris laetitia* seriously will have to tackle these questions, since "[i]n every situation, when dealing with those who have difficulties in living God's law to the full, the invitation to pursue the *via caritatis* must be clearly heard" (AL 306). Whatever the suitable structures look like which are found for this, regardless of that, the fact is that all structures here must fail unless individuals can be found in these structures: matured personalities who are able to maintain relationships and who are willing to enter into a debate. Pope Francis finds clear words of warning here: "For this reason, a pastor cannot feel that it is enough simply to apply moral laws to those living in 'irregular' situations, as if they were stones to throw at people's lives. This would bespeak the closed heart of one used to hiding behind the church's teachings, 'sitting on the chair of Moses and judging at times with superiority and superficiality difficult cases and wounded families'" (AL 305). There is a need to contrast this distorted image of pastoral work with a personal ideal of willingness to discuss, care and a welcoming fundamental attitude. This is something which we can ultimately only ask our workers in pastoral work to take to heart. However, then we would have to presume, and indeed could presume with high hopes, that they make this fundamental stance their own and that we work together and with passion on *demanding pastoral work*.

Remarried Divorcees

The foundation of these considerations, finally, also permits the question to be approached of how the church is to deal with those individuals who have entered into a new civil marriage after having divorced and who express a desire to receive the sacrament of Reconciliation and the Eucharist. *Amoris laetitia* leaves little room for doubt as to what Pope Francis wishes to say with regard to this question of the entire ductus of the Exhortation. A discussion has nonetheless been unleashed particularly in this regard, which however has been clarified once more at the latest by the above-mentioned letter of the Pope of 5 September 2016 to the Delegate of the Buenos Aires Pastoral Region, Bishop Alfredo Fenoy.

Particularly when it comes to these individuals, Pope Francis makes a strong case for *accompanying, discerning and integrating*, on the basis of the fundamental statement: "No one can be condemned for ever, because that is not the logic of the Gospel!" (AL 297) As he explains in the above-mentioned letter, he is concerned to "go out to encounter those who are at a distance, and, once found, to start down the road of welcome, accompaniment, discernment, and integration into the ecclesial community. We know that this is tiresome, that it entails a pastoral approach 'person to person' that isn't satisfied with programmatic, organizational, or legal interventions, however necessary they may be."[3]

It is made unambiguously clear what he means here by "discernment", as he states in *Amoris laetitia*: "The Church possesses a solid body of reflection concerning mitigating factors and situations. Hence it can no longer simply be said that all those in any 'irregular' situation are living in a state of mortal sin and are deprived of sanctifying grace." (AL 301) *Amoris laetitia* therefore does not contain an automatic mechanism, either towards admitting all remarried divorcees across the board, or towards excluding them from the sacraments. Footnote 336 (AL 300) makes it clear that the manner in which a person has got themselves into this situation, which is to be adjudged on an individual basis, may also favour the possibility of receiving the sacraments. Footnote 351 (AL 305) furthermore points out that the sincere efforts of the individual in question to find a way with the church may justify their receiving the sacraments. In the context of the preparations for the synodal journey, the German bishops presented in 2014/2015 arguments entitled "Theologically-responsible and pastorally-suitable ways to accompany remarried divorcees", and these have been largely confirmed by *Amoris laetitia*. These reflections lead one to the conclusion that: "It would certainly be wrong to indiscriminately admit to the sacraments all believers whose marriages have broken up and who have civilly divorced and remarried. There is, rather, a need for differentiated solutions which do justice to the individual case and then come to bear when a marriage cannot be annulled."[4]

The bishops of the Buenos Aires Pastoral Region stress here that "it's not convenient to speak of 'permission' to receive the sacraments, but about a personal and pastoral process of discernment".[5] On the proviso of this process of discern-

---

3 *Letter of Pope Francis*.

4 SEKRETARIAT DER DEUTSCHEN BISCHOFSKONFERENZ (ed.): *Die pastoralen Herausforderungen der Familie im Kontext der Evangelisierung*, Bonn: Sekretariat der Deutschen Bischofskonferenz, 2014 (Arbeitshilfen; 273), 42-76, here 76.

5 *Basic Criteria for the Application of Chapter Eight of the Post-Synodal Apostolic Exhortation Amoris Laetitia*, Buenos Aires, 5 September 2016, available from https://cruxnow.com/global

ment, "*Amoris Laetitia* opens up the possibility of access to the sacraments of Reconciliation and the Eucharist." This at least is the interpretation of the above named bishops of the Post-Synodal Apostolic Exhortation, referring to these two remarks. Pope Francis confirms these statements with highly-welcome clarity: "There are no other interpretations".

With the Tailwind of *Amoris Laetitia*

The significance of these statements is ultimately underlined by the remark of Pope Francis: "Finally, I would like to recall that *Amoris laetitia* was the fruit of the labor and prayer of the whole Church with the mediation of two synods and of the Pope. For that reason I recommend a complete catechesis of the Exhortation that will certainly aid in the growth, consolidation, and sanctity of the family."[6] This, finally, leads us to the starting point of our considerations, to the fruit of the synod and to the wish for it to "give hope and joy to many families in the world, guidance to pastors and pastoral workers, and a stimulus to the work of evangelization" (*Relatio Synodi*, 94). According to the words of Pope Francis, in this regard "[e]ach country or region, moreover, can seek solutions better suited to its culture and sensitive to its traditions and local needs." (AL 3) The task which arises from this for us as pastors and pastoral workers is undoubtedly demanding, and it has only been possible in this brief essay to name a small number of aspects related to these tasks, albeit they are central in nature. With his cordial tone, his accessible language and his openness to the further development of pastoral work, Pope Francis has however certainly fulfilled a wish of the synod: He has given us a strong stimulus for this pastoral work. What we now need to do is to use this tailwind for pastoral work.

-church/2016/09/18/guidelines-buenos-aires-bishops-divorcedremarried; accessed 07.02.2017.

6 *Letter of Pope Francis*.

Amoris Laetitia: On the Need for a Contextual Theology and Inculturation in Practice

George S. Worgul

How are the local churches to care for divorced and remarried Catholics in view of the charge Pope Francis issued in *Amoris laetitia*?[1] Chapter 8 of *Amoris laetitia* has become a much debated question among many Episcopal Conferences around the globe as well as individual local dioceses. The text rightly underscores discernment and conscience as crucial forces in this complicated and challenging process. Few if any commentators have taken issue with the theme of accompaniment and what might be understood as merciful empathy. However, vigorous and surprisingly nasty claims, criticisms and even accusations of heresy have been present when the question of sacramental Eucharistic communion for those who are divorced and remarried without a declaration of nullity is raised.[2] In a real sense, the reactions to *Amoris laetitia* chapter 8 on this question are a revisiting of the debates, arguments and conflicts present during the two sessions of the Synod on the Family. Pope Francis did not intervene during the Synod to halt debate and dialogue. Similarly, in *Amoris laetitia* he directs local episcopal conferences and the local diocese to craft their response to this pastoral issue.

The present conflict on the issue of communion for the divorced and remarried without a decree of nullity invites us to revisit the debates surrounding different understandings of conscience within the episcopal magisterium and the theological magisterium. At the same time, this "micro" focus discloses a more profound and pervasive "macro" challenge already articulated on November 10, 2015 by Francis when he emphasized to the Italian church leadership gathered in Fiorenza

---

1 FRANCIS: *Post-Synodal Exhortation Amoris Laetitia*, 2016, available from https://w2.vatican.va/content/dam/francesco/pdf/apost_exhortations/documents/papa-francesco_esortazione-ap_20160319_amoris-laetitia_en.pdf; accessed 20.02.2017.

2 Cardinal Burke has proposed the possibility of inaugurating a "formal act of correction" to Pope Francis. Cf. D. HITCHENS: "Cardinal Burke: We Will Make 'Formal Act of Correction if Pope Doesn't Issue Amoris Clarification", 16.11.2016, available from www.catholicherald.co.uk/news/2016/11/16/cardinal-burke-we-will-make-formal-act-of-correction-if-the-pope-doesnt-make-amoris-clarification; accessed 20.02.2017.

that we are not living in "an era of change but the change of an era".[3] Where one stands on the issue of this paradigm shift predicts one's answer to the pastoral challenges of the divorced and remarried in the life of the Christian community.

The Conscience Debate

The understanding of conscience seemingly implicit in *Amoris laetitia* might be judged a return to the theological vision of conscience being articulated by moderately progressive moralists immediately prior to the Second Vatican Council and until the papacy of John Paul II. Some representatives of this interpretation were my professor Canon Louis Janssens[4] in Leuven, Josef Fuchs[5] and Bernard Häring[6] in Rome or Richard McCormick[7] and Charles Curran[8] in the USA.

---

3 Cf. J.J. McELWEE: "Catholicism Can and Must Change, Francis Forcefully Tells Italian Church Gathering", in: *National Catholic Reporter*, 10.11.2015, available from www.ncronline.org/news/vatican/catholicism-can-and-must-change-francis forcefully-tell s-italian-church-gathering; accessed 20.02.2017.

4 Cf. D.L. CHRISTIE: *Adequately Considered: An American Perspective on Louis Janssens' Personalist Morals*, Leuven-Grand Rapids, MI: Peeters, 1990 (Louvain Theological and Pastoral Monographs; 4); L. JANSSENS: "Teleology and Proportionality: Thoughts about the Encyclical Veritatis Splendor", in: J.A. SELLING /J. JANS (eds.): *The Splendor of Accuracy. An Examination of the Assertions Made by Veritatis Splendor*, Grand Rapids, MI: William B. Eerdmans, 1994, 99-113; J.A. SELLING/F. BOCKLE/R. BURGGRAEVE et al. (eds.): *Personalist Morals: Essays in Honor of Professor Louis Janssens*, Leuven: Leuven University Press, 1988.

5 Cf. J. FUCHS: "Gewissen und Gefolgschaft", in: *Stimmen der Zeit* 207 (1989), 308-320; translated in English as "Conscience and Conscientious Fidelity", in: C.E. CURRAN (ed.): *Moral Theology: Challenges for the Future: Essays in Honor of Richard A. McCormick, S.J.*, New York: Paulist Press, 1990, 108-124.

6 B. HÄRING: *Free and Faithful in Christ: Moral Theology for Priests and Laity*, Middlegreen, Slough: St. Paul Publications, 1978, 224-301 (chapter 6: "Conscience: The Sanctuary of Creative Fidelity and Liberty"); ID.: "Reciprocity of Consciences: A Key Concept in Moral Theology", in: R. GALLAGHER/B. McCONVERY (eds.): *Conscience: Studies in Honour of Seán O'Riordan, C.Ss.R.*, Dublin: Gill and Macmillan, 1989, 60-72.

7 R. McCORMICK: "Church Teaching and Conscience", in: C.E. CURRAN (ed.): *Conscience*, New York: Paulist Press, 2004 (Readings in Moral Theology; 14), 103-109.

8 C.E. CURRAN: "The Christian Conscience Today", in: C.E. NELSON (ed.): *Conscience: Theological and Psychological Perspectives*, New York: Newman Press, 1973, 134-142; ID.: "Conscience in the Light of the Catholic Moral Tradition", in: C.E. CURRAN (ed.): *Conscience*, 3-24 (chapter 1). See also his essay written for the Canon Law Society of America's seminar on The Role of Law in the Church: ID.: "Law and Conscience in the Christian Context", in: J.E. BIECHLER (ed.): *Law for Liberty: The Role of Law in the Church Today*, Baltimore, MD: Helicon Press, 1967, 156-171

Some current exemplars of this vision of conscience would be Cardinals Cupich[9], Kasper[10] and Marx[11], as well as professors Lawler and Salzman[12] (Creighton), and the Bishops of the Buenos Aires Pastoral Region in a Sept 5, 2016 directive[13] tacitly approved in a letter by Pope Francis.[14]

Alternatively, most of the opposition to *Amoris laetitia*'s implicit understanding of conscience seems to follow the expression of conscience which flows throughout the writings of John Paul II and Benedict XVI.[15] Some exemplars of this vision of conscience who have reacted to *Amoris laetitia* would be the Americans: Cardinal Burke[16], Archbishop Chaput of Philadelphia[17] (who has been appointed the head of the National Conference of Catholic Bishops committee for the implementation of AL), George Weigel[18] (Ethics and Public Policy Cen-

---

[9] Cf. J.J. McELWEE: "Chicago's Cupich on Divorce: Pastor Guides Decisions, but Person's Conscience Inviolable", in: *National Catholic Reporter*, 16.10.2015, available from https://www.ncronline.org/news/vatican/chicagos-cupich-divorce-pastor-guides-decisions-persons-conscience-inviolable; accessed 21.02.2017.

[10] Cf. J. BENTZ: "Cardinal Kasper: Can the 'Remarried' now Receive Communion? 'Yes. Period'", 24.10.2016, available from https://www.lifesitenews.com/news/cardinal-kasper-amoris-laetitia-changes-everything-on-communion-for-remarri; accessed 21.02.2017.

[11] Cf. "Cardinal Marx Rejects the Dubia", 22.12.2016, available from http://biblefalseprophet.com/2016/12/22/cardinal-marx-rejects-the-dubia/; accessed 21.02.2017

[12] Cf. M.G. LAWLER/T.A. SALZMAN: *Sexual Ethics: A Theological Introduction*, Georgetown: Georgetown University Press, 2012. Also ID.: "Following Faithfully: The Catholic Way to Choose the Good", in *America* (22.01.2015), available from www.americamagazine.org/issue/following-faithfully; accessed 21.02.2017.

[13] Cf. "Guidelines of Buenos Aires bishops on divorced/remarried", 18.09.2016, available from https://cruxnow.com/global-church/2016/09/18/guidelines-buenos-aires-bishops-divorcedremarried/; accessed 21.02.2017.

[14] Cf. "What Pope Francis Said about Communion for the Divorced-and-Remarried", 13.09.2016, available from http://www.catholicnewsagency.com/news/what-pope-francis-said-about-communion-for-the-divorced-and-remarried-42513/; accessed 21.02.2017.

[15] Cf. JOHN PAUL II: *Veritatis Splendor*, 1993, available from http://w2.vatican.va/content/john-paul-ii/en/encyclicals/documents/hf_jp-ii_enc_06081993_veritatis-splendor.html; accessed 21.02.2017, and for Benedict cf. B.P. BRADSHAW: "Truth and Conscience in the Thought of Joseph Ratzinger and Dignitatis Humanae", available from http://www.frben.com/documents/truth_and_conscience_in_the_thought_of_joseph_ratzinger_and_dignitatis_humanae.pdf; accessed 21.02.2017.

[16] Cf. an excerpt from March 7, 2015 address that Cardinal Burke gave at the Society for the Protection of Unborn Children Youth Conference, Southport, England: R.L. BURKE: "Conscience, the Infallible Guide to Holiness of Life", 22.01.2016, available from http://thewandererpress.com/catholic/news/frontpage/conscience-the-infallible-guide-to-holiness-of-life/#more-13145; accessed 21.02.2017.

[17] Cf. the Archdiocesan Guidelines for implementing *Amoris laetitia* promulgated by Chaput: "Pastoral Guidelines for Implementing *Amoris Laetitia*, Archdiocese of Philadelphia, July 1, 2016", available from http://archphila.org/wp-content/uploads/2016/06/AOP_AL-guidelines.pdf; accessed 21.02.2017.

[18] Cf. Weigel's interesting interpretation of *Amoris laetitia*: G. WEIGEL: "Pope Francis on Love,

ter), Matthew Schmitz (editor, *First Things*), Joseph Shaw (Oxford) representative of 45 Catholics requesting the College of Cardinals to avoid possible heresy in *Amoris laetitia*[19], and let us not forget the thirteen cardinal signatures to a letter addressed to Francis during the synod[20].

Wherein lies the differences in these two apparently conflicting understandings of conscience? Fortuitously, E. Christian Brugger in the *Catholic World Report* (Sept 20, 2016)[21] and Lawler/Salzman in the *National Catholic Reporter* (Sept 7, 2016)[22] have offered clear and accurate summaries of the differences with Brugger endorsing the alleged interpretation in line with John Paul II and Lawler/Salzman aligning themselves with Pope Francis.

Lawler/Salzman appeal to the inviolability of conscience which they claim was established by Thomas Aquinas and affirmed in *Gaudium et spes* and *Dignitatis humanae*. They postulate that one's understanding of the relationship between the subjective and objective dimensions of morality underpin one's understanding of conscience and its relationship to truth or magisterial teaching.

Lawler/Salzman clearly frame the argument. "Is conscience subjective and internal and truth objective and external, whereby the subjective and internal conscience must obey and conform to the objective and external truth? Or does conscience include both the objective and subjective realms, whereby conscience discerns and interprets its understanding of objective truth and exercises that understanding in the subjective judgment of conscience?"

Lawler and Salzman embrace the latter position. They also claim that this should not be labeled relativism. "In this formulation, truth exists 'in myself,' not in a relativist sense that denies objective and universal truth, but in the sense of the intrinsic human dignity of the person and the authority of conscience. Conscience

Marriage, and the Family", 08.04.2016, available from http://www.nationalreview.com/article /433832/pope-francis-marriage-document-defends-catholic-teaching; accessed 21.02.2017.

19 Cf. C. CHRETIEN: "Full Text of 45 Theologians' Appeal to Correct Amoris Laetitia's Errors Revealed", 28.07.2016, available from https://www.lifesitenews.com/news/full-text-of-45-theo logians-appeal-to-correct-amoris-laetitias-errors-revea; accessed 21.02.2017. Full text of the 45 theologians available from http://2n613ar7ekr056c3upq2s15c.wpengine.netdna-cdn.com/w p-content/uploads/2016/07/45-theologians-censure-AL.pdf; accessed 21.02.2017.

20 Cf. S. MAGISTER: "Thirteen Cardinals Have Written to the Pope", 12.10.2015, available from http://chiesa.espresso.repubblica.it/articolo/1351154?eng=y; accessed 21.02.2017.

21 Cf. E.C. BRUGGER: "The Catholic Conscience, the Argentine Bishops, and 'Amoris Laetitia'", 20.09.2016, available from http://www.catholicworldreport.com/Item/5069/the_catholic_consc ience_the_argentine_bishops_and_amoris_laetitia.aspx; accessed 21.02.2017. N.B., all quotations are from this article.

22 Cf. M.C. LAWLER/T.A. SALZMAN: "In Amoris Laetitia, Francis' Model of Conscience Empowers Catholics", 07.09.2016, available from https://www.ncronline.org/news/theology/amor is-laetitia-francis-model-conscience-empowers-catholics; accessed 21.02.2017. N.B., all quotations are from this article.

must internalize the values reflected in the norm, see their relevance to the human person in all her particularity, and go through the process of understanding, judgment, decision and action."

Lawler and Salzman explain the role of "objective norms" in this manner. "The essential point for conscience as object-orientation is the relevance of the objective norm from the perspective of the inquiring subject in light of the understanding of all the circumstances in a particular historical cultural context. The implications of this perspective on the relationship between conscience as object-orientation and objective norms is that conscience should be guided by those norms but the authority of conscience is not identified with whether or not it obeys the objective norm."

Lawler and Salzman marshal *Dignitatis humanae* to support this claim. "Otherwise, *Dignitatis humanae* could not advocate for religious freedom, where 'every man has the duty, and therefore the right, to seek the truth in matters religious in order that he may with prudence form for himself right and true [objective] judgments of conscience, under use of all suitable means.'"

If mere obedience to objective norms was the sole role of conscience, then conscience that leads people to follow religious traditions other than the Roman Catholic Church could never be tolerated. That religious pluralism is recognized and affirmed in *Dignitatis humanae* shifts authority from the objective norm to conscience as object-orientation, informed by objective norms, where the hermeneutical lens of the conscience as subject-orientation facilitates the process of understanding, judgment and decision of conscience.

Lawler and Salzman claim that this hermeneutical perspective resonates with the basic perspective witnessed in B. Häring. In the context of Häring's overall approach to moral theology, God's call to all women and men and each person's response of a moral life, conscience must be free and inviolable, and "the church must affirm the freedom of conscience itself". Church doctrine is at the service of women and men in their sincere conscience search for goodness, truth and Christian wholeness; conscience is not at the service of doctrine.

E. Christian Brugger, J. Francis Cardinal Stafford Professor of Moral Theology at St. John Vianney Theological Seminary, has issued a strong negative critique of Lawler and Salzman as well as of the Argentine Bishops. He avers that any account of conscience, therefore, that sets it in opposition to freedom (à la Salzman and Lawler) or makes it indifferent to objective truth (à la Argentine bishops) has misconceived not only conscience and moral truth, but human nature, the doctrine of creation and the Christian moral life.

Brugger begins by rejecting proportionalism which he claims is being presumed in the Lawler/Salzman argument. He represents proportionalism this way: "common to all proportionalists is the insistence that intending evil as an end or means (what defenders refer to variously as 'premoral evil', 'ontic evil', 'dis-value', etc.) does not by that fact make an action morally wrong. If there are 'morally relevant circumstances' justifying the commission of the evil – what they call 'proportionate reasons'... – then it can rightly be chosen." He continues, "[p]roportionalism denies the existence of intrinsically evil actions, types of behavior that when freely chosen always constitute a disorder of the will. If there are no intrinsically wrongful types of action, then the Church, when it has taught that there are (e.g., adultery), has taught illicitly. And so whereas according to the Church's teaching, conscience never rightly deliberates over whether or not to have sex with someone other than one's valid spouse, conscience in the proportionalist account may indeed (in fact sometimes must) remain open to it. Why? Because if there are proportionate reasons for doing so, then under the circumstances it may be the right thing for me to do."

Brugger claims that conscience in the Catholic view does indeed stand in obedience to the moral law. But this obedience is not servile and passive, not the obedience of a slave to his master. It is the obedience of a scientist to the truth, or a famished man to a feast, or the ear to sound and the eye to color, or an explorer to his longed-for destination, or of a hunting dog to his quarry. Conscience is made for moral truth. It searches for, finds, probes and understands more deeply, then directs action as best as it can in accord with it. How can this be a threat? Is a hand a threat to a glove, or a key to a lock? A healthy conscience doesn't close us down and restrict us. It opens us up to the good and ultimately to God. It makes possible the flourishing of the gift of freedom.[23] Furthermore, Pope John Paul II's apostolic exhortation *Familiaris consortio* expresses this same perspective, being wholly rooted in both the truth of sexuality and marriage as taught by the church and the obligation of the laity to obey that truth. Almost nowhere in *Familiaris consortio* does the church's teaching on the inviolable primacy of individual conscience, even in sexual matters, appear. Such an absence unjustly ignores the long-standing Catholic tradition fundamentally strengthened at the Second Vatican Council.

The Paradigm Shift

In turning now from the micro debate on conscience to the macro challenge of the church in the change of an era or the paradigm shift from modernity to post-modernity, the core challenge of our times is disclosed. The last two papal reigns have responded to the paradigm shift by strong resistant opposition. Now it seems that Pope Francis is urging the church to move from negation to engagement and accompaniment.

23 See JOHN PAUL II, General Audience, Aug. 17, 1983, 2, in: *Insegnamenti* 6/2 (1983), 256.

Among the many impacts of post-modernity, key elements might be a master narrative replaced by multiple narratives, a claim of universal non-historical truth replaced by historical meaning systems, and doctrinal identity replaced by experience of solidarity and ethical living. It is not surprising that inculturation and contextuality would emerge as powerful forces as the church engages an increasingly globalized and post-modern world. This is strongly underscored in Pope Francis' *Evangelii gaudium*.[24]

Evangelii gaudium, the "Joy of the Gospel", is the Apostolic Exhortation that Pope Francis wrote after the New Evangelization Synod called and completed during Pope Benedict's reign. It's key theme is that the "Joy of the Gospel" is the fruit of an encounter with Jesus. This encounter with Christ is the source of authentic personal fulfillment. This authentic joy contrasts with the emptiness of consumerism and materialism.

Francis wants the church to move beyond primary concern with institutional maintenance and embrace anew its missionary vocation with greater evangelical commitment. Francis links the call to evangelization with the Gospel's social message. The Gospel should guide our attitudes towards money, inequality, the inclusion of the poor, etc. (cf. EG 115-117).

Francis understands that the human person is always situated in a culture: "nature and culture are intimately linked". Grace supposes culture, and God's gift becomes flesh in the culture of those who receive it. Rather than the culture changing the Gospel, it is the Gospel that permeates the culture. Therefore, inculturation is presented less as an adaptation of the Gospel and more as an insertion of the Gospel in the culture.

Interestingly, the practice of popular piety (cf. EG 122-126) is suggested by Pope Francis as a prime model of a practice of a Christian faith that is truly inculturated. Once the Gospel has been inculturated in a people, in their process of transmitting their culture the Gospel faith is also transmitted in new forms. Popular piety is a true expression of the spontaneous missionary activity of the people of God. Popular piety enables us to see how the faith, once received, becomes embodied in a culture and is constantly passed on. The practices of popular piety offer deep insight into inculturation and the Gospel and provide a rich source for theological insight. Would not the popular living out of the Gospel among those divorced and remarried offer a rich source for reflection and discernment?

Evangelii gaudium refuses to reduce the Gospel to its expression in any one culture which culture then becomes normative for the others. EG 117 notes:

---

24 Cf. FRANCIS: *Evangelii Gaudium*, 2013, available from http://www.vatican.va/evangelii-gaudium/en/; accessed 21.02.2017.

> While it is true that some cultures have been closely associated with the preaching of the Gospel and the development of Christian thought, the revealed message is not identified with any of them; its content is transcultural. Hence in the evangelization of new cultures, or cultures which have not received the Christian message, it is not essential to impose a specific cultural form, no matter how beautiful or ancient it may be, together with the Gospel. The message that we proclaim always has a certain cultural dress, but we in the Church can sometimes fall into a needless hallowing of our own culture, and thus show more fanaticism than true evangelizing zeal.

He continues:

> We cannot demand that peoples of every continent, in expressing their Christian faith, imitate modes of expression which European nations developed at a particular moment of their history, because the faith cannot be constricted to the limits of understanding and expression of any one culture. It is an indisputable fact that no single culture can exhaust the mystery of our redemption in Christ. (EG 118)

One should expect that cultural diversity will lead to multiple expressions of ecclesial life. Cultural diversity does not diminish church unity. While historically, certain cultures have been closely associated with evangelization and development of Christian thought, revelation should not be identified with any of them. No culture exhausts the mystery of salvation. More positively stated, the diversity and pluralism of cultures can result in deeper insights and understanding of the Gospel. Cultural diversity may also lead to different pastoral practices surrounding marriage and any challenges linked to it within local contexts.

Evangelization requires inculturation if the Gospel is to be heard, understood and take root in a culture. Frequently, the bridge building image was utilized to describe the inculturation process. The missionary, carrying the Gospel, would travel across the bridge into a culture and work at expressing the Gospel in the language, thought patterns, and social structures/institutions of a people insofar as these cultural phenomenon and practices were not sinful or demonic. However, the bridge was almost always assumed to function as a "one way street". There was little or no consciousness that the people who received the message might themselves cross the bridge into other cultures. There was little or no consciousness that new and different insights and understandings of the Gospel might arise as it was proclaimed and lived in this new cultural context. A fresh understanding and living of the Gospel might be shared with other communities in the church as cross cultural fertilization becomes more pervasive. Increasingly, both Christian inculturated religious experience and wisdom, spirituality and truth from an evangelized's own non-Christian religious experiences which might further illumine our Christian faith and understanding.

Presently, there is a growing recognition that the bridge connecting cultures is not one way, nor even two ways. A globalized world of easy and rapid communication witnesses multiple bridges with a plethora of interchanges and crossovers.

This "new evangelization" might redesign the concerns and change or develop the existing interpretation of the Gospel or dramatically impact the shape and form of Christian communities and practices. True inculturated evangelization potentially enriches and transforms each local church and therefore the whole church. Therefore, inculturation is more than a one-way bridge. Inculturation is multidimensional. One should expect that once the Gospel has been inculturated in any particular culture, people go back across the bridge and walk in many directions and bring the fruit of inculturation into the many cultures around the globe. In an era marked by pervasive globalization and readily accessed information to expect anything less would be naïve.

So while the questions surrounding divorce and remarriage and communion are very important, a more foundational issue also stands before us – and how we answer these macro challenges will deeply chart any micro responses. How can we have truly inculturated and contextual understandings of what we call marriage? Might it be possible to admit that we evangelized non-western cultures with the Gospel and with our western cultural understanding of marriage and this master narrative of marriage was understood to be true everywhere and for all time?

In a certain sense, we theologians of the West suffer from what I would call unconscious intellectual colonialism. Perhaps you have heard some of the following examples. A Theology Faculty member at a European University, "they are very bright for an African"; a Theology Faculty member at an American University, "some of those Asia students have grown so much, they are now thinking like Americans"; a Theology faculty member in Canada, "do those Africans have an African Philosophy? Does it correspond any of the great philosophers, Aristotle, Plato, Hegel, Heidegger?"

Unconscious intellectual colonialism attempts to control both the method and content of thinking. It uncritically presumes that the West has a normative master narrative which is the reference point for all others to master and imbibe and make their own. Isn't it evocative to read African and Asian thinkers and see how almost all often frame their thinking and writing in relation to the issues, methods and content of the West. Fortunately, a few non-western theologians have taken up the challenge of doing theology in their own world and culture.

Unconscious intellectual colonialism thwarts true inculturation. At best, it will allow superficial adaptation. *Evangelii gaudium* strongly asserts that the Gospel is not tethered to any one culture. Nonetheless, it may fall short in not recognizing the controlling influence of unconscious intellectual colonialism. If true evangelization is to be accomplished, this pernicious remnant of colonialism must be negated. The antidote to unconscious intellectual colonialism is the dialogue of inculturation wherein the Gospel in encountered in a people's own language, thought patters, and social structures/institutions. This form of dialogue is only in a gestational period. Let us hope it matures quickly, and specifically takes up the living of conjugal love and family life.

A first step theologians might take is to undertake the arduous and creative challenge of imagining a truly non-colonial, non-imperialistic theological education that is culturally and cross culturally rooted and therefore deeply engaged with a diversity of religious experiences. This may only be possible if theologians make the unconscious intellectual colonialism control them consciously and embrace a more open perspective. This may be the necessary activity of theologians living not in an era of change but the change of an era.

In the end, many challenges concerning marriage engaged by *Amoris laetitia* are rooted in a different understanding of conscience. However, *Amoris laetitia* invites us to face the challenge of a living in communities that have different understandings and practices of marriage that are inculturated and contextualized in the local churches. Perhaps this is the call of theological reflection and married life in the change of an era. Perhaps the synodality, dialogue, and decentralization endemic in the vision of *Amoris laetitia* are a practical response to living in an era of postmodernity which witnesses diversity and plurality to be normative rather than exceptional. *Amoris laetitia* in this sense is a model for theological and pastoral reflection not only on questions, issues and theology of marriage and family but on all of ecclesial shared life and communion. Contextuality and inculturation will be driving forces in shaping the new era of communal ecclesial life as expressed in the local churches in their real cultural contexts.

Amoris Laetitia and the Development of Catholic Theological Ethics: A Reflection

Todd A. Salzman & Michael G. Lawler

Introduction

On March 19, 2016, Pope Francis published his response to the two Synods on Marriage and Family of 2014 and 2015, his Apostolic Exhortation *Amoris laetitia*. In this essay we extract three topics from the Exhortation and reflect upon their meaning for Catholic theological ethics: the ancient Catholic doctrine on the authority and absolute inviolability of the informed personal conscience, which governs the entire Exhortation, what Francis calls "gradualness", and two great Gospel commandments he constantly emphasizes, "Love your neighbor as yourself" (Mt 19,19) and "Judge not" (Mt 7,1). Because we believe it to be the doctrinal key to the Exhortation's contribution to Catholic theological ethics, we deal at length with its teaching on conscience and deal with the other two topics as they arise. The overall contribution of the three topics is examined as they relate to what Francis calls "irregular situations", divorce and remarriage without annulment, contraception, cohabitation before marriage, and homosexual relations.

1 Conscience

Already in the thirteenth century, Thomas Aquinas established the authority and inviolability of conscience. "Anyone upon whom the ecclesiastical authorities, in ignorance of the true facts, imposes a demand that offends against his clear conscience, should perish in excommunication rather than violate his conscience."[1] For any Catholic in search of the good and the true, no clearer statement on the authority and inviolability of personal conscience could be found. Aquinas goes further and insists that even the dictate of a mistaken conscience must be followed and that to act against such a dictate is immoral and sinful. "To believe in Christ", he argues, "is good in itself and necessary for salvation; all this does not win the

[1] THOMAS AQUINAS: *In IV Sent.*, dist. 38, q. 2, art. 4.

will unless it be recommended by reason. If the reason presents it as bad, then the will reaches to it in the light, not that it really is bad in itself, but because it appears so because of a condition that happens to be attached by the reason apprehending it."[2]

Seven hundred years later, the last hundred of which saw the rights of personal conscience much ignored and even suppressed in the Catholic Church, *Gaudium et spes* issued a clarion cry in its defense. "Conscience is the most secret core and sanctuary of a man. There he is alone with God whose voice echoes in his depths. In a wonderful manner conscience reveals that law which is fulfilled by love of God and neighbor." (GS 16) *Dignitatis humanae*, the Decree on Religious Freedom, went further to assert the inviolability of conscience. "In all his activity a man is bound to follow his conscience faithfully, in order that he may come to God for whom he was created. It follows that he is not to be forced to act contrary to his conscience. Nor, on the other hand, is he to be restrained from acting in accordance with his conscience, especially in matters religious." (DH 3) In the 1960s, these were seldom-voiced words in Catholic magisterial circles, but they are words deeply rooted in the Catholic moral tradition and, indeed, constitutive of it.

From Aquinas above, we see immediately that conscience is related to reason, and its understanding is situated in Aquinas' anthropology. Closely following Aristotle, he considers the human person to be a unitary being endowed with a body and a rational soul that vivifies it. Reason distinguishes humans from all other animals, and the rational soul has two powers, intellect and will, intimately related and involved in the process of knowledge. All knowledge begins with experience[3] and proceeds through understanding to judgment and decision, which is then actualized in action. Conscience is the act of practical judgment that something is right or wrong, moral or immoral, to be done or not done. Conscience is, as Robert Smith comments, "the act of practical judgment on a particular moral issue... that commands us to do this or not to do that".[4]

Conscience, then, comes at the end of a rational process which is a process of experience, understanding, judgment, decision. This process includes a natural grasp of moral principles that Aquinas calls *synderesis*, though the Greek is more correctly *synteresis*. "Though the habits which inform conscience are many", he argues, "nevertheless they all take effect through one chief habit, the grasp of prin-

---

2 THOMAS AQUINAS: *Summa Theologiae*, I-II, 19, 5. Henceforth cited as ST.

3 See ST I, 79, 2. For an excellent summary, see K.L. SCHMITZ: "St. Thomas and the Appeal to Experience", in: *Proceedings of the Catholic Theological Society of America* 47 (1992), 1-20.

4 R.J. SMITH: *Conscience and Catholicism: The Nature and Function of Conscience in Contemporary Roman Catholic Theology*, Lanham, MD: University Press of America, 1998, 12.

ciples called *synderesis*."[5] Aquinas never makes these principles clear anywhere because, as Jean Porter argues, his "general theory of goodness requires him to hold that the first principle of practical reasoning is self-evident to all".[6] Cardinal Joseph Ratzinger, in a 1991 speech, interpreted the medieval tradition as offering two levels to the concept of conscience, *synteresis* (which he suggests is better rendered as *anamnesis*) and conscience. *Synteresis* or *anamnesis* is "an inner repugnance to evil and an attraction to the good. The act of conscience applies this basic knowledge to the particular situation".[7] To make a practical judgment of conscience, then, involves both a grasp of the first principles of practical judgment (*synderesis*) and a gathering of as much evidence as possible, consciously weighing and understanding the evidence and its implications, and finally making as honest a judgment as possible that this action is to be done and that action is not. Since this process ends with a judgment about what is good or evil, right or wrong, we call it a *moral* process. A *moral* action is one that comes as the right outcome of such a process and an *immoral* action is one that comes as the wrong outcomes of such a process. It is commonplace theologically to insist that, in order to be right and moral, conscience must be informed; that formation is precisely the process from gathering the necessary informational evidence to judgment we have just outlined.

Since conscience is a practical judgment that comes at the end of a deliberative process about the relationship of means to ends, it necessarily involves the virtue of prudence, by which "right reason is applied to action".[8] Aquinas locates prudence in the intellect[9] along with *synderesis* and *conscientia*. *Synderesis* provides the first principles of practical reason, prudence discerns those principles, applies them to particular situations, and enables conscience to make practical judgments that this is the right thing to do on this occasion, toward this person, and with this good intention.[10] Prudence, therefore, needs to know "both the general moral principles of reason and the individual situation in which human actions take place".[11] Prudence is a *cardinal* virtue around which all other virtues pivot, integrating both agents and their actions.[12] Because prudence controls the judgments that precede the exercise of all other moral virtues, and must precede them if they are to be

---

5 ST I, 79, 13.

6 J. PORTER: *The Recovery of Virtue: The Relevance of Aquinas for Christian Ethics*, Louisville: Westminster/John Knox, 1990, 85-86.

7 J. RATZINGER: "Conscience and Truth", 8, available from http://www.ewtn.com/library/curia/ratzcons.htm; accessed 02.02.2017.

8 ST II-II, 47, 5.

9 ST II-II, 47, 1.

10 See ST II-II, 47, 6.

11 See ST II-II, 47, 3.

12 See ST I-II, 61, 2 and 3.

moral, Aquinas holds that "no moral virtue can be possessed without prudence, since it is proper to moral virtue to make a right choice".[13]

Unfortunately, in the human condition all judgments, even the most prudential practical judgments of conscience, can be in error. That raises the question of the erroneous conscience noted above and so, at this point, we need to introduce some important distinctions. Ethicists note that there are two poles in every moral judgment. It is always a free, rational human *subject* who makes a judgment, and so one pole of the judgment is a subjective pole; but every subject makes a judgment about some objective reality, cohabitation or homosexual actions, for instance, and so there is always also an objective pole. Subjects arrive at their judgments either by following the rational process outlined above or by somehow short-changing that process. In the first case, the subject arrives at a right moral understanding and conscience-judgment about the object; in the second case, the subject arrives at a wrong or erroneous understanding and conscience judgment about the object. If a decision to act follows a right understanding and judgment about the object, then conscience is also said to be right; if it follows an erroneous understanding and judgment, then conscience is also said to be erroneous.

If the rational error of understanding and judgment can be ascribed to some moral fault, taking "little trouble to find out what is true and good" (GS 16), for instance, or negligent failure to be sufficiently attentive to the necessary experience, to gather the necessary evidence, to engage in the necessary deliberation, to take the necessary advice, then the wrong understanding and the practical judgment of conscience flowing from it are both deemed to be culpable and cannot be morally followed.[14] If the error cannot be ascribed to some moral fault, then both the understanding and the practical judgment of conscience flowing from it are deemed to be non-culpable and not only can but must be followed, even contrary to church authority, as we saw Aquinas arguing above. Subjects are bound not only *to conscience* but also *for* conscience, that is, they must do all in their power to ensure that conscience is right. Any negligence in the search for rightness is immoral. There is one final distinction to be added here. The morality of an action is largely controlled by the subject's intention. A good intention, giving alms to the poor *because* the poor need help and to help them is the right and Christian thing to do, results in a moral action. A bad intention, giving alms to the poor *because* I want to be seen and to be praised by men (Mt 6,2-5; see Lk 18,10-14), will result in an immoral action.

A decision of right conscience is a complex process. It is an *individual* process, but far from an *individualistic*, exclusively subjective process. The Latin

---

13 ST I-II, 65, 1.

14 See ST I-II, 19, 6.

word *con-scientia* literally means "knowledge together", perhaps better rendered as to "know together". It suggests what human experience universally demonstrates, namely, that being freed from the prison of one's individual self into the company of others is a surer way to come to right knowledge of moral truth and right moral judgment of what one ought to do or not do. This community-basis of the search for Christian truth, conscience, and moral action builds a sure safeguard against both an isolating egoism and a subjective relativism that negates all universal truth. The community dimension of consciences has been part of the Christian tradition since Paul, who clearly believed in the inviolability and primacy of conscience (1Cor 10,25-27; 2Cor 1,12; 4,2; Rom 14,23). Bernard Häring calls it "the reciprocity of consciences".[15] It is within this reciprocity of consciences that church authority functions, not indeed guaranteeing conscience (past errors preclude that simplistic claim) but informing it to a right practical judgment. We are instructed here by Cardinal Newman's famous comment in a letter to the Duke of Norfolk. "If I am obliged to bring religion into after-dinner toasts (which indeed does not seem the right thing), I shall drink to the Pope if you please, still to conscience first and to the Pope afterwards."[16]

The Catholic faithful, the International Theological Commission recently teaches, "have an instinct for the truth of the Gospel, which enables them to recognize and endorse authentic Christian doctrine and practice, and to reject what is false".[17] "Banishing the caricature of an active hierarchy and a passive laity", the Commission continues, "and in particular the notion of a strict separation between the teaching church (*Ecclesia docens*) and the learning church (*Ecclesia discens*), the Council taught that all the baptized participate in their own proper way in the three offices of Christ as prophet, priest, and king. In particular it taught that Christ fulfills his prophetic office not only by means of the hierarchy but also via the laity."[18] The attainment of moral truth in the Catholic tradition, therefore, involves a dialogical process in the communion-church between the "bishops down to the last member of the laity" and, when that process has been conscientiously completed, even the last member of the laity is finally "alone with God whose voice echoes in his depths" (GS 16) and has to make that practical judgment and decision of conscience that this is what *I* must believe or not believe, do or not

---

15 B. HÄRING: *Free and Faithful in Christ: Moral Theology for Clergy and Laity*, New York: Seabury, 1980, vol. 2, 25.

16 J.H. NEWMAN: "Letter to the Duke of Norfolk", 10, available from, http://www,newmanreader.org/Works/anglicans/volume2/gladstone/sec; accessed 02.02.2017.

17 INTERNATIONAL THEOLOGICAL COMMISSION: *Sensus Fidei in the Life of the Church*, 2014, 2, available from http://www.vatican.va/roman_curia/congregations/cfaith/cti_documents/rc_cti_20140610_sensus-fidei_en.html; accessed 02.02.2017.

18 Ibid. 4.

do. Back to Newman's dictum, and indeed also Aquinas': first conscience and afterwards the Pope.

Having made that practical judgment and decision of conscience, no Catholic is "to be forced to act in a manner contrary to his conscience. Nor... is he to be restrained from acting in accordance with his conscience, especially in matters religious" (DH, 3) and, we might add, moral. Theologian Joseph Ratzinger, later Pope Benedict XVI, points out that "not everything that exists in the church must for that reason be also a legitimate tradition... There is a distorting as well as legitimate tradition." The long-standing adherence of the church to teachings on the taking of interest on loans, on slavery, and on religious freedom are well-known examples of distorting traditions that it now rejects. Ratzinger concludes to what is obvious: "consequently tradition must not be considered only affirmatively but also critically".[19] The *Catechism of the Catholic Church* places the Church's teaching beyond doubt: Catholic women and men have "the right to act in conscience and in freedom so as personally to make moral decisions" (1782). A well-informed, and therefore well formed, conscience is the long-established Catholic way to choosing the true and the good.

1.1 Subject-Orientation and Object-Orientation of Conscience

It is common in contemporary theological ethics to distinguish between what is called the subject-orientation and the object-orientation of conscience and to argue that the former is primary and the latter secondary. Two judgments are embedded in every conscientious moral action, the first about the person or subject *who* is acting and about her/his moral goodness, the second about *what* is to be done and about its moral correctness or rightness. We are in complete agreement with Joseph Fuchs when he states that "the conscience's genuine and therefore primary interest is the moral goodness of the personal subject as such. And it is solely this personal morality that is morality in the true and original meaning of the word."[20] This subject-orientation of conscience is, therefore, to be held as primary and every other use, "moral norm", "moral action", for instance, is used analogously to this original meaning. The subject, however, expresses and fulfills her/his moral goodness only when she/he acts morally correctly or rightly in the external, objective world. It is clear, therefore, both that the conscience has also an object-orientation and that this object-orientation is secondary to its primary subject orientation. Human subjects seek in conscience to do what is morally correct or right in the external world. They so seek, however, not in order to follow some

[19] J. RATZINGER: "The Transmission of Divine Revelation", in: H. VORGRIMLER (ed.): *Commentary on the Documents of Vatican II*, New York: Herder, 1969, vol. 3, 185.

[20] J. FUCHS: *Christian Morality: The Word Becomes Flesh*, Dublin: Gill and MacMillan, 1987, 125.

external, authoritatively-taught ethical system but to be faithful to and to advance their own goodness in relationship to God, neighbor, and self. Again, we are in agreement with Fuchs. "Moral truth" is something arrived at by the practical judgment of conscience and is, therefore, to be understood not as something existing in itself to be discovered by the conscience but as something existing only within the moral subject.[21] Which of these two models of conscience, the primacy of the objective-orientation or primacy of the subjective-orientation of conscience and moral action, we now ask, is in the forefront in *Amoris laetitia*?

1.2 Amoris Laetitia *and Conscience*

Both models of conscience and moral action are evident in the Catholic Church and in the theologies of its ethicists. Those who prioritize an objective-orientation argue that moral norms *must* be followed and, therefore, control the subjective conscience. Those who prioritize a subjective-orientation argue to the contrary that the subjective conscience is free and that, when it makes a moral decision, it *must* take into consideration not only relevant moral norms but also immediate, concrete, circumstances which can lessen or even override moral norms and thus extenuate moral culpability. The two models are clearly evident in efforts to interpret *Amoris laetitia*.

In his "Pastoral Guidelines for Implementing Amoris Laetitia" Archbishop Chaput of Philadelphia writes that "Catholic teaching makes clear that the subjective conscience of the individual can never be set against objective moral truth as if conscience and truth were two competing principles for moral decision making".[22] That assertion is a "moral truth in itself" assertion, an objective-orientation of conscience assertion, obligating the subjective conscience simply to obey the moral truth in itself without any discernment. It is contrary to Catholic teaching. The *Catechism of the Catholic Church* makes authentic Catholic teaching clear. "Imputability and responsibility for an action", it teaches, "can be diminished and even nullified by ignorance, inadvertence, duress, fear, habit, inordinate attachments, and other psychological or social factors" (1734). When speaking of masturbation, it clearly teaches that "to form an equitable judgment about the subject's moral responsibility and to guide pastoral action, one must take into account the affective immaturity, force of acquired habit, conditions of anxiety, or other psychological or social factors that lessen or even extenuate moral culpability" (2352). Any conscience decision must discern not only the moral truth in

---

21 Ibid.

22 ARCHDIOCESE OF PHILADELPHIA: *Pastoral Guidelines for Implementing Amoris Laetitia*, July 1, 2016, available from http://archphila.org/wp-content/uploads/2016/06/AOP_AL-guidelines.pdf; accessed 02.02.2017.

itself but also any and every relevant circumstance. Pope Francis clearly teaches this in several different ways in *Amoris laetitia.*

Speaking of those in the "irregular situation" of being divorced and remarried without annulment, he acknowledges both that they "can find themselves in a variety of situations, which should not be pigeonholed or fit into overly rigid classifications leaving no room for personal and pastoral discernment" (AL 298). In a footnote that became instantly famous, he cites the Second Vatican Council's judgment that if they take the option of living as brother and sister the church offers them, "it often happens that faithfulness is endangered and the good of the children suffers".[23] For these reasons, the Pope continues, "a pastor cannot feel that it is enough simply to apply moral laws to those living in 'irregular' situations, as if they were stones to throw at people's lives. This would bespeak the closed heart of one used to hiding behind the Church's teachings, 'sitting on the chair of Moses and judging at times with superiority and superficiality difficult cases and wounded families'." (AL 305) Acknowledging the influence on a conscience judgment of the various concrete factors and circumstances he has enumerated, the Pope advises that "individual conscience needs to be better incorporated into the Church's praxis in certain situations which do not *objectively* embody our understanding of marriage" (AL 303, emphasis added). His argument, of course, applies not only to marriage and divorce and remarriage, about which he is specifically speaking, but also to every other concrete personal moral situation.

It is clear that Francis holds and teaches what the Catholic Church teaches but has been reticent to speak about in recent centuries, namely, a subjective- rather than an objective-orientation of conscience. To make a genuine conscience-judgment, as he argues in his *Evangelii gaudium*, we need a "harmonious objectivity", in which the internal and external realities of people's concrete lives, which "simply are", are in continuous dialogue with intellectual ideas, which must constantly be "worked out". Intellectual ideas disconnected from concrete realities, Francis judges, "give rise to ineffectual forms of idealism and nominalism, capable at most of classifying and defining, but certainly not calling to [moral] action. What calls us to [moral] action are realities illuminated by reason." (EG 232-233) His adherence to a subjective – rather than to an objective-orientation of conscience probably explains the absence from his Exhortation of the commonly cited requirement of *debitum obsequium* to magisterial teaching, doctrinal and moral. Austin Flannery translates this phrase as "loyal *submission*", the *Code of Canon Law* translates this phrase as "due *respect*" and, similarly, the phrase *religiosum obsequium* as "religious *respect*".[24]

---

[23] See GS 51.

[24] See *Lumen gentium*, in: A. FLANNERY (ed./trans.): *Vatican Council II: The Conciliar and Post Conciliar Documents*, Collegeville, MN: Liturgical Press, 1992, 25.

The translation of the Latin *obsequium* by the English "submission", however, is debated and, therefore, not compelling. In the 1983 Canon Law Society's official English translation of the *Code of Canon Law*, *debitum obsequium* is translated as "due respect" (can. 218), and *religiosum obsequium* as "religious respect" (can. 752 and can. 753).[25] In the 1997 Canon Law Society's official English translation of the *Code of Canon Law*, however, *debitum obsequium* is translated as "due submission" (can. 218), and *religiosum obsequium* as "religious submission" (can. 752 and can. 753).[26] There is a world of difference between "submission" and "respect" and, we suggest, Pope Francis shows his preference for "respect" and the inviolability of personal conscience in the beginning of his Exhortation when he teaches that "we have been called to form consciences, not to replace them" (AL 37). This, we suggest, is but an extension into the specifically lay area of marriage and family of the plea he made in *Evangelii gaudium* for a discerning, consultative church. That discernment requires, first, an understanding of the difficult circumstances and realities of people's lives, the "weaknesses" he calls them some fifteen times,[27] and, second, the offering of support and spiritual nourishment to weak people to enable them and their consciences to advance *gradually* into Christian maturity.

2 Irregular Situations

Traditionally in Catholic sexual ethics there is no parvity of matter; every sexual sin is a mortal sin. *Amoris laetitia* challenges that position. The church, however, Francis argues, "possesses a solid body of reflection concerning mitigating factors and situations. Hence it can no longer simply be said that all those in any 'irregular' situation are living in a state of mortal sin and are deprived of sanctifying grace." He learned from the Synod Fathers, he says, that "factors may exist which limit the ability to make a decision" (AL 301). Even Aquinas, he points out, "recognized that someone may possess grace and charity, yet not be able to exercise any one of the virtues well".[28] It all depends, he argues, on the person's understanding the "inherent values" behind a law or her/his concrete situation which may "not allow him or her to act differently and decide otherwise without further sin" (AL 301). The *Catechism* teaches the universal Catholic doctrine: "imputability and responsibility for an action can be diminished or even nullified by ignorance, inadvertence, duress, fear, habit, inordinate attachments, and other psychological or social factors" such as "affective immaturity, force of acquired

25 *Code of Canon Law*, Washington, DC: Canon Law Society of America, 1983.

26 *Code of Canon Law*, Washington, DC: Canon Law Society of America, 1999.

27 See AL, Chapter Eight, "Accompanying, Discerning, and Integrating Weakness", 291-312.

28 ST I-II, 65, 3, ad 2 and ad 3; *De Malo*, 2, 2.

habit, conditions of anxiety or other psychological or social factors" (1735 and 2352). Francis applies these teachings to the consideration of various "irregular situations".

2.1 Communion for the Divorced and Remarried without Annulment

The topic of sacramental communion for the divorced and remarried without annulment was the topic most hotly debated at the Synods and the topic about which the Bishops were most divided. In their final document, by a margin of 187 yes to 72 no votes (72% yes), they proposed a "logic of integration" for re-establishing the divorced and remarried into communion with the church, including possible sacramental communion.[29] On a vote of 178 yes and 80 no (69% yes), they agreed that full integration should depend on the divorced and remarried being "subjectively certain in conscience" about their freedom to take sacramental communion,[30] and, on a vote of 190 yes and 64 no (75% yes) that certain conscience should depend on an internal forum process accompanied by a priest or counselor.[31] Francis takes those decisions of the Synods and argues that "conversation with the priest, in the internal forum, contributes to the formation of a correct judgment on what hinders the possibility of a fuller participation in the life of the Church and what steps can be taken to re-establish it and make it grow". To avoid any suspicion of laxity, favoritism, or double standard, this discernment must include "humility, discretion and love for the Church and her teaching, in a sincere search for God's will and a desire to make a more perfect response to it" (AL 300).[32] Any conscience or internal forum judgment about divorce, remarriage without annulment, and partaking of communion, in other words, must be a community-based but ultimately subjective-conscience judgment made by the couple themselves.

2.2 Contraception

The topic of contraception has divided opinion in the Catholic Church since the publication of Pope Paul VI's *Humanae vitae* in 1968. Its treatment in *Amoris laetitia* focuses on the situation in which a State imposes contraception on its citizens and Francis condemns that imposition as a gross violation of both individual and couple consciences. State intervention in birth policy challenges "the upright

---

29 See SYNOD OF BISHOPS: *The Final Report of the Synod of Bishops to the Holy Father, Pope Francis*, 2015, 84, available from http://www.vatican.va/roman_curia/synod/documents/rc_synod_doc_20151026_relazione-finale-xiv-assemblea_en.html; accessed 02.02.2017.

30 Ibid. 85.

31 Ibid. 86.

32 See canon 916 and commentary in J.A. CORIDEN ET AL. (eds.): *The Code of Canon Law: A Text and Commentary*, New York: Paulist Press, 1985, 653.

consciences of spouses who have been generous in transmitting life" and "may lead them, for sufficiently serious reasons, to limit the number of their children", and "the Church strongly rejects the forced State intervention in favor of contraception, sterilization, and even abortion" (AL 42). Francis refers to Paul VI's *Humanae vitae* 14, but highlights "the need to respect the dignity of the person in morally assessing methods of regulating birth..." rather than citing the text from *Humanae vitae* on the specific prohibition of artificial birth control.[33] Indeed, the *Relatio Synodi* 58, cited in *Amoris laetitia*, mentions "natural methods for responsible procreation". This reference to natural methods, however, is noticeably absent from the Exhortation itself.[34] In addition, the Exhortation references John Paul II's *Familiaris consortio* 14, which lauds children as the "precious gift of marriage" (AL 42), but nowhere does it mention the absolute inseparability of the unitive and procreative meanings of sexual intercourse so emphasized by Paul VI in *Humanae vitae* 11 and 12 and so central to his banning of all artificial contraception. Without specifically abrogating Paul VI's much-controverted teaching, Francis comes down on what to some is a new, but in reality is an old though recently magisterially ignored, Catholic principle of the absoluteness and inviolability of an informed conscience. Decision about family planning, Francis insists, "fittingly takes place as the result of a consensual dialogue between the spouses" and the decision flows from an informed conscience "which is 'the most secret core and sanctuary of a person' where 'each one is alone with God whose voice echoes in the depth of the heart'" (AL 222)[35]. The Second Vatican Council taught that the married couple "will make decisions [about the transmission of life] by common counsel and effort... *The parents themselves and no one else should ultimately make this judgment in the sight of God*" (AL 222, emphasis added).[36] This firm principle has always assumed a couple's accompaniment by a priest in making their conscience judgment and Francis reinforces this in his decree that any conscience or internal forum solution should ultimately be the decision of the couple assisted by the counsel of a priest. Again, since a priest represents his church community, a community-based subjective-conscience judgment.

2.3 Cohabitation

The approach to sex, marriage, and family of contemporary Western women and men, including a large majority of Catholics, has largely collapsed. When the *Lineamenta* for the 2015 Synod on Marriage and Family was distributed, the first

---

33 AL 82, 222.

34 *Relatio synodi*, 2014, 58, available from http://www.vatican.va/roman_curia/synod/documents/rc_synod_doc_20141018_relatio-synodi-familia_en.html; accessed 02.02.2017.

35 See GS 16.

36 See GS 50.

reaction of Catholic Marriage Care in England, charged with the marriage preparation of those wishing to marry in the Catholic Church, was that "nearly all couples attending our marriage preparation courses are cohabiting, and many have children...the couple asking to be married in the Church and not already living together is a rarity."[37] There are multiple reasons for such an approach to sex, marriage, and family, but they are not elaborated in *Amoris laetitia* and need not detain us here. Francis contents himself with the undisputed judgment that "in some countries, *de facto* unions are very numerous, not only because of a rejection of values concerning the family and matrimony, but *primarily* because celebrating a marriage is considered too expensive in the social circumstances. As a result, material poverty drives people into *de facto* unions." (AL 294, emphasis added)[38] Nowhere in his Exhortation does Francis condemn cohabitation in blanket fashion. In contradistinction to the *Final Report* from the Synods which condemns all cohabitation,[39] he makes a distinction between "cohabitation which totally excludes any intention to marry" (AL 53) and cohabitation dictated by "cultural and contingent situations" like poverty (AL 294). Borrowing from Jesus' treatment of the Samaritan woman and Saint John Paul II's "law of gradualness", he accepts the latter "in the knowledge that the human being 'knows, loves and accomplishes moral good by different stages of growth" (AL 295).[40] The church must never "desist from proposing the full ideal of marriage, God's plan in all its grandeur". Aware of all the psychological, historical, cultural, and "even biological" mitigating circumstances, she must also never desist from accompanying "with mercy and patience the eventual stages of personal growth as these progressively appear" (AL 307). Again the law of gradualness. The biblical Jesus leaves his followers with two commandments: first, the great commandment, "You shall love your neighbor as yourself" (Mt 19,19; see Jn 15,16), which is "much more than all whole burnt offerings and sacrifice" (Mk 12,33); second, the commandment, "judge not that you be not judged" (Mt 7,1; Lk 6,37).[41] The Catholic Church and Catholics in general, Francis argues, must heed these commandments even if, in his pregnant phrase, "in the process, her shoes get soiled by the mud of the street" (AL 308).

---

37 See the editorial "Winding Journey to Wedlock", in: *The Tablet* (12 December, 2013).

38 Anyone interested in cohabitation statistics may consult M.G. LAWLER: "Cohabitation in the Catholic Church", in: M.G. LAWLER: *Marriage in the Catholic Church: Disputed Questions*, Collegeville, MN: Liturgical Press, 2002, 162-192.

39 See *The Final Report*, 25.

40 See JOHN PAUL II: *Familiaris consortio*, 34.

41 See AL 306 and 308.

2.4 Homosexual Action

The final irregular situation Francis chooses to dwell on is the situation occasioned by the phenomenon of homosexuality. His treatment is brief and he drops the more positive language found in the earlier Synod documents. "'Every sign of unjust discrimination' is to be carefully avoided, particularly any form of aggression and violence." (AL 250)[42] This specific proscription of *unjust discrimination* has left the door open for some to argue that *just discrimination* against homosexual persons is permitted, a conclusion that surely is contrary to the two commandments he so emphasizes "love your neighbor as yourself" and "judge not". To the much-controverted questions of homosexual marriage, he gives an unequivocal answer. "*De facto or same-sex unions*... may not simply be equated with marriage", and "there are absolutely no grounds for considering homosexual unions to be in any way similar or even remotely analogous to God's plan for marriage and family" (AL 251). The basis for this judgment should be read as a positive claim for the benefits of heterosexual marriage and not just as a condemnation of same-sex unions. "It is legitimate and right", Francis argues, "to reject older forms of the traditional family marked by authoritarianism and even violence, yet this should not lead to a disparagement of marriage itself, but rather to the rediscovery of its authentic meaning and its renewal." (AL 53)

The grand plan of *Amoris laetitia* is the rediscovery of the authentic meaning and the renewal of Christian marriage and family, for "the Christian proclamation on the family is good news indeed", and "the joy of love experienced by families is also the joy of the Church" (AL 1). It is unfortunate, however, that Francis did not choose to recognize the joy of genuine love experienced by same-sex couples and chose instead to contrast it with the joy of love experienced by opposite-sex couples. We wonder if, when he wrote his brief comments on same-sex unions in paragraphs 52 and 53, he had not already thought about paragraph 314 where he asserts, correctly, that God "dwells deep within the marital love that gives him glory". He cannot possibly be asserting that God dwells within love in marriage and does not dwell within the love between two same-sex persons, for the universal and unchallenged Christian position is the biblical position: "God is love" and "if we love one another, God abides in us and his love is perfected in us" (1 Jn 4,8 and 12). We judge that, despite the negative judgments about their unions, there is good news for gays and lesbians in Francis' Exhortation. That good news lies in two things that run throughout and color the entire document, the theme of gradualness and the theme of the authority and inviolability of personal conscience.

The theme of gradualness applies to the extent that, as mutually-loving gay and lesbian couples demonstrate that their unions, whether called marriage or not,

[42] See *The Final Report*, 2015, 78 and *Catechism of the Catholic Church*, 2358.

are as loving and interpersonally fruitful as heterosexual unions, Catholics and their church will become as comfortable with them as with communion for the divorced and remarried without annulment. Indeed, there is extensive sociological evidence that the majority of Western Catholics are already comfortable with gay and lesbian marriages. Francis' judgment that "adoption is a very generous way to become parents", his exhortation "I encourage those who cannot have children to expand their marital love to embrace those who lack a proper family situation", and his further judgment that "adopting a child is an act of love, offering the gift of a family to someone who has none" can all be applied to homosexual as well as heterosexual unions.[43] The common and uninformed wisdom that asserts that gay and lesbian parents are bad for the proper development of their children is universally controverted by the scientific evidence that shows that the children of gay and lesbian parents fare as well as the children of heterosexual parents.[44] And as for conscience, the theme of the freedom and inviolability of an informed personal subjective-conscience applies as much to the decision of gays and lesbians to enter a loving union and to adopt children as it applies to any other conscience or internal forum decision.

3 Conclusion

There are, of course, other items of interest in *Amoris laetitia* but limitation of space precludes dealing with them here. There is Francis' ubiquitous emphasis on poverty and its effects on marriages and families, especially on the women and children in families worldwide. He insists that Christian marriage demands that husband and wife be equal in their marriages and families. "Every form of sexual submission", the Pope argues, "must be clearly rejected. This includes all improper interpretations in the passage in the Letter to the Ephesians where Paul tells women to 'be subject to your husbands'. This passage mirrors the cultural categories of the time." But, "as Saint John Paul II wisely observed: Love excludes every kind of subjection whereby the wife might become the servant or the slave of her husband." (AL 156) We already noted his judgment about the influence of poverty preventing couples from entering into marriage in the first place.

There remains much work to be done to draw out the full anthropological, normative, and ethical methodological implications of *Amoris laetitia* for Catholic

---

43 AL 179; see also 180.

44 See the Policy Statement of the AMERICAN PSYCHOLOGICAL ASSOCIATION: "Sexual Orientation, Parents, and Children", 2004, available from http//www.apa.org/pi/lgbc/policy/parents.html; accessed 02.02.2017, and the report of the AMERICAN ACADEMY OF PEDIATRICS: "Gay and Lesbian Parents", 2005, updated in 2015, available from https://healthychildren.org/English/family-life/family-dynamics/types-of-families/Pages/gay; accessed 02.02.2017. Both these reports offer extensive and useful bibliography.

sexual ethics, but it is clear that it will stimulate debate around the moral issues involved in irregular situations that appeared magisterially settled with the publication of John Paul II's *Veritatis splendor*. The three items we have focused on in the grand plan of *Amoris laetitia* will be in the forefront of that theological debate and reflection: first, the reinstatement of the importance of an informed conscience in making moral decisions of any sort and of its absolute inviolability in proceeding to the action judged to be moral in the internal forum; second, the gradualness of growing into life, Christian life, and marital life it presents and takes for granted; third, the emphasis on the virtues of love, mercy, and non-judgment of other people and their situations. We have no doubt that in *Amoris laetitia* Pope Francis has pointed the way, not to any abrogation of Catholic ethical doctrine but to a renewed, gospel, and therefore Catholic, way to approach it.

The Law of Gradualness or the Gradualness of Law? A Critical Analysis of *Amoris Laetitia*

Branislav Kuljovsky

Introduction

Ever since its release on the 8th of April 2016, the apostolic exhortation of Pope Francis has stirred conflicting reactions not only among Catholic scholars but also among the highest representatives of the church. Some welcomed the new document with keenness and excitement; others expressed their displeasure and even an outright critique.[1] The main bone of contention represents the document's eight chapter entitled "Accompanying, Discerning and Integrating Weakness", which elaborates pastoral perspectives on the situation of people living in irregular situations, i.e. in a manner that the church deems morally evil. However, this pastoral proposal is underpinned, explicitly or implicitly, by certain ethical assertions. This paper will focus on the analysis of these ethical underpinnings of the pope's pastoral suggestions. More specifically, it will address a particular question of whether the document's concrete elaborations of the "law of gradualness", through the conceptions of discernment and conscience, does avoid what it explicitly intends to reject, namely the "gradualness of law".[2] Two assumptions are implicit to the question about the distinction between these two concepts: first, that there truly exists an intelligible and significant difference between them, otherwise it would be nonsensical to make the distinction; and second, that one of

1 For a glimpse at a disparate reception of the document until approximately August 2016, cf. S. GOERTZ/C. WITTING: "Wendepunkt für die Moraltheologie? Kontext, Rezeption und Hermeneutik von Amoris laetitia", in: S. GOERTZ/C. WITTING (eds.): *Amoris laetitia – Wendepunkt für die Moraltheologie?*, Freiburg-Basel-Wien: Herder, 2016, 48-60. Undoubtedly, the main development in the debate occurred in November 2016 with the publication of five *dubia* (doubts) formulated by four cardinals (Burke, Brandmüller, Caffarra, and Meisner) and sent to Pope Francis on 19 September 2016. They requested an authoritative clarification over some confusing interpretations of AL.

2 Cf. FRANCIS: *Amoris laetitia*, 2016, 295, 300, available from https://w2.vatican.va/content/dam/francesco/pdf/apost_exhortations/documents/papa-francesco_esortazione-ap_20160319_amoris-laetitia_en.pdf; accessed 02.05.2017.

them is good, thus it is to be accepted, and the other is bad, thus it is to be rejected. Although the primary purpose of this paper is not to provide an argument for why the "gradualness of law" is problematic, its incompatibility with certain principles of Catholic moral teaching will become obvious throughout the text. Primarily, this paper will argue that the two explicit passages in *Amoris laetitia* (AL 295 and 300) that put these two conceptions – "the law of gradualness" and "the gradualness of law" – in opposition to each other are but rhetoric, i.e. *Amoris laetitia*'s concrete application of the principle of the "law of gradualness" as a tool for a pastoral approach to the so-called irregular situations entails "gradualness in law". Secondarily, it will also argue that erasing this distinction is in direct contradiction to the previous teaching of the church's magisterium, which firmly preserved it. To achieve this purpose, the article will proceed in two steps: first, it will carefully elucidate the distinction between the two concepts through a detailed study of the previous documents of the magisterium; second, it will discuss some prominent concepts of *Amoris laetitia* in order to demonstrate that the aforementioned distinction is not preserved.

1 The Distinction Between the Law of Gradualness and the Gradualness of Law

1.1 A Trivial Question?

To start with, it might seem that the meaning of the concept of gradualness is spontaneously obvious to everyone. However, a quick look at the explanations of gradualness by some Synod Fathers, published in various Catholic newspapers around the time when the "law of gradualness" first started to resonate at the 2014 Synod of Bishops, will quickly prove this assumption wrong. For example, Cardinal Vincent Nichols of Westminster noted that "the 'law of graduality'[3] is a law of pastoral moral theology which *permits* people, all of us, to take one step at a time in our *search for holiness* in our lives". Or, Cardinal Reinhard Marx of Munich and Freising told reporters that "the idea of graduality could help the Church develop a *new* way of speaking about sexuality... We cannot have always 100 percent, and I would say good and bad, that's not so easy to make the difference... There is a development, a way, in the biography or in a relationship and so on."[4]

3 Different materials use different modalities of the English expression for "gradualness", such as "graduality" or "gradualism". These notions refer to the same reality. Since the official English translation of AL uses the term "gradualness", the present paper will use this expression. However, direct quotations with different versions of this expression will not be amended.

4 F.X. ROCCA: "Family Synod: Participants Emphasise Importance of 'Graduality' in Morality Discussions", in: *Catholic Herald* (08.10.2014), available from http://www.catholicherald.co.uk/news/2014/10/08/family-synod-participants-emphasise-i

A list of similar statements about gradualness from senior church representatives could be easily enlarged. As obvious as it seems it is not clear how these general statements about gradualness, such as a progressive "search for holiness" or "development in a relationship", translate into a concrete method for evaluating human behavior as morally good or evil. Do they, for example, imply that one is allowed to steal as long as he or she always intends to steal less than the previous time; or that one is allowed to live promiscuously as long as he intends to continuously decrease the amount of sexual partners; or that a husband may allow himself a love affair as long as he envisions to keep the promise of fidelity in the long run? Even though such implications might flow from the previously mentioned explanations of the principle of gradualness, it is not quite clear whether this is what the two Synod Fathers quoted had in mind. Nonetheless, what is clear is that the concept of gradualness did not fall from heaven during the last two Synods on the family and, therefore, it is surely not a "new" idea. Rather it has been pondered quite extensively in the previous statements of the magisterium. They also provide us with a careful and intelligible distinction between the concepts of the "law of gradualness" and the "gradualness of law".

1.2 Gradualness at the 1980 Synod on the Family

Interestingly enough, the term gradualness made a noticeable appearance at another Synod of Bishops on marriage and family some 36 years ago. Just like at recent Synods, gradualness came to the fore in the first days of the Synod, during which the Synod Fathers from around the world delivered 162 interventions.[5] The notion of "gradualness in the pedagogy of the faithful" was suggested as a potential tool to bridge the gulf between the official teaching of the church and the experience of the faithful, specifically with regard to the norm prohibiting artificial means of contraception, decreed by the 1968 encyclical *Humanae vitae*.[6]

---

mportance-of-graduality-in-discussion-of-moral-issues/; accessed 02.0.2017; emphasis added. Cf. J.L. ALLEN: "The Synod's Key Twist: The Sudden Return of Gradualism", in: *Crux* (08.10.2014), available from https://cruxnow.com/church/2014/10/08/the-synods-key-twist-the-sudden-return-of-gradualism/; accessed 02.02.2017.

5 For the most complete compilation of these contributions, cf. J. POTIN (ed.): *Aujourd'hui la famille: Principaux documents du Synode des Evêques 1980*, Paris: Centurion, 1981. For a systematic summary of the speeches according to a geographical distribution, cf. J. FRISQUE: *Le Synode sur la famille: L'apport des églises locales*, Brussels: Prospective international, 1981. A selection of 15 interventions was also published in SYNODE DES ÉVÊQUES 1980: *La Famille*, Paris: Le Cerf, 1980, 61-136.

6 Cf. J. GROOTAERS/J.A. SELLING: *The 1980 Synod of Bishops "On the Role of the Family": An Exposition of the Event and an Analysis of Its Texts*, Leuven: Peeters, 1983 (Bibliotheca Ephemeridum Theologicarum Lovaniensium; 64), 95, 109. Some African bishops were suggesting the same principle – "la pédagogie progressive de Dieu" – with regard to the question of polygamy. Cf. J. FRISQUE: *Le Synode sur la famille*, 18.

The alleged author of this notion at the Synod was the then Superior General of the Jesuits, Pedro Arrupe.[7] Similarly, during the second week of the 1980 Synod, when the Synod Fathers worked in eleven language-based *circuli minores*, gradualness was again proposed in relation to the questions of the transmission of life. What role did this notion play in these discussions about sensitive ethical issues?

The notion of "gradualness" was suggested as a conception underpinning a pastoral process of Christian education that should present the church's moral teaching as an ideal toward which Christian marriage should strive. The Spanish-speaking discussion Group C concluded that "the opportunity was offered to underscore the necessity of providing for an education in love appropriate to the period of life and an education in sexuality in a Christian perspective".[8] The French-speaking Group A proposed that in pastoral praxis, the norm of *Humanae vitae* should be presented as a highly noble Christian ideal towards which the spouses progress gradually.[9] Gradualness thus stood for the notion that conversion was a dynamic and gradual process that does not happen overnight but takes place through progressive stages. It implies that not everyone is at the same stage of conversion as well as not everyone can be expected to be equally mature in his or her Christian faith. As a result, not everyone can be expected to uphold the "ideal" norm prohibiting contraception.

Given its importance in the synodal discussions, it comes as no surprise that the notion of gradualness also features prominently in the final text voted on by the Synod Fathers – a list of 43 advisory *Propositiones* prepared for presentation to John Paul II.[10] However, since the propositions represent a common syn-

---

7 Cf. B.L. MARTHALER: "The Family in Global Perspective: Synod 1980", in: *The Living Light* 18 (1981), 72. Joseph Selling traces the notion of gradualness even further back to the post-*Humanae vitae* period. According to him, gradualness is implicit in the interpretation of the encyclical that views it as putting forth an "ideal" teaching. Cf. J. GROOTAERS/J.A. SELLING: *The 1980 Synod of Bishops*, 262 note 135. This interpretation is found for instance in the "The Statement of the Presidential Council of the Italian Bishops' Conference" from 10 September 1968. Cf. J. HORGAN: *Humanae Vitae and the Bishops*, Shannon: Irish University Press, 1972, 68. Daniel Bogner even states that in "the tradition of Catholic moral thinking the notion [gradualness] has played a role for several centuries." D. BOGNER: "Angedeuteter Wandel: Die Ambivalenz von 'Gradualität'", in: S. GOERTZ/C. WITTING (eds.): *Amoris laetitia*, 203.

8 J. GROOTAERS/J.A. SELLING: *The 1980 Synod of Bishops*, 127.

9 Cf. SYNODE DES ÉVÊQUES 1980: *La Famille*, 147, 149.

10 After the failure of the 1974 Ordinary Synod of Bishops to produce a final coherent document, this procedure was abandoned and replaced by the process of drafting *Propositiones*. The Latin text of the propositions can be consulted in the Selling-Grootaers' book. Cf. J. GROOTAERS/J.A. SELLING: *The 1980 Synod of Bishops*, 345-365. The English version, containing the votes of the bishops on each proposition, was first published in *National Catholic Reporter* (USA). Later it was reproduced in three consecutive issues of *The Tablet*. Cf. "The Synod Propositions", in: *The Tablet* 235/7334, 7335, 7336 (1981), 116-118, 141-142, 164-167. This text will be the main reference point for this paper. For the French translation, cf. "Les 43

thetic statement of all the Synod Fathers, they naturally manifest, contrary to the more individual contributions during the discussions, an influence of the differing viewpoints at the Synod.[11] As a result, despite certain incoherencies, already the *Propositiones* text includes all the relevant elements that will later be part of official Church documents.

Gradualness is discussed in two propositions. First, Proposition 7 stipulates a general principle of gradual conversion or development towards the fullness of stature of Christ.

> It [the conversion] is a dynamic process. It begins with the love of God poured into our hearts through the Spirit. That love leads us to choose Christ whose paschal mystery reveals the father, and *it slowly integrates God's gifts and the demands of his absolute definitive love into all of human life...* Pastoral and educational guidance must patiently lead the faithful... from what they have received of Christ's mystery to*a richer understanding of it* and *a fuller integration of it* in their lives and conduct.[12]

A difficulty comes when the acknowledgement of this general principle of a "slow integration of God's demands" is practically applied in Proposition 24 to "the moral norms taught by the Church", more specifically to the norm of *Humanae vitae*.[13] Proposition 24 first acknowledges that "many Christian couples... feel unable[14] to obey the moral norms taught by the Church due to their weakness and objective difficulties". Subsequently, it states that the concrete educational approach of priests, who "should keep in mind the law of gradualism... should aim to help couples to see clearly that the teaching of *Humanae vitae* is normative for the ex-

---

propositions du Synode des évêques sur la famille", in: *La Documentation catholique* 78/1809 (1981), 537-550.

11 It must be noted that Grootaers and Selling have strongly criticized the process of the textual reduction of the final *Propositiones* for its non-transparency, especially with regard to the work of the committee for incorporating the *modi* (objections and suggestions of the bishops for revision of the text) and drawing up the *Expensio modorum* (the official commentary on the incorporation of the *modi* on the first version of the text). Their analysis suggests that those in charge of the Synod might have manipulated the final text according to their liking. Cf. J. GROOTAERS/J.A. SELLING: *The 1980 Synod of Bishops*, 156, 168-169, 257-258 note 129, 294-296.

12 "The Synod Propositions", in: *The Tablet* 235/7334 (1981), 116-117 (emphasis added).

13 Grootaers states that this proposition was "one of the most difficult texts coming from the 1980 Synod for the simple reason that, to put it mildly, it was a product of compromise." J. GROOTAERS/J.A. SELLING: *The 1980 Synod of Bishops*, 144.

14 Instead of the expression "feel [*sentiunt*] unable", the first draft of the Proposition 24 contained "are [*sunt*] unable". This change from *sunt* to *sentiunt* had for purpose, as the Synod's relator Cardinal Ratzinger explained, to avoid the condemned proposition of Jansenius that some of God's commandments are impossible for the justified person to fulfill. Cf. P. HEBBLETHWAITE: "Echoes of Old Showdown Haunt New Encyclical", in: *National Catholic Reporter* (27.08.1993), 13.

ercise of their sexuality, and to work sincerely in creating the right conditions for the *fulfillment of these norms*". Moreover, this educational approach "has to lead the couple on a human journey that involves the consciousness of sin, the desire to keep the law not just as an ideal for the future, and the ministry of reconciliation". Likewise, "[i]n following the law of gradualism, neither priests nor couples should set up a false dichotomy between the doctrine and pastoral practice".[15]

These formulations suggest that gradualness in pastoral praxis cannot justify even a provisional diminishing of the demands of the doctrine, i.e. violating moral norms taught by the church. Even in difficult life circumstances it is not permissible to break the norm against contraception on the basis that one holds that norm in high esteem as an ideal to be achieved gradually in the future. The demand of *Humanae vitae* is not a mere ideal, as if using contraception to limit responsibly the size of one's family would be just "less of an ideal" but not moral evil, and thus permissible.

Yet, a few other statements included in this proposition compromise such a straightforward meaning. It, for example, states that this educational approach "will mix constancy with *patience*, courage, humility and complete confidence in God's mercy; ...there should be neither fear nor anxiety, but just the love that casts out fear". "*Patience*, sympathy and *time*" are also required simply because "the conjugal act involves the free will of two persons who must come to grips with each other's conduct and opinions".[16] These formulations suggest that in some situations pastors should be patient with the couple, which might mean that provisionally they may even permit breaking the norm against contraception. Thus, Proposition 24 is not completely coherent in spelling out the implications of the notion of gradualness for the pastoral-pedagogical guidance of the faithful. A much more coherent position was presented in several official documents of the church.[17]

1.3 Gradualness in the Official Documents of the Church

The first explicit formulation of the distinction between the "law of gradualness" and the "gradualness of law" is found in the Synod's closing homily on 25 October 1980 delivered by John Paul II. After repeating that gradualness cannot mean

15 "The Synod Propositions", 118 (emphasis original).

16 Ibid. (emphasis added).

17 The following documents discuss the notion of gradualness most explicitly: John Paul II's closing homily of the 1980 Synod of Bishops, no. 9 and no. 34 of the 1981 Post-Synodal Apostolic Exhortation *Familiaris consortio* (FC), no. 103 of the 1993 encyclical *Veritatis splendor* (VS), no. 75 of the 1995 encyclical *Evangelium vitae* (EV), as well as the 1997 *Vademecum* (i.e. practical guidelines) for confessors concerning some aspects of the morality of conjugal life issued by the Pontifical Council for the Family.

"keeping the law as a mere 'ideal' to be obeyed in the future", John Paul II urges that "difficulties [in fulfilling the law] must constantly be overcome".[18] He adds that

> ...the 'law of gradualness,' as it is called, is not possible unless a person sincerely obeys the divine law and seeks those benefits that are protected and promoted by that law. For the 'law of gradualness' (or gradual progress) cannot be the same as 'gradualness of the law' as if there were various grades or forms of commandment for different men [sic] and circumstances in the divine law. All couples are called to holiness in marriage according to the divine plan; and the dignity of this vocation becomes effective when a person is able to respond to the command of God with a serene mind, trusting in divine grace and his [sic] own will.[19]

In addition, FC 34 states that "husbands and wives should first of all recognize clearly the teaching of *Humanae vitae* as indicating the norm for the exercise of their sexuality, and... they should endeavor to establish the conditions necessary for observing that norm".

John Paul II situates the "law of gradualness" here within the process of sincere obedience of the divine law and search for the good promoted by that law, a process to which all couples are invited. Such a process of "continuous permanent conversion" requires, as FC 9 states, "an interior detachment from every evil and an adherence to good in its fullness".[20] John Paul II makes clear in these passages that the anthropological truth about the progressive nature of human development cannot imply that pastors may advise as permissible what is considered to be an

---

[18] This assertion is also included almost literally in FC 34: "They [married people] cannot however look on the law as merely an ideal to be achieved in the future: they must consider it as a command of Christ the Lord to overcome difficulties with constancy." JOHN PAUL II: *Familiaris consortio*, 1981, 34, available from http://w2.vatican.va/content/john-paul-ii/en/apost_exhortations/documents/hf_jp-ii_exh_19811122_familiaris-consortio.html#_ftnref95; accessed 02.02.2017. Similarly, *Veritatis splendor* 103 teaches that "[i]t would be a very serious error to conclude ... that the Church's teaching is essentially only an 'ideal' which must then be adapted, proportioned, *graduated* to the so-called concrete possibilities of man [sic] ...". JOHN PAUL II: *Veritatis splendor*, 1993, 103, available from http://www.vatican.va/holy_father/john_paul_ii/encyclicals/documents/hf_jp-ii_enc_06081993_veritatis-splendor_en.html; accessed 02.05.2017, emphasis added.

[19] "Pope's Final Address to the Synod", in: *The Tablet* 234/7321 (1980), 1081. The last two sentences of this quote were taken verbatim into *FC* 34.

[20] In the same sense, the 1997 *Vademecum* teaches that "the law of gradualness" "consists of requiring a *decisive break* with sin together with a *progressive path* towards total union with the will of God and with his loving demands", and warns that this should "not be confused with the 'gradualness of the law' which would tend to diminish the demands it places on us". PONTIFICAL COUNCIL FOR THE FAMILY: *Vademecum for Confessors Concerning Some Aspects of the Morality of Conjugal Life*, 1997, 9, available from http://www.vatican.va/roman_curia/pontifical_councils/family/documents/rc_pc_family_doc_12021997_vademecum_en.html; accessed 02.02.2017, emphasis original.

immoral behavior. He clarifies that the "law of gradualness" cannot imply that there are different moral precepts for different people depending on how difficult their life circumstances are. Such a view would precisely amount to the "gradualness of law".

As a result, according to John Paul II, the way the "law of gradualness" should be legitimately applied in pastoral praxis, for example in relation to the norm of *Humanae vitae*, is that the spouses deliberating the means to responsibly control the size of their family should not just recognize the norm against contraception as an ideal to be achieved one day in the future, but they should try to observe it immediately. If the spouses then fail to observe the norm, due to their weakness or other difficult life circumstances, the law of gradualness should remind the priests or pastoral workers not to judge or admonish the spouses, but rather to kindly and patiently encourage and inspire them anew to follow the good protected by the norm. In no case can the law of gradualness entitle them to license morally evil kinds of behavior. However, a question still arises as to what precisely then the *processus dynamicus* – the slow integration of the demands of God's absolute love – about which Proposition 7 speaks, stands for if one is always expected to seek to implement the moral norm in its fullness regardless of circumstances. After all, even FC 34 speaks clearly of certain dynamism in accomplishing moral good:

> But man [sic], who has been called to live God's wise and loving design in a responsible manner, is an historical being who day by day builds himself up through his many free decisions; and so *he knows, loves and accomplishes moral good by stages of growth.*[21]

Thus, is there not a tension, on the one hand, between acknowledging human historicity and accomplishment of moral good by stages of growth or through a slow integration and, on the other hand, requesting that the moral good protected by specific moral norms be sought in each and every human action? Or, as certain theologians argue, did John Paul II's requirement that difficulties in fulfilling the law must be constantly overcome render "void the concept of gradualness"?[22]

To fully comprehend these seemingly conflicting statements in relation to "the law of gradualness", one needs to elucidate the understanding of such terms as "law", "demands" or "norms" and their relationship to the evaluation of human behavior within the Catholic moral tradition. More specifically, it is necessary to provide at least a short consideration of the Catholic moral teaching on moral absolutes.

---

21 FC 34 (emphasis added).

22 T. KNIEPS-PORT LE ROI/R. BURGGRAEVE: "New Wine in New Wineskins: Amoris Laetitia and the Church's Teaching on Marriage and Family", in: *Louvain Studies* 39 (2016), 295.

1.4 Gradualness and Moral Absolutes

The expression "moral absolutes" refers to specific moral norms that prohibit certain kinds of actions, "which, per se and in themselves, independently of circumstances, are always seriously wrong by reason of their object".[23] This means that, as possible objects of human choice, these types of actions identified by moral absolutes, are specified "without employing in their description any morally evaluative terms".[24] In other words, these norms exclude not only "needless" acts of city destroying against noncombatants and combatants alike, or intercourse with the "wrong" person or "selfish" exclusion of children from marriage, but every act so directed.[25] A good label for these absolutes would also be "exceptionless moral norms".[26] The church's moral tradition has termed the types of actions prohibited by these exceptionless moral norms as "intrinsically evil" (*intrinsece malum*).[27]

In the post-*Humanae vitae* period, increasingly some prominent Catholic moral theologians started to question the nature, specific number or even the very existence of moral absolutes.[28] This dissent prompted John Paul II to the publication of his 1993 encyclical *Veritatis splendor* (VS), "the central theme" of which

---

[23] JOHN PAUL II: *Reconciliatio et paenitentia*, 1984, 17, available from http://w2.vatican.va/content/john-paul-ii/la/apost_exhortations/documents/hf_jp ii_exh_02121984_reconciliatio-et-paenitentia.html; accessed 02.02.2017. See also the address of John Paul II to the international congress of moral theologians: "...nell'ambito di quelle [humana] attività, esistano atti che siano sempre e comunque in se stessi e per se stessi illeciti...Tutta la tradizione della Chiesa ha vissuto e vive basandosi sulla convinzione contraria a questa negazione." JOHN PAUL II: *Discorso di Giovanni Paolo II ai partecipanti al congresso internazionale di teologia morale*, 1986, 3, available from https://w2.vatican.va/content/john-paul-ii/it/speeches/1986/april/documents/hf_jp-ii_spe_19860410_teologia-morale.html; accessed 02.02.2017.

[24] W.E. MAY: *An Introduction to Moral Theology*, Huntington, IN: Our Sunday Visitor, 2007, 142.

[25] Cf. SECOND VATICAN COUNCIL: *Gaudium et spes*, 1965, 80, available from http://www.vatican.va/archive/hist_councils/ii_vatican_council/documents/vat-ii_const_19651207_gaudium-et-spes_en.html; accessed 02.02.2017.

[26] J. FINNIS: *Moral Absolutes: Tradition, Revision, and Truth*, Washington, DC: Catholic University of America Press, 1991, 3.

[27] Cf. VS 80. It must be noted that the term "*intrinsece malum*" has its origin only in the sixteenth century, which, however, does not mean that the theme of the actions wrong *per se* cannot be found for example in the thought of the patristic authors, such as Saint Augustine. This is due to the fact that the theme of moral absolutes is connected to the general conception of morality. Cf. S. PINCKAERS: *Ce qu'on ne peut jamais faire: La question des actes intrinsèquement mauvais; Histoire et discussion*, Fribourg: Éditions Universitaires Fribourg, 1986 (Études d'éthique chrétienne; 19), 21, 63.

[28] Several authors describe this evolution within Catholic moral theology. Cf. J.A. SELLING: *Reframing Catholic Theological Ethics*, Oxford: Oxford University Press, 2016, 19-22.; S. PINCKAERS: *The Sources of Christian Ethics*, Washington, DC: Catholic University of America Press, 1995, 305; J.E. SMITH: *Humanae Vitae: A Generation Later*, Washington, DC: Catholic University of America Press, 1991, 194-195, 198.

was to restate, "with the authority of the Successor of Peter... *the universality and immutability of the moral commandments*, particularly those which prohibit always and without exception *intrinsically evil acts*".[29] The encyclical attempted to set forth an argument against new trends in Catholic moral theology (teleologism, consequentialism, or proportionalism) that reject moral absolutes and the notion of intrinsically evil acts as understood by the Catholic moral tradition. Elucidating all the individual issues and differing positions related to the immense academic discussion on the question of moral absolutes during the last half-century cannot (due to the available space) be the purpose of the present exposition.[30] Rather the present section will analyze the conception of moral absolutes in *Veritatis splendor* and *Evangelium vitae* (EV) and point to its relevance for the understanding of the "law of gradualness".

Discussing the universal and immutable nature of natural law, *Veritatis splendor* makes a distinction between positive and negative precepts of the law. According to VS 52, the positive precepts for example include the following: "it is right and just, always and for everyone, to serve God, to render him the worship which is his due and to honour one's parents as they deserve". Although these precepts are "universally binding" and "unchanging", John Paul II explains that "[t]hese universal and permanent laws... are applied to particular acts through the judgment of conscience". As a result, although one may never choose to act in contradiction with the positive precepts, the concrete content of human action in a given situation, as determined by the positive precepts, "depends on the cir-

29 VS 115 (emphasis original).

30 There are, roughly speaking, three strains within Catholic moral theology that have been part of the academic discussion in the post-conciliar and more specifically post-*Humanae vitae* period: (1) the classical natural law theory represented by such authors as Elizabeth Anscombe, Russel Hittinger, Ralph McInerny, Janet E. Smith, etc.; (2) the new natural law theory represented by Germain Grisez, John Finnis, Joseph Boyle, William E. May, etc; and (3) the revisionist theories – proportionalism or consequentialism (which most of the time also claim to be a version of the natural law), represented by people like Richard A. McCormick, Joseph Fuchs, Louis Janssens, Charles Curran, etc. Obviously this is a very simplified and incomplete categorization that does not do justice to the differences among individual authors. All three approaches claim the support of Thomas Aquinas for their respective theories, however, only the revisionists, while acknowledging that there are some kinds of moral absolutes (e.g. some "transcendental principles" or "formal norms" or norms described in morally evaluative language), deny that there are any "intrinsically evil acts" in the strong sense, and corresponding to them, specific moral absolutes. The main difference between the traditional and new natural law theory seems to lie in their different analyses of human action, especially their different views of what is the origin of morality (the "is-ought" debate) and what constitutes an "object" of human action (*finis operis* vs. *finis operantis*). Cf. W.E. MAY: *Moral Absolutes: Catholic Tradition, Current Trends, and the Truth*, Milwaukee, WI: Marquette University Press, 1989; S. PINCKAERS: *Ce qu'on ne peut jamais faire*; J. FINNIS: *Moral Absolutes: Tradition, Revision*; J.E. SMITH: *Humanae Vitae*, 194-229, 340-370.

cumstances". This means that a precept such as "care for your wife and family" will translate into a different set of actions for different husbands depending on their life circumstances.[31] There will always be a potential for growth in achieving the fullness of the good protected by this norm because the perfect fulfillment of positive precepts can only be achieved in the eschaton.

On the other hand, the pope states that there are negative precepts of the law, such as we find in Matthew 19, 17-18 – "you shall not murder, you shall not commit adultery, you shall not steal, you shall not bear false witness" – "which forbid a given action *semper et pro semper* [i.e. always and in each instance], without exception, because the choice of this kind of behavior is in no case compatible with the goodness of the will of the acting person, with his vocation to life with God and to communion with his neighbor" (VS 52).[32] In other words, while the commandment of love does not have in its dynamic any higher limit, it does have a lower limit, beneath which the commandment is broken. There are certain kinds of behavior that can never be properly chosen even if they are motivated by a remote good end. As a result, the negative norms that prohibit these specific kinds of behavior cannot be graduated to the possibilities and circumstances of an individual person.

---

31 These kinds of moral norms are more or less what the revisionist moral theologians believe to be the only moral absolutes, true always and in all circumstances. They commonly call these norms "formal" and include among them such general and abstract principles as the great commandment "love God and your neighbor as yourself", the golden rule "treat others as you would like them to treat you", or the first principle of natural law "do good and avoid evil". In addition, they also include here norms expressed positively in the language of virtue such as be honest, be just, be chaste, etc. Finally, formal absolute norms also include more specific norms but described in morally qualified language, i.e. mere tautologies such as "you must not kill *unjustly*" or "you must not have sex with the *wrong* person or for the *wrong* reasons", etc. Cf. L. JANSSENS: "Norms and Priorities in a Love Ethics", in: *Louvain Studies* 6/3 (1977), 207-210, 216; R.M. GULA: *Reason Informed by Faith: Foundations of Catholic Morality*, New York: Paulist Press, 1989, 286-289; T.E. O'CONNELL: *Principles for a Catholic Morality*, New York: Seabury, 1978, 157-161; J. FUCHS: *Christian Ethics in a Secular Arena*, Washington, DC: Georgetown University Press, 1984, 72; R.A. MCCORMICK: *Notes on Moral Theology 1965-1980*, Washington, DC: University Press of America, 1981, 578-579.

32 According to the revisionist position, the norms of this kind can refer either to merely tautological statements (e.g. murder means only *unjust* killing and adultery only *wrongful* sex) or to mere "material norms" which however are relative because "we can have a proportionate reason to depart from the norm". L. JANSSENS: "Norms and Priorities in a Love Ethics", 217. Yet, the encyclical has in mind precisely what the revisionists would call negative "material norms" (although many of them would still deny that this is what the encyclical teaches), but contrary to the revisionist view, it teaches that these kinds of actions, qualified as morally evil according to their object (*ex objecto*), are never to be deliberately chosen by the acting agent's will because they are never capable of being "ordered to the good [of the person] and to the ultimate end, which is God" (VS 79).

It is in line with this distinction between the positive and negative precepts (exceptionless moral norms) of the moral law that we find in EV 75 the following reference to the principle of gradualness.

> In this sense, the negative moral precepts have an extremely important positive function. The "no" which they unconditionally require makes clear the absolute limit beneath which free individuals cannot lower themselves. At the same time they indicate the minimum which they must respect and from which they must start out in order to say "yes" over and over again, a "yes" which will *gradually* embrace the entire horizon of the good (cf. Mt 5:48). The commandments, in particular the negative moral precepts, are the beginning and the first necessary stage of the journey towards freedom. As Saint Augustine writes, 'the beginning of freedom is to be free from crimes… like murder, adultery, fornication, theft, fraud, sacrilege and so forth. Only when one stops committing these crimes (and no Christian should commit them), one begins to lift up one's head towards freedom. But this is only the *beginning* of freedom, not *perfect* freedom.'[33]

These texts elucidate the apparent tension between recognizing a dynamic element in one's moral growth toward the entire horizon of the good protected by the moral norm and the requirement to constantly seek that norm in fullness, and thus give gradualness its proper meaning.

First of all, it is clear that the dynamic process or, in other words, adaptation (graduation) according to the concrete possibilities of an individual person, pertains to the fulfillment of the positive precepts of the moral law. This still does not mean that one can dispense at any time from seeking to embody the positive precepts of the law (as if one could choose not to love one's neighbor), only that enacting the positive norm, and thus seeking the good it promotes, will take different forms of action depending on the concrete possibilities of the individual person. The law of gradualness is a legitimate description of a continuous enacting of the good promoted by the positive precepts of the moral law such as "love your neighbor", the most perfect representation of which was manifested on the cross at Golgotha. Human beings, as historical beings, will attain the full and perfect accomplishment of such law only in eternity. In this sense no one can really say, as current Archbishop of Vienna Cardinal Schönborn rightly remarked, that he or she has already achieved the perfection to which the Christian message invites us.[34] Yet, such an understanding of gradualness requires a decisive break

---

33 JOHN PAUL II: *Evangelium vitae*, 1995, 75, available from http://w2.vatican.va/content/john-paul-ii/en/encyclicals/documents/hf_jp-ii_enc_25031995_evangelium-vitae.html; accessed 02.02.2017, emphasis added.

34 Cf. C. CARD. SCHÖNBORN: "Was ist Gradualität? Kardinal Schönborn erklärt", in: *Radio Vatikan* (23.06.2015), available from http://de.radiovaticana.va/news/2015/06/23/was_ist_gradualität_kardinal_schönborn_erklärt/1153444; accessed 02.02.2017. Cf. IDEM: "Kardinal

with morally evil action (*intrinsece malum*) identified by moral absolutes. In other words, the continuous development towards the full horizon of the moral good can never take the form of specific kinds of behavior considered morally evil regardless of one's circumstances and motivations. Thus, for example, one can never graduate the norm prohibiting sexual intercourse with an unwilling partner (rape) as if one could permit it as long as its brutality diminishes in time or as long as one finds oneself in a difficult life circumstance, or as long as one feels unable, due to his/her weakness, to avoid it.

The following scheme may help understand these two conceptions:

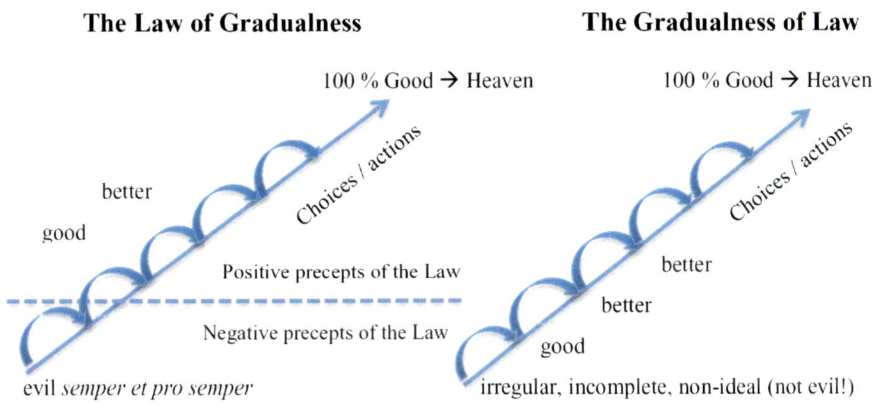

Ultimately these two concepts assume a different understanding of moral law and the negative consequences for the good of the human person and society that follow from breaking that law, especially the exceptionless moral norms. This logically results in different pastoral praxis with regard to people engaging in

Schönborn: Schritt für Schritt in die Ehe", interview by Bernd Hagenkord, in: *Katholische Kirche Erzdiözese Wien* (08.10.2014), available from https://www.erzdioezese-wien.at/site/menschenorganisation/lebendigekirche/familie/bischofssynodezurfamilie/article/39312.html; accessed 02.02.2017. It must be noted that Cardinal Schönborn's distinction between the "law of gradualness" and the "gradualness of law" is unclear. On the one hand he states: "The law is not gradual. There is no stealing more or stealing less. Stealing is stealing – the seventh commandment is the seventh commandment. And lying is lying." On the other hand, in relation to cohabiting couples, i.e. couples engaged in actions of fornication, he does not say similarly "the sixth commandment is the sixth commandment". Rather, he states that "many people achieve the full form of marriage only gradually" and makes a distinction between gradualness of law, which is illegitimate, and gradualness in "fulfilling God's law". Yet, it is difficult to grasp how the legitimacy of gradual "fulfilling" of God's norm (against premarital sex) is different from "gradualness of law", since in the given situation both terms simply imply that engaging in fornication is just less of an "ideal" or "full form" and therefore permissible. The Cardinal's thought on gradualness clearly lacks a full appreciation of the distinction between positive precepts of the moral law and moral absolutes.

actions prohibited by the absolute moral norms. Whereas "the law of gradualness" requires us to recognize the moral evil and make everything possible, with the help of God's grace, to overcome it, "the gradualness of law" would most probably remind us of our final destination and, as long as this ideal is kept in mind, for the time being, due to our weakness, immaturity or other difficult circumstances, we can "legitimately" continue to act in contradiction to the moral absolutes.

2 The Concept of Gradualness in *Amoris Laetitia*

The following section will analyze how the concept of gradualness is presented in the controversial eighth chapter of the exhortation. Whereas until now gradualness was invoked in relation to the teaching of *Humanae vitae*, Pope Francis uses it in relation to the norms against non-marital sexual relationships. The core sections discussing this conception can be found in AL 295, which deals with civilly married and cohabiting couples, and AL 300, which deals with the divorced and remarried. In both cases, while elaborating his pastoral propositions, the pope explicitly upholds the "law of gradualness" and rejects the "gradualness of law". Moreover, using this distinction he directly refers to John Paul II's FC 9 and 34. This seems to imply not only that Pope Francis posits an intelligible difference between the two conceptions but also that he wants to stay in a certain continuity with his predecessor's position. Yet, the following section will argue that *Amoris laetitia* does not maintain the same distinction between these two conceptions of gradualness as upheld in the previous teaching of the church. Moreover, it will argue that Pope Francis' understanding of such concepts as "discernment", "conscience", or "moral law" implies "gradualness in law".

2.1 Civilly Married and Cohabiting Couples

With regard to the cohabiting and civilly married, AL 294 first states that their situations require "a constructive response seeking to transform them into opportunities that can lead to the full reality of marriage and family in conformity with the Gospel". These couples "need to be welcomed and guided patiently and discreetly". Subsequently, the text mentions Jesus' encounter with the Samaritan woman from the fourth chapter of John's Gospel (cf. Jn 4,1-26) as an example for such a patient and discreet way of approaching these couples. Then comes the explicit reference to the law of gradualness in AL 295:

> Along these lines, Saint John Paul II proposed the so-called 'law of gradualness' in the knowledge that the human being 'knows, loves, and accomplishes moral good by different stages of growth' [FC 34]. This is not a 'gradualness of law' but rather a *gradualness in the prudential exercise of free acts on the part of subjects who are not*

> *in a position to understand, appreciate, or fully carry out the objective demands of the law.* For the law is itself a gift of God which points out the way, a gift for everyone without exception; it can be followed with the help of grace, even though each human being 'advances gradually with the progressive integration of the gifts of God and the demands of God's definitive and absolute love in his or her entire personal and social life.' [FC 9][35]

First of all, one observes here an interesting fact. While Pope Francis refers here significantly to *Familiaris consortio*, he does not adopt the most crucial point, namely John Paul II's distinction between the "law of gradualness" and the "gradualness of law". Instead, while the "gradualness of law" is rejected, without explaining what it actually is, a completely new definition of the "law of gradualness" is coined. This new explanation seems to imply that as long as an individual or a couple is "not in a position to understand, appreciate or fully carry out" the objective demands of the law (in this case a norm prohibiting premarital sex) it is legitimate not to ask from them an *immediate effort* to observe the norm (i.e. stop engaging in premarital sex) since, after all, human beings accomplish the moral good by stages. Even though the text states that the law is "a gift for everyone" that "can be followed with the help of grace", which is a reference to the teaching of the Council of Trent,[36] it adds that God's demands are integrated gradually. Since God's demand in question here concerns the prohibition of premarital sex, this provision entails that to different people, according to their circumstances (level of advancement), the demand of prohibiting premarital sex apply differently.[37] Consequently, no meaningful qualifier could set the proposed notion of gradualness here apart from the idea of "gradualness of law". In this sense, Pope Francis' reference to *Familiaris consortio* appears misleading because he argues for a position that is actually in contradiction to the one upheld by John Paul II.

35 AL 295 (emphasis added).

36 In its "Decree on justification" during the sixth session (13 January 1547), the Council of Trent speaks in chapter 11 that "no one, however justified, ought to think that he is exempt from the observance of the commandments, nor should he use that rash statement, forbidden by the fathers under anathema, that the commandments of God are impossible of observance by one who is justified. For God does not command the impossible, but... he gives his aid to enable you." Accordingly, the Council solemnly declares in canon 18: "If anyone says that the commandments of God are impossible of observance even by a person justified and established in grace: let him be anathema." (N.P. TANNER [ed.]: *Decrees of the Ecumenical Councils*, vol. 2, Washington, DC: Georgetown University Press, 1990, 675, 680.)

37 Other scholars hold such an interpretation of this text possible. Cf. T. KNIEPS-PORT LE ROI/R. BURGGRAEVE: "New Wine in New Wineskins", 295. Cf. J. FINNIS/G. GRISEZ: *The Misuse of Amoris Laetitia to Support Errors Against the Catholic Faith: A Letter to the Supreme Pontiff Francis, to All Bishops in Communion with Him, and to the Rest of the Christian Faithful*, 21.11.2016, 9–10, available from http://www.twotlj.org/OW-MisuseAL.pdf; accessed 02.02.2017.

2.2 Divorced and Remarried Couples

The second instance where Pope Francis explicitly appeals to the distinction between the "law of gradualness" and the "gradualness of law" can be found in the long section dealing with the idea of discernment of irregular situations, specifically AL 300:

> Given that gradualness is not in the law itself (cf. FC 34), this *discernment* can never prescind from the Gospel demands of truth and charity, as proposed by the Church.[38]

This actual quote is immune to any accusation of "the gradualness in law". Rather, by referring again to *Familiaris consortio*, it gives the impression of preserving the distinction between these two conceptions. Yet, the crucial term in the text is "discernment", which is the catchword of the entire eighth chapter of *Amoris laetitia*. So how does Pope Francis conceive of this "special discernment" (AL 301) which should never prescind from the Gospel demands of truth and charity, thus presumably from the truth of the exceptionless moral norm against non-marital sexual unions?

The pope teaches us that the "responsible personal and pastoral discernment of particular cases" is the only possible approach if we consider "the immense variety of concrete situations" of the divorced and remarried couples. No "new set of rules" can be provided. So what are the pastors supposed to discern? The pope states that this discernment should recognize that "since 'the degree of responsibility is not equal in all cases' [*Relatio Finalis*, 51], the consequences or effects of a rule need not necessarily always be the same" (AL 300). This statement, as do many others in *Amoris laetitia*, exhibits a certain ambiguity. For example, it is unclear whether "the degree of responsibility" refers to the responsibility for the failure of the first marriage or to the responsibility for engaging in a new non-marital relationship that includes sexual intimacy; these are two different things.[39] The fact that one is not responsible for the failure of his or her previous marriage does not justify his or her free engagement in other evil action, i.e. a sexual relationship with someone else than a legitimately married spouse. If we assume that the pope has in mind the latter sense (responsibility for entering a new non-marital sexually active relationship), pastors are now supposed to discern (or only assist the couple to discern)[40] the imputability of guilt for one's evil action, an issue dis-

---

38 AL 300 (emphasis added).

39 This ambiguity comes mainly from AL 298 which enumerates a variety of situations of the divorced and remarried in order to argue that their situation cannot be pigeonholed into rigid classifications. These examples, however, relate either to the circumstances of the failure of the first marriage or the difficult situation in the second relationship.

40 While most of AL's references to the notion of "discernment" imply that discernment is the task of the pastors (e.g. no. 79, 243, 293, 297-299, 302, 304), some instances (e.g. no. 37, 300, 303)

cussed in AL 301-303.[41] However, although the church indeed "possesses a solid body of reflection concerning mitigating factors" (AL 301) limiting responsibility for one's evil action, the way it is used in *Amoris laetitia* seems to depart from the traditional understanding.

The idea of mitigating factors is about identifying possible factors limiting one's exercise of free will and one's knowledge of the good and evil. Until now the discernment of the mitigating factors was supposed to serve in rightly judging the penitents' culpability retrospectively in order to determine an appropriate penance and help them deal with these factors so that they can start freely choosing rightly again. *Amoris laetitia* seems to suggest that now pastors should assess subjective culpability in order to direct prospective action without either seeking to remove the factors by appropriate instruction (in case of ignorance) or encouraging the penitents to overcome them (in case of psychological or sociological factors affecting one's freedom of choice). As a result, people may continue to engage in evil actions without ever becoming sufficiently responsible for them.[42] In the case of divorced and remarried couples, since they are not fully responsible for violating the norm against adultery, due to mitigating circumstances, they are not guilty of grave sin. Consequently, they may receive Holy Communion.[43] How does *Amoris laetitia* support such an understanding of discernment?

First of all, *Amoris laetitia* does not state clearly that people should always try to overcome, with the grace of God, the difficulties (factors) that hinder them from freely and knowingly avoiding the evil and pursuing the good, promoted by

suggest that it is the role of one's personal conscience.

41 Some authors even suggest that the notion of God's mercy in AL cannot concern only the question of discerning the degree of one's subjective guilt. Cf. S. GOERTZ/C. WITTING: "Wendepunkt für die Moraltheologie", 80-83.

42 Cf. C.E. BRUGGER: "Five Serious Problems with Chapter 8 of Amoris Laetitia", in: *The Catholic World Report*, (22.04.2016), available from http://www.catholicworldreport.com/Item/4740/five_serious_problems_with_chapter_8_of_iamoris_laetitiai.aspx; accessed 02.02.2017. Defending AL's continuity in its teaching on personal guild, Stephan Ernst as well as Rocco Buttiglione fail to completely consider the above-mentioned critique, namely that AL does not anymore require the penitent to overcome the factors limiting his or her responsibility in order to start choosing rightly again and sin no more, in faith that God never commands the impossible and offers us the necessary grace to fulfill his will. Cf. S. ERNST: ""Irreguläre Situationen" und persönliche Schuld in Amoris laetitia: Ein Bruch mit der Lehrtradition?", in: S. GOERTZ/C. WITTING (eds.): *Amoris laetitia – Wendepunkt für die Moraltheologie*, 136-159; R. BUTTIGLIONE: "The Joy of Love and the Consternation of Theologians: Some Comments on the Apostolic Exhortation Amoris Laetitia", in: *L'Osservatore Romano* (19.07.2016), available from http://www.osservatoreromano.va/en/news/joy-love-and-consternation-theologians; accessed 02.02.2017.

43 This is most clearly suggested in the footnote 351: "In certain cases [of subjective non-culpable sin], this [the Church's help towards a person's growth in God's grace] can include the help of sacraments" (AL 305 note 351).

the moral absolutes. Choosing to do moral evil, whether culpably or inculpably, always involves harm to the good of the person, regardless of the circumstances and further noble motivations.[44] Instead of demanding that pastors encourage the penitents to break with morally evil actions (a purpose of amendment), *Amoris laetitia* names "sincere search for God's will" and "more perfect response to it" (AL 300) as the conditions for the right execution of the pastors' discernment of the penitent's degree of responsibility.

Referring to the avoidance of evil action (i.e. adultery) as merely a "more perfect response" implies that failing to avoid this evil, is just a "less perfect action" but no evil. Such a language undermines the church's teaching on moral absolutes and leads to the gradualness of law.[45] Moreover, with such statements as "search for God's will", *Amoris laetitia* gives the impression that God's will is something unknown to the individual person, something different from the revealed moral order taught by the Catholic Church. Such a dichotomy between individual conscience and the church's doctrine[46] is even more explicitly presented in the section describing the role of individual conscience:

> ...conscience can do more than recognize that a given situation does not correspond objectively to the overall demands of the Gospel. It can also recognize with sincerity and honesty what for now is the *most generous response* which can be given to God, and come to see with a *certain moral security* that it is *what God himself is asking* amid the concrete complexity of one's limits, *while yet not fully the objective ideal.*[47]

According to this passage, individual conscience can discern with certain moral security, amid the complexity of one's limits, that God is asking him or her to engage in a morally evil action, an action prohibited by a moral absolute. Obviously, a discernment of God's will would be legitimate if we understood the "search for

---

44 Cf. VS 63. One of the frequent misunderstandings spread out by the revisionist moral theologians is their view that there is a radical difference between what they call the personalist values and the moral (natural) law of God, as if the latter's precepts were directed against the good of the human person. Often they read this dichotomy into the history of Catholic moral theology. Cf. S. GOERTZ/C. WITTING: "Wendepunkt für die Moraltheologie", 13-35, 90-91. For a view that counters such a dichotomy, cf. J.E. SMITH: *Humanae Vitae*, 54-67.

45 AL never states that to knowingly and willfully engage in non-marital sexual actions is always morally evil regardless of one's circumstances or motivations. Rather it portrays such way of behaving as "irregular" (AL 78, 298, 301, 305), "incomplete" (AL 291), non-"ideal" (AL 292, 298, 303, 307, 308), "imperfect" (AL 78, 296,), or non-"full" (AL 76, 291, 292, 293, 294, 295, 297, 303, 306, 307, 308). If one's action is deemed to be a "less full ideal," it implies that one cannot evaluate such action as morally evil *per se*. Consequently, AL's opting for such a language undermines the existing teaching of the church on the moral absolutes.

46 Bogner also identifies this dichotomy in AL but sees a solution in a revision of the "inappropriate" moral doctrine of the Church. Cf. D. BOGNER: "Angedeuteter Wandel", 205-206.

47 AL 303 (emphasis added).

God's will" within the framework of what we defined earlier as positive precepts of the law. However, even in this case, one can never discern in conscience that God asks us to direct our will against the positive precepts of the law as if God would ask us "not to love our neighbor". It only means that the concrete realizations of the positive precepts like "honor your parents" or "love your spouse" must be discerned by every individual's conscience and may lead to different actions. Their fulfillment includes an unlimited potential for growth. Since *Amoris laetitia* speaks here about people living in extra-marital sexual unions, it is clear that the "search for God's will", the "special discernment" and the "conscience's recognition of God's will" involves here a process of deliberating whether, due to the existing difficult circumstances (mitigating factors), the penitent may legitimately continue violating the norm against adultery. This proposition implies that there may be different norms applicable to different people depending on their possibilities, which clearly amounts to the "gradualness of law". Thus, if this analysis is correct, Pope Francis' refusal of the "gradualness of law" in AL 300 in relation to the situation of divorced and remarried couples is again devoid of meaning and his reference to John Paul II's *Familiaris consortio* misleading.

Finally, apart from the notion of discernment, there is another element in *Amoris laetitia* that leads to "the gradualness of law". It is the implicit denial of moral absolutes most expressly presented in AL 304 quoting a section from Aquinas' *Summa Theologiae* I-II, q. 94, art. 4 on the general principles of natural law. AL 304 interprets this section as follows: "It is true that general rules set forth a good which can never be disregarded or neglected, but in their formulation they cannot provide absolutely for all particular situations." In this context, the "general rule" in question stands for the exceptionless moral norm against adultery. Since no rule can provide absolutely for all particular situations, there can be no norm anymore "which forbid a given action *semper et pro semper*".[48] This section in Aquinas' *Summa* is not a new discovery of Pope Francis. The revisionist moral theologians have been using this one text for decades to deny the existence of moral absolutes.[49] Critiquing these revisionist attempts, other scholars

48 VS 52.

49 Cf. L. JANSSENS: "Ontic Evil and Moral Evil", in: *Louvain Studies* 4/2 (1972), 155; F. SCHOLZ: "Problems on Norms Raised by Ethical Borderline Situations: Beginnings of a Solution in Thomas Aquinas and Bonaventure", in: C.E. CURRAN/R.A. MCC ORMICK (eds.): *Readings in Moral Theology: Moral Norms and Catholic Tradition*, v. 1, New York: Paulist, 1979, 163; R.A. MCCORMICK: *The Critical Calling: Reflections on Moral Dilemmas Since Vatican II*, Washington, DC: Georgetown University Press, 2006, 358, note 5. In addition, this passage from Aquinas was similarly interpreted in the 2009 document of the International Theological Commission on universal ethics. Cf. INTERNATIONAL THEOLOGICAL COMMISSION: *In Search of a Universal Ethic: A New Look at the Natural Law*, 2009, 53, available from http://www.vatican.va/roman_curia/congregations/cfaith/cti_documents/rc_con_cfait

have argued that Thomas as well as Scripture, Church Fathers, and all teachers of Catholic morality until mid-twentieth century unambiguously affirmed the truth of moral absolutes, a fact witnessed to by those who laid their lives rather than even once violate a commandment of God.[50]

Conclusion

This paper sought to demonstrate that Pope Francis' rejection of the "gradualness of law" in AL 295 and 300 is only a rhetorical device devoid of meaning. In view of this aim, the first part of the paper traced the notion of gradualness back to the first Synod on family in 1980 and, through a careful study of several magisterial documents, it elucidated the difference between the "law of gradualness" and the "gradualness of law", considering the Catholic moral teaching about the exceptionless moral norms, as defended in John Paul II's encyclical *Veritatis splendor*. A careful analysis of the eighth chapter of *Amoris laetitia* in the second part revealed that Pope Francis' new definition of gradualness in relation to cohabiting and civilly married couples, his elaborations of the concepts of discernment and conscience, as well as his understanding of the moral norms, imply the "gradualness of law," and thus stand in contradiction not only to his own words in AL 295 and 300 but also to the teaching of the magisterial documents of Pope John Paul II. Moreover, since the "gradualness of law" goes hand in hand with the denial of moral absolutes, as this paper strived to demonstrate, *Amoris laetitia* risks standing not only in opposition to John Paul II's magisterial teaching but also in opposition to what he and many other believed to be the fundamental principles of the Catholic moral tradition.

---

h_doc_20090520_legge-naturale_en.html#2.5._The_application_of_the_common_precepts: _historicity_of_the_natural_law; accessed 02.02.2017. No wonder that after AL such interpretations of this section in Aquinas multiply. Cf. K.-W. MERKS: "Grenzzäune mit Löchern? Über die Allgemeingültigkeit moralischer Normen", in: S. GOERTZ/C. WITTING (eds.): *Amoris laetitia – Wendepunkt für die Moraltheologie*, 181-183, 189-192.

50 For a counter-interpretation of this section in Aquinas, cf. J. FINNIS: *Aquinas: Moral, Political, and Legal Theory*, Oxford: Oxford University Press, 1998, 163-164; ID.: *Moral Absolutes*, 90-91; S. PINCKAERS: *Ce qu'on ne peut jamais faire*, 131-134; G. GRISEZ: *Christian Moral Principles*, Chicago, IL: Franciscan Herald, 1983 (The Way of the Lord Jesus; 1), 268-269. For a concise exposition of Aquinas' teaching on moral absolutes, cf. W.E. MAY: *An Introduction to Moral Theology*, 170-175.

How Can We "Make Room for the Consciences of the Faithful"?

Timothy Radcliffe, OP

Pope Francis wrote in *Amoris laetitia*, that the Church must "make room for the consciences of the faithful, who very often respond as best they can to the Gospel amid their limitations, and are capable of carrying out their own discernment in complex situations" (AL 35). First of all, I shall ask what it means to have a conscience. Then I shall test my theory by asking how the faithful might exercise their conscience in the hotly disputed question, as to whether the divorced and remarried might ever receive communion.

What is the Conscience?

Our understanding of conscience is related to our conception of being human. Today, and especially in the West, the tendency is to think of ourselves as essentially private and solitary beings. We have relationships with other people through our families, our work, our ethnic or national communities, but it is usually assumed that these do not determine my identity. The "American dream" is that I am free to be whoever I want. Such a highly individualistic understanding of being human yields a view of conscience as essentially private. It is my private instinct for the truth, which protects me from being taken over by any community: the nation, the party or even the Church.

This view is only partially true. The International Theological Commission of the Church published a wonderful document on the *sensus fidei*, the personal understanding of the faith of every baptised person.[1] It quotes the First letter of St. John: "You have been anointed by the Holy One and all of you have knowledge", "the anointing that you received from Christ abides in you and so you do not need anyone to teach you" (1Jn 2,20.27). The Second Vatican Council taught:

---

1 INTERNATIONAL THEOLOGICAL COMMISSION: *Sensus Fidei in the Life of the Church*, 2014, available from http://www.vatican.va/roman_curia/congregations/cfaith/cti_documents/rc_cti_20140610_sensus-fidei_en.html; accessed 12.12.2016.

"Conscience is the most secret core and sanctuary of a human being. There he is alone with God, whose voice echoes in his depths."[2]

This personal grasp of the truth of the gospel protects us from being blindly swept up in the mob. Cardinal Ratzinger described how as a young seminarian he studied Blessed John Henry Newman, the great doctor of conscience: "We had experienced the claim of a totalitarian party, which understood itself as the fulfilment of history and which negated the conscience of the individual. One of its leaders had said, 'I have no conscience. My conscience is Adolf Hitler.'"[3] So the individual conscience resist all totalitarian claims, even of the Church. As Newman famously said: "I shall drink...to the Pope, if you please, – still, to Conscience first, and to the Pope afterwards."[4]

But this is only half the truth. I am human through the relationships that I have with other people. Conscience is a *con-scientia*, a knowing with other people. My identity is not completely private. Belonging to my family, my culture and above all the Church, forms me to know the truth.

So a healthy conscience is nurtured by the interplay between my attention to what God teaches me in the depths of my heart, and my openness to what the Church teaches me in many different ways. Ultimately these are not in competition, because I can only be a strong individual through belonging to community, and a community will only be vigorous if it enables the faithful to flourish in their individuality.

So in seeking to hear the voice of the Lord, each of us turns inwards, to the core of our being where we are addressed by the Lord, and outwards, to the wisdom that is granted to the whole community of Christ's Body. This is a dynamic process, because we are all always at the beginning of discerning what the Lord says to the churches. We rarely hear the voice of the Lord with utterly clarity. Usually we hear just an echo, a whisper, like Elijah on the mountain. John Henry Newman wrote: "So the gift of conscience raises a desire for what it does not itself fully supply... It creates in them [human beings] a thirst, an impatience, for the knowledge of that Unseen Lord, and Governor, and Judge, who as yet speaks to them only secretly, who whispers in their hearts, who tells them something, but not nearly so much as they wish and as they need."[5]

Note those wonderful words of Newman: God whispers to his friends, and tells us something, but "not nearly as much as they wish and as they need". And so a

---

2 *Gaudium et spes*, 16.

3 H. GEISSLER: 'Conscience and Truth in the writings of John Henry Newman", s.a., 1, available from http://www.newmanfriendsinternational.org/newman/wp-content/uploads/2013/05/conscience-and-truth-in-the-writings-of-blessed-jhn.pdf; accessed 12.12.2016.

4 Letter to the Duke of Norfolk.

5 J.H. NEWMAN: *Sermons Preached on Various Occasions*, London, 1908, 66.

mature conscience does not give us simple answers to moral questions. It is the voice of the Lord summoning me on a journey towards the truth. The possession of a conscience is never static. We learn to hear the word of the Lord, as the Good Shepherd summons us out of the narrow confines of our egoism into the wide open spaces of the divine life.

We do this by a twofold journey, inwards to the core of our being where God is, and outwards, transcending all self-centredness. If we focused solely on the privacy of the conscience, then it might tell me only what I want to hear. If we focused solely on its communal dimension, then my personal dignity as a child of God would be imperilled. It is like breathing. We need to breathe in and out if we are to be alive. A healthy conscience lives by this rhythm, folding me inwards into the core of my being, and propelling me outwards into the community of Christ's body.

Breathing in

Let us consider with absurd rapidity what is involved with the inward and outward breathing of our conscience. The great expert on the journey inwards is St Ignatius of Loyola. His understanding of discernment is central to Pope Francis' understanding of conscience in *Amoris laetitia*.

First of all there is what Ignatius calls "indifference". This does not mean that I am indifferent to what course of action I must take, but that I really stand poised between the alternatives, ready to accept whatever is the Lord's will. If I am divorced and remarried, and wondering whether it is right to receive communion, I must genuinely open myself to the possibility that the Lord's will might be that I go or that I do not go. If I have already loaded the dice and decided that I have the right to go, then I am not opening myself to the Lord's voice. I have to imagine that either option might be a good and right one, for imagination is central to the Ignatian process of discernment.

A second element is what Newman calls "consolation and desolation". I quote my friend James Martin SJ: "If you are in accord with God's presence within you, you will feel a sense of rightness, of peace, of what Ignatius calls 'consolation'. It is an indication that you are on the right path."[6] If you incline towards what is not the Lord's will, then you will feel unhappy, ill at ease.

This is a journey into freedom which is a sharing in the joy of the Lord. That is the heart of Pope Francis' position. Becoming free is long and arduous, the birth pangs of heaven's happiness. He writes: "Moral education has to do with cultivating freedom... The virtuous life thus builds, strengthens and shapes freedom, lest

[6] J. Martin: *The Jesuit Guide to (Almost) Everything: A Spirituality for Real Life*, New York: HarperOne, 2010, 308.

we become slaves of dehumanizing and antisocial inclinations. For human dignity itself demands that each of us 'act out of conscious and free choice, as moved and drawn in a personal way from within'." (AL 267) True freedom is more than the freedom to decide what to do. It is doing what the Lord asks of us. Discernment seeks to liberate us from all the ways in which we may fool ourselves and pretend that what I *want* to do is the voice of God. The Lord *wants* me to have another glass of wine or slice of cheesecake!

Slowly we learn to say, like Mary, "Behold the handmaid of the Lord". So in this process, we need to be accompanied by people whom we can trust to challenge the ways in which we fool ourselves, and help us to keep travelling. Like the young Samuel, we need people like the high priest Eli to discern when we are listening to the Lord and when we are listening to our egocentric fantasies.

Breathing Out

This interior journey is only half the story. We also seek the truth by opening ourselves to the teaching of the Church. Newman argued that the Church is kept in the truth by the balance of several authorities. There is the authority of the tradition, which is in the care of the hierarchy. There is the authority of reason, which he saw as entrusted to above all to the universities. There is the authority of devotion, which is the knowledge of God given by prayer and experience. This belongs to the whole people of God. Pope Francis has also spoken of the authority of the poor and there is the authority of the great saints, like St Catherine of Siena and St Teresa of Avila, underlined by Pope Emeritus Benedict.

Each of these is needed, but each can become deceptive if it becomes so dominant as to exclude the others. In the history of the Church they are always mutually correcting each other, like someone balancing on a bicycle. Sometimes one authority speaks too loudly and so the Church needs to attend more to the others. If reason becomes the absolute authority, then one ends up with an arid rationalism; if devotion and experience become the sole authority, then Newman thought that one falls into superstition. And if the authority of Church government and tradition becomes too strong then, Newman asserted, the danger was "ambition and tyranny".[7] All creativity would be stifled. In recent centuries, the Church has tended to overemphasize the authority of the hierarchy and tradition and marginalise the theologians and the voice of the laity. We have an expression in English, that the role of the laity is "to pay, pray and obey". It is interesting that when Cardinal Burke reacted to *Amoris laetitia*, it was precisely in stressing just

7 *Via Media*, xli, quoted by N. LASH: "Authors, Authority and Authorization", in: B. HOOSE (ed.): *Authority in the Roman Catholic Church: Theory and Practice*, London: Ashgate, 2002, 62.

one of the three authorities identified by Newman. He asserted: "What's binding is the Tradition. Ecclesial authority exists only in service of the Tradition."[8]

So the conscience develops through a never ending process of discernment in which several voices are in dialogue: The Word of God in the scriptures, the magisterium, the voice of reason, the voice of the saints, and the voice of God in my own heart. To have a healthy conscience is to let this conversation take us where it will, for the Holy Spirit, Jesus tells us, is "like the wind. It blows where it chooses, and you hear the sound of it, but you do not know where it comes from or where it goes." (Jn 3,8) Newman's theory of the development of doctrine argues that this evolution when authentic, though unpredictable and surprising, is never a betrayal of the tradition.

Making Room for the Conscience of the Laity

So then, how do we make room for the conscience of the laity? In at least two ways. First of all, as John Henry Newman asserts, by listening to the people of God. Richard Gaillardetz wrote: "The great attention that the Roman Catholic Church has given to the *teaching* acts of the bishops needs to be matched by equal attention to the *listening* process of the bishops. If the bishops are the authoritative teachers of the apostolic faith, it is only because they are first hearers."[9] The International Theological Commission wrote: "Not only do they [the laity] have the right to be heard, but their reaction to what is proposed as belonging to the faith of the Apostles must be taken very seriously, because it is by the Church as a whole that the apostolic faith is borne in the power of the Spirit."[10] If a teaching of the Magisterium is not well accepted, then the bishops must ask why. Is it badly expressed or partial?

Secondly, the Church needs to listen to the voice of individual Christians, who have wrestled to discover what is the Lord's will, often despite being criticised and even silenced by the Church. St Catherine of Siena struggled to bring healing to a divided Church at great personal cost. Dorothy Day endured painful attacks when she campaigned against the support of the American hierarchy for the war in Vietnam. Jean Vanier needed vast personal courage and faith to establish the *L'Arche* communities and help the Church to respond to the needs and gifts of the disabled. So the Church should listen to the voice of the laity, the *sensus fidelium*, and the voice of individual lay people, the *sensus fidei* of individual baptised people.

---

8 Interview with Edwin Pentin in: *National Catholic Register* (15.11.2015).

9 R.R. Gaillardetz: *Teaching with Authority: A Theology of the Magisterium in the Church*, Collegeville: Liturgical Press, 1997, 84 – 85.

10 International Theological Commission: *Sensus Fidei*, 74.

Amoris Laetitia

How does this apply to the admission to communion of the divorced and remarried? Let us begin by asking what it does *not* mean. First of all, it is not Pope Francis' intention to change the Church's rules. Francis is not saying that whereas it used to be the rule that in no case could a divorced and remarried person, not living with their spouse as brother and sister, receive communion but now the rule is changed so that this is sometimes permissible. Nor is he saying that a priest may dispense someone from the rule, nor that my own conscience may free me from obedience to the rule. He is inviting us to go a step deeper. Our conscience discerns in all the mess and complexity of our human lives how the Lord summons each of us to freedom and maturity and graces our journey.

People have become so captured by the image of Catholic morality as submission to rules that many people find it hard to grasp what the Pope is doing. I once gave a lecture on sexual ethics to five hundred teenagers in Mauritius, in bad French, attempting to get beyond just thinking of sexual ethics in terms of rules, good and necessary though rules are. It was a disaster. All they want to know was what is permitted and what is forbidden!

But if the rules are not changed, what is there for the conscience to do? If a first marriage is indissoluble, and is not annulled, then how can a formed conscience lead to any other conclusion than that a divorced and remarried couple must either refrain from sex or else refrain from communion? If the first marriage is, as the Church teaches, indissoluble, then for such a couple to have sex is to commit adultery. This seems to be the view of Archbishop Chaput of Philadelphia, if I have understood correctly the pastoral guidelines which he issued to the diocese in July 2016.

What, therefore, can the formed conscience do except submit? But Archbishop Bergoglio worked for years in the poor barrios of Buenos Aires, where few people were married, and where people's lives did not conform to the rules. He had to start where people are, with all the mess and confusion that human beings created, and find a way forward. He listened to the people of God, as Newman said that we must. When he was on sabbatical in Germany, he discovered the painting of Our Lady, Untier of Knots, and prayed to her to untie this knot. As he writes in *Amoris laetitia*: "No one can be condemned for ever, because that is not the logic of the Gospel!" (AL 297) So how might there be a way forward?

My belief is that it lies in the very nature of marriage. It is the *free* consent of two people to give themselves to each other. Their freedom is not just a juridical necessity if the contract is to be valid. Marriage is a profound expression of what it means for us to be free, and to enter into God's own freedom. We freely give ourselves to another person for ever. But both Pope John Paul II in *Familiaris consortio* and Pope Francis today recognise that we live in a society in which such a pure freedom is often undermined. Extreme individualism and prolonged adolescence make it hard today freely to give yourself to another with mature freedom. And this gift of oneself is difficult to maintain with a lack of housing in which people can live together in dignity, violence within the family and the lack of social support for the institution of marriage. The Church believes that it belongs to our dignity as God's children that we can make vows to God and to each other, but contemporary culture militates against our fidelity.

The Church has always recognised that where there is a clear lack of freedom and maturity, the marriage can be annulled. But there are many other cases where it is not so clear. Pope Francis, quoting Pope John Paul II, writes that there are "those who have entered into a second union for the sake of the children's upbringing, and are sometimes subjectively certain in conscience that their previous and irreparably broken marriage had never been valid" (AL 298). There is no formal annulment, but someone's conscience recognises that the full meaning of a marriage, as a free consent, was somehow lacking. So already we are moving beyond the simple black and white of Archbishop Chaput's position that either the first marriage was valid or it was not.

Amoris laetitia edges us more deeply into this ambiguous area, in which freedom has been only partially exercised. Many people cannot deny the validity of their first marriage. It would seem wipe out so much that was so good, and maybe the presence of love over many years. It looks like a rejection of the children of the union. But looking back, one can see elements of immaturity, of unfreedom, which mean that sustaining the relationship was somehow beyond the couple. Surely this is where conscience might come into play. Accompanied by understanding pastors, after prayer and dialogue and a recognition of failures and sin, someone might conclude that obedience to the Lord's summon to life and freedom might include a return to the Eucharist, the medicine for the wounded pilgrim.

Jean-Paul Vesco, the Dominican bishop of Oran in Algeria, clarifies what is at issue.[11] Bishop Vesco is a firm champion of the indissolubility of marriage. If we give ourselves to another person with free consent for ever then that it is not a relationship that can be dissolved by the Church. But, if I understand him correctly, it may die. A marriage may be ended by the death of the husband or wife. In a similar way, a relationship may die. The union of two people, freely given, may become irreparably damaged, so that a common life simply is no longer possible. St John Paul II recognises this in *Familiaris consortio*. Vesco takes a further step and argues that in this case there may be a rupture which is similar to death.

---

[11] J.-P. Vesco: *Tout amour véritable est indissoluble: Plaidoyer en faveur les divorcés- remariés*, Paris: Cerf, 2015.

After such a mortal crisis of a relationship, some people manage to rebuild their lives with another person. He writes: "On ne choisit pas de se remarier, on choisit de retrouver un chemin de vie après un échec humain douloureux dans lequel on a peut-être une part de responsabilité."[12] Let us rejoice that a painful failure has not crushed them. With the grace of God, they have found love again and this second love may endure and have its own indissolubility. They are a sign for the Church that the death of the first marriage is not the end of the story. They have not given up in their hope for a union which is indeed is indissoluble.

What about a return to the table of the Eucharist? This is a matter of obedience to their conscience, accompanied by the Church. The conscience, we have seen, is the voice of God calling us to truth and freedom. And so the first stage is to be truthful about one's own responsibility for the death of the first relationship. Was one just to the other person, and to one's children? How free were the two to love each other? If one is really truthful in the examination of what has happened, then maybe a full public reintegration into the community should be possible, as in the Orthodox Churches, leading to communion. Bishop Vesco arrives at a conclusion which is virtually identical with that of *Amoris laetitia*. His contribution is to clarify how this pastoral solution might be reconcilable with the Church's abiding teaching on the indissolubility of marriage.

It is time to conclude. How are we to make room for the conscience of the faithful? This conscience is founded on the gift of the Holy Spirit at baptism. We share the life of God and so we know the things of God. But Newman reminds that often we only know partially. We hear the whisper of God's voice. To hear that voice more clearly, then we need to make a journey inwards, in which, as St Ignatius taught us, we undo the deceits of the heart so as to know God's will more clearly. We also make a journey outwards, beyond our own egocentric delusions and listen to those who have authority in the Church: the hierarchy, the guardians of the tradition, the thinkers who ponder on the Word of God and examine the tradition of the Church, and the experience of the whole Church, the *sensus fidelium*.

The conscience of the faithful works in this discernment in two ways. First of all, the people of God do indeed seem to be summoning us to show a profound welcome to those who are divorced and remarried. Pope Francis learned in the barrios of Buenos Aires just how difficult it is for many people today even to marry in the first place, and how hard are the pressures on marriage everywhere. Even the most holy people can find that they are in mess. There must be a way forward.

Secondly, we must help the faithful to form good and true consciences. As the encyclical says, "We have been called to form consciences, not to replace them."

---

12 Ibid. 24

(AL 37). The community of the Church will be strong if she raises individuals with strong personal consciences. If the faithful lose the courage to hearken to the voice of the Lord speaking in their hearts, then the whole Church will be weakened. But this listening means daring to hear what the pastors of the Church say, what the Word of God in the scriptures says, what the saints and the thinkers say. When we do this, then we hear the quiet whisper of the Lord summoning us to freedom and God's own joy.

Sin, Repentance and Conversion in *Amoris Laetitia*

Nadia Delicata

In his 2013 interview with Fr. Antonio Spadaro, SJ, Pope Francis famously replied to the question "Who is Jorge Mario Bergoglio?" with first, a silent pause, and then the following:

> I do not know what might be the most fitting description. ... *I am a sinner*. This is the most accurate definition. It is not a figure of speech, a literary genre. I am a sinner.
>
> ... [T]he best summary [of who I am], the one that comes more from the inside and I feel most true is this: *I am a sinner whom the Lord has looked upon*. ... I am one who is looked upon by the Lord. I always felt my motto, *Miserando atque eligendo* [By Having Mercy and by Choosing Him], was very true for me.

To emphasize his point further, Pope Francis added:

> [T]he painting of '*The Calling of St. Matthew*' by Caravaggio... That finger of Jesus, pointing at Matthew. That's me. I feel like him. Like Matthew...
>
> *"I am a sinner, but I trust in the infinite mercy and patience of our Lord Jesus Christ, and I accept in a spirit of penance.* [1]

These words of Pope Francis, that reflect the heart of the Christian life – becoming aware of one's sinfulness through the experience of God's salvific mercy that brings rebirth in Christ – reflect the spirit of this papacy and therefore also of its body of teachings. As I will proceed to argue, it is not just highly significant that Pope Francis chose to tie the closing of the Synods of the Family, which sought to deliberate on some of the deepest wounds in the church, with a Jubilee of Mercy, but even the Apostolic Exhortation *Amoris laetitia* must be read through this lens of the universal, and simultaneously deeply personal, human experience of sinfulness to which God responds with infinite mercy. Indeed, as the story of the

---

1 A. SPADARO: "Intervista a Papa Francesco", in: *La Civiltà Cattolica* 3918 (2013), 449-478. English translation: A. SPADARO: "A Big Heart Open to God: The Exclusive Interview with Pope Francis", in: *America: The National Catholic Weekly* 209/8 (September 30, 2013), 14-38, emphasis added; available from http://www.americamagazine.org/pope-interview; accessed 13.12.2016.

adulteress who washed Jesus' feet teaches, the experience of God's mercy presupposes a profound experience of contrition since the greater the sinfulness, the more profound the conversion (cf. Lk 7,48). Thus, if Pope Francis' consistent call for witnessing God's mercy in the church is palpable in the pastoral wisdom of *Amoris laetitia*, it follows that the Apostolic Exhortation also seeks to foster a robust theology of sin where the personal God-human relationship, rather than description of individual acts, is central. The role of the minister who accompanies is, first and foremost, to mediate this paradoxical dual experience where, through the palpable experience of sin, each one of us is invited to discover God who always seeks us, always calls us, always loves us.

In the first part, I will present, albeit briefly, this theology of sin as retrieving the quintessentially Christian experience of salvation. Sin is presented, first and foremost, not as a particular act, but as an internal disposition that distances the human from God, just as salvation is, first and foremost, the experience of God-with-us who takes on "death" as effect of all our sinfulness to make, once again, possible for us eternal life. This understanding of sin evident in the context of soteriology does not only permeate the tradition but is also synthesized boldly in the heart of Ignatian spirituality in which, as a Jesuit, Pope Francis is imbued.

Next, I will offer a brief textual analysis of fragments from the eighth chapter of *Amoris laetitia* where this retrieval of a relationship-grounded hamartiology is most apparent. It is, in fact, on the basis of the progressive healing and purification of this relationship with God that the repentant slowly becomes able, not only to properly "name" his or her deepest sin, but also to boldly shed tears and ask forgiveness, and thus to experience the fullness of God's mercy through absolution in the sacrament of reconciliation and the partaking of the Eucharist.

Yet, the reception of the Eucharist does not merely represent how the individual has been blessed by Christ's salvific grace. It also symbolizes the experience of communal salvation and divinization that is "the source and summit" of being *ecclesia* (*Lumen gentium*, 11). Lastly, therefore, I will suggest possible room for development and ongoing diocesan pastoral discernment so the theology of sin, repentance and conversion emphasized in *Amoris laetitia* moves beyond a seeming narrow focus on the individual to retrieve a more robust communal dimension as evident in the earliest Christian communities.

1 The Retrieval of a Robust Theology of Sin

The *Catechism of the Catholic Church* explains "the reality of sin" thus:

> Sin is present in human history; any attempt to ignore it or to give this dark reality other names would be futile. To try to understand what sin is, one must first recognize *the profound relation of man to God*, for only in this relationship is the evil of sin

> unmasked in its true identity as humanity's rejection of God and opposition to him, even as it continues to weigh heavy on human life and history. (386)

As the Jesuit theologian Piet Schoonenberg argues, this understanding of sin is profoundly scriptural since, "from the way the bible uses all the words [for sin], it is quite evident that sin is against God himself".[2] If in the Greco-Roman, Stoic mindset "sin" is against "an essential law of nature", in the Jewish mindset the divine ruler chooses his people and is bonded with them through "a loving covenant". Going against God's laws – or against laws in one's nature that is created by God – is the same as going against God himself. Nor is this understanding foreign to the New Testament. Quite the contrary: in the Fourth Gospel in particular, the "firstfruits of the gospels",[3] but also the most eschatological of the New Testament writings, sin is equated with denying Christ himself: "Those who believe in him are not condemned; but those who do not believe are condemned already, because they have not believed in the name of the only Son of God" (Jn 3,18). This contrary disposition recalls the sin against the Holy Spirit in the Synoptic tradition (cf. Mk 3,28-29, Mt 12,31-32, and Lk 12,10) and in both Johannine and Synoptic traditions it is evident that what is at stake is the reception of the theological virtues and of the Holy Spirit himself who transforms human hearts to a state of divinization.

This is why even when we describe specific human actions as sinful, rather than as merely "immoral", fundamentally we are speaking of the disposition towards or against God that flows from the human "heart" – the inner centre of the person – as revealed in the particular act. It is not the disobedience of laws that is first and foremost "sinful" even though, following Stoic natural law, most of the tradition would recognize that wrong action is most certainly "unreasonable" because contrary to human nature and our natural *telos*. Rather, what at its core is properly "sinful" is the exercise of freedom that, in flowing from the human heart, symbolically denies our being creatures made in the image of God and to find fulfillment in God alone, thus effectively contradicting our relational nature as inherently dependent on God. Actions are "sinful" and not only "wrong" because they are a willful denial of the good ordered to ultimate finality and therefore to God himself. As the First Gospel puts it:

> Do you not see that whatever goes into the mouth enters the stomach, and goes out into the sewer? But what comes out of the mouth proceeds from the heart, and this is

---

2 P. SCHOONENBERG: *Man and Sin: A Theological View*, trans. John Donceel, Notre Dame, IN: University of Notre Dame Press, 1965, 7.

3 ORIGEN: *Commentary on the Gospel According to John*, trans. Ronald E. Heine, Washington, DC: Catholic University of America Press, 1989, 1993 (The Fathers of the Church; 80 and 89), 1.37.

> what defiles. *For out of the heart come evil intentions*, murder, adultery, fornication, theft, false witness, slander (Mt 15,17-19, emphasis added).

This profoundly existential and relational reality of sin is strongly evident in the Ignatian tradition, marked by the *Spiritual Exercises* that Ignatius of Loyola understood as "every way of preparing and disposing the soul to rid itself of all inordinate attachments, and, after their removal, of seeking and finding the will of God in the disposition of our life for the salvation of our soul".[4] Here it becomes evident how Pope Francis' spirituality, marked by the acknowledgement of sinfulness and the wonder at being "chosen", reflects the spiritual journey of the *Exercises* that in itself can be understood as a renewal of the traditional pilgrimage of the catechumenate in Lent. Thus, the Christian retreats internally from daily life – whether literally in an actual thirty-day retreat or, more metaphorically through the nineteenth annotation, for a retreat in everyday life – to undergo again the quintessential Christian task of repentance or "purgation" to prepare to receive "illumination" that in the Ignatian charisma is marked by becoming "contemplatives in action" and therefore by being personally commissioned for a particular labour for the Kingdom by God.

> Four Weeks are assigned to the Exercises given below. This corresponds to the four parts into which they are divided, namely: the first part, which is devoted to the consideration and contemplation of sin; the second part, which is taken up with the life of Christ our Lord up to Palm Sunday inclusive; the third part, which treats of the passion of Christ our Lord; the fourth part, which deals with the Resurrection and Ascension; to this are appended Three Methods of Prayer.[5]

According to this highly traditional schema, the first major task of the Christian life is purgation from sin made possible in the infinite mercy of God. But God's infinite mercy is made most palpable precisely in the Christ event; thus from the Second Week to the Fourth, the retreatant contemplates the Incarnation and the life of Christ culminating in the epitome of the experience of salvation which is the empty tomb. Together, therefore, purgation and illumination prepare the Christian for his or her individual mission. Yet, what distinguishes the *Exercises* as a modern spiritual classic is precisely that, as a master of the inner life, Ignatius recognized that sin and the evil it implies can take many guises that are not immediately evident to the spiritual novice. Thus, Ignatius proposes "Rules of Discernment" that are distinct for both stages of spiritual formation.

---

4 IGNATIUS OF LOYOLA: *The Spiritual Exercises of St. Ignatius: Based on Studies in the Language of the Autograph*, trans. Louis J. Puhl, Westminster, MD: Newman Press, 1951, 1.

5 Ibid. 4.

> In the case of the First Week, where the focus is on sin, Ignatius proposes the following distinction that hinges precisely on how it is not merely the "objective", or overt, reality of sin that shackles, but also the deeper internal torment that prevents the sinner from receiving grace:
>
> In the case of those who go from one mortal sin to another, the enemy is ordinarily accustomed to propose apparent pleasures. He fills their imagination with sensual delights and gratifications, the more readily to keep them in their vices and increase the number of their sins. With such persons the good spirit uses a method, which is the reverse of the above. Making use of the light of reason, he will rouse the sting of conscience and fill them with remorse.
>
> In the case of those who go on earnestly striving to cleanse their souls from sin and who seek to rise in the service of God our Lord to greater perfection, the method pursued is the opposite of that mentioned in the first rule. Then it is characteristic of the evil spirit to harass with anxiety, to afflict with sadness, to raise obstacles backed by fallacious reasonings that disturb the soul. Thus he seeks to prevent the soul from advancing. It is characteristic of the good spirit, however, to give courage and strength, consolations, tears, inspirations, and peace. This He does by making all easy, by removing all obstacles so that the soul goes forward in doing good.[6] (314-315).

Thus, the rules of discernment are grounded in learning how to recognize the signs of the presence of evil or good spirits in the human heart. These signs that the person who accompanies must always be able to read to accompany the retreatant are of "consolation" and "desolation" that Ignatius describes schematically as follows:

> *Spiritual Consolation.* I call it consolation when an interior movement is aroused in the soul, by which it is inflamed with love of its Creator and Lord, and as a consequence, can love no creature on the face of the earth for its own sake, but only in the Creator of them all. It is likewise consolation when one sheds tears that move to the love of God, whether it be because of sorrow for sins, or because of the sufferings of Christ our Lord, or for any other reason that is immediately directed to the praise and service of God. Finally, I call consolation every increase of faith, hope, and love, and all interior joy that invites and attracts to what is heavenly and to the salvation of one's soul by filling it with peace and quiet in its Creator and Lord.
>
> *Spiritual Desolation.* I call desolation what is entirely the opposite of what is described in the third rule, as darkness of soul, turmoil of spirit, inclination to what is low and earthly, restlessness rising from many disturbances and temptations which lead to want of faith, want of hope, want of love. The soul is wholly slothful, tepid, sad, and separated, as it were, from its Creator and Lord. For just as consolation is the opposite of desolation, so the thoughts that spring from consolation are the opposite of those that spring from desolation.[7] (316-317).

6 Ibid. 314-315.

7 Ibid. 316-317.

Yet, if in the First Week sinfulness or distance from God is characterized by vice or anxiety, Ignatius suggests that the evil spirit changes tactics in the Second Week and therefore the signs of desolation also become more difficult to recognize. This is because, through succeeding the First Week's closing meditation on Christ's call to follow him, the Second Week corresponds more closely to the more advanced stage of the spiritual path, where the evil one tempts through mimicking the experience of consolation:

> When the one who is giving the Exercises perceives that the exercitant is being assailed and tempted *under the appearance of good*, then is the proper time to explain to him the rules of the Second Week, which we mentioned above. *For commonly the enemy of our human nature tempts more under the appearance of good when one is exercising himself in the illuminative way.* This corresponds to the Exercises of the Second Week. He does not tempt him so much under the appearance of good when he is exercising himself in the purgative way, which corresponds to the Exercises of the First Week.[8]

From this brief look at the *Spiritual Exercises* it becomes apparent that the "accompaniment" and "discernment" that characterizes the Ignatian tradition assumes a careful pondering of one's relationship with God in order to become aware of one's true guilt and thus to seek purgation not merely from "objective" or obvious sins, but from what lies buried in one's heart stultifying a generous response to God. The First Week in particular presents a process of truly naming or discerning one's deepest sin, through which the sinner can arrive to contrition that seeks not only re-"integration" in the life of the church but first and foremost in his or her innermost being. In line with the rest of the Christian tradition, the *Exercises* assume as well that such integration is possible only in receiving God's infinite and undeserved mercy.[9]

Yet, it is also evident that, analogous to the task of the First Week of the *Spiritual Exercises*, *Amoris laetitia* too suggests that persons in complex life situations and relationships must be encouraged, with the help of the church, to ponder God's infinite love and simultaneously how one's personal response to that love is hindered by the cold chasm of one's innermost sinfulness. In light of God's desire for human freedom, the person being accompanied on a journey to wholeness

---

8 Ibid. 10, emphasis added.

9 This process can be summarized in the Second Exercise of the First Week where Ignatius gives precise instructions to "record" all sins, contemplate their "gravity", "loathsomeness" and "malice", recognize oneself as a source of "corruption and contagion" for others, acknowledge how one does not deserve to live at all, and yet, notwithstanding this wickedness, one arrives to the humble awareness that God himself through all his creatures, not only "permits" the sinner to live but "sustains" his life. Ignatius suggests that the retreatant concludes the exercise "with a colloquy, *extolling the mercy of God our Lord, pouring out my thoughts to Him, and giving thanks to Him that up to this very moment He has granted me life.* I will resolve with His grace to amend for the future" (*Spiritual Exercises*, 56-61, emphasis added).

must face those sins and patterns of resistance to respond in love and indeed even recognize – in line with Pope Francis' powerful insight that Matthew is not only forgiven, but forgiven through being *chosen* – that notwithstanding the complexity of any life situation, Christ always calls every sinner to follow him.

2 A Robust Hamartiology in *Amoris Laetitia* 8

In line with the understanding of sin as profoundly relational and the process of discerning one's true sinfulness evident in the Ignatian tradition, in his interview on *Amoris laetitia* published in *La Civiltà Cattolica*, Cardinal Schönborn also states: "I believe that a fundamental point in the elaboration of AL is that *all of us – no matter in what abstract category we may be classified – are called to beg for mercy*, to desire conversion."[10] This implies that if we are to find prove that the same robust theology of sin, whose heart is the human response to God's merciful call, permeates *Amoris laetitia*, then it must do so most clearly in paradigmatic passages of the eighth chapter, dedicated to outlining a pastoral journey or new "catechumenate" of "Accompanying, discerning and integrating weakness". As Cardinal Schönborn makes clear: "The family is *en route*. I believe that this is the bedrock of the entire document. This way of looking at things... is biblical realism, the way of looking at human beings that Scripture gives us."[11]

I will focus on three key passages, all between the controversial paragraphs 300-305, where this robust theology of sin is most evident. Moreover, I will argue that precisely through interpreting these passages as reflecting a robust theological, rather than merely casuistical or act-based understanding of sin, the passages must be interpreted as strongly situated within the ecclesial tradition that always sought to rehabilitate – and not create distance from – the sinner. After all there is no greater scandal in the church than a stubborn refusal to encourage the sinner to drink of God's infinite mercy always graciously given.

First passage from paragraph 300:

> What we are speaking of is a process of accompaniment and discernment which guides the faithful to an awareness of their situation before God. Conversation with the priest, in the internal forum, contributes to the formation of a correct judgment on what hinders the possibility of a fuller participation in the life of the Church and on what steps

10 A. SPADARO: "Conversazione con il Cardinale Schönborn sull'Amoris Laetitia", in: *La Civiltà Cattolica* 3986 (2016), 130-152. Excerpt available in English translation as A. SPADARO: "The Demands of Love: A Conversation with Cardinal Schönborn about 'The Joy of Love'", in: *America: The National Catholic Weekly* 215/4 (August 15-22, 2016), 23-27, emphasis added; available from http://www.americamagazine.org/issue/demands-love; accessed 13.12.2016.

11 Ibid.

> can foster it and make it grow. Given that gradualness is not in the law itself (cf. *Familiaris consortio*, 34), this discernment can never prescind from the Gospel demands of truth and charity, as proposed by the Church.

This passage presents an accurate depiction of the purpose of Christian discernment: "awareness of the situation before God" which implies "correct judgment on what hinders fuller participation in the life of the church". In other words, this passage points to a precise "naming" of one's sin, of the sin that, at its most fundamental existential level, separates the sinner from God and the Christian community. The naming of this sin goes beyond a mere description of how the situation might appear externally but calls for a proper examination of conscience where the emphasis is first and foremost on evaluating one's internal disposition towards God. This does not mean that the "objectivity" or outward, concrete manifestation of the situation must be ignored or bracketed. But it does mean that what is in the human heart – our desire or otherwise to respond with contrition and courage to God's mercy – is not always immediately or clearly perceptible through external actions. While actions reflect who we are and in turn also form us, they are also conditioned by a context that is contingent and often beyond our complete control. Hence, the traditional teaching on mitigating factors that *Amoris laetitia* presents in paragraphs 301-302:

> The Church possesses a solid body of reflection concerning mitigating factors and situations. Hence it is can no longer simply be said that all those in any "irregular" situation are living in a state of mortal sin and are deprived of sanctifying grace. . . .
>
> [A] negative judgment about an objective situation does not imply a judgment about the imputability or culpability of the person involved.

Second passage from paragraph 303:

> [C]onscience can do more than recognize that a given situation does not correspond objectively to the overall demands of the Gospel. It can also recognize with sincerity and honesty what for now is the most generous response which can be given to God, and come to see with a certain moral security that it is what God himself is asking amid the concrete complexity of one's limits, while yet not fully the objective ideal. In any event, let us recall that this discernment is dynamic; it must remain ever open to new stages of growth and to new decisions which can enable the ideal to be more fully realized.

This passage moves beyond the Thomistic principle, grounded in a virtue ethic, that what we do, or how we act, shapes who we become. It also recognizes – once more through a Christian realism – that how we act in every circumstance requires a decision in prudence that responds as fittingly as possible to the exigencies of the concrete context and circumstances. In addition, the Ignatian emphasis on responding to God's specific call to the individual sinner is palpable in the emphasis given in the passage that "moral security" comes from knowing – presumably through the experience of consolation – "that it is what God himself is asking". Thus, as *Amoris laetitia* is making clear, conscience can no longer be understood – as was the temptation of a manualist theology influenced by Nominalism – merely or solely through the measure of external laws. The judgment of conscience is ultimately of one's situation before God, and even more, of one's most loving response to God in the particular situation. Vatican II's understanding of conscience, that retrieves the centrality of *synderesis* as the first principles of practical reason – "do good and avoid evil" – also reclaims as true ground for a realist moral judgment one's desire and orientation to God, our absolute finality. Yet how this desire is lived as authentically as possible through concrete actions in a constantly shifting environment, requires ongoing discernment and therefore the constant willingness for spiritual purification that we strive our utmost to make increasingly (but never fully) manifest in concrete choices.

Third passage from paragraph 305, that includes the now famous footnote 351 on the reception of the sacraments:

> Because of forms of conditioning and mitigating factors, it is possible that in an objective situation of sin – which may not be subjectively culpable, or fully such – a person can be living in God's grace, can love and can also grow in the life of grace and charity, while receiving the Church's help to this end. (Footnote 351)[12] Discernment must help to find possible ways of responding to God and growing in the midst of limits.

This seemingly paradoxical conclusion of paragraph 305 – that a person can be living in God's grace even if the situation in which he or she is living is "objectively" (or concretely and manifestly) disordered – must be understood in the context of what has been presented thus far: where sin is, first and foremost, the truthful judgment of the state of one's relationship with God that is made manifest in actions whose righteous external execution is not always fully possible or within our control. The limitations imposed on us by our past life choices and life situations effectively limit the decisions that we can, in prudence, take. But they do not limit our openness to receiving God's mercy and grace and therefore the possibility of reconsidering, through the new eyes of the Holy Spirit, the reality of the situation that imposes itself upon us. God himself infuses virtues through

---

[12] Footnote 351 reads: "In certain cases, this can include the help of the sacraments. Hence, 'I want to remind priests that the confessional must not be a torture chamber, but rather an encounter with the Lord's mercy' (*Evangelii Gaudium*, 44). I would also point out that the Eucharist 'is not a prize for the perfect, but a powerful medicine and nourishment for the weak' (*ibid.*, 47)."

which, in the words of Reinhold Niebuhr, I can learn "to accept the things I cannot change, courage to change the things I can, and wisdom to know the difference".

Hence, as the Bishops of the Buenos Aires Pastoral Region in their Directive on *Amoris laetitia* addressed to the regional clergy note:[13]

> If one arrives at the recognition that, in a particular case, there are limitations that diminish responsibility and culpability (cf. 301-302), particularly when a person judges that he would fall into a subsequent fault by damaging the children of the new union, *Amoris Laetitia* opens up the possibility of access to the sacraments of Reconciliation and the Eucharist (cf. notes 336 and 351). *These in turn dispose the person to continue maturing and growing with the aid of grace.* (emphasis added)

Yet, as the Bishops also note (9), when members of the community who are "subjectively" open to grace but "objectively" burdened by a situation that remains ambiguous return to partaking in the Eucharistic meal, this could still pose challenges in the wider ecclesial community.

The Eucharist is, by definition, a communal meal of thanksgiving. As Pope Francis makes clear in *Evangelii gaudium* and once more in footnote 351 of *Amoris laetitia*, our weaknesses are such that as an ecclesial community we do not just come together to be witnesses of the Final Banquet, but also to be nourished by the Body and Blood of Christ for our ongoing journey. Nonetheless, participation in the Eucharist in itself communicates the desire to receive God's mercy and respond to it authentically. When, for whichever reason, there are grounds on which that authenticity is not immediately evident on the basis of "irregular" external circumstances that might threaten the sacramental understanding of the Christian life, the possibility of scandal remains. Does this weaken (or even question) the contribution of *Amoris laetitia* as some critics have argued?

3 The Ecclesial Community's Role in the Individual Members' Sin, Conversion and Repentance

Undoubtedly *Amoris laetitia* offers much wisdom on how families, irrespective of their weaknesses or even "irregularities", must be accompanied in the internal forum. Yet the risk of the internal forum is precisely that: that it becomes too "in-

---

13 BISHOPS OF THE BUENOS AIRES PASTORAL REGION: *Directive to the Regional Clergy*, September 5, 2016. Published by the Argentinean Blog "The Wanderer" and the Spanish news service InfoCatólica. English translation by Matthew Cullinan Hoffman of LifeSiteNe ws.com. Republished on Crux website with the response issued by Pope Francis, September 18, 2016: https://cruxnow.com/global-church/2016/09/18/guidelines-buenos-aires-bishops-div orcedremarried/; accessed 13.12.2016. The directive was highly praised by the Pope: "The document is very good and thoroughly specifies the meaning of chapter VIII of *Amoris Laetitia*. There are no further interpretations. I am confident that it will do much good."

ternal", to the extent that it might appear as if the truly ecclesial character of the Christian life is somewhat "bracketed" or denied. Lest such individualistic interpretations of the Christian life are to be unnecessarily encouraged, it is evident that the understanding of sin, as not only a personal offence against God but also as brokenness in the brotherhood and sisterhood of the ecclesial community itself through an impoverished witness of the Christian life, must also be safeguarded.

Amoris laetitia does not seem to say much on this point although, in line with the tradition where the priest in the confessional represents the ecclesial community, perhaps it presupposes the minister's role of accompaniment as representing the church as a whole.[14] However, in its pivotal third paragraph it specifies clearly that the application of the Exhortation's pastoral insights must be discerned and extended according to the specific needs of each diocese.[15] In this regard, the Directive of the Bishops of the Buenos Aires Pastoral Region offers wise pointers for other dioceses to consider. They write:

> [A]t the same time one must not cease *to accompany the community*, so that it might grow in a spirit of understanding and welcoming, without creating confusion regarding the teaching of the Church on the indissolubility of marriage. The community is an instrument of mercy that is "undeserved, unconditional, and free" ([AL] 297) (9, emphasis added).

The bishops recognize that it is not sufficient for the church to accompany individuals in their journey to holiness. The Christian life is a communal journey and as such, the entire community requires accompaniment to grow in the wisdom of discernment in order to become true witnesses of God's mercy, not only *ad extra* in the world but also *ad intra* among the church's brothers and sisters. As Cardinal Schönborn alerts us, not only the individual sinner but the ecclesial community as

---

14 As Kenan Osborne has argued, however, after Trent, "[t]he priest may represent the community, but the format of the sacrament [of confession] was so privately structured that this representational and social aspect of the church came to be almost unnoticed. In the new ritual, the rite for individual reconciliation (form I) does not clearly do justice to the basic thrust of the documents of Vatican II, which stated that a communal nature of sacramental celebration is to be preferred over a more private celebration." (K. OSBORNE: *Reconciliation and Justification: The Sacrament and Its Theology*, Eugene, OR: Wipf and Stock, 2001, 240).

15 It reads: "Since 'time is greater than space', I would make it clear that not all discussions of doctrinal, moral or pastoral issues need to be settled by interventions of the magisterium. Unity of teaching and practice is certainly necessary in the Church, but this does not preclude various ways of interpreting some aspects of that teaching or drawing certain consequences from it. This will always be the case as the Spirit guides us towards the entire truth (cf. *Jn* 16:13), until he leads us fully into the mystery of Christ and enables us to see all things as he does. *Each country or region, moreover, can seek solutions better suited to its culture and sensitive to its traditions and local needs.* For 'cultures are in fact quite diverse and every general principle … needs to be inculturated, if it is to be respected and applied' (*Gaudium et Spes*, 44)" (emphasis added).

a whole must be willing to discern and undergo an examination of conscience to ascertain that its attitude towards the sinner – towards each one of us – reflects divine mercy, and not the *hubris* of self-righteousness and bigotry:

> It is necessary to enter into the concrete dimension of life in order to "discern the body," begging for mercy. It is possible that the one whose life is in accordance with the rules lacks discernment, and eats his own judgment. It is possible, in certain cases, that the one who is in an objective situation of sin can receive the help of the sacraments. We come to the sacraments as beggars, like the tax collector at the back of the Temple who does not dare to lift his eyes. The Pope invites us not only to look at the external conditions (which have their own importance), but also to ask ourselves whether we have this thirst for a merciful pardon, so that we may respond better to the sanctifying dynamism of grace.[16]

Moreover, for the repentant himself or herself, the church has always established rituals of re-institution that mark their return to the sheepfold. In the early church these rituals of public penance mimicked the catechumenate while in particular after Trent they took on a much less public dimension through priestly absolution. Yet, in particular in the case of "irregular" unions, especially in the case of the divorced and remarried where their legal status is necessarily a public affair, it could be argued that the process of healing and re-integration needs to be marked by a "public" ecclesial symbolic gesture if their "objective" status of irregularity is not to cause scandal, even in the case of subjective repentance. In fact, this is precisely what the Orthodox Order of the Second or Third Marriage presupposes: it is "somewhat different than that celebrated as a first marriage and it bears a penitential character. Second or third marriages are performed by 'economy' – that is, out of concern for the spiritual well being of the parties involved and as an exception to the rule, so to speak".[17]

Perhaps, to offer a fuller pastoral response to the needs of the community and therefore precisely "by economy", at the discretion of local bishops, in Roman Catholic dioceses too there could be incorporated rituals of penitence and celebration that, in exceptional cases, recognize not only the full re-integration into the ecclesial community of members in so-called "irregular" unions but also the goodness of their new relationships even if they can never embody the perfection of sacramental marriage. After all, this is precisely what "the help of the sacraments" of Reconciliation and the Eucharist would imply if, as Pope Francis is suggesting, in exceptional cases those in complex familial situations could participate fully in them.

16 A. SPADARO: "The Demands of Love".

17 J. MATUSIAK: "Divorce and Remarriage: Questions and Answers about Orthodoxy", available from the Orthodox Church in America website, https://oca.org/questions/sacramentmarriage/divorce-and-remarriage; accessed 13.12.2016.

4 Conclusion

The message of *Amoris laetitia* is profound in its gospel clarity and simplicity. The "Joy of Love" must be made alive through lives that witness it. We are all sinners called to trust in the infinite mercy and patience of our Lord Jesus Christ. We are all called to accept this fundamental existential truth in a spirit of contrition and penance, but also in the courage of knowing that even in our weakness, even in our "objective" "irregularities" we remain chosen. The robustness of the theology of sin that *Amoris laetitia* calls us to ponder, demands the willingness to receive with grace and dignity our ultimate vocation in God – even in the messiness of everyday life.

The Sacrament of Marriage: A Dogmatic Theologian Reads *Amoris Laetitia*

Peter Hünermann

1 Introduction

Seldom has a papal and synodal teaching document been so strongly criticized by cardinals, bishops, theologians, and philosophers, as well as in the public discussion in the media, as the Post-Synodal Apostolic Exhortation *Amoris laetitia* of Pope Francis.[1]

This text is accused of "unclarity", a "lack of seriousness", and a kind of "Jesuitical dialectic" that sows "confusion" among the faithful. It is also accused of deviation from the Church's teaching, that is to say, of heresy.

In response to these charges, I shall discuss the treatment of the sacrament of matrimony in *Amoris laetitia*. The relevant chapters, 3 and 8, will be interpreted in relation to the preceding and following chapters. This will at the same time allow us to grasp the line of argument and the precise conceptual work of Pope Francis.

2 The Dogmatic Characterization of the Post-Synodal Exhortation in the Introduction (AL 1-7)

In his introduction (AL 1-7), the Pope has presented a theologically exact and conceptually precise characterization of this document.

AL 1 explains the initial words that function as its title. Despite the many signs of a crisis of marriage, the Christian proclamation about the family is truly *good news* – Gospel.

AL 2 defines the ecclesial process that generated *Amoris laetitia*: "The *Synod process* allowed for an examination of the situation of families in today's world, and thus for a broader vision and a renewed awareness of the importance of marriage and the family. The complexity of the issues that arose revealed the need for

---

1 Quotations from the official English tradition, available from https://w2.vatican.va/content/dam/francesco/pdf/apost_exhortations/documents/papa-francesco_esortazione-ap_20160319_amoris-laetitia_en.pdf; accessed 12.12.2016.

continued open discussion of a number of *doctrinal, moral, spiritual, and pastoral questions*." The Pope emphasizes the ecclesial process, the synodal path that led to this document, and he himself adheres strictly to this process. The *Relatio synodi* of 2014 and the *Relatio finalis* of 2015, the approved summaries of the discussions by the bishops, are quoted continuously. The first point he mentions is the consensus of the Synod Fathers that not only spiritual and pastoral questions needed to be studied in greater depth, but "doctrinal and moral" questions too. The latter term refers to dogmatic and moral-theological changes that concern the problems involved and the solutions and answers that have been given up to now. The reason for this deeper study is the complexity of the problems, which emerged in the answers of the People of God and in the words of the bishops who took part in the Synod. Trusting in the assistance of the Holy Spirit, the Pope says: "The thinking of pastors and theologians, if faithful to the Church, honest, realistic, and creative, will help us to achieve greater clarity."

He then describes the spectrum of the debate by the bishops and holders of responsibility in the Church, as well as the debate in the public sphere. The positions "range from an immoderate desire for total change without sufficient reflection or grounding, to an attitude that would solve everything by applying general rules or deriving exaggerated conclusions from particular theological considerations." This excludes two extremes. On the one hand, the wish to change everything without sufficient reflection or grounding – that is to say, without looking more deeply at what precisely must be changed in the teaching and praxis that have prevailed up to now. This would lead to a total relativism that surrendered the faith to temporary circumstances.

On the other hand, we have the opposite extreme, which has also been upheld by bishops and theologians, namely to resolve the complexity of the problems concerning marriage and the family "by applying general rules". The Pope adds: "or deriving exaggerated conclusions from particular theological considerations". Obviously, the reason why the conclusions are exaggerated is that they are extended beyond the appropriate area of their validity. It became clear during the Synod that these two positions, which are characterized as extremes, were unacceptable. The consensus of the Church and of the pastors is located between these two boundaries.

AL 3 explains this. In the history of the transmission of the faith, there can be differing positions with differing accentuations. The plurality of cultures leads to differentiating features in the tradition of the faith. This kind of plurality belongs to the unity of teaching and praxis of the Church.

Amoris laetitia itself is characterized as an element and an outcome of this synodal path: it is meant to bring together the contributions made by the two last Synods on the family. At the same time, the Pope wishes to add "other considerations as an aid to reflection, dialogue and pastoral practice, and as a help and encouragement to families in their daily commitments and challenges".

Accordingly, he does not describe this synodal process as an intervention by the magisterium (AL 3). This term denotes the resolution of a doctrinal, moral, or pastorally contentious question by a declaration of the magisterium; and these declarations can have varying degrees of authority. In view of the complexity and the *de facto* difficulties of the given situation, it is clear that the "synodal path" is intended to confirm the general unity of the faith that finds expression both in the faith of the people and in the ordinary magisterium of the bishops (and hence in that of the Pope too).[2]

In AL 4, Pope Francis employs the image of the "multifaceted gem" to illustrate the view of marriage and the family that is shared by believers.[3]

> Here our model is not the sphere, which is no greater than its parts, where every point is equidistant from the center, and there are no differences between them. Instead, it is the polyhedron, which reflects the convergence of all its parts, each of which preserves its distinctiveness. Pastoral and political activity alike seek to gather in this polyhedron the best of each. There is a place for the poor and their culture, their aspirations and their potential. Even people who can be considered dubious on account of their errors have something to offer which must not be overlooked. It is the convergence of peoples who, within the universal order, maintain their own individuality; it is the sum total of persons within a society, which pursues the common good, which truly has a place for everyone.
>
> To Christians, this principle also evokes the totality or integrity of the Gospel which the Church passes down to us and sends us forth to proclaim … The good news is the joy of the Father who desires that none of his little ones be lost … The Gospel is the leaven which causes the dough to rise and the city on the hill whose light illumines all peoples. The Gospel has an intrinsic principle of totality.[4]

In AL 5, the Pope makes a link between this document and the Jubilee Year of the Mercy of God. He describes the structure of the text in AL 6.[5] In AL 7, he speaks about how various groups of readers will tackle the various chapters, and refers at

2 See Pope Francis' discourse on October 17, 2015 marking the fiftieth anniversary of the establishing of the Synod of Bishops, available from: http://papa-francesco_20151017_50.anniversario-sinodo.html; accessed 12.12.2016.

3 See FRANCIS: *Post-Synodal Exhortation* Evangelii Gaudium, 2013, 236-237. The Pope employs this image in EG in relation to the common good and to social peace in the world. He also applies it in EG to the evangelizing Church and to the Gospel itself.

4 EG 236-237.

5 In *Amoris laetitia*, the Pope speaks basically as a pastor, not as a professor of dogmatics. He addresses first and foremost the People of God and the pastors. This is why his exposition of the contents of *Amoris laetitia* emphasizes chapters 4-7, which contain the *explicatio mysterii.* For a reading from the perspective of dogmatics, however, it is chapters 3 and 8 that occupy the foreground.

the end to chapter 8. He hopes that all readers will feel most strongly addressed by this chapter, because its theme is the ecclesial ordering of marriage and family, which is renewed by being taken to a deeper level.

Let us summarize what the introduction tells us. *Amoris laetitia* is a synodal document; but this means that Pope Francis has given the Extraordinary Synod of 2014 and the Ordinary Synod of 2015[6] a different function than that intended by Paul VI. Pope Francis did not want merely a body that would give him advice. The bishops were challenged, both in the Extraordinary and in the Ordinary Synod of Bishops, to present their testimony to the faith and their understanding of the faith as pastors commissioned by the Lord, after the testimony to the faith of the People of God with regard to faith and family had been gathered in. Accordingly, the Pope quotes many, many pages of the summaries that were voted upon in the two Synods, as autonomous sources of the testimony to the faith given by the pastors of the Church. He does not go beyond the boundaries that were posited in these summaries, for example by making a statement about homosexual partnerships. Where he adds something, his additions are precisely marked, and he justifies them.

In view of the crisis of marriage and the family,[7] the one faith of the Church with regard to marriage and the family was to be the theme, as this is attested in the faith of the People of God and in the teaching of the pastors. This faith is inherently many-layered and plural, but it is one. With regard to the authoritative bearers of testimony that *Amoris laetitia* goes on to quote – scripture, tradition, and recent declarations by the magisterium – it must be noted that the process of tradition operated in the Synod in such a way that it itself excluded the two extreme positions that are characterized in AL 2.

This "synodal process" is the formalized process of bearing testimony to the faith and the teaching of the ordinary magisterium, in order to arrive – in view of

6 On the difference in canon law between an Extraordinary and an Ordinary Synod of Bishops, see J. LOFFELD: "Prozessverläufe und divergente theologische Erkenntnisorte – die außerordentliche und ordentliche Bischofssynode 2014/15", in: J. KNOP/J. LOFFELD (eds.):*Ganz familiär: die Bischofssynode 2014/2015 in der Debatte,* Regensburg: Friedrich Pustet, 2016, 43-62.

7 See already the Preparatory Document: *III Extraordinary General Assembly. Pastoral Challenges to the Family in the Context of Evangelization*, 2013, 2: "Concerns which were unheard of until a few years ago have arisen today as a result of different situations, from the widespread practice of cohabitation, which does not lead to marriage, and sometimes even excludes the idea of it, to same-sex unions between persons [...]. Within the Church, faith in the sacramentality of marriage and the healing power of the Sacrament of Penance show signs of weakness or total abandonment." Available from http://www.vatican.va/roman_curia/synod/documents/rc_synod_doc_20131105_iii-assemblea-sinodo-vescovi_en.html; accessed 12.12.2016.

the crisis – at a deepening of the common testimony to the faith and of the praxis of the Church.[8]

3 The Results of the Synodal Process from a Dogmatic Perspective: Chapters 3 and 8

These results, carefully gathered together and justified, are to be found in chapter 3: "Looking to Jesus – the vocation of the family" and in chapter 8: "Accompanying, discerning and integrating weakness".

3.1 The Dogmatic Significance of Chapter 3: "Looking to Jesus – the Vocation of the Family"

The dogmatic significance of chapter 3 can be seen both from the summary of the contents with which it begins and from the position of this chapter in the sequence of the argumentation. Let us begin by locating this chapter in its context.

Chapter 1, "In the light of the Word" (AL 8-30), presents all the many-layered reality of the relationship between husband and wife, marriage and family, including earning one's living, daily work, and the whole sphere of the erotic, as this is depicted in the Bible and in the New Testament. It is a "path of love and joy", but also "a path of suffering and blood".

The second chapter, "The experiences and challenges of families" (AL 31-57), confronts the reader with the situation of marriage and the family today and sketches particularly urgent problems and challenges. These two chapters thus show us a picture of marriage and family both in the testimony of scripture and in the contemporary situation.

A decisive further step is taken in the introduction to the third chapter, "Looking to Jesus: the vocation of the family" (AL 58-70). What we meet here is the Gospel, "the heart of Christ's message"[9] about marriage and the family. This is the "mystery" of marriage and the family in the mystery of Christ and the Church (AL

---

8 On this, see Pope Francis' discourse at the opening of the Synod on October 5, 2015, available from http://w2vatican.va/content/francesco/it/speeches/2015/october/documents/papa-francesco_20151005-padri-sinodali.htm; accessed 12.12.2016, as well as his discourse at the close of the Synod on October 24, 2015.

9 This expression is taken from EG 34. – With regard to the theological explanation, the Pope adds in EG 36: "All revealed truths derive from the same divine source and are to be believed with the same faith, yet some of them are more important for giving direct expression to the heart of the Gospel. In this basic core, what shines forth is *the beauty of the saving love of God made manifest in Jesus Christ who died and rose from the dead.* In this sense, the Second Vatican Council explained, 'in Catholic doctrine there exists an order or a "hierarchy" of truths, since they vary in their relation to the foundation of the Christian faith.'"

59). In formal terms, according to AL 60, this brief chapter contains a summary of the Church's teaching about marriage and the family.

This teaching is not presented in the manner of a theoretical statement from the perspective of uninvolved third parties, so to speak. Rather, it is presented from "the gaze of Jesus", who "looked upon the women and men whom he met with love and tenderness... as he proclaimed the demands of the Kingdom of God". The text speaks here of the specific perspective of seeing and speaking that John XXIII called "pastoral teaching" at the solemn opening of the Second Vatican Council in October 1962.[10]

After this introduction, the Church's teaching is set out in six sections; the passage about the sacrament of matrimony occupies the central place here (AL 71-75). Pope Francis did not himself formulate the summary of the central statements of faith that scripture and tradition attest with regard to marriage and the family. He adopts them almost in their entirety from the *Relatio synodi* of 2014 and the *Relatio finalis* of 2015.

The first section (AL 61-66) discusses the *testimony of scripture,* and summarizes it from various perspectives:

- statements about marriage as a good gift of creation and of grace (1 Tim 4,4; 1 Cor 7,7; Heb 13,4; 1 Cor 7,5);
- about its indissolubility as "a concession by God", who heals hardened hearts via the path of the cross (Mt 19,8.6.3);
- about Jesus, who leads marriage and the family back to their original form and to perfection (Mk 10,1-12; Eph 5,21-32; Gen 1,26f.; Rev 19,9);
- and who bears witness to this in his public ministry (Jn 2,1-11; Lk 10,38; Mt 8,14; Mk 5,41; Lk 7,14f.; Jn 4,1-30; Jn 8,1-11);
- finally, the incarnation of the Word and Jesus' growing up in a human family are mentioned (Prologue to John and the infancy narratives of the synoptics).

These statements are summarized in AL 66 in words of Paul VI: "The covenant of love and fidelity lived by the Holy Family of Nazareth illuminates the principle which gives shape to every family, and enables it better to face the vicissitudes of life and history. On this basis, every family, despite its weaknesses, can become a light in the darkness of the world..."

In the second section (AL 67-70), Pope Francis summarizes the statements about *marriage and the family in the documents of the Church.*

He begins with the Second Vatican Council and the relevant post-conciliar texts. He quotes Paul VI's *Humanae vitae* and John Paul II's *Gratissimam sane*

[10] See P. HÜNERMANN/B.-J. HILBERATH: *Herders Theologischer Kommentar zum II. Vatikanischen Konzil*, vol. 5, Freiburg: Herder, 2007, 482-490, esp. 486-88. For a more precise conceptual explanation, see P. HÜNERMANN: *Sprache des Glaubens – Sprache des Lehramts – Sprache der Theologie,* Freiburg-Basel-Wien: Herder, 2016 (Quaestiones Disputatae; 274).

and *Familiaris consortio,* as well as Benedict XVI's encyclicals *Deus caritas est* and *Caritas in veritate.* The core affirmations that he cites are devoted to the mystery of marriage and the family in the mystery of Christ.[11]

These statements from the documents of the magisterium are collected and quoted in the *Relatio synodi* of 2014 and the *Relatio finalis* of 2015. This entire section consists of a sequence of sections from these two synodal documents. It is obvious that what we read here is the shared view of faith held by the representatives of the worldwide college of bishops and by the Pope with regard to the mystery, namely, to the gospel of marriage and the family in scripture and in tradition.

Under the heading: "The sacrament of matrimony" (AL 71-75), these constitutive elements of the doctrine of the faith are employed to set out the meaning and importance of the sacrament of marriage. By way of introduction, AL 71 – with another quotation from the *Relatio finalis* of 2015 – shows that, and how, marriage belongs to the mystery of the Holy Trinity, the mystery of the Father, of Jesus Christ, and of the Church, and at the same reveals this mystery. AL 72 then provides an exact outline of the sacrament of marriage:

> The sacrament of marriage is not a social convention, an empty ritual or merely the outward sign of a commitment. The sacrament is a gift given for the sanctification and salvation of the spouses, since "their mutual belonging is a real representation, through the sacramental sign, of the same relationship between Christ and the Church. The married couple are therefore a permanent reminder for the Church of what took place on the cross; they are for one another and for their children witnesses of the salvation in which they share through the sacrament." Marriage is a vocation, inasmuch as it is a response to a specific call to live conjugal love as an imperfect sign of the love between Christ and the Church. Consequently, the decision to marry and to have a family ought to be the fruit of a process of vocational discernment.

Let us take these points one by one. The sacrament is not simply a traditional social custom, an empty rite born of the religious piety of earlier times. This cites

[11] With regard to *Humanae vitae,* he underlines that Paul VI emphasizes the inherent bond between marital love and life: "Married love requires of husband and wife the full awareness of their obligations in the matter of responsible parenthood... The exercise of responsible parenthood requires that husband and wife, keeping a right order of priorities, recognize their own duties towards God, themselves, their families and human society." Pope Francis writes that the Apostolic Exhortation *Familiaris consortio,* the Letter to Families *Gratissimam sane,* and the catecheses of John Paul II "defined the family as 'the way of the Church'. He also offered a general vision of the vocation of men and women to love." Pope Francis writes that the encyclical *Deus caritas est* of Benedict XVI "returned to the topic of the truth of the love of man and woman, which is fully illuminated only in the love of the crucified Christ"; and in the encyclical *Deus caritas est,* "he highlighted the importance of love as a principle of life in society, a place where we learn the experience of the common good".

the first extreme position, which is employed as a negative foil to the following remarks. The second extreme position is also mentioned: marriage is not the mere external sign of an obligation. Marriage is not an external contract that concerns the *jus in corpus* on the part of the husband and on the part of the wife. – I refer here to the characterization of marriage according to *Casti connubii* (1930), which I shall discuss in a later section of this paper. But what then is the sacrament of marriage? "Marriage is a *vocation,* inasmuch as it is a response to a specific call to live conjugal love as an imperfect sign of the love between Christ and the Church."

Every sacrament has an earthly reality as a sign. This earthly reality is the conjugal love that finds expression in the covenant of love between two persons. This, however, is "an imperfect sign of the love between Christ and the Church". To live marriage as a sign of the covenant between Christ and the Church is called a "vocation". As a technical term, "vocation" in the New Testament means that a human being is addressed by the word of God himself,[12] by his good news of the Kingdom of God that Jesus Christ proclaims. "Vocation" therefore includes the "covenant of every human being with Christ in the Church" – the universal vocation, but also the individual vocation of each one to follow Jesus Christ and to collaborate in a special way in the mission of Jesus Christ. In the sacrament of baptism, the universal element of vocation receives its expression; in the sacrament of marriage, the special element of vocation receives its expression. The notion of the sacrament of marriage as a "thing" or a "power" is rejected. The central point is that the love of the marriage partners not only points to the love of Christ for the Church; rather, this love is present and efficacious in the love of the marriage partners (AL 73). This is the operative presence of the crucified and risen Lord, which is present in the living out of marital love. At the same time, the partners "are called to respond to God's gift with commitment, creativity, perseverance and daily effort. They can always invoke the assistance of the Holy Spirit who consecrated their union, so that his grace may be felt in every new situation that they encounter" (AL 74). This means that there is a very strong resemblance between Christian marriage and the eucharist.

This understanding of Christian marriage as a sacrament – and indeed, as a vocation – means, first of all, that the sacrament of matrimony has its roots in baptism. This is why it is the partners themselves who administer the sacrament to each other. And this is why a non-Christian married couple who come to faith do not need to get married again after baptism, "since by the reception of baptism their union automatically becomes sacramental".[13] In the next three sections,

12 See K.L. SCHMIDT: "καλέω etc.", in: *Theologisches Wörterbuch zum Neuen Testament*, vol. 3, Stuttgart: Kohlhammer, 1953, 488-538, esp. 489-495.

13 AL 75. The Spanish text reads: "automaticamente sacramental".

always with extensive quotations from the texts of the *Relationes* of the Extraordinary and the Ordinary Synods, the Pope sketches three consequences of this.

1. "Imperfect situations" exist (AL 76-79). The keyword of the *semina verbi* allows these to be called "pre-Christian situations". These exist in various cultures and religious traditions, as well as in the forms of exclusively civil marriages. Since the order of redemption illuminates and fulfills the order of creation, the Church's task is to see this as an opportunity "to accompany the persons concerned to the sacrament of matrimony, where this is possible" (AL 77). The entire text of this section is a compact tissue of quotations from the *Relatio synodi* of 2014, the *Relatio finalis* of 2015, and the Apostolic Exhortation *Familiaris consortio* of John Paul II.

2. Pope Francis thematizes the second consequence under the heading: "The transmission of life and the rearing of children". The dispute from the beginning of the twentieth century about the definition of the goal of marriage is taken up in a new manner here. The Pope refers to the *Catechism of the Catholic Church* (2366) and to *Gaudium et spes* 48, and writes: "The child who is born 'does not come from outside as something added on to the mutual love of the spouses, but springs from the very heart of that mutual giving, as its fruit and fulfilment'." With a reference to *Humanae vitae* he states: "From the outset, love refuses every impulse to close in on itself; it is open to a fruitfulness that draws it beyond itself. Hence no genital act of husband and wife can refuse this meaning, even when for various reasons it may not always in fact beget a new life." He also quotes *Donum vitae*: "A child deserves to be born of that love, and not by any other means, for 'he or she is not something owed to one, but is a gift' (CCC 2378), which is 'the fruit of the specific act of the conjugal love of the parents' (*Donum vitae* II, 8)." Finally, no. 83 rejects the attempt to justify abortion on the basis of the woman's rights over her own body; and no. 84 defends the education and formation of children as a primary right and as a duty of the parents. Finally, in the last section, entitled: "The family and the Church", the family is thematized as a "domestic church". The core affirmation runs as follows: "The Church is a family of families, constantly enriched by the lives of all those domestic churches." This too is a quotation from the *Relatio finalis* of 2015.

Let us sum up: On the basis of the testimony of scripture (section 1) and tradition (section 2), the sacrament of marriage is characterized as a mystery in the mystery of Christ and of the Church (section 3). In the next three sections (4 to 6), the historicity of this mystery, and its unfolding into fruitfulness and the family, and ultimately into the ecclesial dimension, are affirmed.

3.2 *The Dogmatic Significance of Chapter 8: "Weakness to Be Accompanied, Discerned and Integrated"*

3.2.1 Preliminary Consideration

Chapter 8 is about *church order* (*Kirchenordnung*).[14] Chapter 3 summarized the testimony of faith to the sacrament of marriage and the unfolding of this sacrament in the mystery of Christ and of the Church; the topic of chapter 8 is the guiding principles of the comprehensive church order, as the title of this chapter shows. The church order is characterized by pragmatic maxims. One must accompany the fragility (of marriage and the family). One must discern the numerous and individually distinct situations of the married couples and their relatives, their success and their failure, their difficulties, and so on. Ultimately, the entire pragmatism aims at an "integration" of the married couple and of their family, with all its weaknesses, its success and its failure, into the mystery of Christ and of the Church.

It is not only the title of chapter 8 that shows that it is about church order. We see this also from the subheadings in the chapter.

Finally, the meaning and significance of chapter 8 emerge from its position in the sequence of the preceding chapters. Building on chapter 3, as I have described it above, the fourth chapter begins an explanation of the constitutive elements of this sacrament. The third chapter culminates in the remarks about the *sacramentum,* the mystery of marriage and the family in the mystery of Jesus and Christ and the Church, or of the Holy Trinity. The fourth chapter starts to explain in more detail the constitutive elements of this sacrament. The description of the mystery follows the *explicatio mysterii,* taking the individual elements one by one.

When the eighth chapter thematizes church order, it refers to the preceding explanations and sums up the corresponding mode of behavior in the Church, so that the entire presentation can be concluded with the ninth chapter, on the spirituality of marriage and the family.

---

14 "Church order" is understood here in the sense of the English-language expression "Faith and Order". In other words, it embraces more than canon law alone. The "order" of the Church is not only legal in the sense of canon law, but essentially includes also moral-ethical and creedal-spiritual elements. "Church order" thus means more than simply a *lex fundamentalis.* It includes not only canon law, but also customs and modes of conduct, the ethos of the People of God and of Church governance. This is the complex that is referred to in the traditional formula of *fides et mores*; Neo-Scholasticism narrowed it down to faith and morals in moral theology. Originally, the Latin noun *mores* designates the intentional modes of conduct that have become a rule, in the sense of the English noun: "mores", includes conduct, and lifestyle.

3.2.2 The Guidelines of Church Order

After the introduction (AL 291-295), which displays the entire spectrum of the existing forms of successful sacramental marriages and families, but also the distortions or contradictory forms, the first section thematizes the basis of modes of conduct in the Church, under the heading: "Gradualness in pastoral care" (AL 293-295). AL 293 takes up the special contemporary situation, which had already been presented in chapter 2, and draws the consequence that: "As members of the Church, they too need pastoral care that is merciful and helpful." This means "accompanying weakness", as the title of chapter 8 puts it. This care urgently requires a discerning pastoral dialogue, in order "to distinguish elements in their lives that can lead to a greater openness to the Gospel of marriage in its fullness".

The goal of this discernment is "to transform" these situations "into opportunities that can lead to the full reality of marriage and family in conformity with the Gospel" (AL 294). When he speaks of this process and of the guidelines for the Church's action, the Pope has recourse to the term "law of gradualness", which John Paul II employs in *Familiaris consortio* "in the knowledge that the human being 'knows, loves and accomplishes moral good by different stages of growth'". Cardinal Schönborn had introduced this term into the synodal discussion, appealing thereby to Thomas Aquinas, *Summa Theologiae* II/II, q. 24, a. 9; q. 183, a. 4. Thomas speaks in both these passages of *incipientes, proficientes et perfecti.*[15]

The next section, "The discernment of 'irregular' situations" (AL 296-300), takes up a group of problems that concern today's church order. Canon law understands "irregularity" to mean a permanent hindrance to the reception of ordination as bishop, priest, or deacon.[16] When Pope Francis puts this adjective in inverted commas, it is clear that he is using the canon law term in a broader sense, with regard to marriages of Christians that do not correspond to the sacramental character of matrimony.

---

15 It is regrettable that no mention was made of the New Testament affirmations about this growth in faith, nor of the great theological tradition, the "stepped path" whereby the attempt was made in the patristic period, the Middle Ages, and in the Modern Period to grasp this conceptually. Both Karl Rahner and Hans Urs von Balthasar had taken up this topic already before 1939. See K. RAHNER: "Über das Problem des Stufenweges zur christlichen Vollendung", in: *Schriften zur Theologie,* vol. 3, Einsiedeln-Zürich-Köln: Benziger, 1956, 11-34.

16 When the Code of Canon Law lists the reasons for an irregularity of this kind, after mentioning mental or physical illness, apostasy or schism, it mentions in the third place "a person who has attempted marriage, even only civilly, while either impeded personally from entering marriage by a matrimonial bond, sacred order, or a public perpetual vow of chastity, or with a woman bound by a valid marriage or restricted by the same type of vow" (CIC 1983, can. 1040). On the model of these canons and of their subsequent elaboration, there are various regulations that specify that divorced and remarried persons must not hold any catechesis or preaching, that they are not to undertake any ecclesial offices, etc.

In order that an appropriate judgment may be made in this entire sphere, the Pope at once recalls the fundamentally pragmatic orientation of the Church's action from New Testament times onwards. Exclusion and renewed integration have occurred throughout Church history. One is inevitably reminded of 1 Cor 5,1-5: the licentious man who cohabits with his father's wife is excluded from the community, so that his flesh may be destroyed, *in order that* his spirit may be saved on the day of the Lord. Equally important in this context is the development of the sacrament of penance through the debate between Novatian and Cornelius about the exclusion and possible reintegration of the *lapsi*[17] This concerned members of the Church who had denied the faith under persecution, and the possibility of their reconciliation. In AL 297, drawing on the words of the Synod Fathers in the *Relationes,* and with an explicit reference to *Familiaris consortio,* the Pope confirms the correctness of the "exclusion" because of irregularity, for example "if someone flaunts an objective sin as if it were part of the Christian ideal... he or she can in no way presume to teach or preach to others". At the same time, he emphasizes the "general consensus" of the Synod Fathers on the following point: "'In considering a pastoral approach towards people who have contracted a civil marriage, who are divorced and remarried, or simply living together, the Church has the responsibility of helping them understand the divine pedagogy of grace in their lives and offering them assistance so they can reach the fullness of God's plan for them,' something which is always possible by the power of the Holy Spirit." Examples in AL 298 illustrate this. With regard to integration, "a new set of general rules, canonical in nature", is not possible. All that is possible is an accompaniment "which guides the faithful to an awareness of their situation before God", and "discernment can recognize that in a particular situation no grave fault exists" (AL 300 and footnote 336). The Pope refers to the *Catechism of the Catholic Church*, no. 1735: "imputability and responsibility for an action can be diminished or even nullified by ignorance, inadvertence, duress, fear, habit, inordinate attachments, and other psychological or social factors".

This means that at the end of this section, in AL 300, the Pope has taken a very decisive step to exclude what he had already rejected in the introduction to *Amoris laetitia* as the second extreme. To what does this exclusion refer? In the Church's tradition, from the *Nicomachean Ethics* of Aristotle and its reception in the Middle Ages onwards, philosophers and theologians had maintained that "adultery" counted as an "intrinsically evil act", which is always *per se* evil, independently of all the specific circumstances. This position overlooked the fact that although Aristotle and the medieval theologians who received him did indeed reject taking external circumstances into account – with whom, where, and for how long the

---

17 See J.S. ALEXANDER: "Novatian/Novatianer", in: TRE, vol. 24, 678-682.

adultery had been committed – they were nevertheless aware of numerous internal or subjective elements that reduced the guilt, for example, if the act took place in the heat of passion, out of fear or ignorance, and so on.[18]

In the dispute about ethical or moral-theological theories that appear to derive – or do in fact derive – evil exclusively from the consequences of an action, John Paul II adopts this position in *Familiaris consortio* (1981) and subsequently in *Veritatis splendor*. This led to strongly polarized discussions.[19]

The result of the intensive theological discussions can be summarized as follows: There are intrinsically evil actions that are not conditioned by external circumstances, but that are indeed conditioned by internal, subjective elements.

In the next section, "Mitigating factors in pastoral discernment" (AL 301-303), the Pope and the Synod Fathers in the two *Relationes* once again confirm the result of the theological discussion. The Pope refers here to Thomas Aquinas and the *Summa Theologiae* I/II, q. 65, a. 3 ad 2 and 3; *De malo* q. 2, a. 2; and to texts from the pontificate of John Paul II in the 1980s, as well as to a text issued by the Pontifical Council for the Interpretation of Legislative Texts in 2000.

In the following section, "Rules and Discernment" (AL 304-306), the Pope takes up the relationship between the general ethical principles and rules, on the one hand, and the personal responsible decision of conscience, on the other hand. The two authorities belong together in their differentness and in their indissoluble bond. By way of explanation, the Pope quotes the observation by the International Theological Commission that: "natural law could not be presented as an already established set of rules that impose themselves *a priori* on the moral subject; rather, it is a source of inspiration for the deeply personal process of making decisions".

The conclusion of chapter 8 – "The logic of pastoral mercy" (AL 307-312) – is a passionate appeal by the Pope to put the preceding reflections into pastoral practice, with all the love of the Good Shepherd.

On the dogmatic basis of the Church's teaching about marriage and the family, as this is presented in chapters 3 and 8, *Amoris laetitia* sets out in the ninth chapter the outlines of a spirituality of marriage and of the family that correspond to the deeper understanding of these realities. In a strictly articulated "vertical plan", the Pope sketches a spiritual path that replaces the *itinerarium mentis in Deum* –

---

[18] On these problems, see S. HERZBERG: "Das Lehrstück von den In-sich-schlechten Handlungen bei Aristoteles", in: *Theologie und Philosophie* 91 (2016), 196-214, and the secondary literature cited there.

[19] See *Herder Korrespondenz* 36 (1985) with all five statements, and a further statement in: *Herder Korrespondenz* 37 (1986). – P. CARLOTTI: *"Veritatis splendor": Aspetti della recezione teologica*, Rome: LAS, 2001 (Biblioteca di scienze religiose; 167).

a form with Neo-Platonic roots, profoundly shaped in the Church's tradition by Pseudo-Dionysius – by an *itinerarium in Deum* through a deepened *caritas.*

After this examination of *Amoris laetitia,* read with the eyes of a dogmatic theologian, we shall attempt in the final section of this paper to identify the dogmatic consolidations, clarifications, and innovations that AL has brought with regard to the sacrament of marriage and to the family.

4 The Doctrinal Consolidations, Clarifications, and Innovations of *Amoris Laetitia*

4.1 Preliminary Methodological Remark

Our starting point is the core affirmations in the third chapter, in AL 72: "The sacrament is a gift given for the sanctification and salvation of the spouses, since 'their mutual belonging is a real representation, through the sacramental sign, of the same relationship between Christ and the Church.'... Marriage is a vocation, inasmuch as it is a response to a specific call to experience conjugal love as an imperfect sign of the love between Christ and the Church. Consequently, the decision to marry and to have a family ought to be the fruit of a process of vocational discernment."

We contrast this with the basic definition of the sacrament of marriage in *Casti connubii,* because we find there a summary of the previous basic elements of the doctrine of marriage in the Latin Church.[20] No. 10 states: "From God comes the very institution of marriage, the ends for which it was instituted, the laws that govern it, the blessings that flow from it; while man, through generous surrender of his own person made to another for the whole span of life, becomes, with the help and cooperation of God, the author of each particular marriage, with the duties and blessings annexed thereto from divine institution."

Casti connubii and *Amoris laetitia* share the following theological foundations. (*a*) The origin of the human being and of his marriage lies in God, as does the restoration of the creation and of marriage through Jesus Christ. (*b*) Both documents speak of the gift of one's own person to one's marriage partner as a decisive element. There are, however, striking differences in the way in which the two papal documents link these two constitutive realities. We read in *Casti connubii*: "Matrimony was not instituted or restored by man but by God; not by man were the laws made to strengthen and confirm and elevate it but by God, the

[20] Quotations here follow DH 3700-3724, and the edition with commentary by Fr. Franziskus Hürt, SJ, the author of the encyclical: *Litterae encyclicae Nr. I, Leo XIII. et Pius XI. De matrimonio christiano, "Arcanum divinae sapientiae" 10. Febr. 1880, "Casti connubii" 31. Dec. 1930,* ed. F. Hürt SJ, Rome: Gregorian University, 1945. – English translation from the Vatican website (which, however, has a divergent numbering of the paragraphs).

Author of nature, and by Christ Our Lord by Whom nature was redeemed, and hence these laws cannot be subject to any human decrees or to any contrary pact even of the spouses themselves."[21] The text then states explicitly that the freedom of the partners "regards only the question whether the contracting parties really wish to enter upon matrimony or to marry this particular person; but the nature of matrimony is entirely independent of the free will of man, so that if one has once contracted matrimony he is thereby subject to its divinely made laws and its essential properties.[22] This is the Augustinian view of marriage – namely, that this *contract* is to be made for the sake of the three goods of *proles, fides* and *sacramentum.* The mutual fidelity is permeated here by a notion of "ownership", when *fides* primarily concerns the prohibition against more than one partner sharing the *jus in corpus.*[23]

The third *bonum,* the *sacramentum,* designates "the indissolubility of the bond and the raising and hallowing of the contract by Christ Himself, whereby He made it an efficacious sign of grace".[24] It is explicitly affirmed that stability and indissolubility belong in varying degrees to individual marriages, but apply in a special degree to Christian marriages.

The abstract juridical affirmations of *Casti connubii* are toned down when the encyclical states that "love in the home" means that the couple must help each other to grow in love, "on which indeed dependeth the whole Law and the Prophets... This determined effort to perfect each other, can *in a very real sense,* as the Roman Catechism teaches, be said to be the chief reason and purpose of matrimony, provided matrimony be looked at not in the restricted sense as instituted for the proper conception and education of the child, but more widely as the blending of life as a whole and the mutual interchange and sharing thereof."[25]

The "restricted sense" left its mark on the public image of marriage, which dominated in preaching, pastoral care, canon law, and theology. Such a marriage does not exist for modern human beings, when they look at the cultural history of humankind. Marriage as an unchangeable divine law that is present in the human being himself – so that one would have to have recourse to the construction of a divine dispensation from the divine law, if one wished to make sense of the

---

21 *Casti connubii*, 5.

22 Ibid. 6.

23 See ibid. 19: "conjugal honor...consists in the mutual fidelity of the spouses in fulfilling the marriage contract, so that what belongs to one of the parties by reason of this contract sanctioned by divine law, may not be denied to him or permitted to any third person; nor may there be conceded to one of the parties anything which, being contrary to the rights and laws of God and entirely opposed to matrimonial faith, can never be conceded."

24 Ibid. 31.

25 Ibid. 23f.

polygamy of a figure like Abraham – is unthinkable for the modern human being, who finds the whole idea crazy.

4.2 The Theological Innovations with Regard to the Sacrament of Marriage

The *first* innovation lies in the starting point in the view of marriage that *Casti connubii* itself calls the *verissima ratione,* the *primaria matrimonii causa et ratio,* namely, the *totius vitae communio. Amoris laetitia* calls this the "mutual belonging" of the marriage partners. This designates the comprehensive, bodily, total relation of love that binds together husband and wife in marriage. This reality, the *covenant of life,* this marital love itself, is the expression of the relationship of love between Christ and the Church, fulfilled and perfected in the event of the Passion and the mysteries of Easter. The "imperfect signs of conjugal love" belong to this mystery. This shift had already been made by *Gaudium et spes* 48f. and *Lumen gentium* 11. *Amoris laetitia* spells out the individual facets of this relationship, especially in chapters 4-7.

Secondly, the sacrament of marriage is a *covenant of life,* not simply a contract. It involves a consent that "is not only a requirement of the law, but something that also entails an ethical obligation".[26] A covenant (*fœdus* in the Roman legal terminology) is an obligation that is entered into in good faith, and that obligates both in moral-ethical terms and in legal terms. This bids farewell to the juridical construction of the divinely preordained contract. When a marriage is evaluated, more must be involved than the question whether the wedding was legally valid.

Thirdly, marriage, as a covenant of life, is exposed to many risks, which are directly connected to the finitude and temporality of the covenant. The sacrament of marriage is threatened by moral and legal failure in every situation, down to the most everyday situations. The accumulation of offenses against good faith can pile up to such an extent that the mutual belonging is no longer merely at risk, but in fact no longer exists. The bishops who gathered for the Synod and the Pope himself have uncovered, with a remarkable perspicacity, this risk in the modern historical and societal situation. The sacrament is seen as a reality that exists in history.

Fourthly, the imperfection and the risk show us the reason for the gradualness, since the living of the sacrament in people's life histories involves a realization

[26] See I. RIEDEL-SPANGENBERGER: "Ehebund", in: A. FREIHERR VON CAMPENHAUSEN/I. RIEDEL-SPANGENBERGER/F. REINHOLD SEBOTT (eds.): *Lexikon für Kirchen- und Staatskirchenrecht,* Paderborn: Schöningh, 2001, vol. 1, 5001f. – CIC 1983, can. 1055 §1, 1058 §2, 1063 §4, explicitly adopts this concept.

of the covenant of life that must be deepened and renewed in the various phases and situations in life. At the beginning, there is the loving testing of the divine vocation to the covenant of life with this particular partner. At the end, there is the completion in the hour of death, as an entering, full of hope, into communion with the Father, the Son, and the Holy Spirit. And in all the various phases, there are various forms of possible failure.

Fifthly, the imperfection and fragility of the covenant of life open our eyes to the at least partial and analogous realization of marriage in other forms of union.

Sixthly, the sacrament of marriage is not seen as a "thing", as a "power", that exists *in* the Church. This sacrament belongs to the Church; it is the Church *qua* domestic church. According to *Lumen gentium* 1, the Church is in Christ "as it were the sacrament, or sign and instrument, of the most intimate union with God and of the unity of the entire human race". This leads here to a new view of the sacraments: the individual sacraments are forms of realization of the Church in faith, mysteries in the mystery of Christ and the Church.

The orientation of the sacrament of marriage to the fruitfulness that transcends conjugal love in the divine gift of children, and the development into a family, transmits a holistic theological image of marriage and the family that is new.

When we look back over these innovations, we see that very many individual elements of this understanding in faith of marriage and the family as a sacrament had already appeared and were accepted in the period between *Casti connubii* and *Amoris laetitia.* But the true innovation of *Amoris laetitia* consists in the fact that it succeeds in integrating these very different elements into one new holistic image. This is what must be said about the believing understanding of the sacrament of marriage in chapter 3.

A number of innovations, corrections, and clarifications are found in the eighth chapter, and these are very important for the Church's praxis with regard to the sacrament of marriage and the family – since it is in praxis that the new understanding must be articulated.

First, Casti connubii is essentially concerned about the official act of witnessing a wedding and the determination of the validity of a wedding on the occasion of a remarriage, which is sanctioned with the exclusion from reception of the sacraments. But the guidelines for the praxis in *Amoris laetitia* embrace all the phases, from encouraging a person to get married, down to death, and each phase is accompanied personally. The requirement that we accompany the fragility of marriage demands a fundamental transformation of pastoral activity.

Secondly, Amoris laetitia explains two ethical or moral presuppositions that were implied in the previous pastoral activity of the Church: a) "Intrinsically evil actions" do not exclude internal subjective circumstances that reduce or remove guilt; b) although the human being is obliged in conscience to observe general ethical principles and commandments, and to behave accordingly, knowledge of this fact can never replace the decision of his conscience, which he must take personally – because the universality of moral principles and commandments can never reach fully into the individuality or particularity of the individual situations and actions. Both authorities remain. They are at one and the same time distinct *and* inseparable.

Thirdly, these two clarifications explain why *Amoris laetitia* does not quote certain passages from *Familiaris consortio, Veritatis splendor,* and the *Catechism of the Catholic Church*: it is because these contain an erroneous interpretation of intrinsically evil actions. Statements from *Humanae vitae* are not quoted, because they contain an extension of the common natural ethical law into the particularity of individual actions.

Do We Expect Too Much? A Reflection on Expectations and Marriage in *Amoris Laetitia*[1]

Stephanie Höllinger

The fragility of interpersonal relationships, especially marriages, is becoming an increasingly common human experience. The most striking indicator of this phenomenon is the consistently high divorce rates nowadays, especially in West European countries and the US. Separation, divorce and remarriage have become an inevitable reality and are, therefore, no longer fringe phenomena. For this reason, political, social and scientific discourses have long been addressing this issue in an attempt to understand the underlying processes. Thus, the main focus of their investigations is usually not to determine exact numbers or concrete procedures in cases of separation and divorce, but rather to analyse the specific reasons that might be substantially relevant in regard to these developments in contemporary relationships. Ecclesial and theological reflections have also been influenced by these deliberations, which in recent decades have led to intense and controversial discussions. Today, the reality of separation, divorce and remarriage and the question of successful (re)marriages and relationships are still regarded as pressing issues and they sometimes result in significant tensions between believers. Whereas some are hoping for change and progress in doctrine, others want to see existing doctrine confirmed and thereby strengthened.

Hence, a great deal of attention, both inside and outside the Catholic Church, was drawn to the two Synods of Bishops[2] convened by Pope Francis, which were followed by the Postsynodal Apostolic Exhortation *Amoris laetitia* on 19

1 I would like to thank my colleague Nenad Polgar, whose thoughts about language and content helped to greatly improve and enrich this article. Furthermore, I want to thank Prof. Sigrid Müller and Prof. Gunter Prüller-Jagenteufel for attentively reading and providing comments on this manuscript.

2 See esp. III Extraordinary General Assembly: *Relatio Synodi* (18 October 2014); XIV Ordinary General Assembly: *Relatio Finalis* (24 October 2015). Hereafter, references to *Relatio Synodi* in the text are abbreviated RS, while *Relatio Finalis* is abbreviated RF.

March 2016[3]. One of the most distinctive characteristics of this synodal process was evident right from the preparatory stages, which for the first time in church history involved presynodal consultations. Right from the start, the importance of including the everyday experiences of Catholic believers from around the globe was considered indispensable,[4] and this was ultimately also echoed in the eagerly awaited exhortation. Pope Francis drew a true-to-life picture of human relationships that depicts "the reality of the family today in all its complexity, with both its lights and shadows" (RS 5, cited in AL 32). Fundamental to the Pope's reflection was the idea "that there is no stereotype of the ideal family, but rather a challenging mosaic made up of many different realities, with all their joys, hopes and problems" (AL 57).

In accordance with this pivotal intention of focusing on the complexity of human life, *Amoris laetitia* not only offers insights into recent positive developments related to marital life (e.g. equitable distribution of responsibilities, greater valuation of communication, etc., see esp. AL 32, 38), but also a critique of ways of life, working patterns and social structures (see esp. AL 33, 39-56) that have a profoundly negative impact on families and can be a source of severe difficulties.[5] Taking into account the many obstacles faced by intimate relationships,[6] this arti-

---

3 FRANCIS: *Amoris laetitia* (19 March 2016). Hereafter, references to *Amoris laetitia* in the text are abbreviated AL.

4 Besides positive reactions to this innovative step of synodal preparations and the motive of actively listening to the ambiguity of family experiences that underlies it, it should be noted that these consultations have also been criticised. Some of the main points of criticism included the incomprehensibility of certain questions, the non-publication of the results and difficulties in relation to the national reports (in terms of time and organisation). See e.g. E. DAVIES: "Understanding Families as Gifts rather than as Problems", in: *INTAMS Review* 22/1 (2016), 67-70; D. HAYES: "Never Expecting Too Much, Never Being Satisfied with Too Little", ibid. 94-97.

5 The theological reception of *Amoris laetitia* shows an ambivalent interpretation of this cultural critique. It fluctuates between "too blurred and pessimistic" and "surprisingly concrete". One example that makes this ambiguity clear is a comparison of two articles, both published in *Herder Korrespondenz*. While A. Wollbold criticises the analysis of the present-day situation in the exhortation, due to its length and cultural pessimism, S. Orth emphasises that this critical approach is very precise, but at the same time not the main focus of the document. See S. ORTH: "Franziskus: Nachsynodales Schreiben 'Amoris laetitia'", in: *Herder Korrespondenz* 70/5 (2016), 9-10; A. WOLLBOLD: "Ermutigung zu Seelsorge", in: *Herder Korrespondenz* 70/6 (2016), 13-14.

6 *Amoris laetitia* points to several aspects of marital and family life that are also mentioned in scientific discourses (esp. sociological research) as special challenges for marriage and family: an increase in endogenous and exogenous stressors (AL 33), an abundance of choices and options (AL 40), changes in the economy/social exclusion (AL 44), decline of multigenerational households/growth of single-parent families (AL 49), alternatives to marriage (AL 53), etc. The following works provide a solid sociological overview: E. MONYK: *Lieber alleine oder zu zweit?: Die individualistische Lebensweise von Singles und kinderlosen Paaren*, Vienna:

cle focuses on a specific perspective that is repeatedly mentioned by Pope Francis and seems especially noteworthy in the context of the high likelihood of separations and divorces in the present day: namely, the exhortation's explicit argument that "[a]mong the causes of broken marriages are unduly high expectations about conjugal life" (AL 221), because it "is not helpful to dream of an idyllic and perfect love needing no stimulus to grow" (AL 135). Consequently, a tension is created between the often challenging reality and the strived-for perfection within a relationship with a partner, and this seems to have a great impact on interpersonal relationships. This leads to the question that this article focuses on: "Do we expect too much (when it comes to our personal beliefs about a harmonious family life)?" In the following, the question is dealt with in three consecutive steps: (1) outlining excessively high expectations as a serious source of conflict in contemporary marriages and families, (2) reflecting on the possible backgrounds to these expectations and (3) presenting helpful attitudes, in particular for dealing with the problem of excessively high expectations as raised in *Amoris laetitia*.

1 Excessively High Expectations as a Source of Conflict

The exhortation notes a specific problem that originates in human beliefs about how a relationship should ideally be formed. These beliefs are a central object of research in the field of cognitive psychology, where they are commonly termed cognitions. According to this specific branch of psychology, cognitions have an impact on personal life, because within concrete marital or family experiences they usually do not remain abstract images, but instead become goals that the individuals wish to realise in their relationship with their partner. In other words, individual cognitions have an effect on intimate relationships.

Although, as psychologists regularly admit, this is a common process, certain cognitions may become extremely problematic and sometimes even result in drastic consequences for personal life. This is especially evident in situations where a confrontation with these cognitions is unavoidable, as for instance is the case when the two people involved do not share the same thoughts about a particular issue pertaining to a harmonious life together, or when one of the partners has rigid standards which cannot be fulfilled entirely within the relationship. If there is no way of finding compromises that would satisfy both partners, the expectations[7] remain unfulfilled and can place great strain on the relationship. Hence,

LIT, 2007 (Sozialanthropologie des städtischen Lebens; 2); R. PEUCKERT: *Familienformen im sozialen Wandel*, Opladen: Leske + Budrich, 1991.

[7] This branch of psychological research distinguishes between five types of cognitions. The relevant type in relation to the description above is generally associated with the term "standards". These are cognitions about how something (a situation/relationship/person) should be. In other

unfulfilled expectations are an extraordinary challenge for marriage and family, and the effects can result in serious conflicts that sometimes make separation or divorce appear inevitable.[8]

Although no explicit references to these findings from cognitive psychology can be found in *Amoris laetitia*, the Synods of Bishops have demonstrated a keen sense for the risks of excessively high expectations that are examined in greater depth in the exhortation. In other words, the reflection on problematic expectations and their possible consequences for marital and family life was already present in the *Lineamenta*[9] and finally came to a fuller fruition in the exhortation. Especially in the latter document, excessively high expectations are regarded as a cause of serious problems within intimate relationships and are, therefore, explicitly regarded as one of the causes of separation and divorce (see AL 221). This is why Pope Francis does not merely describe the difficulties related to excessively high expectations; he also inquires into their possible roots, as well as attitudes that will allow spouses to successfully deal with problems together. He even goes beyond most current psychological and theological reflections on this topic.

2 Possible Backgrounds to Excessively High Expectations

Although the topic of expectations is not covered within a particular chapter and no systematic approach to it can be found in the document, a summary of *Amoris laetitia* reveals at least four noteworthy ideas concerning the backgrounds

words, the term "expectation" in ordinary language usually evokes an association that is related to the scientific use of the term "standards". This observation can also be made with regard to *Amoris laetitia*. This article therefore uses the term "expectations" while being aware that the technical term for this in psychology is "standards". For further explanation see D.H. BAUCOM/N. B. EPSTEIN/S.L. SAYERS/T. SHER: "The Role of Cognitions in Marital Relationships: Definitional, Methodological, and Conceptual Issues", in: *Journal of Consulting and Clinical Psychology* 57/1 (1989), 31-38, here 31-34; D.H. BAUCOM/N.B. EPSTEIN: *Cognitive-Behavioral Marital Therapy*, New York: Brunner/Mazel, 1990, 47-90.

8 For an overview, see e.g. G.J.O. FLETCHER/J.A. SIMPSON: "Ideal Standards in Close Relationships: Their Structure and Functions", in: *American Psychological Society* 9/3 (2000), 102-105; P. NOLLER/S.R.H. BEACH/S. OSGARBY: "Cognitive and Affective Processes in Marriage", in: K.W. HALFORD/H.J. MARKMAN (eds.): *Clinical Handbook of Marriage and Couples Intervention*, Chichester: John Wiley & Sons, 1997, 43-71; E. WUNDERER/K.A. SCHNEEWIND: "The Relationship between Marital Standards, Dyadic Coping and Marital Satisfaction", in: *European Journal of Social Psychology* 38/3 (2008), 462-476.

9 The problem of excessive expectations is explicitly mentioned in RF 8: "In great areas across the planet, cultural situations affecting the family display a conflicting character, even under the extensive influence of mass media. On the one hand, marriage and the family are held in high esteem and the idea still prevails that the family represents a safe haven for the most profound and gratifying sentiments. On the other hand, the concept of the family is marred by excessive expectations and, consequently, exaggerated claims on each other."

to relationship-specific expectations: images of perfect marriages and family life conveyed by society and media, emotionally undesirable developments resulting from experiences in the family of origin, individualistic tendencies and ecclesial distance from experienced reality are noted in the exhortation as factors that are responsible for the emergence of excessively high expectations. In the following, these four influencing factors, namely (1) media/social, (2) familial, (3) individualistic and (4) ecclesial influences, are briefly described.

2.1 Media/Social Influences

Directly quoting the Episcopal Conference of Chile,[10] the Exhortation points out the "deceptive consumerist propaganda" (AL 135) which presents all too perfect images of the family that rarely correspond to reality. Media and society constantly create ideals that stimulate unrealistic beliefs about personal relationships. In other words, they tend to define what a perfect marriage or family should look like (see AL 135) and this, in turn, can result in dubious standards for personal life becoming dominant – dubious, because they often do not reflect daily circumstances and challenges.

Films and TV shows, for example, usually do not consider the complexity of everyday tasks, such as the often stressful situation of having to simultaneously manage household chores, go to work, raise children and have an intact and loving relationship with one's spouse. In contrast to this, mass media often focus only on one or two of these areas and frequently presents a happy ending to fictional tensions or conflicts. Thus, a direct comparison of one's personal marital and family life with these simplistic images can lead sooner or later to frustration and great disappointment, because life, with its unpredictable challenges and misfortunes, can be easily misinterpreted as deviation from this supposed "normality".

2.2 Familial Influences

Pope Francis dedicates two paragraphs (AL 239-240) to the topic of "old wounds". In these passages, he considers the importance of experiences within the family of origin as another possible factor that affects expectations. If, for instance, parents or other adult family members lack emotional maturity (see AL 239) or the feeling of unconditional love is not experienced at a young age (see AL 240), this can have a profound effect on the development of children

---

10 See Episcopal Conference of Chile: *La vida y la familia: regalos de Dios para cada uno de nosotros* (21 July 2014), 3: "No existen las familias 'perfectas' que nos propone la propaganda falaz y consumista. ... La propaganda consumista muestra una fantasía que nada tiene que ver con la realidad que deben afrontar, en el día a día, los jefes y jefas de hogar que con tanto sacrificio acuden a sus trabajos para 'ganarse la vida'".

and lead to untenable beliefs about love. The exhortation mentions the following specific threats:

> an insatiable love that screams or cries when it fails to get what it wants. Others love with an adolescent love marked by hostility, bitter criticism and the need to blame others; caught up in their own emotions and fantasies, such persons expect others to fill their emptiness and to satisfy their every desire. (AL 239)

According to *Amoris laetitia* childhood experiences can have a significant effect on individual beliefs, including the emergence of excessively high expectations. Constant exposure to such problematic concepts of love at an early age sometimes leads to non-critical internalisation of these beliefs and, if there is no adequate reflection later on, could distort future family life. Hence, Pope Francis argues that "[u]nresolved issues need to be dealt with and a process of liberation must take place" in order to stop these inadequate tendencies which "can re-emerge and hurt a marriage" (AL 240) in adult life.

2.3 *Individualistic Influences*

The exhortation also highlights the problem of "an extreme individualism" that is "leading in some cases to the idea that one's personality is shaped by his or her desires, which are considered absolute" (RS 5, cited in AL 33). In other words, personal expectations are sometimes regarded as the ultimate point of reference and combined with the demand that the partner should adapt to them. Therein lies the danger of total dominance and encroachment. One's own expectations become the only acceptable guidelines for the relationship, although the partner might have very different wishes and desires. Thus, Pope Francis notes the problem of subjective absolutization:

> There are those [people] who feel themselves capable of great love only because they have a great need for affection, yet they prove incapable of the effort needed to bring happiness to others. They remain caught up in their own needs and desires. In such cases, emotions distract from the highest values and conceal a self-centredness that makes it impossible to develop a healthy and happy family life. (AL 145)

A distinct egoism tends to enhance illusions of an invariably perfect relationship that disregard the anthropological condition of limitations[11] and remain blind to

---

[11] S. ORTH: "Heilsame Selbstkritik", in: *Herder Korrespondenz* 70/5 (2016), 4-5, 5. Orth, for example, highlights the "remarkable statements on theological anthropology" [translated by the author] ("[mit] bemerkenswerte[n] Aussagen zur theologischen Anthropologie") in *Amoris laetitia*, where the references to human "limitations" seem to be an especially important element. In total, an explicit usage of the term "limitation[s]" can be found thirteen times in the text (AL 37, 49, 100, 107, 113, 238, 269^2, 277, 283, 305, 323, 325).

human finitude. This leads to the fallacious belief that personal expectations are realistic conditions, which ought to be fulfilled without any exception. More precisely, this belief in the existence of the unlimited human being can become a major factor behind the development of excessively high expectations.

However, this disposition leads to severe problems, including the risk of encroachment. The ignorance of human limitations fosters the desire for egoistic possessiveness (see AL 127) that in all probability leads to excessive demands towards one's partner and a need for the unconditional and immediate realisation of these demands. Furthermore, this neglect of limitations creates great potential for conflict, and ignores the possibility of the growth of the partner and of marital and family life. A fixed anthropological image that expects (instant) perfection arises and results in frustration and resignation as two people get to know each other more closely and discover more of each other's weaknesses.

2.4 Ecclesial Influences

Finally, Pope Francis also argues for a "healthy dose of self-criticism" (AL 36)[12] that "calls for missionary conversion by everyone in the Church" (RS 32, cited in AL 201). Beside the emphasis on procreation and the lack of support for young married couples, in this paragraph (AL 36) he also highlights the problem of the ecclesial image of marriage and family, which has become more and more detached from everyday life.[13] He argues that the Catholic Church has

> proposed a far too abstract and almost artificial theological ideal of marriage, far removed from the concrete situations and practical possibilities of real families. This excessive idealization, especially when we have failed to inspire trust in God's grace, has not helped to make marriage more desirable and attractive, but quite the opposite. (AL 36)

This is one of the most distinctively novel aspects of the Post-Synodal Exhortation and reacts implicitly to critiques that were previously made by a number of theologians. R. Ammicht Quinn, for instance, talks about three ideologies within the Christian proclamation: (1) "ideology of fertility", i.e. reproduction as the primary legitimation of sexuality, (2) "ideology of cells", i.e. marriage and family as the single core of society and (3) "ideology of fusion", i.e. marriage and family as

---

12 For additional insights into the self-critical voice of Pope Francis, see also G.P. DI NICOLA/A. DANESE: "Notes on Amoris laetitia", in: *INTAMS Review* 22/1 (2016), 3-14, 8; S. ORTH: "Heilsame Selbstkritik", 4-5.

13 See also S. ORTH: "Heilsame Selbstkritik", 5; S. Orth: "Nachsynodales Schreiben", 9.

the ideal image.[14] In relation to these three aspects, M. Heimbach-Steins presents the following conclusion:

> The threefold idealisation of marriage and family in the Christian proclamation mirrors a partial denial of social reality. The concern to give clear guidance and unambiguous normative instructions in order to support people in the way they live their lives should certainly not be disdained. But it will necessarily fail if it no longer bridges the tensions between ideal and reality.[15]

Amoris laetitia expresses similar concerns with unwavering clarity and consequently presents the inner-ecclesial approach in terms of a "cold bureaucratic morality" (AL 312), without denying or even disparaging the doctrine of marriage itself. Quite to the contrary, it emphasises, "that in no way must the Church desist from proposing the full ideal of marriage, God's plan in all its grandeur" (AL 307; see also AL 308). In other words, the doctrine still needs to be an important point of orientation, but since the uncritical reception of perfect images draws the attention away from existing marital and family challenges, the church also has to remain open to different life experiences. In this sense, the importance of both an awareness of reality and the ideal of marriage and family is asserted.[16] The final paragraph of *Amoris laetitia* also makes this point, with exceptional vividness:

---

14 R. AMMICHT QUINN: "Vom Leben für andere: Frauenfragen als Beziehungsfragen?: Überlegungen aus der Perspektive theologischer Ethik", in: M. HEIMBACH-STEINS/G. CYPRIAN (eds.): *Familienbilder: Interdisziplinäre Sondierungen*, Opladen: Leske + Budrich, 2003, 59-68, at 66. The three terms have been translated by the author and refer to the German terms (1) "Fruchtbarkeitsideologie", (2) "Zellenideologie" and (3) "Verschmelzungsideologie".

15 M. HEIMBACH-STEINS: "Die Idealisierung von Ehe und Familie in der kirchlichen Moralverkündigung", in: K. HILPERT (ed.), *Zukunftshorizonte katholischer Sexualethik*, Freiburg i. Br.-Basel-Vienna: Herder, 2011 (Quaestiones Disputatae; 241), 300-309, here: 307-308. The quotation was translated by the author of this article and relates to the following passage in the original text: "Die dreifache Idealisierung von Ehe und Familie in der kirchlichen Verkündigung spiegelt eine partielle Verweigerung gegenüber der sozialen Wirklichkeit. Das Anliegen, das dahinter zu vermuten ist, eine klare Orientierung, eindeutige normative Weisungen zu geben, um Menschen in ihrer Lebensgestaltung zu unterstützen, ist keinesfalls gering zu schätzen. Aber es muss scheitern, wenn die Spannung zwischen Ideal und Wirklichkeit nicht mehr überbrückt werden."

16 Interestingly, this assertion also reflects the structure of the exhortation. On the one hand, the Christian ideal of marriage is discussed several times, especially in the third (AL 58-88) and eighth (AL 291-312) chapters. On the other hand, the orientation towards marital and family challenges and their possible influences, described in the second chapter (AL 31-57), tries to take the world of women and men today seriously. Furthermore, many passages include calls for pastoral care based on reality. This is especially prominent in the sixth (and second -longest) chapter (AL 199-258), in which the actual situation of couples is again specifically described on the basis of practical examples, and deeper pastoral perspectives are developed.

> As this Exhortation has often noted, no family drops down from heaven perfectly formed; families need constantly to grow and mature in the ability to love. … Our contemplation of the fulfilment which we have yet to attain also allows us to see in proper perspective the historical journey which we make as families, and in this way to stop demanding of our interpersonal relationships a perfection, a purity of intentions and a consistency which we will only encounter in the Kingdom to come. It also keeps us from judging harshly those who live in situations of frailty. All of us are called to keep striving towards something greater than ourselves and our families, and every family must feel this constant impulse. Let us make this journey as families, let us keep walking together. What we have been promised is greater than we can imagine. May we never lose heart because of our limitations, or ever stop seeking that fullness of love and communion which God holds out before us. (AL 325)

Thus, the confrontation with reality needs a perspective that couples and families can align themselves with in hopeful expectation. In other words, the ideal remains indispensable as the point of orientation, although at the same time, and this is Pope Francis' main critique, it should not become a relentless standard demanding that the perfection implied by the ideal should be necessarily and continuously accomplished without any deviation. More precisely, as Di Nicola and Danese have stressed, it has become necessary for the church to start from "the concrete reality of women and men, without denying the ideal – lofty and never fully attained – of Trinitarian harmony, but accompanying the bumpy road that is taken by those who live in complex and traumatic situations".[17]

3 Helpful Attitudes towards Excessively High Expectations

When "it becomes apparent that the reality is more limited and challenging than one imagined" (AL 221), this realisation can, especially within intimate relationships, be experienced as a great disappointment and disruption against the background of personal expectations. Without wishing to make a crude generalisation, separation and divorce might be regarded as the only possible way to cope with this (see AL 221), which could conceivably lead to a search for a new partner who meets the individual's personal expectations without exception. In this case, it is not the beliefs themselves that are strongly questioned, but rather their realisation by the partner. Such an approach, however, remains thoroughly futile in the long term and seems very likely to lead to similar exasperation and disillusionment within a new relationship or remarriage.

Hence, it can be assumed that excessive expectations may entail drastic consequences which could perhaps be avoided through appropriate support and joint reflections. This idea is also expressed in the fourth chapter of *Amoris laetitia*

---

17 G.P. Di Nicola/A. Danese: "Notes on Amoris laetitia", 12.

(esp. AL 89-119). In reference to the hymn to love (1 Cor 13,4-7), Pope Francis describes "some of the features of true love" (AL 90) and, according to Orth, presents a detailed meditation[18] on this biblical text. Through this incremental approach, Pope Francis relates the Pauline exploration of love to the contemporary understanding of marriage and family. In the course of doing so, he highlights "that Paul wants to stress that love is more than a mere feeling. Rather, it should be understood along the lines of the Hebrew verb 'to love'; it is 'to do good'" (AL 94). Hence, the Exhortation delineates attitudes in service of a harmonious life within marriage and family. According to this particular emphasis, and the awareness of the difficulty of excessive expectations, this passage offers various insights that could help partners to successfully deal with their problems. In particular, the following attitudes, which are noteworthy in relation to the overall context, can be discerned: (1) abandonment of egoism, (2) acceptance of differences, (3) forgiveness and (4) hope.

3.1 Abandonment of Egoism

In addressing patience (1 Cor 13,4) as the first feature of love within the contemporary context of love and marriage (see AL 91-92), Pope Francis names an element that seems to play a crucial role when it comes to successful attitudes towards personal expectations. Within the scope of this particular feature, the Exhortation does not primarily accentuate that which is typically associated with patience (esp. temporal endurance, perseverance, etc.), but instead introduces a notion that could also be described as the abandonment of egoism:

> Being patient does not mean letting ourselves be constantly mistreated, tolerating physical aggression or allowing other people to use us. We encounter problems whenever we think that relationships or people ought to be perfect, or when we put ourselves at the centre and expect things to turn out our way. (AL 92)

The paragraph excludes two extremes: on the one hand, the exhortation disassociates itself from radical submissiveness and makes it unambiguously clear that patience must not be misinterpreted as sacrificial selflessness and acceptance of aggression and injustice.[19] Quite the contrary: for Pope Francis, to love one another implies that "we must first love ourselves", which is "a psychological prerequisite

---

[18] S. Orth: "Nachsynodales Schreiben", 9.

[19] Although this article primarily focuses on the problem of excessively high expectations, it should not be understood as an appeal to absolute modesty. As Pope Francis also points out, there are limits to abandoning one's own expectations: "The ideal of marriage cannot be seen purely as generous donation and self-sacrifice, where each spouse renounces all personal needs and seeks only the other's good without concern for personal satisfaction. We need to remember that authentic love also needs to be able to receive the other…" (AL 157; see also AL 92). The balance between giving and receiving is strongly emphasised and outlined as an essential factor

for being able to love others" (AL 101). On the other hand, the document does not disregard the problem of excessively high expectations that are often tightly intertwined with egoistic traits, as was previously argued in connection with the possible backgrounds to these traits. More precisely, the attempt to impose one's own beliefs, without recognising the expectations of the spouse, is a highly self-centred process that could lead to encroachment and blind dominance over the partner. With regard to the danger of these extremes and in order to avoid tensions, Pope Francis endorses the importance of a well-balanced oscillation between the expectations of oneself and one's partner.

With this balance between the two extremes of submissiveness and dominance serving as the crucial foundation, in the following paragraphs Pope Francis focuses especially on the second aspect, especially in the reflections on the passages about love that is not "boastful" (1 Cor 13,4) (see AL 97-98) and "does not insist on its own way" (1 Cor 13,5) (see AL 101-102). In both passages, the exhortation clarifies that the abandonment of egoism is an indispensable condition for orienting oneself towards the other person. A critical introspection with respect to often blind demands and inflated desires can thus be an important step towards pursuing a successful marital and family life. First and foremost, one's own expectations have to be critically examined and, if required, carefully revised without tilting into a total abandonment of oneself for the "benefit" of the other (see AL 92, 157).

3.2 Acceptance of Differences

In close connection with the abandonment of egoism, Pope Francis notes the pertinence of the acceptance of differences. Thus, patience and, going along with it, cautious reflection and adequate distance from personal beliefs, as well as an orientation towards one's partner, do not take firm form until

> I recognize that other people also have a right to live in this world, just as they are. It does not matter if they hold me back, if they unsettle my plans, or annoy me by the way they act or think, or if they are not everything I want them to be. Love always has an aspect of deep compassion that leads to accepting the other person as part of this world, even when he or she acts differently than I would like. (AL 92)

The invitation to accept the spouse despite his or her differences implies a general openness that, again, goes beyond one's ego and disentangles oneself from a self-centred view. In this regard, "love is not jealous" (1 Cor 13,4) (see AL 95-96) or

in the specific context of the subchapter "Violence and Manipulation" (AL 153-157). For this reason, it is also recommended that partners share and talk about their different beliefs about each other and their prospective life together right from the stage of marital preparations (see AL 209).

envious, but rather appreciates the strengths and celebrates the merits of the partner (see esp. AL 95). This also includes the fact that love "is not arrogant or rude" (1 Cor 13,4) (see AL 99-100) and tries to understand the other's weaknesses and empathise with possible setbacks that he or she may encounter (see esp. AL 100, 105).

However, the acceptance which *Amoris laetitia* is propounding does not aim at an enforced harmony, but rather embraces the anthropological limitations of oneself and one's partner. For this reason, Pope Francis is emphasising the importance of a "kind look" that "helps us to see beyond our own limitations, to be patient and to cooperate with others, despite our differences" (AL 100; see also AL 128).

The two attitudes, abandonment of egoism and acceptance of differences, merge in this particular thought and underscore the relevance of the insight that the "unity that we seek is not uniformity, but a 'unity in diversity', or 'reconciled diversity'" (AL 139). Both are intended to enable us to distance ourselves from personal expectations and to create a holistic image of the other that includes positive as well as negative traits and experiences.

3.3 Forgiveness

Although abandonment of egoism and acceptance of differences seem to have a beneficial effect in terms of expectations, conflicts and violations in relationships with other people can never be completely eliminated. This essential aspect is also addressed when Paul points out that love is not "resentful" (1 Cor 13,5). In contrast, the element of forgiveness (see AL 103-108) has to be cultivated, "which is rooted in a positive attitude that seeks to understand other people's weaknesses and to excuse them" (AL 105).

This dimension highlights the importance of supplementing the attitude of forgiveness with an attitude of general acceptance of differences in the event of disagreement and dispute. More precisely, it is not about simply acknowledging the weaknesses of the spouse, but, in the light of "[l]ove bears all things" (1 Cor 13,7), to understand them as a part of the whole person, who is, like every other human being, always limited and imperfect. Thus, failings should be recognised and in cases of troubles and conflicts excused as "part of a bigger picture. We have to realize that all of us are a complex mixture of light and shadows" (AL 113).

However, it is not only the partner that is a part of this complex mixture, but also oneself. The exhortation makes this clear by arguing

> that being able to forgive others implies the liberating experience of understanding and forgiving ourselves. Often our mistakes, or criticism we have received from loved ones, can lead to a loss of selfesteem. We become distant from others, avoiding af-

> fection and being fearful in our interpersonal relationships. Blaming others becomes falsely reassuring. We need to learn to pray over our past history, to accept ourselves, to learn how to live with our limitations, and even to forgive ourselves, in order to have this same attitude towards others. (AL 107)

In other words, it could be argued that the two aforementioned attitudes culminate in this dimension of forgiveness. In leaving a blind egoism behind and accepting differences between oneself and the other person lie two important conditions for forgiveness. Firstly, forgiving oneself and accepting one's personal limitations, which, secondly, is the indispensable foundation for fully forgiving one's partner's limitations.

3.4 Hope

Finally, the perspective of hope supplements the first three attitudes. In contrast to a static and fixed image of the human being, in *Amoris laetitia* (see AL 116-117) this dimension strongly emphasises the idea of alteration. For Pope Francis the phrase "love... hopes all things" (1 Cor 13,7) "speaks of the hope of one who knows that others can change, mature and radiate unexpected beauty and untold potential. This does not mean that everything will change in this life." (AL 116). Consequently, changes can happen or not and can be either negatively or positively experienced, depending on the respective situation. Therein lies, without a doubt, the possibility that people, and also relationships, develop in a certain direction which can also lead to, at least initially, misery, grief or hopelessness (see AL 116). By taking this fact into consideration, the simple idea of a change can provoke a grave and thoroughly frightening uncertainty.

However, paradoxically, in these situations it can be helpful to trust in this particular idea, which also includes the hope of overcoming difficulties. Due to its valuable dynamics, this means, in the context of marriage and family, that the relationship with the partner is not fixed, but has the potential to be changed or improved. The attitude of hope in the exhortation hence includes a clear plea against resignation and despair, although this certainly requires commitment and sometimes even hard work. For this reason, Pope Francis underscores this aspect again in the sixth chapter in relation to pastoral perspectives, particularly regarding premarital preparations (AL 205-211):

> In any event, if one partner clearly recognizes the other's weak points, he or she needs to have a realistic trust in the possibility of helping to develop the good points that counterbalance them, and in this way to foster their human growth. This entails a willingness to face eventual sacrifices, problems and situations of conflict; it demands a firm resolve to be ready for this. (AL 210)

In relation to successfully dealing with excessive expectations, this attitude of hope urges people to believe in and consciously work towards their shared future, even in hard times. Looking forward with a positive attitude, while still being aware of and accepting the limitations of oneself and one's partner, generally results in a greater ability to solve problems and a greater capacity for growth, rather than stagnancy and resignation.

4 Conclusion: Do We Expect too Much?

In the light of *Amoris laetitia* the question "Do we expect too much?" can definitely be answered in the affirmative, especially when we talk about excessively high expectations that are proving to be a heavy burden for marriage and family, since they are too far removed from reality and do not fully take into account everyday challenges and human limitations. Consequently, these expectations usually remain unfulfilled and put heavy strains on intimate relationships that may lead to separation and divorce. No other document by the Catholic Church has ever touched on the topic of expectations in such an explicit way; in fact, even theological discussions of it are rare. However, the Exhortation explores this issue seriously and invites couples "to discuss what each expects from marriage, what they understand by love and commitment, what each wants from the other and what kind of life they would like to build together" (AL 209) while they are still at the stage of preparing for their marriage.

At the same time, Pope Francis not only points out the risks of excessively high expectations, but also inquires deeper into the possible backgrounds to this specific problem and attitudes that are helpful in relation to it. In other words, he does not aim to formulate rigid doctrinal conclusions,[20] but aims at a sapiential approach which Cardinal Kasper illustrates with the following picture: *Amoris laetitia* develops "a pastoral conception that is not characterised by a raised forefinger but an outstretched helping hand".[21] This sapiential approach by Pope Francis seems to consist in three steps: (1) acknowledging reality as it is (i.e. acknowledging the problem of excessively high expectations), (2) reflecting on it in the light of what is central to Christian tradition (i.e. reflecting in particular on the ecclesial image of marriage and family and the possible background to this image in relation to excessively high expectations) and (3) offering guidance whose

[20] See also W. KASPER: "'Amoris laetitia': Bruch oder Aufbruch?: Eine Nachlese", in: *Stimmen der Zeit* 234/11 (2016), 723-732, here: 724–725. In this article, Kasper emphasises the "new realistic, biblical and pastoral tone" [translated by the author] ("neuer realistischer, biblischer und pastoraler Ton") of the Exhortation, which does not intend to criticise, moralise or indoctrinate.

[21] Ibid. 724. The quotation was translated by the author of this article and relates to the following passage in the original text: "[Aus dieser Grundlegung folgt] eine pastorale Konzeption, für die nicht der erhobene Zeigefinger, sondern die ausgestreckte helfende Hand charakteristisch ist."

unfinished character implicitly invites further reflection (i.e. highlighting helpful attitudes with respect to excessively high expectations).

The originality of this approach is especially evident when contrasted with the tendency to closed-off theological discussions that is common in other magisterial documents. *Amoris laetitia* chooses a different path by remaining open to continuous reflection on teaching and "the immense variety of concrete situations", which makes it "understandable that neither the Synod nor this Exhortation could be expected to provide a new set of general rules, canonical in nature and applicable to all cases" (AL 300). In other words, Pope Francis has prompted the church to enter the discussion on this issue with its own distinctive voice, but the dynamics of this call are different; instead of pushing the church into the position to "defend the truth", it ought to initiate a learning–teaching process. In turn, this learning–teaching process includes the positive perspective of growth and development, which not only has great value for church doctrine itself, but furthermore has to be lived up to within our personal relationships, for example in marriage and family: "[N]either spouse can expect the other to be perfect. Each must set aside all illusions and accept the other as he or she actually is: an unfinished product, needing to grow, a work in progress." (AL 218)

Part II

AMORIS LAETITIA – PERSPECTIVES ON AND FOR DIVORCED AND REMARRIED PERSONS

Divorce and Remarriage: A Reading of *Amoris Laetitia* from a Theological-Ethical Perspective[1]

Martin M. Lintner

1 Divorce and Remarriage: From *Gaudium et Spes* to *Familiaris Consortio*

The Second Vatican Council in part two of its Pastoral Constitution on the Church in the Modern World *Gaudium et spes* (GS) deals with some problems of special urgency. The first chapter is dedicated to the issue of marriage and family. In no. 47 the Pastoral Constitution indicates some elements and developments which obscure the dignity of the institution of marriage and family:

> Yet the excellence of this institution is not everywhere reflected with equal brilliance, since polygamy, the plague of divorce, so-called free love and other disfigurements have an obscuring effect. In addition, married love is too often profaned by excessive self-love, the worship of pleasure and illicit practices against human generation. Moreover, serious disturbances are caused in families by modern economic conditions, by influences at once social and psychological, and by the demands of civil society. Finally, in certain parts of the world problems resulting from population growth are generating concern.

It is interesting that divorce is named as a plague but the document doesn't speak about remarriage after divorce. Obviously, at that period of time it was not yet "an evil... affecting more and more Catholics as well",[2] as later described by John Paul II. The Sacred Congregation for Doctrine of Faith addressed this issue in 1973, publishing a short letter "regarding the indissolubility of marriage" (April 11).[3] The letter laments a "dissemination of new opinions which seek to deny

1 The author wishes to thank specially Sr. Joyce-Mary Fryer OSM for the correction of the English text.

2 JOHN PAUL II: *Familiaris Consortio,* 1981, 84, available from: http://w2.vatican.va/content/john-paul-ii/en/apost_exhortations/documents/hf_jp-ii_exh_19811122_familiaris-consortio.html; accessed 13.12.2016.

3 Available from http://www.vatican.va/roman_curia/congregations/cfaith/documents/rc_con_cfaith_doc_19730411_indissolubilitate-matrimonii_en.html; accessed 13.12.2016.

or to put in doubt the doctrine regarding the indissolubility of marriage". Even though the document is not referring explicitly to divorced and remarried couples but speaks of "those who live in an irregular union" as well as of the increasing situations of the faithful having only a civil marriage or living together without any marriage, it notes the growing number of people who got remarried after divorce. The Congregation responded on two levels. Firstly, it admonished "all those entrusted with teaching religion in schools or institutes of any grade, as well as those who serve as officials in ecclesiastical tribunals, [to] remain faithful to the doctrine of the Church on the indissolubility of marriage and act in accord with this doctrine in their ecclesiastical tribunals."

Secondly, regarding the administration of the Sacraments, it addressed the local Ordinaries and insisted on two aspects, "on one hand, to encourage the observance of the discipline in force in the Church, and on the other hand, to act so that pastors of souls show particular solicitude toward those who live in an irregular union, seeking to resolve these cases through the use of the approved practices of the Church in the internal forum, as well as other just means." Anyhow, the letter didn't clarify or explain what was meant by "the approved practices of the Church in the internal forum".

Several Bishops' Conferences dealt with this issue and proposed the following practice of confession: to admit divorced and remarried couples to the sacraments of Reconciliation and the Eucharist the situation being if they repented and intended to end their sexual intercourse. In this case they could be admitted to those sacraments but only in a church where they were not known so as to avoid creating scandal amongst the faithful.[4]

Pope John Paul II in his Post-Synodal Apostolic Exhortation *Familiaris consortio* (FC), no. 84, adopted this idea,[5] discounting one of the proposals made by the V. Ordinary General Assembly of the Bishop's Synod on the Christian Family (1980):

---

4 See B. PETRÀ: "Amoris laetitia: Un passo avanti nella Tradizione", in: *Il Regno* 61 (2016), 243-251, here 243.

5 In regard to the conditions for the admission of divorced and remarried to the sacraments of Reconciliation and Eucharist (separation or – in the cases that they can't separate for serious reasons – complete sexual continence, cf. FC 84, also BENEDICT XVI: *Sacramentum Caritatis*, 2007, 29 [available from http://w2.vatican.va/content/benedict-xvi/en/apost_exhortations/documents/hf_ben-xvi_exh_20070222_sacramentum-caritatis.html; accessed 13.12.2016], where sexual continence is not obliged as it is in FC 84, but simply encouraged), notice the following: The obligation to sexual continence anyhow has not a long tradition, since John Paul II in FC 84 is referring only to his own homily of October 25, 1980. Only in 1998 card. Joseph Ratzinger demanded this expressly with reference to the "approved practice of the Church" of which the CDF was speaking in 1973 (cf. J. RATZINGER: "Introduzione", in: CONGREGAZIONE PER LA DOTTRINA DELLA FEDE [ed.]: *Sulla pastorale dei divorziati risposati*, Vatican City, 1998 [Documenti, commenti e studi; 17], 17-18).

> The Synod declared its wish that a new and deeper study be initiated into the pastoral care of these [divorced and remarried] faithful, "taking account of the practices of the Eastern Churches", so that pastoral kindness can be brought more clearly to the fore.[6]

Nevertheless, John Paul II in FC 84 introduced some significant differentiations:

> Pastors must know that, for the sake of truth, they are obliged to exercise careful discernment of situations. There is in fact a difference between those who have sincerely tried to save their first marriage and have been unjustly abandoned, and those who through their own grave fault have destroyed a canonically valid marriage. Finally, there are those who have entered into a second union for the sake of the children's upbringing, and who are sometimes subjectively certain in conscience that their previous and irreparably destroyed marriage had never been valid.

Further, he recognizes that "various reasons can, unfortunately, lead to the often irreparable breakdown of valid marriages" (FC 83) and that there may also be situations where, "for serious reasons, such as for example the children's upbringing, a man and a woman cannot satisfy the obligation to separate" (FC 84). He strongly emphasizes that involved people are not excluded from the community of the Church and that they are allowed to receive the sacraments of Reconciliation and Eucharist if they repent and "take on themselves the duty to live in complete continence, that is, by abstinence from the acts proper to married couples" (ibid.). Otherwise, all concerned people would be "unable to be admitted thereto from the fact that their state and condition of life objectively contradict that union of love between Christ and the Church which is signified and affected by the Eucharist" (ibid.). Quite correctly it may be observed that there is a logical inconsistence in the argumentation owing to the pastoral duty, "for the sake of truth" to discern carefully the different situations. However, this requested differentiation of the situations is rarely taken into account when it comes to disciplinary procedures.

2 From *Familiaris Consortio* to *Amoris Laetitia*

It is well known that despite the strong criticism made by many theologians and the serious concerns of many bishops, the Roman Magisterium frequently and strictly insisted on maintaining its position. In *Veritatis splendor* (VS), John Paul II rejected the "so-called 'pastoral' solutions contrary to the teaching of the Magisterium" (VS 56). Such solutions would mean to "justify a 'creative' hermeneutic according to which the moral conscience is in no way obliged which in every case would be initiated by a particular negative precept" (ibid.). John Paul II criticized

[6] Quoted in K. SCHEMBRI: "The Orthodox Tradition on Divorced and Remarried Faithful: What can the Catholic Church Learn?", in: *Melita Theologica* 65 (2015), 121-141, 123.

this ethical position according to which "beyond the doctrinal and abstract level, one would have to acknowledge the priority of a certain more concrete existential consideration. The latter, by taking account of circumstances and the situation, could legitimately be the basis of certain exceptions to the general rule and thus permit one to do in practice and in good conscience what is qualified as intrinsically evil by the moral law."

The Pope defended the position that "there is profoundly imprinted upon it [the conscience] a principle of obedience vis-à-vis the objective norm which establishes and conditions the correspondence of its decisions with the commands and prohibitions which are at the basis of human behaviour" (VS 60).[7]

At the basis of this argumentation any remarriage after divorce has to be judged exclusively according to the normative prohibition of adultery, i.e. of any sexual relationship outside of a continuing valid marriage. It would represent an obstinate persistence in manifestly grave sin which prohibits the reception of the sacraments of Reconciliation and Holy Communion (cf. CIC 1983, can. 915), independently of the individual disposition of the concerned persons and of the very singular conditions of circumstances and situations. The *Catechism of the Catholic Church* (CCC), in this sense, affirms that "the remarried spouse is then in a situation of public and permanent adultery" (CCC 2384), and the Pontifical Council for Legislative Texts in its declaration *Concerning the Admission to Holy Communion of the Faithful Who Are Divorced and Remarried* (2000) explains that the fact of the "objective contradiction" of their situation to the union of the love between Christ and the Church which is represented as a sacrament and signified by a valid marriage would be sufficient to identify this situation as sinful, regardless of the subjective responsibility. It is important to note that one of the main arguments of the Magisterium's position was based on the commitment of the Church to remain faithful to the truth of the Gospel and the doctrine of the indissolubility of marriage. Despite the fact that John Paul II in FC 84 spoke of the obligation of pastors, "for the sake of truth", to exercise careful discernment of situations, the emphasis was put on the commitment of the Church to the truth of the doctrine on marriage.

3 The Reception of *Familiaris Consortio* 84 in *Amoris Laetitia* 8

Pope Francis shares the profound attitude of his predecessor, John Paul II, for a special pastoral care for remarried couples, expressed by the latter in FC 84 as follows:

---

7 This passage is a quotation from JOHN PAUL II: *Encyclical Letter* Dominum et Vivificantem, 1986, 43, available from http://w2.vatican.va/content/john-paul-ii/en/encyclicals/documents/hf_jp-ii_enc_18051986_dominum-et-vivificantem.html; accessed 13.12.2016.

The Church, which was set up to lead to salvation all people and especially the baptized, cannot abandon to their own devices those who have been previously bound by sacramental marriage and who have attempted a second marriage. The Church will therefore make untiring efforts to put at their disposal her means of salvation.[8]

In the light of this pastoral attitude *Familiaris consortio* already opened a way to those who were not able to satisfy the obligation to separate from the second non valid union, i.e. to persist in the second marriage, but to abstain from sexual intimacy. This solution was obviously not in complete concordance with the pure doctrine of the indissolubility of marriage from which there would derive the obligation of separation. Further, *Familiaris consortio* urged that concerned people be integrated as much as possible into the life of the Church and "to make sure that they do not consider themselves as separated from the Church, for as baptized persons they can, and indeed must, share in her life" (FC 84). Therefore, it is not surprising at all that Pope Francis in *Amoris laetitia* (AL 298) widely cites the respective passage of FC 84.

But *Amoris laetitia* goes beyond *Familiaris consortio*,[9] for example citing more reasons than the upbringing of children, so that a concerned couple can't be obliged to separate viz. a second union may be "consolidated over time, with new children, proven fidelity, generous self giving, Christian commitment, a consciousness of its irregularity and of the great difficulty of going back without feeling in conscience that one would fall into new sins" (AL 298).

While FC 84 expresses the Church's confidence "that those who have rejected the Lord's command and are still living in this state will be able to obtain from God the grace of conversion and salvation, provided that they have persevered in prayer, penance and charity", *Amoris laetitia* is convinced that "the grace of God works also in their lives [i.e. of those who participate in the Church's life in an incomplete manner] by giving them the courage to do good, to care for one another in love and to be of service to the community in which they live and work" (AL 291).

The document, however, recognizes that "the Holy Spirit pours into their hearts [of divorced and remarried] gifts and talents for the good of all" (AL 299) and, therefore, basically shows an attitude of appreciation for affected persons[10] and for how they try to respond as best they can to their moral commitments (cf.

---

8 See B. PETRÀ: "Amoris laetitia", 247.

9 For a detailed comparison of FC and AL see E.-M. FABER/M. M. LINTNER: "Theologische Entwicklungen in *Amoris laetitia* hinsichtlich der Frage der geschiedenen Wiederverheirateten", in: S. GOERTZ/C. WITTING (eds.): *Amoris laetitia – Wendepunkt für die Moraltheologie?*, Freiburg i. Br.: Herder, 2016 (Katholizismus im Umbruch; 4), 279–320.

10 See E.-M. FABER/M. M. LINTNER: "Theologische Entwicklungen in *Amoris laetitia*", 290.

AL 37). Pope Francis emphasizes that even in "an objective situation of sin – which may not be subjectively culpable, or fully such – a person can be living in God's grace, can love and can also grow in the life of grace and charity, while receiving the Church's help to this end" (AL 305).

Precisely at this point he adds a note affirming that "in certain cases, this can include the help of the sacraments" (AL 305, note 351). It is quite evident that *Amoris laetitia* aims to go beyond *Familiaris consortio* in regard to the disciplinary consequences for divorced and remarried people. Even in regard to the demand of sexual abstinence, *Amoris laetitia* recognizes that "in such situations, many people, knowing and accepting the possibility of living 'as brothers and sisters' which the Church offers them, point out that if certain expressions of intimacy are lacking, 'it often happens that faithfulness is endangered and the good of the children suffers' (GS 51)" (AL 298, note 328).

While *Familiaris consortio* urges the Church to discern the different situations but does not recognize that there are different consequences for different situations,[11] *Amoris laetitia* affirms the pastoral need as well as the moral requirement to recognize that the "consequences or effects of a rule need not necessarily always be the same" (AL 300), and maintains that "this is also the case with regard to sacramental discipline, since discernment can recognize that in a particular situation no grave fault exists" (ibid., note 336). If it is not surprising that *Amoris laetitia* quotes widely FC 84 where the document speaks about the Church's pastoral commitment for divorced and remarried couples and admonishes it to differentiate carefully the different situations, likewise it is not surprising that *Amoris laetitia* stops quoting FC 84 at that point where John Paul II reaffirms the Church's practice of not admitting divorced persons who have remarried independently of their situation to reception of the Eucharist. As one might say, *Amoris laetitia* stops to cite *Familiaris consortio* where its argumentation becomes inconsistent.

4 *Amoris Laetitia*: Going beyond *Familiaris Consortio* and, at the Same Time, Remaining Faithful to the Long Tradition of Moral Theology

There are serious theological-ethical reasons and arguments for not excluding divorced and remarried persons categorically from the sacraments of Reconciliation and Eucharist. These reasons, which were partly expressed already in the aforementioned passages of *Amoris laetitia*, should be emphasized more clearly in the following section. In order to do so, three main arguments will be briefly reexamined. These advocate in favour of the position which refutes any possibility

[11] See E. SCHOCKENHOFF: *Chancen zur Versöhnung? Die Kirche und die wiederverheirateten Geschiedenen*, Freiburg i. Br.: Herder, 2011, 19-20.

of allowing divorced and remarried couples to the sacraments of Reconciliation and Eucharist unless they practise sexual abstinence:[12]

1. A second marriage after divorce would present a persisting situation of a grave objective sin, namely of public and permanent adultery (cf. FC 84; CCC 2384).
2. The Church is committed to the doctrine of indissolubility of marriage and, therefore, its practice, seen as based upon Sacred Scripture, is an expression of "fidelity to Christ and to His truth" (FC 84).
3. The Church is committed not to lead into error and confusion the faithful and, therefore, in order to avoid any uncertainty regarding the Church's teaching about the indissolubility of marriage (cf. FC 84) and any scandal, "understood as an action that prompts others towards wrongdoing"[13], she cannot admit concerned people to the Eucharist.

4.1 The Significance of Conscience in AL

(a) The Distinction between the Objective and Subjective Level of an Ethical Judgment

With regard to the first argument, there is the very illuminating passage quoted already from AL 305:

> Because of forms of conditioning and mitigating factors, it is possible that in an objective situation of sin – which may not be subjectively culpable, or fully such – a person can be living in God's grace, can love and can also grow in the life of grace and charity, while receiving the Church's help to this end.

Pope Francis is affirming a basic ethical argument, namely the distinction between the objective and subjective level of an ethical judgment. The CCC clearly recognizes this distinction in two passages, quoted in AL 302: The first passage says that "imputation and responsibility for an action can be diminished or even nullified by ignorance, inadvertence, duress, fear, habit, inordinate attachments, and other psychological or social factors" (CCC 1735); the second one mentions "affective immaturity, force of acquired habit, conditions of anxiety or other psychological or social factors that lessen or even extenuate moral culpability" (CCC

---

[12] For a detailed and critical explanation of these different arguments pro and contra from the perspective of moral theology see: M.M. LINTNER: "Geschieden und wiederverheiratet: Zur Problematik aus theologisch-ethischer Perspektive", in: M. GRAULICH/M. SEIDNADER (eds.): *Zwischen Jesu Wort und Norm: Kirchliches Handeln angesichts von Scheidung und Wiederheirat*, Freiburg i. Br.: Herder, 2014 (= Quaestiones disputatae; 264), 193-215.

[13] PONTIFICAL COUNCIL FOR LEGISLATIVE TEXTS: *Declaration Concerning the Admission to Holy Communion of Faithful Who Are Divorced and Remarried*, 2000, 1, available from http://www.vatican.va/roman_curia/pontifical_councils/intrptxt/documents/rc_pc_intrptxt_doc_20000706_declaration_en.html; accessed 13.12.2016.

3252) as factors which may mitigate moral responsibility. Karl Rahner noticed in an article on the crisis of the Sacrament of confession, that the Church in theory has always recognized the differentiation of an objective situation of sin and of subjective grave sin, but in her practice for centuries she has neglected the difference.[14] The sincere intentions and an accurate evaluation of motives of the acting subject form part of the ethical quality of a moral act. Furthermore, the new modern awareness of various possible psychological or social conditions and limitations of the subject shows clearly the need to take anew into account this basic differentiation. The Church already "possesses a solid body of reflection concerning mitigating factors and situations" (AL 301). If the term "sin" is normally used to refer to the personal culpability of a moral subject, it indicates that this person freely, deliberately, and intentionally is doing something ethically wrong or omitting something ethically right. Therefore, *Amoris laetitia* correctly concludes that "a negative judgment about an objective situation does not imply a judgment about the imputation or culpability of the person" (AL 302). Of course, at this point one could ask critically if, in order to avoid any ambiguity, the term "sin" should be used (see Pope Francis in AL 305) to express a negative judgment about a situation that is in objective contradiction to what is morally right. What matters at this point, anyhow, is to recognize that it "can no longer simply be said that all those in any 'irregular' situation are living in a state of mortal sin and are deprived of sanctifying grace" (AL 301).

(b) The Nature of a Human Person and its Actions as Basis for Moral Standards

A further aspect regards the objective standards of the moral quality of human acts. GS 51, referring to the question of responsible transmission of life and affirming that "the moral aspects of any procedure does not depend solely on sincere intentions or on an evaluation of motives, but must be determined by objective standards" that are "based on the nature of the human person and his acts". It is interesting, but also revealing, that Paul VI in *Humanae vitae* (HV), no. 10, linguistically changes this notion slightly but with serious consequences, when he speaks with regard to the objective moral order of the "very nature of marriage and its use" (*ipsa matrimonii eiusque actuum natura*), not rather of the "nature of the human person and his acts" (*personae eiusdem actuum natura*).[15] The objective standards cannot be deduced simply by the nature of the institution of marriage and of marital acts because every act has to be understood as the act of a person,

---

14 Cf. K. RAHNER: "Warum man trotzdem beichten soll: Zur Situation des Bußsakraments", in: *Entschluss* 35 (1980/9-10), 4-12, here 5.

15 See: M. M. LINTNER: "Die Morallehre des Zweiten Vatikanischen Konzils: Kontinuität und Diskontinuität am Beispiel der Lehre über Ehe und Familie", in: J. ERNESTI/L. HELL/G. KRUCK (eds.): *Selbstbesinnung und Öffnung für die Moderne: 50 Jahre II. Vatikanisches Konzil*, Paderborn: Schöningh. 2013, 95-122.

i.e. of a moral subject who acts with certain motives and intentions as well as with its limitations and conditional dispositions. What really matters is not some kind of immanent morality of an institution like marriage or of marital acts but the person who acts and who is the subject of an institution. For centuries the traditional moral theology understood marriage as a contract whose object is the "matrimonial consent [that] is an act of the will by which each party gives and accepts perpetual and exclusive rights to the body, for those actions that are of themselves suitable for the generation of children"[16]. This so-called *ius in corpus* for too long a time has impeded the accusation of sexual violence or indecent assault within the marriage. Quite rightly Pope Francis in *Amoris laetitia* – quoting Paul VI – clearly denounces that there are situations of sexual violence and manipulation within marriage itself.

> Hence it must be clearly reaffirmed that "a conjugal act imposed on one's spouse without regard to his or her condition, or personal and reasonable wishes in the matter, is no true act of love, and therefore offends the moral order in its particular application to the intimate relationship of husband and wife" (HV 13) (AL 154).

It is evident that the doctrine of marriage of *Gaudium et spes* marks a significant turning point in understanding marriage not as contract, but as a covenant of personal love. Therefore, the morality of an act has to be judged by standards of personal love like trust, mutual respect, honour, fidelity and generous self giving, etc. It is only rational to recognize – as Pope Francis does for example in AL 298 that such personal values of love and partnership can be lived and witnessed also in expressions of a relationship which does not correspond (yet or completely) to the institutional or sacramental marriage. The criterion of regularity or irregularity is not a sufficient or adequate one for an ethical discernment of the different and often very complex situations of partnership and family realities. It is remarkable that Pope Francis in AL uses the term "irregular" emphasised by the use of punctuation marks and accompanied by the adverb "so-called". Cardinal Schönborn also in his presentation of *Amoris laetitia* explored this matter:

> In the ecclesial discourse on marriage and the family there is often a tendency, perhaps unconscious, to discuss these realities of life on the basis of two separate tracks. On the one hand there are marriages and families that are 'regular', that correspond to the rules, where everything is 'fine' and 'in order', and then there are the 'irregular' situations that represent a problem. Already the very term 'irregular' suggests that

[16] CIC 1917, can. 1081 § 2: "Consensus matrimonialis est actus voluntatis quo utraque pars tradit et acceptat ius in corpus, perpetuum et exclusivum, in ordine ad actus per se aptos ad prolis generationem." English translation: *The 1917 or Pio-Benedictine Code of Canon Law: In English Translation with extensive scholarly apparatus*, ed. E.N. PETERS, San Francisco: Ignatius Press, 2001.

> such a distinction can be made very clearly. Those, therefore, who find themselves on the side of the 'irregular' families, must live with the fact that the 'regular' families are on the other side. I am personally aware of how difficult that is for those who come from a 'patchwork' family, due to the situation of my own family. The discourse of the Church in this regard may cause harm and can give rise to a sensation of exclusion.[17]

Finally, there remains a strong suspicion that the demands of sexual abstinence in a second marriage after divorce (cf. FC 84 et al.) present a remnant of the aforementioned narrow understanding of the bond of marriage as a contract that implies the exclusivity of sexual acts.

(c) The Notion of Conscience in Amoris Laetitia

In the past, by considering the actual conditions of the acting subject and taking into account the circumstances of the situation this was often suspected by the Roman Magisterium of subjectivism and situational ethics (cf. e.g. VS 34, 36, 47, 52). Quite rightly the Magisterium stressed that the moral judgment of an acting person can never ignore objective moral standards, but, at the same time, by emphasizing the objective ethical dimension and by identifying this dimension primarily with the nature of actions and with moral norms the individual moral judgment was rather reduced to an act of obedience to moral norms. The function of conscience from this perspective was understood to be a transformation of the actual concrete situation to the objective moral order.[18] If an authentic interpretation of the objective moral order were subjected to the exclusive competence of the Magisterium the result would be that the "subjective conscience must always submit to, and obey, the objective 'truth' of magisterial teaching"[19].

Without denying the essential role of the objective moral dimension, Pope Francis makes clear that "it is reductive simply to consider whether or not an individual's actions correspond to a general law or rule, because that is not enough to discern and ensure full fidelity to God in the concrete life of a human being" (AL 304).

This passage shows that the relationship of moral rules and general principles with concrete life situations and circumstances has to be integrated within the broader question of how a moral subject can be faithful to God's will which

---

[17] C. CARD. SCHÖNBORN: *Presentation of the Post-Synodal Apostolic Exhortation Amoris Laetitia: The Logic of Pastoral Mercy*, 08.04.2016, available from https://press.vatican.va/content/salastampa/en/bollettino/pubblico/2016/04/08/160408a.html; accessed 13.12.2016.

[18] Cf. A. AUTIERO: "*Amoris Laetitia* und das sittliche Gewissen: Eine Frage der Perspektive", in: S. GOERTZ/C. WITTING (eds.): *Amoris laetitia*, 95-113.

[19] M.G. LAWLER/T.A. SALZMAN: In Amoris Laetitia, Francis' Model of Conscience Empowers Catholics, in: *National Catholic Reporter* (07.09.2016), available from https://www.ncronline.org/news/theology/amoris-laetitia-francis-model-conscience-empowers-catholics; accessed 13.12.2016.

is not just expressed in moral norms. The acting person has to understand what "God Himself is asking amid the concrete complexity of one's limits" (AL 303) and question how he or she can offer a more proper response to God. From this perspective conscience is a place where one becomes aware of his or her situation before God (cf. AL 300) who can be found not in external moral rules but rather in the heart of human beings.[20]

This concept of conscience follows GS 16, quoted in AL 222, where conscience is seen as "the most secret core and sanctuary of a person. There each one is alone with God, whose voice echoes in the depths of the heart". In *Amoris laetitia* we find basically an existential-ethical notion of conscience. It is seen first of all as place of encounter and dialogue with God and, as such, moral subjects in fidelity to their conscience are capable of responding as best as they can to God's will amid their limitations and of carrying out their own discernment in complex situations (cf. AL 37). Conscience is seen as an ability to recognize the deep values of the Gospel and its ethical implications for one's own life. In other words: One learns to look at one's life "with the eyes of the faith" or "with the eyes of Jesus". It is evident that behind this notion of conscience are the Ignatian principles of spiritual discernment and of indifference. An inner dialogue with God besides a critical confrontation with other persons helps not only to find appropriate moral solutions but also to become aware of one's situation before God, to listen to God's voice and His commandments. The aim is to learn what the Gospel demands from a person and to enable him or her to respond as best as is possible to the Gospel amid existential conditions.

(d) The Relationship between Conscience and Moral Norms

AL 296-300 stresses the demand for an accurate differentiation of the various situations. As a logical consequence this requires taking into consideration the mitigating factors in the pastoral discernment and the consequences as well as the sanctions of moral acts (cf. AL 301-312). In those cases and situations which do not objectively embody the Church's moral teaching or correspond to a general moral rule we have to differentiate whether it is a situation of personal sin or not. This is a matter which involves more than mere knowledge or ignorance of the rule (cf. AL 301). Firstly, the process of discernment has to consider personal motives and intentions as well as mitigating factors and situations, and, secondly, it has to recognize that "a subject may know fully well the rule, yet has great difficulty in understanding 'its inherent values', or be in a concrete situation which does not allow him or her to act differently and decide otherwise without further sin" (AL 301).

[20] Cf. A. AUTIERO: "*Amoris Laetitia* und das sittliche Gewissen: Eine Frage der Perspektive", 103.

Beside the fact that certainly a moral subject can sin and be morally guilty, there are other possibilities: the moral responsibility can be diminished or even nullified by various factors, e.g. by ignorance of a moral norm or by an existential inability to recognize the authentic value of a norm or to be convinced of it. In these cases, the person has an erroneous conscience as has been already noted (cf. AL 301). Furthermore, AL 301 mentions the case that one could "be in a concrete situation which does not allow him or her to act differently and decide otherwise without further sin". Even though AL doesn't mention explicitly the principle of *Epikeia*[21], in the case exemplified one has to exercise exactly this virtue.[22] A person in a concrete situation has to do justice to the authentic intention and spirit of a moral norm, more than to its letter. Conscience is the ability to recognize the authentic meaning of a norm as well as the very specific requirements of a complex situation and to know the needs of the involved person. Therefore, one can find solutions which are appropriate to this very singular complex situation. Quoting Thomas Aquinas, AL 304 affirms that the more we go into concrete situations the more general principles may be found to be insufficient, inadequate or even found to fail: "Although there is necessity in the general principles, the more we descend to matters of detail, the more frequently we encounter defects."

In this instance conscience has not merely a role to apply a general rule to a particular situation, but to mediate between a general rule and a concrete situation, and to judge how a moral good that is the object of a moral rule or principle can be realized as best as possible for a moral subject who is in a concrete situation. Therefore conscience includes both the objective and subjective dimensions. It "discerns and interprets its understanding of objective truth and exercises that understanding in the subjective judgment of conscience".[23] As AL 300 affirms, there is an "immense variety of concrete situations", so that it is not possible to provide any "set of general rules, canonical in nature and applicable to all cases". This does not entail either the denial of the binding force of general norms or moral subjectivism, but it means the ability to recognize the impossibility of subsuming all single situations under a general rule (cf. AL 2), and acknowledge the competence of the individual conscience in the process of understanding, judging and deciding how to respond as far as is possible to what God demands (cf. AL 37). "The only moral solution to any and every situation is a path of careful discernment accompanied by a priest and a final judgment of personal conscience that commands us to do this or not to do that (AL 300-305). Only such an in-

---

21 See G. VIRT: "Moral Norms and the Forgotten Virtue of Epikeia in the Pastoral Care of the Divorced and Remarried", in: *Melita theologica* 63 (2013), 17-34.

22 Cf. A. SPADARO: ""Amoris Laetitia": Struttura e significato dell'Esortazione apostolica postsinodale di Papa Francesco", in: *Civiltà Cattolica* 167 (2016), 122.

23 M.G. LAWLER/T.A. SALZMAN: "In Amoris Laetitia".

formed conscience can make a moral judgment about the details of any and every particular situation."[24]

Of course in this concept we find a scepticism towards the attitude of deriving undue conclusions from particular theological considerations (cf. AL 2). Therefore, it is not just a matter of exception to moral rules, but of realizing with wisdom and understanding in a correct way the deeper understanding of morality.[25]

(e) The Significance of the Formation of Conscience and of the Internal Forum

There is no surprise that after this conversion "to conscience as object-orientation, informed by objective norms, where the hermeneutical lens of the conscience as subject-orientation facilitates the process of understanding, judgment and decision of conscience",[26] Pope Francis stresses the need to accurately form the conscience: "Naturally, every effort should be made to encourage the development of an enlightened conscience, formed and guided by the responsible and serious discernment of one's pastor, and to encourage an ever greater trust in God's grace" (AL 303).

AL 300 gets to the heart of this:

> What we are speaking of is a process of accompaniment and discernment which "guides the faithful to an awareness of their situation before God. Conversation with the priest, in the internal forum, contributes to the formation of a correct judgment on what hinders the possibility of a fuller participation in the life of the Church and on what steps can foster it and make it grow. Given that gradualness is not in the law itself (cf. FC 34), this discernment can never prescind from the Gospel demands of truth and charity, as proposed by the Church. For this discernment to happen, the following conditions must necessarily be present: humility, discretion and love for the Church and her teaching, in a sincere search for God's will and a desire to make a more perfect response to it" (*Relatio Finalis* 2015, 86).

With regard to persons who are living in so-called "irregular" situations, the Congregation for the Doctrine of the Faith in 1973 (as mentioned above) needed "to show particular solicitude toward those who live in an irregular union, seeking to resolve these cases through the use of the approved practices of the Church in the internal forum, as well as other just means"[27].

---

24 Ibid.

25 Cf. the second report of the *Circulus Germanicus* (14.10.2015) during the III. General Assembly 2015; available from https://press.vatican.va/content/salastampa/it/bollettino/pubblico/2015/10/14/0784/01688.html#germ; accessed 13.12.2016.

26 M.G. LAWLER/T.A. SALZMAN: "In Amoris Laetitia".

27 SACRED CONGREGATION FOR THE DOCTRINE OF THE FAITH: *Letter Regarding the Indissolubility of Marriage*, 1973, available from http://www.vatican.va/roman_curia/congregations/cfaith/documents/rc_con_cfaith_doc_19730411_indissolubilitate-matrimonii_en.html; accessed 13.12.2016.

The *internal forum*, however, can be non-sacramental and sacramental.[28] In the context of the non-sacramental *internal forum* the pastor has to help a person to evaluate his or her life *coram Deo*, i.e. in the presence of God, to know God's will, to deepen and strengthen his or her trust in God, to take responsibility according to his or her possibility within a concrete situation, to encourage him or her to do his or her best etc. The sacramental *internal forum* is the sacrament of Penance. It is strictly requested only if someone is aware of having committed a grave or mortal sin. *Amoris laetitia* offers a clear ethical framework for discerning situations and cases and for helping persons to become aware if their situation is an objective contradiction to the Church's doctrine and whether or not the person is subjectively culpable or not (cf. AL 305). It stresses the mission of the Church to offer the sacraments as a help towards a growth in faith, grace, and humanity.

At this point the much quoted crucial passage of AL 303 should be emphasised:

> It is possible that in an objective situation of sin – which may not be subjectively culpable, or fully such – a person can be living in God's grace, can love and can also grow in the life of grace and charity, while receiving the Church's help to this end.

In footnote 351, Pope Francis affirms that "in certain cases, this can include the help of the sacraments", and he adds a quotation of his Apostolic Exhortation, *Evangelii gaudium*: "Hence, 'I want to remind priests that the confessional must not be a torture chamber, but rather an encounter with the Lord's mercy' (no. 44). I would also point out that the Eucharist 'is not a prize for the perfect, but a powerful medicine and nourishment for the weak' (no. 47)". Pope Francis makes clear that in some ways he had changed this paradigm even much earlier. The Church feels obliged to offer the help of the sacraments in imitation of Jesus Christ who demands a profound logic and practice of integration and reinstating, not of casting off (cf. AL 296).

4.2 Mercy and the Fidelity to Christ and to His Truth

At this point the second argument in favour of the previous position of the Magisterium should be re-examined, i.e. that the Church is committed to the doctrine of the indissolubility of marriage and, therefore, its practice which is seen to be based upon Sacred Scripture, would be an expression of "fidelity to Christ and to His truth" (FC 84). In *Amoris laetitia* the ideal of marriage stamped by its commitment to exclusivity and stability is not at all brushed aside. Pope Francis affirms that "in order to avoid all misunderstanding, I would point out that in no way must the Church desist from proposing the full ideal of marriage" (AL 307), but, with

[28] Cf. B. PETRÀ: "Amoris laetitia", 245–247.

the same vigour, he stresses that "'without detracting from the evangelical ideal, there is a need to accompany with mercy and patience the eventual stages of personal growth as these progressively appear', making room for 'the Lord's mercy, which spurs us on to do our best'" (AL 308; with quotations from EG 44).

Pope Francis never tires of pointing out that God's mercy is part of the truth of the Gospel. He calls it "the beating heart of the Gospel" (AL 309).[29] "Mercy is revealed truth itself and... is 'the core of the revelation of Jesus Christ'".[30]

Mercy, therefore, has never to be misunderstood as pastoral leniency but is a demand of revealed truth. It requires one to look at the reality of people's lives "with the same eyes with which Christ looked at it, as he walked among the people of his time" (*Relatio finalis* 2015, 56), and with an "attitude... of humility and understanding in order to accompany each and every family so that each family might discover the best way to overcome the obstacles it encounters" (ibid.).

If, as Pope Francis affirms, "the Lord's mercy spurs us on to do our best" (cf. AL 308), our witness to mercy requires us to accompany people on their gradual process of human and spiritual growth (cf. AL 293–295). Self-critically, Pope Francis admits that too often the Church "puts so many conditions on mercy that we empty it of its concrete meaning and real significance" (AL 311).

The Church is committed to the whole truth of the Gospel and, therefore, has to reach out to everyone without exception (cf. AL 309). Mercy requires an accurate distinction of different situations in order to measure up to the complexity and singularity of each situation and to the persons involved in them. It also requires us to accompany these persons in order to integrate them, as far as possible, into the Church's life and, ultimately, into communion with God for the Church is seen as the basic sacrament of God's communion with all human beings.

---

29 This is a quotation from FRANCIS: *Misericordiae Vultus: Bull of Indication of the Extraordinary Jubilee of Mercy*, 2015, 12, available from https://w2.vatican.va/content/francesco/en/apost_letters/documents/papa-francesco_bolla_20150411_misericordiae-vultus.html; accessed 13.12.2016. Cf. also FRANCIS: *The Name of God is Mercy*, New York: Random House, 2016; M.M. LINTNER: "Miserando atque eligendo: Zur Spiritualität der Barmherzigkeit bei Papst Franziskus", in: M.M. LINTNER/J. ERNESTI/M. MOLING (eds.): *Papst Franziskus – Herausforderung für Theologie und Kirche*, Brixen-Innsbruck: Tyrolia, 2016 (Brixner Theologisches Jahrbuch; 6), 71-87.

30 XIV ORDINARY GENERAL ASSEMBLY OF THE SYNOD OF BISHOPS: *The Vocation and Mission of the Family in the Church and the Contemporary World: Instrumentum Laboris*, 2015, 68, available from http://www.vatican.va/roman_curia/synod/documents/rc_synod_doc_20150623_instrumentum-xiv-assembly_en.html; accessed 13.12.2016.

4.3 Caring for the Weak, Fragile and Broken Persons as Expression of a Strong Faith

Similarly, the answer to the third above mentioned argument is recognised, this being that the Church is committed to avoid leading the faithful into error and confusion and, therefore, in order to avoid any uncertainty regarding the Church's teaching about the indissolubility of marriage and any scandal, she cannot admit concerned people to the Eucharist. Even though Pope Francis confesses to "understand those who prefer a more rigorous pastoral care which leaves no room for confusion", he points out that he "sincerely believe[s] that Jesus wants a Church attentive to the goodness which the Holy Spirit sows in the midst of human weakness" (AL 308). Again, the Church is committed to the whole truth of the Gospel in which we encounter Jesus who said: "It is not the healthy who need a doctor, but the sick. I have not come to call the righteous, but sinners" (Mk 2,17). Therefore, the "Christian community's care of such persons is not to be considered a weakening of its faith and testimony to the indissolubility of marriage, rather, such care is a particular expression of its charity" (AL 243). As Pope Francis stresses, mercy means to choose the *via caritatis*, which means not to judge nor condemn the other, but to "remain ever open to new stages of growth and to new decisions which can enable the ideal to be more fully realized" (AL 303) and "to find possible ways of responding to God and growing in the midst of limits. By thinking that everything is black and white, we sometimes close off the way of grace and of growth, and discourage paths of sanctification which give glory to God. Let us remember that 'a small step, in the midst of great human limitations, can be more pleasing to God than a life which appears outwardly in order, but moves through the day without confronting great difficulties' (EG 44)" (AL 305).

Pope Francis strongly warns that lack of mercy or putting conditions on mercy until emptying it of its concrete meaning and real significance presents "the worst way of watering down the Gospel" (AL 311).

5 Summary

Amoris laetitia shows that there are good pastoral, theological, and ethical reasons to discern attentively situations, to accompany divorced and remarried couples and to integrate them as far as possible into the life of the Church by trying to identify and overcome possible obstacles. Beside the special pastoral and spiritual care for these couples, *Amoris laetitia* has indeed opened up new possibilities in the discipline concerning reception of the sacraments by the divorced and remarried. According to *Amoris laetitia*, the Church does not categorically further exclude them from the sacraments of Reconciliation and Eucharist, even without strictly demanding sexual abstinence.

From a theological-ethical perspective there are at least three main aspects which present a new development in *Amoris laetitia* by comparison to the Magisterium's doctrinal teaching since *Familiaris consortio*, which are, however, in full accordance with the long tradition of moral theology, which is supported by reference to Thomas Aquinas.[31]

First of all, Pope Francis overcomes a deep sceptical attitude towards the competence of the conscience of the faithful which has characterized the Church's position in past papacies. In AL conscience has a significant role. The issue of conscience runs like a red thread through the whole document. For the first time it is mentioned in no. 37, in a very self-critical statement:

> We [the Church]... find it hard to make room for the consciences of the faithful, who very often respond as best they can to the Gospel amid their limitations, and are capable of carrying out their own discernment in complex situations. We have been called to form consciences, not to replace them.

Therefore, "individual conscience needs to be better incorporated into the Church's praxis in certain situations which do not objectively embody our understanding of marriage" (AL 303).

Secondly, *Amoris laetitia* points out the importance of conscience not only for the discernment of situations but also for the clarification of personal responsibility and culpability (cf. AL 298-312). The document stresses the need to differentiate the objective and the subjective dimension. The basic notion of conscience is that of a subjective competence able to recognize how to realize, as far as possible, the objective moral standards in a concrete situation with its complexity, limitations, and conditions. In accordance with Thomas Aquinas, a general rule is not able to cover all the details of a singular and complex situation and, therefore, needs to be mediated by the individual conscience with its hermeneutical competence. Pope Francis, following GS 16, understands the experience of conscience first of all as an encounter and dialogue with God and, therefore, as a place of becoming aware of one's situation before God. Conscience is not only a moral occurrence, but it helps to understand and carry out fully God's will in one's life.

The third and, for the *raison d'être* of this paper, crucial aspect is the following: Even though remarriage after divorce may present a serious deviation from the ideal of marriage, marked by a commitment to exclusivity and stability, not ev-

[31] Rodrigo Guerra López in his comment on AL in the Vatican newspaper *L'Osservatore Romano* speaks of an "organic development with creative fidelity"; cf. R. GUERRA LÓPEZ: "Fedeltà creative: Dalla riflessione di Karol Wojtyła all'esortazione 'Amoris laetitia'", in: *Osservatore Romano* (23.07.2016), 5.

ery situation of remarriage after divorce automatically presents a grave sin for the involved moral subjects. The previous position that "the 'objective truth', according to magisterial teaching, is that the couples living in this situation are committing adultery and cannot receive Communion and that their subjective consciences must adhere to this truth"[32], is not sustainable any more. *Amoris laetitia* affirms that concerned people, who live in such situations, may "be living in God's grace, can love and can also grow in the life of grace and charity, while receiving the Church's help to this end, and [what] in certain cases…can include the help of the sacraments" (AL 305 plus note 351).

In sum, *Amoris laetitia* is very clear and consistent in its argumentation so as to draw the conclusion that, in some cases, this document opens up the possibility for divorced and remarried persons to approach the sacraments of Reconciliation and the Eucharist. The counterargument that *Amoris laetitia* would not state this explicitly or that it would be insufficient to state such an important content ambiguously and as a footnote open to misinterpretation sounds unreasonable. Also a footnote is an integral part of this document and – as already stated – the intention and the whole argumentation of *Amoris laetitia* are clear. Therefore, the response of Pope Francis to the Argentinian Bishops, who elaborated some "Basic criteria for the application of chapter 8 of *Amoris Laetitia*"[33], is not surprising. The Bishops wrote:

> (5) Whenever feasible, and depending on the specific circumstances of a couple, and especially when both partners are Christians walking together on the path of faith, the priest may suggest a decision to live in continence. *Amoris Laetitia* does not ignore the difficulties arising from this option (cf. footnote 329) and offers the possibility of having access to the Sacrament of Reconciliation if the partners fail in this purpose (cf. footnote 364 …).
>
> (6) In other, more complex cases, and when a declaration of nullity has not been obtained, the above mentioned option may not, in fact, be feasible. Nonetheless, a path of discernment is still possible. If it comes to be recognized that, in a specific case, there are limitations that mitigate responsibility and culpability (cf. 301–302), especially when a person believes they would incur a subsequent wrong by harming the children of the new union, *Amoris Laetitia* offers the possibility of access to the sacraments of Reconciliation and Eucharist (cf. footnotes 336 and 351). These sacraments, in turn, dispose the person to continue maturing and growing with the power of grace.

Pope Francis in his response affirmed: "There are no other interpretations." [34]

---

32 M.G. LAWLER/T.A. SALZMAN: "In Amoris Laetitia".

33 An English translation is available from https://cvcomment.org/2016/09/18/buenos-aires-bishops-guidelines-on-amoris-laetitia-full-text/; accessed 10.10.2016.

34 See: I. SAN MARTÍN: *Pope okays Argentine doc on Communion for divorced and remarried*, 2016, available from https://cruxnow.com/global-church/2016/09/12/pope-okays-argentine-doc-communion-divorced-remarried/; accessed 10.10.2016.

Accompanying, Discerning and Integrating the Fragility of Couples: Pastors and Theologians at a Crossroads

Arnaud Join-Lambert

For a practical theologian, it is not easy to approach a text like chapter 8 of the Apostolic Exhortation *Amoris laetitia.* In addition to the specific difficulty posed by the complexity of the subject that is discussed in the text, I see a more significant challenge that goes beyond our present topic: What is the status of practical theology? Is it only a question of giving examples of characteristic or tragic situations that are relevant to our topic? Or (as in earlier centuries) ought one to apply the reflections of the moral and dogmatic theologians by giving orientations, or even solutions? That is not why I intend to do here. I propose to place myself alongside the reader of *Amoris laetitia* who seeks to grasp what Pope Francis retains from the synodal process that was launched in 2013, and what he adds to it.

I shall begin by speaking about a fear that some persons experience, and about a disappointment that others experience. Both of these reactions are engendered by *Amoris laetitia* in the field of the pastoral care of divorced and remarried persons. The fact that many people are not completely satisfied with this text may perhaps in itself show that this text, in its own literary genre, is well adjusted to the situation. When I discuss this, I shall also speak of what I have experienced as an expert who was invited by the bishops of Belgium to two consultations in view of the Synods of 2014 and 2015 (1). I would then like to take a step back and approach the difficult question of the impossibility of structuring the relationship between the doctrinal and the pastoral, when these two dimensions are thought of as distinct entities. My hypothesis is that this is an implicit intention on the part of Pope Francis. This path would allow us to get beyond the contemporary impasses in the Catholic magisterium. I shall therefore explore in depth two expressions in *Amoris laetitia*: "certain 'irregular' situations" and "they are not excommunicated", and I shall then examine the situation of children in what the Pope's proposes (2). Finally, since we pastors and theologians are at a crossroads,

I shall take the risk of proposing some perspectives that open up before us, with regard both to reflection and to action (3).

1 It Took Three Years to Arrive at *Amoris Laetitia*

1.1 The Synodal Process

I have been asked to take here the perspective of pastoral theology. I must therefore begin by emphasizing the two great novelties of the Roman Synods on the family. Although the first novelty – namely, holding two sessions on the same theme, with an interval of one year between them – made little impact on lay Christians, it certainly contributed to the emergence of new positions on the part of some Synod Fathers. If we assume that the new participants in the second Synod had also followed what went on at the first Synod, admittedly from the outside, this meant that they were able to bring to maturity their own approach to the questions that had been discussed. It is necessary to give people time, when the questions under debate are sensitive and complex, either in human terms or theologically. This temporal extension of the synodal processes is a recent innovation in the Catholic Church, and expresses powerfully the need for discernment that is addressed from now on to every baptized person. This "discernment" seems to have become the key word of the pontificate of Pope Francis.

From the pastoral point of view, another innovation by Pope Francis is the extension of the traditional consultation, on both occasions, to include all the baptized. One of the greatest novelties of post-conciliar synodality is the consultation of baptized Catholics; the question of the specific ways in which this is done is secondary here. In the past, this was quite simply unthinkable – in the strong sense of that word – both in ecclesiology and in praxis. This is one of the most explicit signs that a theology, and a pastoral care with room for the *sensus fidei,* are being taken seriously. We must however note that this new way of "doing church" and "making the church" has created difficulties that should not be underestimated.[1]

In the case of these Synods on the family, the episcopal conferences had to decide the concrete ways of enacting this consultation and writing a report on it. Sometimes, as in France, the dioceses were free to choose what would be asked and how this would be done. In Belgium, the bishops decided to put the two questionnaires online, without any restrictions about the questions or about access. They took three risks in doing so: first, that the questions would not be understood, because of their theological-ecclesial jargon or because of the topics they evoked; secondly, that a synthesis would be impossible, because of the heterogeneity of

[1] See my remarks on this subject in *Synodes et concile en France: Bilan et perspective*, Paris: Conférence des Évêques de France, 2016 (Documents Épiscopat; 5), 21-23.

the responses and the brief space of time allotted for putting the questionnaires on line and for examining the responses; and thirdly, that pressure groups would swing into action on behalf of their particular interests, so that the outcome of the inquiry would be useless. We can affirm that these three risks also existed on the level of the worldwide church. The Pope and the secretariat of the Roman Synods took one further risk, namely, that the persons who were consulted would be disappointed.

1.2 The Belgian Consultation

In Belgium, the questionnaire was published in two languages on the homepage of the Catholic Church and in the weekly parish magazines. The dioceses encouraged, and to some extent organized, groups who would reply. The examination was entrusted to theologians, and the analysis to a professor of moral theology (Thomas Knieps of the Catholic University of Leuven) and four professors of pastoral theology (Annemie Dillen of the Catholic University of Leuven, Henri Deroitte and myself from the Université catholique de Louvain, and Stijn Van Den Bosche from the International Center *Lumen Vitae*).

1,283 French-language questionnaires were examined at the first consultation in 2014; 184 of these were sent in by groups. 306 Flemish-language questionnaires were examined; 60 of these were sent in by groups. There were some recurrent negative observations about the process itself: the formulation of the questionnaire was unsuitable and incomprehensible for the great majority of the targeted public; the questionnaire was too long and required knowledge that not all parishioners possess; there was insufficient time for a questionnaire of this kind, so that it was not possible to organize groups for a deeper discussion. The responses were often partial, or generalized without specifying in detail which precise question they were referring to. Some people simplified the questionnaire to make it accessible, but sometimes this meant that the questions got distorted. It was impossible to determine how far those who replied were representative of the Catholics in Belgium as a whole. In addition to all these responses, some individual experts and groups of experts sent in their reactions, sometimes partial and sometimes highly developed. The principal effect would thus have been a raising of people's awareness, clearly awakening expectations of an evolution, especially in the subject that brings us together in this symposium.

The fourth sub-question c of question 4, on the number of persons who are separated or divorced and remarried, and on the activity of the local church in their regard ("Are separated couples and those divorced and remarried a pastoral reality in your particular Church? Can you approximate a percentage? How do you deal with this situation in appropriate pastoral programmes?"), received numerous responses, almost all of which expressed a lack of comprehension, or a lack of acceptance, of the ecclesiastical discipline.[2] There was a divergence in the responses with regard to the perception of the way in which these persons live their relationship to the church (sub-question d: "In all the above cases, how do the baptized live in this irregular situation? Are they aware of it? Are they simply indifferent? Do they feel marginalized or suffer from the impossibility of receiving the sacraments?"), and with regard to what they expect (sub-question e: "What questions do divorced and remarried people pose to the Church concerning the Sacraments of the Eucharist and of Reconciliation? Among those persons who find themselves in these situations, how many ask for these sacraments?"). In general terms, we see that the consciousness, the indifference, the feeling of being excluded, and the suffering seem sometimes present and sometimes absent and that, most frequently, they are mixed, as is the case with other feelings. Thc requests of divorced and remarried persons are various and concrete. They ask for the positive benefits of being welcomed, being forgiven, and having the feeling that they have a place in the Church, and they ask for more "Gospel love". They also aspire to be treated in the same way as everyone else and to be able to remain practicing Catholics. The request to be able to receive the sacraments is strong, especially with regard to penance and the eucharist, but sometimes also with regard to matrimony. Some people appeal to the freedom of conscience; others would like to see their new union blessed. Some ask to be given a second chance; and some want the Church to reconsider the way in which it sees divorce. And finally, there are some who would no longer make any request of the Church, either because they believe that they are rejected, or else because they are "sorting things out" on their own.

The second consultation in 2015 received less than half as many responses, and the phenomenon of lobbying was plain to see. Since so many responses came from groups that were not identified, but that we have characterized as "rigorist", it was not possible to extrapolate anything from the proportions of the responses that were received. Besides this, the questions were just as difficult as in the first questionnaire. For example, no. 38, which was relevant to the present topic, runs as follows:

> With regard to the divorced and remarried, pastoral practice concerning the sacraments needs to be further studied, including assessment of the Orthodox practice and taking into account "the distinction between an objective sinful situation and extenuating circumstances" (n. 52 [of the 2014 *Relatio synodi*]). What are the prospects in such a

2 The questionnaire is available from http://www.vatican.va/roman_curia/synod/documents/rc_synod_doc_20131105_iii-assemblea-sinodo-vescovi_en.html; accessed 12.12.2016.

> case? What is possible? What suggestions can be offered to resolve forms of undue or unnecessary impediments?[3]

Apart from the "rigorist" responses that insisted on the strict preservation of current discipline, the great majority of the Belgians who responded expressed the wish that divorced and remarried persons should be able to receive the sacraments, especially penance and the eucharist. Many observed that in any case, many priests did not practice this form of exclusion: they gave communion with a good conscience to persons who were divorced and remarried. Some envisaged the structure of an accompaniment on a spiritual path that, for some persons, could go as far as a sacramental remarriage. For some, it is normal to want a second chance. This would be a lesser evil, and it would be appropriate, in that case, to recognize the values of the new union. But others insisted on the suffering that such a recognition would inflict on the partner who had been abandoned. Others again wanted the divorced and remarried persons not to be shut up in their failure: they should be reintegrated into the community with discernment, and without any judgment. And they should be offered a blessing (something that already occurs in practice). They underlined the freedom of conscience. Some went as far as to propose that the idea of sin should also be suppressed.

We should note that a parallel large-scale investigation of a more academic character was carried out in Flanders by our colleagues at the KU Leuven. This resulted in positions that were clearly more marked, and that were almost unanimous in their lack of understanding of the official Catholic discipline.[4]

1.3 Fears and Disappointments

If we were to sum up the numerous comments that were made after the publication of *Amoris laetitia*, at least in French-speaking Europe and North America, as well as in Germany, we would have to say: "All that trouble – for such a small result!" So much energy, so many meetings, so much work and time – to end up with a text that seems rather banal on a superficial reading, a text that satisfies neither the rigorists who defend the pure doctrine nor those who work on the ground level and are confronted with a multitude of painful situations. Several cardinals, bishops, and traditionalist groups have spoken at length in the media about their dissatisfaction with this text, which "sells off" both doctrine and sacraments. Their statements are characterized by a vocabulary that is linked to fear.

---

3 Available from http://www.vatican.va/roman_curia/synod/documents/rc_synod_doc_20141209_lineamenta-xiv-assembly_en.html; accessed 12.12.2016.

4 Cf. A. DILLEN/T. KNIEPS-PORT LE ROI/K. KRYSINSKA: "A Growing Gap? Catholic Pastoral Workers and Volunteers' Perceptions of Family Life and Church Teaching in Flanders", in: E. OSEWSKA/J. STALA (eds.), *Modern Family: Local and European Perspectives*, Krakow: The Pontifical University of John Paul II, Krakow Press, 159-177.

Others have spoken of their hope that this text will allow them to encounter and to accompany in truth those who live in a situation of failure and suffering. This was the case, for example, with Cardinal Schönborn of Vienna and Cardinal Vingt-Trois of Paris. But the great majority of the priests, deacons, and lay persons who are involved in pastoral work – as well as most of the baptized – seem to be keeping silent. One initial common interpretation was to call this reception a disappointment, since, ultimately, it was not possible to perceive any doctrinal or pastoral change. My hypothesis is that *Amoris laetitia* is a text that is very hard to understand on those points where the expectations were greatest. This is due, not only to the compact nature of the text, but also and above all to its intention to bypass the primary traditional reading that posits an antithesis between the doctrinal and the pastoral. The new attitude to which Pope Francis is inviting us requires such huge shifts that this would be too difficult for most Catholics.

In my following reflections, I shall look at nos. 76-79 of the Apostolic Exhortation *Amoris laetitia,* entitled "Seeds of the Word and imperfect situations," in chapter 3; nos. 241-246 in the section entitled "Casting light on crises, worries, and difficulties" with the subtitle "Accompaniment after breakdown and divorce", in chapter. 6; and nos. 296-312, entitled "The discernment of 'irregular' situations", "Mitigating factors in pastoral discernment," "Rules and discernment," and "The logic of pastoral mercy" in chapter 8. The words employed in these titles already indicate problems that are both theological and pastoral – but also problems of canon law.

2 The Traditional Disjunction between the Doctrinal and the Pastoral as the Root of the Problem

We often read a major criticism of the Second Vatican Council in traditionalist circles and in similar groups: namely, that since this was a "pastoral" council, to use the language of Popes John XXIII and Paul VI, it did not basically involve doctrine (understood as the presentation of dogma and of morality). It is useless to point out – although I do so anyway – that such declarations lack any foundation in history or theology. Pope Paul VI himself rejected such an interpretation as contrary to the project and to the texts of the Council. I do not wish to labor this point, but it is precisely the same type of criticism that we find today among the heirs of these milieus, including bishops and cardinals. They claim that *Amoris laetitia* is a text with an exclusive practical dimension. All that *Amoris laetitia* would demand of us is to improve our pastoral activity in order to be better adapted to the work of evangelization today. With regard to the pastoral care of persons who are divorced and remarried, a little more mercy and accompaniment would be needed, in order to keep these persons in the Church. This means that everyone would agree that "[i]t is a matter of reaching out to everyone" (AL 297). What I have just said scarcely amounts to a caricature of a tension that has persisted since the Council. Let us take a brief look more closely at what "doctrine" might be.

2.1 Amoris Laetitia *and "Doctrine"*

Amoris laetitia employs the noun "doctrine" and the adjective "doctrinal" fourteen times, but it is used at least four times with a negative connotation,[5] and at any rate in a restrictive manner. It suffices to quote no. 59:

> Our teaching on marriage and the family cannot fail to be inspired and transformed by this message of love and tenderness; otherwise, it becomes nothing more than the defense of a dry and lifeless doctrine.

This very clearly indicates an intention to get beyond an antithesis between the doctrinal and the pastoral, or at least, to reduce the distance that separates them. This type of formulation is clearly different from the use of the word "doctrine" to provide a positive justification of the impossibility of giving eucharistic communion to divorced and remarried persons in the Apostolic Exhortation *Familiaris consortio* (1981): "Besides this, there is another special pastoral reason: if these people were admitted to the Eucharist, the faithful would be led into error and confusion regarding the Church's teaching about the indissolubility of marriage."[6] At the beginning of *Amoris laetitia*, Pope Francis himself gives a key to the interpretation of the entire text:

> Unity of teaching and practice is certainly necessary in the Church, but this does not preclude various ways of interpreting some aspects of that teaching or drawing certain consequences from it. (AL 3)

We shall arrive at the fullness of truth only at the end of time. In the present time, we remain marked by our multiple cultural contexts, which make different interpretations possible. The very reason for the existence of the Church is to make

---

5 AL 49: "Rather than offering the healing power of grace and the light of the Gospel message, some would 'indoctrinate' that message, turning it into 'dead stones to be hurled at others'." (The quote is taken from *Conclusion of the Synod of Bishops on the Family: Address of His Holiness Pope Francis*, 24.10.2015, available from http://w2.vatican.va/content/francesco/en/events/event.dir.html/content/vaticanevents/en/2015/10/24/sinodo.html; accessed 12.12.2016.) AL 59: "Our teaching on marriage and the family cannot fail to be inspired and transformed by this message of love and tenderness; otherwise, it becomes nothing more than the defense of a dry and lifeless doctrine." AL 79: "Therefore, while clearly stating the Church's teaching, pastors are to avoid judgments that do not take into account the complexity of various situations." AL 134: "Marital love is not defended primarily by presenting indissolubility as a duty, or by repeating doctrine, but by helping it to grow ever stronger under the impulse of grace."

6 JOHN PAUL II: *Familiaris consortio*, 1981, 84.

it possible for these cultures to be embodied against a horizon of unity, and hence of hope. The theologian François Bousquet has expressed this well in a recent article about the structure of the relationship between dogmatics and praxis:

> The principal function of the Church is in fact to be a body of hope, to make credible the proclamation of the Kingdom that is coming, by giving it proleptically a body and visibility, in the power of an eschatology that has not waited for the end to manifest itself.[7]

Leaving aside the word "doctrine", the Pope has preferred the word "norm" and has emphasized it by employing it twenty-two times, which is strongly present, for example, in no. 301, especially in his quotation from no. 33 of *Familiaris consortio*:

> More is involved here than mere ignorance of the rule. A subject may know full well the rule, yet have great difficulty in understanding "its inherent values" [FC 33], or be in a concrete situation which does not allow him or her to act differently and decide otherwise without further sin. (AL 301)

But "norm" is not the equivalent of "doctrine". The two terms have a different weight in the Catholic Church, theologically, in canon law, and also emotionally.

I propose now to look in detail at three expressions or subjects that reveal the Pope's intention to get beyond the antithesis between the doctrinal and the pastoral. At the same time, we shall see how hard this is to grasp, if the one who reads *Amoris laetitia* is not forewarned.

2.2 "The Discernment of 'Irregular' Situations"

This title of numbers 296 to 300 is emblematic of the tension between the doctrinal and the pastoral – a tension that can go as far as an irreparable fissure, when an antithesis is posited between the two. The Pope employs the adjective "irregular", which locates this question directly in the normative or legal register. This word is used in numbers 297, 301, and 305, and this makes it the official term for subsequent usage. However, the use of inverted commas each time means that this punctuation too becomes part of the language of the magisterium, just as much as the adjective itself. We need to pay attention to these inverted commas.

The title is accompanied by a footnote that we must look at, if we are to grasp the significance of the term itself and to interpret these inverted commas. The note refers to the papal catechesis on June 24, 2015.[8] I quote:

---

7 F. BOUSQUET: "Principe dogmatique et théologie contemporaine?, in: *Recherches de Science Religieuse* 95 (2007), 545-558, here 551.

8 Cf. AL 269, footnote 325.

> Around us we find various families in so-called irregular situations – I don't really like this word – and it causes us to wonder.

I suggest to look at this discourse and listen to it. It is highly significant for understanding the idea of irregularity. The video[9] shows that the words between dashes were not envisaged in the text that had been prepared. I agree with the opinion of Jean-François Chiron and Alain Thomasset that the expressions "various situations of fragility or imperfection" (AL 296) or "complicated situations" (AL 213) do in fact appear to express his thinking better.[10]

The use of inverted commas around "irregular" in *Amoris laetitia* helps the commentators on the Exhortation to understand this term. The official presentation by Cardinal Schönborn employs these inverted commas systematically.[11] But other texts use the term without inverted commas, indicating thereby their disagreement or their lack of understanding. We should not overdo this interpretation. Nor should we turn it into a system. But I believe that we shall learn something that is very valuable for the chapter 8 of *Amoris laetitia*, if we pay attention to the inverted commas.

2.3 "They Are Not Excommunicated"

I believe that Pope Francis' intention to get beyond the tension between the doctrinal and the pastoral can be seen in the sentence: "They are not excommunicated", when we examine the context in which this is said, and the references that are proposed there.

The verb "to excommunicate" is used three times in *Amoris laetitia*, each time in its passive form. The first occurrence is a reference to a catechesis held by Pope Francis on August 5, 2015:

> It is important that the divorced who have entered a new union should be made to feel part of the Church. "They are not excommunicated" and they should not be treated as such, since they remain part of the ecclesial community [261]. (AL 243)

---

9 FRANCIS: "The Family – 20. Wounds", Discourse at the General Audience on June 24, 2015, available from: http://w2.vatican.va/content/francesco/en/audiences/2015/documents/papa-francesco_20150624_udienza-generale.html; accessed 08.12.2016. For the video: 17'12 to 18'30, "cosiddetti irregolari; a me non piace questa parola".

10 J.-F. CHIRON/A. THOMASSET: "Présentation et notes sur le chapitre 8", in: *Exhortation apostolique Post-Synodale du pape François La Joie de l'Amour: Édition présentée et annotée sous la direction du Service national Famille et Société – Conférence des évêques de France – et de la Faculté de théologie du Centre Sèvres*, Namur-Paris, Éditions Jésuites, 2016, 283.

11 Cf. "Cardinal Schönborn's Intervention at Presentation of Amoris Laetitia", available from https://zenit.org/articles/cardinal-schonborns-intervention-at-presentation-of-amoris-laetitia/; accessed 12.12.2016.

> "How can we encourage those parents to do everything possible to raise their children in the Christian life, to give them an example of committed and practical faith, if we keep them at arm's length from the life of the community, as if they were somehow excommunicated?… [270]" (AL 246)

If we look at the discourse as a whole, the suggestions that the Pope makes are even bolder, in keeping with the oral style of these audiences:

> In these decades, in truth, the Church has been neither insensitive nor lazy. Thanks to the in-depth analysis performed by Pastors, led and guided by my Predecessors, the awareness has truly grown that it is necessary to have a fraternal and attentive welcome, in love and in truth, of the baptized who have established a new relationship of cohabitation after the failure of the marital sacrament: in fact, these persons are by no means excommunicated – they are not excommunicated! – and they should absolutely not be treated as such: they are still a part of the Church.[12]

If, however, we understand the term "excommunication" in its usual sense, these words are incomprehensible. The French Larousse dictionary gives the following brief definition: "Exclusion of a member of a religious community to which he belongs."[13] This already shows us the problem. Can a person be both excluded (in the usual sense of this word) and not excluded (according to *Amoris laetitia*)? Things get complicated as soon as we touch on the sacraments and ministries. There is thus a paradox between the papal affirmation that one belongs to the community (in other words, that one is not excommunicated), and being definitively refused access to the sacraments (in other words, that one is excommunicated).

This is not only a question of receiving the sacraments – a matter to which we shall return in the next section. *Amoris laetitia* contains a highly ambiguous passage about certain functions of service in the Church:

> No one can be condemned for ever, because that is not the logic of the Gospel! Here I am not speaking only of the divorced and remarried, but of everyone, in whatever situation they find themselves. Naturally, if someone flaunts an objective sin as if it were part of the Christian ideal, or wants to impose something other than what the Church teaches, he or she can in no way presume to teach or preach to others; this is a case of something which separates from the community (cf. *Mt* 18:17). (AL 297)

If we read this text aright, it states that only some divorced persons who are involved in a new union cannot be catechists or preachers – namely, those who dress up their situation as "part of the Christian ideal". This means that the others are allowed to do so. And this authorizes us to turn the sentence round: "If someone does not flaunt an objective sin…he can presume to teach or preach to

[12] FRANCIS: "The Family – 20. Wounds". For the video: 30' to 30'19.

[13] http://www.larousse.fr/dictionnaires/francais/excommunication/32028; accessed 08.12.2016.

others." This answers the wishes that were most frequently expressed during the consultations before the Synod, for example in Belgium. But it runs counter to the generally held understanding of excommunication, as this is formulated in the dictionaries or in Wikipedia.[14] And it is inconceivable that there could be partial excommunications that are manifested in partial belongings. The Pope's affirmation may be very striking, but ultimately, it can only engender confusion.

The lengthy passages that set out in detail the discernment that must be practiced in this sphere can only accentuate the difficulty of comprehension. I believe that the problem is the author's refusal to employ a doctrinal language with clearly identified referents (accepting the risk that the reader might contest these), while at the same time refusing to reject this language explicitly. The proposal of the path of discernment is in fact more demanding,[15] and is doubtless too complicated. "It is not a question of a 'double morality' where one would have (on the one hand) the strict doctrine and (on the other hand) the supple pastoral care, but rather of the demand that we take the individual situations seriously when the ideal is put into practice."[16]

The third occurrence of "excommunication" permits me to risk formulating a hypothesis about the Pope's position by searching for the keys that he himself offers. AL 299 sets out the specific situation of persons who are divorced and remarried, with a lengthy quotation from no. 84 of the *Relatio finalis* of the 2015 Synod:

> Their participation can be expressed in different ecclesial services, which necessarily requires discerning which of the various forms of exclusion currently practiced in the liturgical, pastoral, educational and institutional framework can be surmounted. Such persons need to feel not as excommunicated members of the Church, but instead as living members, able to live and grow in the Church and experience her as a mother who welcomes them always, who takes care of them with affection and encourages them along the path of life and the Gospel. (AL 299)

Let us recall that this no. 84 of the *Relatio finalis* is one of the numbers that received the highest number of votes against it (72 "no" against 187 "yes"), so that it only just passed the two-thirds threshold of the conciliar tradition (72.2%). In a sense, the Pope is sheltering under the Synod here. He reinforces the authority of his suggestion by appealing to the vote of the bishops.

This number presents a significant pastoral difficulty, because it specifies, not the "various forms of exclusion", but only the spheres of this exclusion – that is to

---

14 https://en.wikipedia.org/wiki/Excommunication; accessed on 08.12./2016.

15 This is also emphasized by C. THEOBALD: "Postface", in: *Exhortation apostolique Post-Synodale du pape François La Joie de l'Amour,* 321-336, here 334-335.

16 J.-F. CHIRON/A. THOMASSET: "Présentation et notes sur le chapitre 8", 288.

say, the liturgy, pastoral care, education, and the ecclesial institution. The reader therefore needs to know what the text specifically refers to, but it is not easy to find this information. In the rest of the text, we have already read in no. 297 that at any rate, catechesis and preaching are included here.

We have to go to no. 300 to find a key with reference to the sacraments, but this key is accessible only to those who know how to read between the lines. The Pope proceeds by means of three references that conceal his meaning, in the manner of a matryoshka doll (or Russian doll):

> What is possible is simply a renewed encouragement to undertake a responsible personal and pastoral discernment of particular cases, one which would recognize that, since "the degree of responsibility is not equal in all cases" [335], the consequences or effects of a rule need not always necessarily be the same [336]. (AL 300)

The Pope adds a personal commentary in footnote 336:

> This is also the case with regard to sacramental discipline, since discernment can recognize that in a particular situation no grave fault exists. In such cases, what is found in another document applies: cf. *Evangelii Gaudium* (24 November 2013), 44 and 47.

The second reference brings us to proposals in the 2013 text about the attitude of openness and welcome that must be developed in all circumstances.[17] In particular, no. 47 of *Evangelii gaudium* contains some sentences about access to the sacraments:

> One concrete sign of such openness is that our church doors should always be open, so that if someone, moved by the Spirit, comes there looking for God, he or she will not find a closed door. There are other doors that should not be closed either. Everyone can share in some way in the life of the Church; everyone can be part of the community, nor should the doors of the sacraments be closed for simply any reason. This is especially true of the sacrament which is itself the "door": baptism. The Eucharist, although it is the fullness of sacramental life, is not a prize for the perfect but a powerful medicine and nourishment for the weak [51].

The reader of *Amoris laetitia* will not notice this reference to baptism and the eucharist, because Pope Francis evokes it only obliquely by means of a footnote referring to another text. When one approaches *Amoris laetitia* from the perspective of practical theology, one may legitimately wonder how such a reader can grasp what is going on in the text here. Nor is this all: we must continue our reading of the matryoshka dolls by examining a third reference. In footnote 51 of *Evangelii gaudium,* the Pope quotes two church fathers, Saint Ambrose of Milan on the forgiveness of sins by means of the eucharist, and Saint Cyril of Alexan-

[17] *Amoris laetitia* refers three times in its footnotes to this no. 47 of *Evangelii gaudium.*

dria on the unworthiness of everyone (himself included) to receive the eucharistic communion.[18]

At the conclusion of this examination of his text, there can be little doubt that Pope Francis is pleading that access to the sacraments should be possible for those in so-called "irregular" situations. But he does not make this plea in a generalized and undifferentiated way. The affirmation that these persons are not excommunicated must be interpreted to mean that they are not definitively excluded from eucharistic communion.[19] But which readers will have undertaken all this journey of exploration that I have just undertaken? There is a risk that those involved in pastoral work will stop short at the first matryoshka doll, and will mistakenly suppose that nothing changes in *Amoris laetitia*

However, the Pope returns insistently to this point in no. 305, on norms and discernment, where he evokes the question of the imputability of sin, with the tension between the objective and the subjective dimensions. Here, he refers once more to numbers 44 and 47 of *Evangelii gaudium.*

> Because of forms of conditioning and mitigating factors, it is possible that in an objective situation of sin – which may not be subjectively culpable, or not fully such – a person may be living in God's grace, can love and can also grow in the life of grace and charity, while receiving the Church's help to this end. [351] (AL 305)

The question of imputability refers in particular to the most contested number of the *Relatio finalis* of 2015.[20] But the question is not located in that text: we must read note 351, which brings a specification about the nature of the Church's help:

> In certain cases, this can include the help of the sacraments. Hence, "I want to remind priests that the confessional must not be a torture chamber, but rather an encounter with the Lord's mercy" (Apostolic Exhortation *Evangelii Gaudium* [24 November 2013], 44 : AAS 105 [2013], 1038). I would also point out that the Eucharist "is not a prize for the perfect, but a powerful medicine and nourishment for the weak" (*ibid.,* 47: 1039).

---

18 Cf. Saint Ambrose, *De Sacramentis,* IV; 6, 28: PL 16, 464: "I must receive it always, so that it may always forgive my sins. If I sin continually, I must always have a remedy": id., op. cit., IV, 5, 24: PL 16, 463: "Those who ate manna died; those who eat this body will obtain the forgiveness of their sins"; Saint Cyril of Alexandria, *In Joh. Evang.,* IV, 2: PG 73, 584-585: "I examined myself and I found myself unworthy. To those who speak thus I say: when will you be worthy? When at last you present yourself before Christ? And if your sins prevent you from drawing nigh, and you never cease to fall – for, as the Psalm says, 'what man knows his faults?' – will you remain without partaking of the sanctification that gives life for eternity?"

19 I note here with regret that the question of the Anointing of the sick was never raised in the synodal process.

20 No. 85 on the imputability of the situation – and thus the question whether or not mortal sin is committed – was adopted by 178 to 80, that is, with a majority of 68.99%.

Our examination of the meandering text and footnotes finally allows us to see the Pope's intention clearly. We are, however, still entitled to wonder if this was the right way to do things, since it risks a confusion that is not favourable to the pastoral exercise of mercy. Nor can such a confusion provide an impetus for the renewal of systematic theology. We do not accuse the Pope of acting according to strategic calculations. This may perhaps be his own way, his style,[21] of getting beyond the sclerosis that is the outcome of the tension among various approaches that claim to have more or less the first right to a doctrine that is supposed to be unchangeable.

2.4 The Children as a Pastoral Priority

I now add a new hypothesis that is generated by the attentive reading of *Amoris laetitia*, namely, that the Pope's pastoral concern for persons in "so-called 'irregular' situations" is motivated just as much (or even more so) by concern for the children of these persons.

When he writes in no. 299 about the goal of integrating divorced and remarried persons into the Church, the quotation from the *Relatio finalis* of 2015 continues: "This integration is also needed in the care and Christian upbringing of their children, who ought to be considered most important." (AL 299) The Synod Fathers, followed on this point by the Pope, speak first of the care and the Christian education of the children. They thus give them symbolically the first place, even before speaking of the situation of remarried adults. This point, which is marginal *per se,* could already be noted in no. 246; it is reinforced further on in the text. It is also remarkable, and indeed astonishing, that the first question that is formulated in the paragraph about the examination of conscience (reflection and repentance) by divorced and remarried persons concerns the children:

> The divorced and remarried should ask themselves: how did they act towards their children when the conjugal union entered into crisis… (AL 300)

This could give the impression that the Church authorities, and especially the Pope, are primarily concerned with the children. Is this to be understood as a concern about the future of the ecclesial institution – a future that would no longer be represented by adults who had experienced marital breakdown? We could make this point in the form of a caricature, as follows: "The worst has come to the worst. So let us do what we can to save what could still have a future."

---

21 To use the theological category that has been developed in recent years by the German Jesuit theologian Christof Theobald.

Let us look more closely at what *Amoris laetitia* says here, by examining the first number that mentions divorce and its consequences. No. 41 quotes no. 10 of the *Relatio synodi* of 2014, where the children are mentioned after the adults:

> "...A crisis in a couple's relationship destabilizes the family and may lead, through separation and divorce, to serious consequences for adults, children and society as a whole, weakening its individual and social bonds" [16]. (AL 41)

When we broaden the picture to take in *Amoris laetitia* as a whole, as well as a number of Pope Francis's discourses, we can see that this is indeed something that concerns him personally. It suffices here to read his catecheses on the family at the Wednesday papal audiences in 2015. For example, when speaking on 24 June of "the hurts that are incurred in family life," he said:

> The depletion of conjugal love spreads resentment in relationships. And often this disintegration "collapses" onto the children. There: the children. I would like to mediate a little on this point. Despite our seemingly evolved sensitivity, and all our refined psychological analyses, I ask myself if we are not just anaesthetizing ourselves to the wounds in children's souls.

I have merely sketched this hypothesis about the priority that *Amoris laetitia* accords to the children. This priority finds a quantitative expression, because the entire text speaks almost unceasingly about the children. In the pastoral care of those in a so-called "irregular" situation, the children are in fact a major criterion of discernment and of the pastoral choices that are to be made. Nos. 245 and 246 are particularly important here. I quote some extracts by way of example:

> The Synod Fathers also pointed to "the consequences of separation or divorce on children, in every case the innocent victims of the situation".[267] Apart from every other consideration, the good of children should be the primary concern, and not overshadowed by any ulterior interest or objective. I make this appeal to parents who are separated: "Never ever take your child hostage!" (AL 245)

> The Church, while appreciating the situations of conflict that are part of marriage, cannot fail to speak out on behalf of those who are most vulnerable: the children who offer suffer in silence. Today, "despite our seemingly evolved sensibilities and all our refined psychological analyses, I ask myself if we are not becoming numb to the hurt in children's souls...Do we feel the immense psychological burden borne by children in families where the members mistreat and hurt one another, to the point of breaking the bonds of marital fidelity?"[269] Such harmful experiences do not help children to grow in the maturity needed to make definitive commitments. For this reason, Christian communities must not abandon divorced parents who have entered a new union, but should include and support them in their efforts to bring up their children. (AL 246)

It does not in any way affect the specifically doctrinal dimension of our theme. And it is easy for the Pope to appeal to theological arguments drawn from sacred scripture, without contradicting a unanimous theological tradition. In this way, he easily wins the unanimous consent of the entire Church. The pastoral priority accorded to the children – something close to the heart of Pope Francis – would displace the paralyzed focal point between the doctrinal and the pastoral dimensions of the situation of these divorced and remarried persons. At any rate, this hypothesis deserves to be studied more deeply.

3 Perspectives after *Amoris Laetitia*

3.1 The Magisterial "Fragility" of the Exhortation

The corpus of the magisterium that is evoked by way of references in order to provide the foundation of chapter 8 of what is only a Post-Synodal Apostolic Exhortation does not enjoy the highest authority in the teaching of the Catholic Church – what we find here are the Apostolic Exhortations *Familiaris consortio* and *Evangelii gaudium,* and catecheses delivered at the weekly papal audiences. This has little weight in a doctrinal reading of the tradition, all the more so, because the quotations or allusions refer most frequently to texts by Pope Francis himself. This is one of the explicit dimensions mentioned in the letter sent by forty-five so-called "theologians" (some of whom are explicit traditionalists) on June 29, 2016.[22] I quote:

> Some commentators have asserted that the document does not contain magisterial teaching as such, but only the personal reflections of the Pope on the subjects it addresses. This assertion if true would not remove the danger to faith and morals posed by the document. If the Supreme Pontiff expresses a personal opinion in a magisterial document, this expression of opinion implicitly presents the opinion in question as one that it is legitimate for Catholics to hold. As a result, many Catholics will come to believe that the opinion is indeed compatible with Catholic faith and morals.

Pope Francis anticipates this potential criticism in no. 3 of AL:

> Since "time is greater than space," I would make it clear that not all discussions of doctrinal, moral or pastoral issues need to be settled by interventions of the magisterium. (AL 3)

Although the first part of this sentence may doubtless be enigmatic for a very large number of readers, the second part is unambiguous and is reinforced by the

---

[22] Available from https://www.lifesitenews.com/news/full-text-of-45-theologians-appeal-to-correct-amoris-laetitias-errors-revea; accessed 08.12.2016.

words: "I would make it clear that not all … " This, however, cannot be taken for granted in the Catholic tradition. Pope Francis relies primarily on the collegial authority of the bishops, which was expressed at the Roman Synods. This is why he quotes at length from the *Relatio Synodi* of 2014 and the *Relation finalis* of 2015, especially when the subjects that he evokes are delicate and complex. And this is why he also refers to documents issued by episcopal conferences.

The fact that the Pope has abandoned the classical construction of texts by the magisterium – proceeding from the doctrinal to the pastoral – has destabilized some theologians and pastors. But Pope Francis does not aim in the least to be abandoning the tradition of the Church. He positions himself explicitly in the continuity of the history of salvation that was inaugurated in the first covenant, and in the Christian revelation that was transmitted in the New Testament and has been penetrated more deeply down through the centuries. He retains what seems to him most appropriate for today's world. The numerous references to Pope John Paul II seek to establish this continuity, especially with the Post-Synodal Apostolic Exhortation *Familiaris consortio* of 1981.

3.2 "An Implementation That is Feeling its Way"[23]

This is the title of an article that was published in the French daily newspaper *La Croix* in June 2016 and that reflects well the timid initiatives that have been undertaken in the sphere of the pastoral care of families. In the western French-speaking area, some dioceses are establishing specific training courses or groups, and these have been given a new élan thanks to the encouragement in *Amoris laetitia*. "Small steps" have been taken here and there. *Amoris laetitia* applies this expression to the education of children, under the title "Patient realism" (AL 271).[24] This applies very well to the present topic too.

It is certainly true that the pastoral mission does not start from zero. And of its very nature, accompaniment is a dynamic process.[25] In his official presentation, Cardinal Schönborn predicted how readers would react to chapter 8: "But what does this mean concretely? Many people ask this question, and rightly so." He suggests that the keys can be found in no. 300, and states that the future disappointment will be due to questions that are badly formulated.[26] I myself would

23 "*Amoris laetitia*, une mise en œuvre à tâtons", in: *La Croix* (30.06.2016), 24-25.

24 "Ordinarily this will be done by proposing small steps that can be understood, accepted and appreciated, while including a proportionate sacrifice. Otherwise, by demanding too much, we gain nothing."

25 "In any event, let us recall that this discernment is dynamic; it must remain ever open to new stages of growth and to new decisions which can enable the ideal to be more fully realized." (AL 303)

26 Other interpretations are possible. For example, Bishop J. KOCKEROLS finds "the hermeneutical key" in no. 312, see *Pastoralia* [Brussels] (2016/6), 10-11, here 11.

choose no. 308 as the hermeneutical key, since it goes beyond details and specific situations. Taking a global view, the Pope appeals for a change of pastoral style:

> I understand those who prefer a more rigorous pastoral care which leaves no room for confusion. But I sincerely believe that Jesus wants a Church attentive to the goodness which the Holy Spirit sows in the midst of human weakness, a Mother who, while clearly expressing her objective teaching, "always does what good she can, even if in the process, her shoes get soiled by the mud of the street" [356 (EG 45)]. (AL 308)

3.3 A Synodality That Must Be Put into Practice

If, however, this change that the Pope desires is to be implemented, precise instruments are required. And since these do not yet exist, everything depends henceforth on the local Churches, which may perhaps sometimes be ill prepared for this task.

It is not by chance that Pope Francis spoke about synodality when he closed the second Synod. I quote his words: "It is precisely this path of *synodality* which God expects of the Church of the third millennium."[27] In 1964, the Catholic Church renewed its own self-understanding in a profound manner. The fruit of the reflections at the Second Vatican Council were set out principally in the Dogmatic Constitution *Lumen gentium.*[28] Much still remains to be drawn from its teaching, and not all of its explicit and implicit orientations have been put into practice. Although the word "synodality" is not found in that text, it is probably one of the terms that best express the options of the conciliar fathers for the future. In 2015, the Jesuit theologian John O'Malley noted with delighted astonishment the appearance of the neologism "synodality" in the English-speaking world, and saw this as a major sign of the reception of the Second Vatican Council.[29] The French-speaking world has become more accustomed to *synodalité* over the past decades.[30] Various speeches by Pope Francis have elaborated this synodality with

---

[27] FRANCIS: "Ceremony Commemorating the 50th Anniversary of the Institution of the Synod of Bishops: Address of His Holiness Pope Francis", 17.10.2015, available from http://w2.vatican.va/content/francesco/en/speeches/2015/october/documents/papa-francesco_20151017_50-anniversario-sinodo.html; accessed 08.12.2016.

[28] Not only in *Lumen gentium.* Éric Boone sees the diocesan synods as an important locus of the reception of the decree *Apostolican actuositatem*; cf. E. BOONE: "Le décret Apostolicam actuositatem: L'engagement des laïcs dans l'Église et dans le monde", in: *Revue Théologique de Louvain* 45 (2014), 562-593.

[29] J. O'MALLEY: "Family Gathering: Rediscovering the Role of the Synod of Bishops", in: *America* (20-27 July 2015).

[30] My colleague, the canon lawyer Alphonse Borras, has recently looked at this idea and analyzed three concrete realizations: the diocesan synod, the diocesan pastoral council, and the synod of bishops; cf. A. BORRAS: "Trois expressions de la synodalité depuis Vatican II", in: *Ephemerides Theologicae Lovanienses* 90/4 (2014), 643-666. I express my gratitude to him here for his suggestions and advice with regard to this *Document Épiscopat.*

a recurrent appeal to make this dimension of the Church more effective. It would be hard to find words more powerful than his in the discourse cited above, or than the following affirmation: "A synodal Church is a listening Church, conscious that listening 'is more than hearing.' It is a reciprocal listening in which each one has something to learn."[31]

With regard to the subject that concerns us here, we can draw a distinction between the local level and the regional or national level. Locally, we must search together for the places and the praxis that build up the future Church that integrates those who are divorced and remarried. If they are believers and are willing to take their place in the Church, they must play their own role in this reflection: this is a theological prerequisite that is based on the baptismal dignity and the divine mercy – it is not in any way a concession to relativism. Synodality, coupled with a collegiality in communion with the Pope, ought to be implemented in the way that is appropriate to episcopal conferences in every culture or context. This desire can be found in several statements made by bishops on the occasion of the two Synods, such as that by Bishop Johann Bonny of Antwerp.

> In their local Churches, the bishops must make a pastoral response to very diverse questions and needs. In the world as a whole, the faithful and their pastors have grasped the opportunity offered by the Synod and by the questionnaire to submit their urgent questions to the Pope and to the bishops. These questions differ from country to country and from continent to continent, but they have a common denominator, namely, the desire that the Church should situate itself in "*the great current of mercy*" (Instrumentum Laboris 68 and 106). It is important that the Synod should acknowledge the local bishops' room for action and their responsibility, which are necessary if they are to formulate adequate responses to pastoral questions in the portion of the people of God that is entrusted to them. The episcopal conferences have a particular role to play here.[32]

There is an echo of this in *Amoris laetitia* in a passage that I have quoted above. It is an orientation for the universal Church:

> Each country or region, moreover, can seek solutions better suited to its culture and sensitive to its tradition and local needs. For "cultures are in fact quite diverse and every general principle... needs to be inculturated, if it is to be respected and applied" [3]. (AL 3)

---

31 FRANCIS: "Ceremony Commemorating the 50th Anniversary of the Institution of the Synod of Bishops".

32 Cf. J. BONNY: *Synod on the Family: Expectations of a Diocesan Bishop*, Antwerp, 2015; available from http://www.associationofcatholicpriests.ie/wp-content/uploads/2014/09/SYNOD-ON-FAMILY-ENG.pdf; accessed 08.12.2016.

4 And now: "A Point of No Return"?

The Council speaks clearly about the task of the pastors and theologians, who are at a crossroads – just like the Church which they are helping to grow in the heart of humankind. The aim of my reflection was to examine *Amoris laetitia* in greater detail, in order to renew the proclamation of the Good News to the women and men, but also to the children, of our age. I have emphasized the new pastoral style of the Apostolic Exhortation, but also how hard it is to understand. It deserves to be worked on by all the baptized who are concerned about their life of faith – not only by priests, deacons, and lay persons who are involved in pastoral work.

"Something has changed in ecclesial discourse", said Cardinal Schönborn at the official presentation of the Exhortation on April 8, 2015. He called *Amoris laetitia* "above all a 'linguistic event,' just like *Evangelii gaudium*". The Archbishop of Vienna began his talk by bringing out the most important point, namely, the style of the text. I quote him:

> In these two hundred pages…, [t]his is his style, and it is his hope that aspects of life are spoken about in the most concrete way possible, especially with regard to the family, one of the most elementary realities of life.

The recurring antitheses between the doctrinal and the pastoral are obsolete. I quote Cardinal Schönborn once more:

> My great joy as a result of this document resides in the fact that it coherently overcomes that artificial, superficial, clear division between "regular" and "irregular", and subjects *everyone* to the common call of the Gospel, according to the words of St. Paul: "For God has consigned all to disobedience, that He may have mercy on all" (Rom. 11, 32).

The inverted commas around the word "regular" are not taken from *Amoris laetitia,* but I find the Cardinal's interpretation legitimate. Pope Francis does not relativize these categories. Rather, he displaces them and thus goes beyond them. "The celebrated 'pastorality' that has been so much discussed since Vatican II does not consist in a simple 'application' of doctrine."[33] We must identify the pastoral contexts in which we should invest, in order that the pastoral style promoted by Pope Francis can take on a concrete form. We may indeed be at a "point of no return", but it is still necessary for the priests, the deacons, and the lay persons who are involved in pastoral work to have the courage to "go out" from their habitual framework of action in order to innovate, in fidelity to the Gospel and listening to the Holy Spirit. Without concrete orientations, however, they may get lost; the Pope himself is aware of this.

---

33 C. THEOBALD: "Postface?, 322.

I believe that it is a matter of urgency now that each local Church should be allowed to make this text its own and to put it into practice in a way that is creative, innovative and in accordance with the culture or cultures of its members. Synodality is without doubt the most urgently required path from now on.

Accompanying Fragility: A Reading of *Amoris Laetitia* from a Pastoral-Psychological Perspective

Paul Galea

Chapter VIII of *Amoris laetitia* is dedicated to accompanying, discerning and integrating weakness (fragility). The subthemes cover the issues of *gradualness in pastoral care* (293-295); *discernment of "irregular" situations* (296-300); *mitigating factors in pastoral discernment* (301-303); *rules and discernment* (304-306); and *the logic of pastoral mercy* (307-312).

1 Understanding the Problem

Any breach of the marriage bond "is against the will of God". But the Church is also "conscious of the frailty of many of her children" (AL 291). The Church must accompany with attention and care the weakest of her children, who show signs of a wounded and troubled love, by restoring in them hope and confidence. To these situations the law of gradualness can be applied (FC 34). This is not a "gradualness of law" but a prudential exercise of free acts on the part of subjects who are not in a position to understand, appreciate, or fully carry out the objective demands of the law (AL 295).

The way forward suggested is that, "[t]he Church does not disregard the *constructive elements* in those situations which do not yet or no longer correspond to her teaching on marriage" (AL 292). The Church has to learn to *"discern"* the "seeds of the Word" also in the "imperfect situations" (cf. AL 76-77). It has to show *respect* also for those signs of love which in some way reflect God's own love (AL 294) to transform them into *"opportunities"* that can lead to the full reality of marriage and family in conformity with the Gospel. Central to *Amoris laetitia* is the issue of *discernment* qualified by *mercy*. In this regard one could speak of two types of discernment, one *pastoral,* the other *personal*.[1]

[1] B. PETRÀ: "I passi da Familiaris Consortio ad Amoris Lætitia: Da *Familiaris Consortio* ad *Amoris Lœtitia*: Un passo avanti nella continuità dell'attitudine pastorale: Il multiforme discernimento del capitolo VIII", in: *Il Regno* (12.05.2016).

Pastoral discernment is a process conducted by bishops as pastors, and by priests, in reaching a sound moral judgment based on the law. *Amoris laetitia* makes it clear that the aim is that of integration, where possible, within the Church's fold, and that there has to be a clear discrimination between one case and another. This means abandoning a "one size fits all" approach and relinquishing the temptation for easy recipes (AL 298).[2]

Personal discernment, on the other hand, is a personal decision also in the attempt to reach a moral judgment to be faithful to God's will but, this time, not separated from one's particular situation or context. This can be part of a process of spiritual direction or pastoral counseling.

These two types of discernment, though having different configurations, are not opposed to each other but complement each other. In the absence of general solutions one logically has to opt for the personal or particular ones. This is central to the exhortation. After all, this is why the faithful seek the help of a pastor to reach a decision. *Amoris laetitia* formally recalls to traditional doctrine when it states that, "[w]e also find it hard to make room for the consciences of the faithful, who very often respond as best they can to the Gospel amid their limitations, and are capable of carrying out their own discernment in complex situations. We have been called to form consciences, not to replace them" (AL 37).

The locus where *personal* and *pastoral* discernment takes place is the *internal forum.* This is where the pastor meets individual consciences. The internal forum is distinct from the external forum as the latter represents the public sphere or governance of the church. The internal forum has two distinct moments, one non-sacramental (e.g., pastoral counseling or spiritual direction) the other sacramental (Penance). Chapter VIII sees these two moments as belonging to the one and same *internal forum.* This distinction is implicit in this document and encouraged: "Individual conscience needs to be better incorporated into the Church's praxis in certain situations which do not objectively embody our understanding of marriage", and that "naturally, every effort should be made to encourage the development of an enlightened conscience, formed and guided by the responsible and serious discernment of one's pastor, and to encourage an ever greater trust in God's grace" (AL 303).

Personal discernment is not meant just to assist the faithful to apply the norm to a particular situation but to help the individual conscience seek the highest good possible in that situation, even though this does not always coincide with the ideal. In this sense, one could envisage two possibilities within the same internal forum itinerary. The first one would be the passage from the non-sacramental phase to the

---

2 BENEDICT XVI: "Address of His Holiness ... [at the] 7th World Meeting of Families," 02.06.2012, sub 5, available from https://w2.vatican.va/content/benedict-xvi/en/speeches/2012/june/documents/hf_ben-xvi_spe_20120602_festa-testimonianze.html; accessed 18.01.2017.

sacramental one, or penance. The other would be when there is no transition, such as when the process ends there in what is known as the conscience solution. In this case there is no need to go to confession in the absence of a moral guilt. This obviously calls for a deeper and more sophisticated form of reasoning together with an appropriate type of pastoral care.

2 Types of Pastoral Care and Functions

Pastoral care is expressed in multiple forms, on a general as well as on a particular level. On the personal level one distinguishes between confession, spiritual direction, and pastoral counseling. The distinction depends on the extent the problems are distanced from explicitly moral issues and verge into more psychological ones. Pastoral care in fact, holds together *religious*, *ethical,* and *psychological* perspectives.[3] Whatever the case, pastoral care more or less typically fulfills any one or more of its traditional functions which are healing, sustaining, guidance and reconciliation.[4]

Healing aims at overcoming some impairment by restoring the person to wholeness. It is advancing beyond the previous condition. Sustaining is helping a hurting person to endure and to transcend a circumstance in which restoration to a former condition or recuperation from that particular condition is either impossible or remote. Guidance is assisting perplexed persons to make confident choices between alternative causes of thought and action, when such choices are viewed as affecting the present and future state of the soul. Reconciliation seeks to re-establish broken relationships between fellow human beings, and between the individual and God. Historically, this has been dispensed through the sacrament of forgiveness and penance and spiritual accompaniment. A closer look at *Amoris laetitia* shows that these four functions are implicit and at times much explicit in its recommendations.

2.1 Healing

The Church, "conscious of the frailty of many of her children... must accompany with attention and care the weakest of her children, who show signs of a wounded and troubled love, by restoring in them hope and confidence..." (AL 291). "Let us not forget that the Church's task is often like that of a field hospital." (AL 291)

3 D.S. BROWNING: "Introduction to Pastoral Counseling": in R.J. WICKS/R.D. PARSONS/D.E. CAPPS (eds.): *Clinical Handbook of Pastoral Counseling,* vol. 1, expanded ed., New York: Paulist Press, 1993, 5-13, here: 5.

4 W.A. CLEBSCH/C.R. JACKLE: *Pastoral Care in Historical Perspective,* New Jersey: Jason Aronson, 1983, 32.

The "field hospital" is a small mobile medical unit, or mini hospital, that temporarily takes care of casualties on-site in military situations or times of disaster, before they can be safely transported to more permanent hospital facilities. The analogy is not a trivial one especially when one considers that "90% of combat deaths occur on the battlefield before the casualty ever reaches a medical treatment facility". Tactical Combat Casualty Care (TCCC) training has driven the casualty fatality rate down to less than 9%.[5] The lesson to be drawn from this analogy is that the closer the treatment available to the site of injury the more effective and dramatic the recovery.

2.2 Sustaining

"Some forms of union radically contradict this ideal, while others realize it in at least a partial and analogous way. The Synod Fathers stated that the Church does not disregard the constructive elements in those situations which do not yet or no longer correspond to her teaching on marriage." (AL 292) In this pastoral discernment, there is a need "to identify elements that can foster evangelization and human and spiritual growth" (AL 293).

2.3 Guidance

"Priests have the duty to 'accompany [the divorced and remarried] in helping them to understand their situation according to the teaching of the Church and the guidelines of the bishop…'" (AL 300). "What we are speaking of is a process of accompaniment and discernment which "guides the faithful to an awareness of their situation before God. Conversation with the priest, in the internal forum, contributes to the formation of a correct judgment on what hinders the possibility of a fuller participation in the life of the Church and on what steps can foster it and make it grow." (AL 300)

"Under certain circumstances people find it very difficult to act differently. Therefore, while upholding a general rule, it is necessary to recognize that responsibility with respect to certain actions or decisions is not the same in all cases. Pastoral discernment, while taking into account a person's properly formed conscience, must take responsibility for these situations. Even the consequences of actions taken are not necessarily the same in all cases". (AL 302)

2.4 Reconciliation

"There are two ways of thinking which recur throughout the Church's history: casting off and reinstating. The Church's way, from the time of the Council of

5 http://www.naemt.org/education/TCCC/tccc.aspx; accessed 18.01.2017.

Jerusalem, has always been the way of Jesus, the way of mercy and reinstatement…The way of the Church is not to condemn anyone for ever; it is to pour out the balm of God's mercy on all those who ask for it with a sincere heart… For true charity is always unmerited, unconditional and gratuitous." (AL 296) "No one can be condemned for ever, because that is not the logic of the Gospel!" (AL 297). "The logic of integration is the key to their pastoral care, a care which would allow them not only to realize that they belong to the Church as the body of Christ, but also to know that they can have a joyful and fruitful experience in it. They are baptized; they are brothers and sisters… " (AL 299)

3 Psychology and Pastoral Care

Since pastoral care holds together religious, ethical, and psychological perspectives, certain cases require more specialized activity, occurring in a more specialized setting and having specific goals. It tends to concentrate more on the psychological blocks and developmental impediments which seem to be stifling personal growth. This kind of pastoral care, which avails of psychotherapeutic skills, can still be considered to be pastoral particularly when it takes place within the moral and religious assumptive world associated with the Judeo-Christian tradition and anthropology, and particularly, within church related activities. These are reflected in the general and fundamental perceptions of the good.

The use of psychology should help us understand the way the persons that are being helped developed the personalities and characters they have. But these psychologies cannot rightfully tell the client which moral and religious values he or she should hold once freedom is gained to make new decisions. In these occasions individuals often need and request the time and attention of the pastor in a structured relationship that may occur within the context of a specific time commitment and designated place. This activity is referred to as pastoral counseling.

3.1 Pastoral Counseling

The focus in pastoral counseling is more on the individual and his or her problems. As Browning explains, "[t]he major new development that has motivated the founding of the pastoral counseling movement has been the insight that most human problems are various mixtures of both conflicted human freedom (psychological) and moral and religious discernment".[6] It is very significant to note these same concepts being reiterated by Pope Francis: "I encourage the faithful who find themselves in complicated situations to speak confidently with their pastors or with other lay people whose lives are committed to the Lord. They may not al-

[6] D.S. BROWNING: "Introduction to Pastoral Counseling", 6

ways encounter in them a confirmation of their own ideas or desires, but they will surely receive some light to help them better understand their situation and discover a path to personal growth. I also encourage the Church's pastors to listen to them with sensitivity and serenity, with a sincere desire to understand their plight and their point of view, in order to help them live better lives and to recognize their proper place in the Church." (Al 312)

3.2 Pastoral Counseling and Other Forms of Companionship

Pastoral counseling shares many things in common with other forms of personal companionship, including "secular" or normal counseling. While equally interested in focusing on the person's relationship with others and with the world, pastoral counseling does so with an eye to the faith dimension in everyday life. It is a self-analysis with a Christian introspection. This is also distinct form spiritual direction and confession as the focus in the latter is mainly on the person's relationship with God. In the sacrament of reconciliation, the process then shifts on a conscientious moral judgment and penance.

3.3 What is Counseling?

Popular portrayals of the psychologist or psychiatrist have encouraged strange and mystical images of the counseling process. Images of couches, bearded men reading the minds have fostered this myth and have persisted till this day. What constitutes counseling is to a large extent a function of the personal characteristics of the counselor and the client, the training and the orientation of the counselor, and the nature of the presenting problem. Cutting across the personal uniqueness of counselor and client, or the various theoretical models employed (behavioral, psychodynamic, existential) counseling is essentially an interpersonal process of a helping sort.[7]

In counseling a professional attempts to help the client or patient develop or rediscover his or her problem-solving skills by using a variety of techniques and approaches that are initiated within the context of this helping, facilitating relationship and interpersonal exchange. The counseling process cannot go forward successfully unless the following essentials are present: (1) a workable, warm counseling relationship, (2) an atmosphere of acceptance and understanding, (3) a show of confidence by the counselor that the client can develop or rediscover problem-solving skills if given enough time and support.

---

7 Cf. R.D. PARSONS/R.J. WICKS: *Counseling Strategies and Intervention Techniques for the Human Services*, 4th edition, Boston: Allyn & Bacon, 1994.

3.4 The Counseling Relationship

A common fear that accompanies a new counselor, and oftentimes the non-professional one, is how to fit the image presented in the popular literature. This creates false expectations by both counselor and client. In soliciting the client's trust and faith in the person's skills, the counselor makes the mistake of pretending to have knowledge and experience one does not possess. This could be particularly true such as when the one doing the counseling is a priest and to whom people attribute competencies related to his sacred status which he does not necessarily have. In spite of this, he is expected to counsel people very often with the limited training the seminary gives him, or with the training in moral theology. What the counselor is expected to do in the first place is to demonstrate interest and bind the relationship. The simplest and most immediate way to do so is to be *authentic*, *respectful,* and *supportive* of the needs of the client.

To be authentic as a counselor implies to shed all role expectations or images. Care and concern are not scripts to be followed as in a play. True concern is to strike a bond with the person and to feel for that person in that moment. The authentic counselor is one who does not hide behind roles, titles or degrees or who uses mechanical responses to fool the clients. Authenticity is to show genuine, appropriate spontaneity while being non defensive. It is a deep form of congruency between thoughts, feelings and actions.

To respect another requires that one truly appreciates and values that person simply because he or she is a human being. This demands looking beyond the behavior of a client (which we may disdain) to the basic goodness and value intrinsic to the person.

This respect is communicated by attending to clients, demonstrating unconditional regard for them (while not necessarily condoning their actions), and accepting their uniqueness. This paves the way to the next step which is to provide the supportive, facilitative environment required for therapeutic growth.

3.5 Acceptance and Understanding

In order for the client to grow and to identify and develop problem-solving skills, the counselor must provide the client with the opportunity to talk. Such an opportunity is promoted by the counselor's use of active listening skills. Although active listening is tedious, time consuming and sometimes ineffective it remains one of the most important operations the counselor must undertake. This goes against seeking quick and easy explanations of a client's statements or behavior. If clients are encouraged to express their opinions, describe their anxieties, fears or anger without fearing retaliation or rejection they will begin to see the counselor as a nonthreatening person. This leads to establishing an efficient working relationship.

It is important for a counselor to provide the conditions that encourage the client to open up and disclose personal information. However, for the relationship to develop the client must feel that the counselor has been attending and accurately understanding what is being disclosed. This process is achieved through the counselor's effective use of *reflection* and *clarification*.

One of the functions of a counselor is to assist clients to better understand their own feelings about certain things. When a reflection is employed, it may be in the form of a question or by means of a simple statement that conveys the counselor's observations. The use of a question in response to a client's question is a reflective technique. In reflecting a question back to a client, the objective is to encourage the expression of personal opinions. In addition, it functions to discourage dependence on the counselor while indicating there are various ways to deal with a problem. As a technique, reflection is important because it forces clients to review their own reflections. Before clients can change or modify their ways of dealing with the world, they must be led to appreciate the intensity of their own feelings, and in this process independence and self-awareness are encouraged.

A second form of feedback comes from the counselor. By listening and withholding judgment, while reflecting on the client's questions, the counselor is communicating a message by indicating that what is said will not bring rejection and that the best route to self-understanding is self-examination. More specific feedback is transmitted in the form of clarification and requests that the client elaborate or expand on particular topics.

3.6 Develop Problem-solving Skills

Once the client's difficulties are defined and the relationship established as a supportive, caring exchange, the process can enter the acting stage. In this stage the counselor's attention s drawn to the identification of a number of alternatives or solutions (i.e. problem solving), supporting the client's attempts at problem resolution (i.e. call to action), and finally, moving the relationship toward increased client independence and eventual termination (i.e. review and termination).

Often, the needed course of action appears obvious to the counselor. However, since the counseling process is more than a mere advice giving, the counselor should resist simply supplying all the answers. If the client is one who is used to accept advice from others – clergy, physician, family – in his own environment, that person would most likely not need counseling. The counselor should increase the client's problem-solving skills and sense of independence so as to be better prepared to avoid or resolve problems in the future. To be effective, the counselor must avoid putting the client in a dependent position. Rather, it is a form of working with the person to discover ways of handling the problem. The counselor should refrain from giving advice except when basic information is required.

Following the identification of potential problem-solving strategies, the client must be encouraged to test these approaches. During this stage of counseling, the counselor needs to be extremely supportive of the client's efforts and not just of the achievements. It is also helpful for the counselor to assist the client in setting clear, concrete goals that are presented in a small, graded fashion. Such a graded approach will increase the probability of success at each level of action.

A brief counseling relationship usually does not result in the formation of a lasting bond between counselor and client. Despite this, the manner in which the relationship is terminated is an important and delicate process. Relationships with clients should not be abruptly or matter-of-factly terminated, as they may cause feelings of rejection or that their problem is of no real importance to the counselor. The counselor may suggest that counseling is available for any future need and remaining questions before bidding the client goodbye.

4 Points of Convergence between the Counseling Process and *Amoris Laetitia*

Having examined the basic characteristics and processes related to counseling it is worth attempting comparisons and points of convergence with the exhortation both implicitly and explicitly. This will be done by quoting excerpts from the text.

4.1 Empathic Understanding

In the first place, the Pope emphasizes the need "to avoid judgments which do not take into account the complexity of various situations" and "to be attentive, by necessity, to how people experience distress because of their condition" (AL 296). Jesus "expects us to stop looking for those personal or communal niches which shelter us from the maelstrom of human misfortune, and instead to enter into the reality of other people's lives and to know the power of tenderness. Whenever we do so, our lives become wonderfully complicated" (AL 308).

4.2 A Non-judgmental Attitude

The divorced who have entered a new union can find themselves in a variety of situations, which should not be pigeonholed or fit into overly rigid classifications leaving no room for a suitable personal and pastoral discernment (cf. AL 298). For this reason, a pastor cannot feel that it is enough simply to apply moral laws to those living in "irregular" situations, as if they were stones to throw at people's lives. This would bespeak the closed heart of one used to hiding behind the church's teachings, "sitting on the chair of Moses and judging at times with superiority and superficiality difficult cases and wounded families" (AL 305).

The church's pastors, in proposing to the faithful the full ideal of the Gospel and the Church's teaching, must also help them to treat the weak with compassion, avoiding aggravation or unduly harsh or hasty judgments. The Gospel itself tells us not to judge or condemn (cf. Mt 7,1; Lk 6,37) (cf. AL 308).

4.3 Unconditional Positive Regard

Respect for the person and acceptance can be expressed when each person is helped to find his or her proper way of participating in the ecclesial community and thus to experience being touched by an "unmerited, unconditional and gratuitous" mercy (AL 297). "At times we find it hard to make room for God's unconditional love in our pastoral activity. We put so many conditions on mercy that we empty it of its concrete meaning and real significance. That is the worst way of watering down the Gospel." (AL 311)

4.4 Empowering for Action

The call for personal responsibility and the empowerment for action are implicit in the exhortation document. However, a few months following the publication it was deemed necessary to make this more explicit, with the Pope's endorsement of the bishops of the Buenos Aires Pastoral Region to a question on this issue. In the first place, it is not convenient to speak of "permission" to receive the sacraments, but rather a process of discernment accompanied by a pastor. It is a "personal and pastoral" (AL 300) discernment.[8]

5 Conclusion

It could be said that *Amoris laetitia* makes a very clear paradigm shift in taking due distance from the external forum as well as from the confessional and move towards personal discernment, autonomy and responsibility. This paradigm resembles very closely the one adopted in the counseling process. In establishing a warm relationship in an atmosphere of acceptance and understanding, given enough time and support, the client can develop or rediscover problem-solving skills. It is perhaps this paradigm shift which is most difficult for some pastors especially those who are trained to use more the confessional rather than the counseling room. However, this does not short change the Gospel ideals and values as

[8] "Directive of the Bishops of the Buenos Aires Pastoral Region to the Regional Clergy", September 5, 2016, available from https://www.lifesitenews.com/images/pdfs/Basic_Criteria_for_the_Application_of_Chapter_VIII_of_Amoris_Laetitia__September_5__2016.pdf; accessed 08.01.2017.

they still form an integral part of personal discernment. The convergence of these recommendations with the counseling techniques is no mere coincidence but the result of experience, common sense and the acknowledgment that free and mature choices are more effective and long lasting than simple compliance with the law.

A second reaction that could be envisaged is the realization that in order to do proper counseling one needs adequate training as well as sufficient time and right disposition. This might also appear intimidating to some. Besides, by empowering laypeople to do this job pastors might feel their capacity to influence others further weakened.

Accompanying fragility starts very early in the life of the couple. *Amoris laetitia* speaks about issues which are of major concern to counseling, such as helping people to commit to marriage (cf. AL 33, 39), fostering personal and affective maturity (cf. AL 40-41) and integrating emotions in one's life, while curbing on their disruptive effect (cf. AL 143-146). But these go beyond the scope of this paper.

Needless to say that the main thrust of this exhortation is in the title itself, "The Joy of Love". *Amoris laetitia* follows in the footsteps of *Gaudium et spes* in integrating conjugal love with the call for salvation. The Pope makes this very explicit when he states that, "[a] love lacking either pleasure or passion is insufficient to symbolize the union of the human heart with God" (AL 142). This is especially true when accompanying fragile or broken relationships. Studies on commitment capture this concept very well as they bring together the emotional and the volitional faculties in a relationship while continuing to feel psychologically "attached" to it. Understood in this way, commitment sees these two categories of intent and attachment as inseparable.[9] *Amoris laetitia* also reiterates that to have one without the other not only makes commitment incomplete but indeed a painful one.

This development poses also a big challenge when applied to concrete situations in such as in canonical legislation governing the Church's external forum. The role of human love in marriage, how this influences matrimonial consent, and what happens when this is absent, are issues that have still to find their proper place in matrimonial jurisprudence. While the gap between the ideal and the real will always remain, the pastoral approach always starts from the latter. In this regard pastoral psychology can be of utmost help not only in understanding and promoting loving relationships but also, particularly in cases of fragility, in offering useful insights to the external forum as well.

---

9 C.E. RUSBULT/D. FARRELL: "A Longitudinal Test of the Investment Model: The Impact on Job Satisfaction, Job Commitment and Turnover of Variations in Rewards, Costs, Alternatives and Investments", in: *Journal of Applied Psychology* 68 (1983), 429-438.

Reflections on Commitment and the Indissolubility of Christian Marriage

Christine Galea

The idea of commitment is central to a marital relationship and provides the foundation for a lasting and joyous partnership. Happy marriages – those which are fruitful, rewarding and nurturing – are built upon mutual and loving respect for the spouses' individuality, but also upon an unwavering fidelity and respect towards the commitment made at the altar. Marriage, as instituted by God, is a faithful, exclusive, lifelong union between one man and one woman, joined in an intimate loving bond; but without a fundamental commitment to love and faithfulness, a marriage has little chance of happiness. When honoured, the commitment itself can be a springboard for growth, progress and mutual development.

Yet, what exactly does commitment entail? What purpose does it serve? How binding is it? And does commitment towards one's spouse over-ride any other commitments a person may have in his or her life? These are some of the considerations I will try and reflect upon in this paper, in which I will try to bring life to these questions through my own personal reflection, based upon my own experience.

Some years ago, in 2010 to be precise, the citizens of Malta were faced with the unenviable task of deciding whether or not divorce legislation would come into effect in our country. The people were firmly divided into three camps: the pro-divorce, those against, and a rather numerous section of the population who were referred to as "floaters". I formed part of an anti-divorce campaign group and we set about valiantly trying to garner as many votes as possible, putting forward some very valid arguments – not only from a religious, but also from a sociological point of view – that marriage is indissoluble, and should remain so.[1] Sadly, just over a year prior to this time, my 27-year long marriage broke down and I was currently undergoing separation proceedings; this had further strengthened my resolve to campaign against the introduction of divorce. In spite of the fact

1 The referendum result went in favour of the proposed Bill and divorce became legalized in Malta on 25 July 2011.

that we had endured a long and difficult struggle to save our marriage, to no avail, I stood firm in my conviction that even though our love had somewhat waned and we were heavily challenged by unsurmountable problems in our relationship, we were still bound by the promises we had pledged at the altar.

During that period of time, I was reading for a Master's degree in Family Ministry. One of the study units I was following was "Theology of Marriage and Sexuality" and my professor, who knew how vociferously, and just how strongly, I was campaigning against the introduction of divorce, set me a different assignment to the rest of the class. In an effort to encourage me to look objectively at both sides of the coin, he requested me to write a paper considering indissolubility as an ideal, rather than a norm – which I did (obtaining a very good grade, might I add).[2] Yet I rebelliously declared in a *nota bene* at the end of my paper, that "my assignment does not reflect my own personal convictions". This, in spite of the fact that, much to my surprise, the research I conducted on the subject, resulted in the discovery of some very convincing exceptions – on three levels: scriptural, theological and juridical – to the doctrine of indissolubility.[3] I would not be fair to myself if I did not acknowledge the fact that, in spite of my hard-held position, I continued to reflect upon the topic long after the assignment was handed in and the result published.

The Value of Commitment Today

As things stand, the way in which the trend is going in our contemporary society, shows clearly that the ideal of commitment to an indissoluble marriage is being severely challenged from every corner, even within the church itself, and there are several newly-held positions, particularly those which try to substantiate that admission to the sacraments for co-habiting couples, or for those persons who enter a second civil marriage – in the case of persons who had previously contracted a valid, sacramental marriage – may be considered as a possibility; and this, not only from the purely legalistic standpoint.[4] The Synods of 2014 and 2015

---

2 C. GALEA: *Indissolubility of Marriage as God's Gift and an Obligation to Fulfill the Task of Commitment: The 'Personalist' Perspective – Is it an Ideal?* Paper presented as part-fulfillment for the Master's Degree in Family Ministry, University of Malta, January 2011.

3 To list these exceptions is outside the remit of this paper. The main sources for my research were K.R. HIMES/J. CORIDEN: "The Indissolubility of Marriage: Reasons to Reconsider", in: *Theological Studies* 65 (2004), 453-499 and M.G. LAWLER: "Divorce and Remarriage in the Catholic Church: Ten Theses", in: K. SCOTT/M. WARREN (eds.): *Perspectives on Marriage: A Reader*, Oxford: Oxford University Press, 2007, 374-388.

4 I am referring to the stand taken by Cardinal Walter Kasper *et alii* during the 2014 and 2015 Synods, when they appealed to early church practice in order to support their view of pastoral practice with civilly remarried and divorced persons and their suggested "toleration" of civil

addressed these and other situations, which Pope Francis refers to as "situations of weakness or imperfection".[5] Taking up this point in his Post-Synodal Apostolic Exhortation, *Amoris laetitia*, he speaks about the importance of accompaniment and discernment in each and every individual case; yet he insists that "this discernment can never prescind from the Gospel demands of truth and charity, as proposed by the Church".[6] John Locke, the English philosopher, once said that "where there is no law, there is no freedom".[7] Pope Francis considers the law itself to be "a gift of God which points out the way ... [and which] can be followed with the help of grace".[8] But it is not "enough simply to apply moral laws" when dealing with wounded spouses and families.[9] Saint John Paul II, in his Apostolic Exhortation, *Familiaris consortio*, had proposed the "law of gradualness",[10] which Pope Francis regards as "a gradualness in the prudential exercise of free acts on the part of subjects who are not in a position to understand, appreciate, or fully carry out the objective demands of the law".[11] Francis confirms this point in his Exhortation, seeing such situations as requiring "a constructive response", in order that this response may serve as an opportunity to lead couples "to the full reality of marriage and family in conformity with the Gospel".[12]

Commitment and the Indissolubility of Marriage

I would like to go on by presenting briefly a couple of points on the relation between commitment and the indissolubility of marriage. To begin with, a look at the etymology of the word "commitment" reveals that the word finds its roots in the Latin *committĕre* – *com*, with, *mittĕre*, to send. To make a commitment is to make a promise or a pledge, to *actually* send my word into another person; when I make a commitment, I dwell in the other person by means of my word. This is an act in itself. The obligation is produced by the promise itself, for the words

marriages following divorce, in line with the Eastern Orthodox theology of *oikonomia* of salvation.

5 FRANCIS: *Amoris Laetitia* [henceforward AL], 12.02.2015, 296, available from https://w2.vatican.va/content/dam/francesco/pdf/apost_exhortations/documents/papa-francesco_esortazione-ap_20160319_amoris-laetitia_en.pdf; accessed 20.12.2016.

6 AL 300.

7 J. LOCKE: *Second Treatise of Civil Government*, available from http://www.constitution.org/jl/2ndtr06.htm (accessed 20.05.2017), Chapter 6, Section 57.

8 AL 295.

9 AL 305.

10 JOHN PAUL II: *Familiaris Consortio*, 22.11.1981, available from http://w2.vatican.va/content/john-paul-ii/en/apost_exhortations/documents/hf_jp-ii_exh_19811122_familiaris-consortio.html (accessed 20.05.2017), 34.

11 AL 295.

12 AL 294.

of promise are "performative". They actually *do* what they say.[13] A willingness to commit has a bearing upon a person's character formation. Sociologists Nock, Sanchez and Wright state that a willingness to commit to exclusivity in marriage signals an acceptance of normative guidelines for good interpersonal behaviour and points to credibility as a dependable, mature citizen. This is because marriage commitment contains both interpersonal and community messages.[14]

According to Margaret Farley, we recognize an obligation to act in a certain way within some particular individual and social commitments which we make, more frequently than in any others. Furthermore, society's tolerance or non-tolerance of certain forms of commitment have a bearing upon how seriously a person honours his or her commitments. For example, does the general tolerance of divorce make the desire for lasting commitment stronger or less strong?[15] Farley outlines various commitments which a person may have, according to his or her role as son or daughter, brother or sister, husband or wife, father or mother: it could be that one is committed to a particular social cause or to one's religious beliefs; to a value, such as beauty, justice, peace; or to caring for a family member who may be ill or disabled; indeed, one may be committed to genuine personal growth. Farley argues: what if lack of commitment and dedication to the marriage or to the family on the part of one spouse impinges upon the personal growth or upon the values and beliefs of the other? Should the second spouse be obliged to remain faithful to the marital covenant?[16] After all, as stated by Günter Virt, "life is always richer than any law or regulation that can be formulated, and our God is a God of life".[17]

Marriage, as the paradigm form of all human friendships should, at its best, mature into an increasingly indissoluble bond between persons.[18] The bond starts

13 J.R. SEARLE: *Speech Acts: An Essay in the Philosophy of Language*, Cambridge, MA: Harvard University Press, 1969, chapters 2 and 3.

14 S.L. NOCK/L.A. SANCHEZ/J.D. WRIGHT: *Covenant Marriage: The Movement to Reclaim Tradition in America*, New Brunswick, NJ: Rutgers University Press, 2008, 79.

15 M.A. FARLEY: *Personal Commitments: Beginning, Keeping, Changing*, revised edition, New York: Orbis, 2013, 5. In this book, Farley explores how commitments, rooted in the story of God's love, are acts of free choice and acts of love by people who strive to be faithful to whom they have claimed to love.

16 M.A. FARLEY: "The Meaning of Commitment", in: K. SCOTT/M. WARREN (eds.): *Perspectives on Marriage*, 344-356. It seems to me that Farley is implying that a lack of commitment of one party necessarily justifies a lack of commitment on the other. Personally, I feel that if one spouse no longer remains committed, then the other spouse would not be justified in saying "I too am no longer committed".

17 G. VIRT: "Moral Norms and the Forgotten Virtue of *Epikeia* in the Pastoral Care of the Divorced and Remarried", in: *Melita Theologica*, 63/1 (2013), 17-34.

18 The bond is indissoluble from the moment of consent, but commitment should increase as the marital relationship matures. As the teaching on the indissolubility of the bond was articulated

to exist at the time when the spouses make a valid consent, but this does not necessarily mean that they are conscious and open to the broader meaning of their marital contract from the very moment they say "yes" on the altar. It is up to the spouses to cultivate and nurture the marital bond in order for their relationship to mature. They have a moral responsibility to keep the attachment alive, in the sense that it thrives as an ideal to work towards, making the commitment something which is to be lived day-by-day and not just a formality which is pronounced once and for all at the altar. Commitment to marriage is a free act of the will, but it is a psychological and emotional attachment as well. If this attachment is not present, or if it is left to die, then the act of committing becomes a mere formality, or perhaps even a lie, for the spouse who loses interest in the marriage and wishes to opt out. Yet, even in the event of marriage breakdown, it is possible for the other spouse to remain faithful to the promise taken at the altar, notwithstanding that this poses great challenges.

One can only hope that together, the spouses will grow to appreciate the intrinsic reality and value of the sacrament and live out its implications through their commitment towards one another, as well as through their participation as a couple in the sacramental and ministerial life of the Christian community. Indeed, Christian marriage is a call for the spouses to commit more deeply to their faith and to grow in their relation to one another in Christ. As Bernard Cooke argues, "the more profoundly Christian a marriage-relationship becomes, the more inseparable are the two persons as loving human beings and the more does their relationship sacramentalize the absolute indissolubility of the divine-human relationship as it finds expression in the crucified and risen Christ".[19] This is a "process", and an awareness of such a process "and the general acceptance of evolution ... are hallmarks of modern Western thought".[20] By taking a look at contemporary church teachings, it is very clear that, from a theological perspective, interesting attempts have been made in recent years to develop a theology of marriage which is less static and less rooted in Canon Law, and which is more evolutionary, dynamic and realistic in nature, as the concept of "process" marriage entails.[21] This should give

by Pope Pius XI in 1930, in his Encyclical Letter, *Casti connubii*, 31 December 1930, paragraphs 31-35, "this inviolable stability, although not in the same perfect measure in every case, belongs to every true marriage"; it is a perpetual and indissoluble bond which is not subject to any civil power.

19 B. COOKE: "What God Has Joined Together...", in: K. SCOTT/M. WARREN (eds.): *Perspectives on Marriage*, 335-343.

20 Ibid.

21 P. GALEA: *Marriage: Quo Vadis?* Paper presented at the National Conference organized by ProgettImpenn, Malta, 7 February 2009. Of course, it is a valid point that Canon Law is itself rooted in the theological reflection on marriage, particularly in *Gaudium et spes* (nos. 47-52). In this document, the council fathers give impetus to help us understand the development of

more leeway to pastors in addressing contemporary issues in marriage and theology could be a further inspiration in developing a matrimonial jurisprudence.[22]

Amoris Laetitia on Commitment

This particular development in the theology of marriage and the family started with Vatican Council II, and is reflected in later papal statements and other magisterial documents, the most recent contribution being *Amoris laetitia*, which in my opinion, provides us with a road-map on how to make marriage a living icon of the love of God. In line with this idea of marriage as a process, Francis points out that the marital decision has to be frequently renewed (since longer life spans now mean that close and exclusive relationships must last for several decades), and that love has to be transformed by passing through several different stages of the life-cycle. For this reason, couples need to "come up with a shared and lasting life project".[23] In order for this project to be realized, the spouses need to foster habits that will help them build a fruitful marriage and rear a strong family, as they learn to commit themselves to find a new honesty in their communication, and foster a deep sense of vocation. The church needs to accompany married couples more and more during this "process" and, integrated into Francis' pastoral plan, is the idea to support spouses "through their instruction in the sacramental grace available to them and in particular, how they can more fully tap into this well-spring of grace, in order that they may experience the power of the sacrament to strengthen their relationship, not just as an idea but as a reality that impacts their daily married life".[24]

Amoris laetitia suggests a pastoral change of approach towards those spouses who, in spite of all their goodwill and effort, are unable to face "the challenge of revealing themselves and coming to know who the other person truly is",[25] with the sad result that their marriage breaks down. Francis taps into the treasure of the church's teachings and confirms that its moral teachings have not changed. He does not say what is a sin and what is not, but he speaks the language of

the church's change of emphasis from too many legal implications, towards a more pastoral orientation with regard to marriage and family in the modern world.

22 J. SELLING: "Marriage as a Sacrament: The Evolution of an Idea", in: R. BURGGRAEVE/K. DEMASURE/M. FOKET/P. WEBER (eds.), *Marriage – Divorce – Remarriage: Challenges and Perspectives for Christians*, Leuven: Peeters, 2007, 157-172.

23 AL 163.

24 ARCHDIOCESE OF PHILADELPHIA: *Pastoral Guidelines for Implementing Amoris Laetitia*, 01.07.2016, available from http://www.collationes.org/doctrinalia-ductu/themata-actualium/item/2334-pastoral-guidelines-for-implementing-amoris-laetitia-archdiocese-of-philadelphia; accessed 20.05.2017.

25 AL 210.

integration. Naturally, an "objective sin" cannot be flaunted as if it were part of the Christian ideal, but for the persons in question whose situation is irreversible, "there can be some way of taking part in the life of the community".[26] After embarking upon a path of discernment, together with the priest who guides them, the spouses must evaluate their particular circumstances to reach a "liveable" goal. Conscious of today's mentality in which autonomy plays such a prominent role, the pope is shifting the responsibility on to the spouses, who need to shoulder more their personal responsibility in arriving at a decision in conscience. This perspective is perfectly traditional, and Francis is encouraging the church to pay more importance to a merciful approach towards couples who are encountering difficult times in their marriage, by stating that "there is need to avoid judgements which do not take into account the complexity of various situations".[27] The accent is on the mercy of God. For reasons known only to them and acknowledged by their spiritual guide, if two people are unable to live up to their marital commitment, and as a consequence, the indissolubility of their marriage becomes an unrealistic burden, then it rests fully upon their shoulders to discern their circumstances honestly and follow the path which God will, in his infinite love and mercy, lead them. This confirms exactly to what extent the pastoral discipline of the church continues to develop in order to suit "the signs of the times" (*Gaudium et spes*, 4).

In *Amoris laetitia*, Francis speaks about the truth about indissoluble marriage, yet, he recalls that we should always have an understanding for people's frailties. This development is very much in line with the approach adopted by Jesus Christ, who always distinguished between the truth and human weakness; and without mincing His words, taught us to respect the former and understand the latter. This particular approach had already been present in earlier teachings of the Magisterium before Francis, however, I am grateful that *Amoris laetitia* has re-inforced this line of thought, because it has helped me to reflect anew upon the balance between lasting commitment/indissolubility of marriage and pastoral solicitude. Yes, commitment is important and it is binding. However, how can one deal with situations when there is no love left in a marriage, or when one spouse is abandoned by the other who has opted out of his or her commitment? Indeed, it is a reflection of God's mercy to enter into a meaningful pastoral dialogue in order to help people who live these difficult situations to "distinguish elements in their lives that can lead to a greater openness to the Gospel of marriage in its fullness".[28]

If I am to be completely sincere, even to myself, I still hold strongly that marriage is indissoluble, and that in the event of a marriage breakdown, legal separation or a declaration of nullity are the only viable options for a practising

---

26 AL 297.

27 AL 296.

28 AL 293.

Catholic. After discerning my own life circumstances, I have chosen to remain living in fidelity to my marital vows, yet I cannot but acknowledge and appreciate that other people may wish – or be compelled – to make different choices. For myself, I remain a firm believer that marriage as a state of life should be a permanent attachment, and I think it could well be that failure to realize such commitment as an inherent element of the marital union, is today leading to the decline in the unity and indissolubility of marriage and encouraging the current attitude towards divorce. In this respect, I feel strongly that it is our duty as Catholics to carry on encouraging couples to continue to grow throughout their lifetimes in a faithful, committed, loving union; to accompany couples in order that they may "enrich and deepen their conscious and free decision to have, hold and love one another for life".[29] As Pope Francis points out, today, it is becoming more and more commonplace for spouses to reason that, if things do not turn out as they wish, there are sufficient grounds for their marriage to end. If this were the case, no marriage would last.[30]

I would like to conclude by saying that in the course of my pastoral work, I am often called upon to minister to couples in difficulty and I have grown to appreciate that dialogue and discernment are key elements of this ministry. In this very delicate and human context, I have come to recognize more the value of moving from trying to "solve everything by applying general rules or deriving undue conclusions from particular theological considerations"[31] to a renewed awareness that reflection upon every individual case and dialogue can serve as an invaluable tool to allow people whose marriages are in trouble to experience the love and mercy of God, even through their extenuating circumstances.

---

29 AL 217.

30 AL 237.

31 AL 2. Traditional moral theology has always taught that the concrete circumstances of one's life differ from person to person and sometimes eliminate the gravity of one's actions.

Canonical Imperatives of Pastoral Care in *Amoris Laetitia* concerning Catholics with Irregular Marital Status

Vincent Mynem C. Sagandoy

1 Introduction

The church has always maintained in her doctrinal position the unitive and indissoluble properties of marriage between a man and a woman and its exclusive ends, that is, for the goods of the spouses and for the procreation and education of children from which the Christian family is established.[1] However, faced with the changing legal systems of countries around the globe and the proliferation of rights group against all forms of discrimination, the church is fully aware of the situations of Catholics who have irregular marital status. The Pope, in his recent Post-Synodal Apostolic Exhortation *Amoris laetitia*, makes no rebuttals but presents these situations as pastoral challenges. He even offers some pastoral insights to the church as to how these situations are to be undertaken with great care. In so doing, the Pope has once again proven himself as a pastor of the universal church by expressing his concern regarding Catholics in irregular marriages with a firm assertion that they are still members of the church and hence are qualified recipients of pastoral care.[2] It is basically from this pronouncement that pastoral care to Catholics in irregular marital situations has been chosen as the topic of this paper.

Briefly, this paper will first present a canonical understanding of pastoral care. Second, the canonical status of Catholics in irregular marriages will be elaborated. Third, the paper will move on to demonstrate the right to pastoral care of Catholics in irregular marital status. And fourth, the obligations to pastoral care to Catholics

---

1 See *Catechism of the Catholic Church: Modifications from Editio Typica*, New York: Doubleday, 1997, 1601 (henceforward CCC); see also *Code of Canon Law: Latin-English Edition*, Washington, DC: Canon Law Society of America, 1989, can. 1055 (henceforward CIC 1983); see also *Lumen gentium*,11 and *Gaudium et spes*, 48.

2 See FRANCIS: *Post-Synodal Apostolic Exhortation Amoris Laetitia*, Pasay City, Philippines: Paulines Publishing House, 2016, 243; henceforward abbreviated as AL.

in irregular marital status will also be demonstrated featuring the canonical imperative of structuring the pastoral care of Catholics in irregular marital situations.

2 Understanding Pastoral Care in the Code of Canon Law

One of the principles for the revision of the Code of Canon Law that were approved by the Synod of Bishops held in 1977 deals specifically with pastoral care.[3] James A. Coriden beautifully summed up this principle in this manner:

> Pastoral care is to be fostered above all, and to that end both the legislation and its application are to be characterized by charity, moderation, humanity, and equity as well as justice. Exhortation and persuasion are to be preferred to an insistence on rights.[4]

The Code of Canon Law is the very instrument that ensures order in the way pastoral care is undertaken visibly and concretely in the church. In the words of St. Pope John Paul II, when he promulgated the Code of Canon Law of 1983, he wrote:

> Since the Church is organized as a social and visible structure, it must also have norms: in order that its hierarchical and organic structure be visible; in order that the exercise of the functions divinely entrusted to it, especially that of sacred power and of the administration of the sacraments, may be adequately organized; in order that the mutual relations of the faithful may be regulated according to justice based upon charity, with rights of individuals guaranteed and well-defined; in order, finally, that common initiatives undertaken to live a Christian life ever more perfectly be sustained, strengthened and fostered by canonical norms.[5]

Viewed from this perspective, pastoral care in the church is neither a mere activity by and upon the discretion of sacred pastors or ministers nor a mere lip-service concept from the church hierarchy. To a canonist, pastoral care is simply the *cura animarum* of all Christian faithful.

It is intriguing, however, that when Catholics with irregular marital status have been characterized as such with a specified way to better pastoral care, it suggests that their very status remains to be a major issue in the church. In this case it is

---

3 "Acts of the Commission for the Revision of the Code", in: *Communicationes* 2 (1969), 77-85, trans. Roger Schoenbechler, O.S.B. quoted in: J. HITE/D.J. WARD: *Readings, Cases, Materials in Canon Law: A Textbook for Ministerial Students,* Collegeville, MN: The Liturgical Press, 1990, 86.

4 J.A. CORIDEN: *An Introduction to Canon Law*, rev. ed., New York-Mahwah, NJ: Paulist Press, 2004, 39.

5 JOHN PAUL II: "Apostolic Constitution *Sacrae Disciplinae Leges*", in *Code of Canon Law: Latin-English Edition,* Washington, DC: Canon Law Society of America, 1989, xxxi.

imperative to recall what has been the position of the church as regard those in irregular marriages.

3 The Canonical Status of Catholics in Irregular Marriages

It was really unfortunate that long before *Amoris laetitia*, Catholics in irregular marriages had to suffer much from exclusion and isolation in the church. First, they were anathemized at the Council of Trent. That is to say, Catholics in irregular marriages were excommunicated and hence forbidden to receive the Sacraments unless the censure is remitted.[6] The irregular situation of such marriage had to suffer for three centuries until the Second Vatican Council. The Council finally has chosen not to use the term again.

Second, at the aftermath of the Second Vatican Council, the status of those in irregular marriages has changed but not until St. John Paul II issued his Apostolic Exhortation *Familiaris consortio* in 1981. In this document, the Pope identified the concerned Catholics as those in "trial marriages", *de facto* free unions, civil marriages without the benefit of the sacrament, divorced but not remarried, and divorced and remarried civilly.[7] The mark of *anathema* was not mentioned but replaced with a specific restriction. Rereading the aforesaid document, only Catholics who divorced and remarried civilly were specified as living in a state of sin for having contradicted the indissolubility of marriage which is the sign of the Covenant and fidelity to Christ. Being in such a state, they were restricted from receiving Holy Communion.[8] The ecclesial communities are simply obliged to encourage them to share more fully and fruitfully in the life of the church as they remain part of it. As with regard to the first three marriage irregularities, no restriction was ever mentioned in the document but only encouragement from both pastors and the ecclesial communities to help them regularize their status in the church.

Third, the restriction towards those in irregular marriages were even promulgated in the New Code of Canon Law in 1983. The canon which deals with restriction on the right to Holy Communion has become the area of debate and even disagreements between pastors and their parishioners, between canonists and pas-

---

6 See COUNCIL OF TRENT, Session XXIV in: N.P. TANNER (ed.): *Decrees of the Ecumenical Councils,* vol. 2:*Trent to Vatican II*, London: Sheed & Ward-Washington DC: Georgetown University Press, 1990, 754-755; see also the definition of the term *anathema* in the canonical tradition in E.N. PETERS (ed.): *The 1917 Pio-Benedictine Code of Canon Law,* San Francisco: Ignatius Press, 2001, can. 2257.

7 JOHN PAUL II: *Apostolic Exhortation* Familiaris Consortio, 1981, 79-84, available from http://w2.vatican.va/content/john-paul-ii/en/apost_exhortations/documents/hf_jp-ii_exh_19811122_familiaris-consortio.html; accessed 10.08.2016.

8 Ibid. 84.

tors, among the clergy themselves especially between the conservatives and the progressives, and among the lay faithful themselves especially between the traditionalists and the liberals. This canon states: "Those who have been excommunicated or interdicted after the imposition or declaration of the penalty and others obstinately persevering in manifest grave sin are not to be admitted to Holy Communion."[9] What this canon refers to as "obstinately persevering in manifest grave sin" is about a person who has committed a sin that is objectively grave, is habitually persisting in doing it despite warning from pastors or church authorities, and such sin is publicly known.[10] In other words, a person is a public sinner, as most commentators would agree, when he/she persists into it just like a hard criminal, a drug syndicate, a corrupt public official, a prostitute, an abortionist, to name a few. It is, in fact, the application of this canon that had placed those Catholics in irregular marriages into this canonical stigma. Some canonists even made a stark generalization that manifest sinners contemplated in this canon would mean to include all Catholics in any irregular marital situations mentioned in *Familiaris consortio* and hence restricted from partaking of the Eucharistic Bread.[11] The reasons for such restriction were those articulated in the same document which states:

> They are unable to be admitted thereto from the fact that their state and condition of life objectively contradict that union of love between Christ and the Church which is signified and effected by the Eucharist. Besides this, there is another special pastoral reason: if these people were admitted to Holy Eucharist, the faithful would be led into error and confusion regarding the Church's teaching about the indissolubility of marriage.[12]

However, as was already expounded above, the restriction and the reasons for such restriction should affect only Catholics who are divorced and remarried civilly.

The same restriction was extended to include the exercise of certain ecclesiastical responsibilities which was introduced into the *Catechism of the Catholic Church* approved by St. Pope John Paul II in 1992.[13] The restriction from the right to receive Holy Communion was also affirmed by the Congregation for the Doctrine of Faith in 1994 to the disappointment of bishops who called for some le-

---

9 CIC 1983, can. 915.

10 See J.M. HUELS: "Title III The Most Holy Eucharist [cc. 897-958]", in: J.P. BEAL/J.A. CORIDEN/T.J. GREEN (eds.): *New Commentary on the Code of Canon Law*, New York-Mahwah, NJ: Paulist Press, 2000, 1110.

11 For further reading of the problematics of this canon see A.N. DACANAY: *The Sacraments of Initiation Baptism, Confirmation, Eucharist: A Commentary on cc. 849-958 of the Code of Canon Law*, Pasig City, Philippines: Anvil Publishing, 2006, 133.

12 JOHN PAUL II: *Familiaris consortio*, 84.

13 See CCC, 1650.

niency.[14] In the final analysis, some canon law commentators place all Catholics in any of the irregular marital situations mentioned in *Familiaris consortio* as manifest sinners or public sinners and subsequently have been denied of their right to receive Holy Communion and to exercise certain ecclesial responsibilities. This interpretation and application of this canon has, in turn, haunted some dioceses around the globe with civil or labor law suits as a consequence.

Finally, in *Amoris laetitia*, it is noticeable that the tone of the document regarding those in irregular marriages has changed. The Holy Father has made it clear: "[I]t can no longer be said that all those in 'irregular' situations are living in a state of mortal sin and are deprived of sanctifying grace."[15] Perhaps the change in the tone can be traced back to the intervention of the German bishops during the recent synods on marriage and family that suggested the omission of the nuancing of those in irregular marital status "as sinful, pure and simple and accordingly calls for conversion".[16] Subsequent to this pronouncement, any ecclesial restriction pertaining thereto has been quashed with the encouragement that they are "to remain part of the ecclesial community".[17] From the hindsight of a canonist, the change of the tone for Catholics in irregular marriages suggests "a point of no return" and hence a subsequent change in canonical status. This is to say precisely that Catholics in irregular marital situations are regular Catholics and what is irregular is their marital situation. Such change, however, does not mean a compromise in the church teaching on Christian marriage and family life. The change suggests rather a more pastoral discretion on the part of local bishops in their respective dioceses as well as pastors and pastoral workers due to "mitigating factors and situations"[18] in each case of irregular marriage. In this regard, pastoral care for Catholics in irregular marriages merits a canonical evaluation underscoring precisely its characteristics as a right and an obligation.

---

[14] See CONGREGATION FOR THE DOCTRINE OF FAITH: *Letter to the Bishops of the Catholic Church Concerning the Reception of Holy Communion by the Divorced and Remarried Members of the Faithful*, 1994, available from http://www.vatican.va/roman_curia/congregations/cfaith/documents/rc_con_cfaith_doc_14091994_rec-holy-comm-by-divorced_en.html; accessed 31.08.2016.

[15] AL 301.

[16] GERMAN BISHOPS' CONFERENCE: *The Vocation and Mission of the Family in the Church and Contemporary World: Response by the German Bishops' Conference to the Questions Aimed at a Response to and an In-Depth Examination of the* Relatio Synodi *in the Preparation Document for the XIV Ordinary General Assembly of the Synod of Bishops of 2015*, 2015, available from http://www.dbk.de/fileadmin/redaktion/diverse_downloads/dossiers_2015/2015-Synode-Lineamenta2015-Antworten-engl.pdf; accessed 25.09.2016.

[17] AL 243.

[18] AL 301.

4 The Right to Pastoral Care of Catholics with Irregular Marital Status

Every Catholic is endowed with rights and obligations in the church which the Code strongly affirms. "By baptism one is incorporated into the Church of Christ and is constituted a person in it with the duties and rights which are proper to Christians in keeping with their condition, insofar as they are in ecclesiastical communion and unless a legitimately issued sanction stands in the way."[19] When referring to Catholics in irregular marriages, their subsequent reinstatement into the ecclesial community since *Amoris laetitia* suggests that they too are qualified in what the canon affirmed. In this sense, it becomes imperative to identify which areas in ecclesial life they may claim the right to pastoral care.

The right to pastoral care is enshrined in the Code in this manner: "The Christian faithful have the right to receive assistance from the sacred pastors out of the spiritual goods of the Church, especially the word of God and the sacraments."[20] The emphasis of this canon is the basic nurturance of the Christian faithful through the Word of God and the reception of the sacraments. A good Catholic despite his/her unfortunate marital status should often find the Word as means for his/her spiritual nourishment. The Holy Father himself attests to this simple truth when he recalls the story of the Samaritan woman and the woman caught in adultery and how Jesus showed compassion and closeness to them despite their frailties.[21] What the Holy Father suggests is a real encounter with Jesus which can be sought through reading and reflection of the Word of God.

Reception to the sacraments is another manifestation of this right. When referring to the condition of those in irregular marriages, reception to the sacraments reflects a more intense personal encounter with Jesus which the Holy Father wishes them to experience more often. The right to the Sacrament of Reconciliation, for instance, is an encounter with Jesus who heals one's wounds. Such encounter should lead one to real conversion and communion with the church and above all with God.

The right to receive the Sacrament of Holy Matrimony is another encounter with Jesus who sustains one's relationship with one's spouse. For Catholics in irregular marriages, real conversion comes into effect through the reception of this sacrament but not too soon. As the Holy Father insists, they are to undergo a process of discernment with the accompaniment of their pastors, pastoral workers, and the ecclesial community. Should their irregularity merit no legal procedure, then they are qualified to receive the sacrament. If undergoing a legal procedure

---

[19] CIC 1983, can. 96.

[20] CIC 1983, can. 213.

[21] AL 38.

especially for the nullity of their previous marriage, by all means they have to approach the proper ecclesiastical authority. For those whose nullity application is denied, the reception to the sacrament of matrimony is unfortunately not available. Such situation does not mean they are excluded from the rest of the ecclesial community. By all means possible, they should remain part of the ecclesial community since they are not excommunicated as the Holy Father assures them.

Still another encounter with Jesus is through the reception of Holy Communion. This encounter is highly commendable as it is a sacrament of Jesus's presence in one's life. It was unfortunate, however, that for a long period of time, Catholics in irregular marriages were not able to enjoy this right due to their canonical status as public sinners. Having been overturned of their status in *Amoris laetitia*, the Holy Father provides for the conditions which the concerned Catholics are to undertake with the pastoral accompaniment of their pastors, other pastoral workers, and the ecclesial community. In this regard, these marriages have to be first regularized should there be a possibility. Otherwise, due discretion is directed to pastors and ministers regarding this right should there be an imminent public scandal to occur and to the detriment of the good order of the ecclesial community.

In the light of the Code and *Amoris laetitia*, the right to pastoral care does not belong to the inviolable rights pertaining to the protection of human dignity. It is a right available to Catholic faithful but subject to certain conditions that need to be fulfilled in each case of irregular marriage. Such conditions, however, need the accompaniment of those whom pastoral care is entrusted.

5 The Obligation to Pastoral Care: Its Agents, its Features, and its Structure

5.1 The Agents of Pastoral Care

In the Code, the obligation to pastoral care is an exercise of sacred powers. "Those who have received sacred orders are qualified, according to the norm of the prescripts of the law, for the power of governance, which exists in the church by divine institution and is also called the power of jurisdiction."[22] This norm affirms the qualification for those eligible for any ecclesiastical position, that is, the required ordination to sacred orders. Hence the bishop is entrusted the pastoral care of a diocese, the *parochus*, which can either be a priest or deacon, is entrusted the care of a parish. Any cleric can also be appointed to the pastoral care of a chaplaincy, a rectory, or any Christian community. In fact, most ministerial functions in the church require ordination to sacred orders as a qualification.

22 CIC 1983, can. 129 §1.

The second paragraph of the same norm also contemplates the cooperation of lay faithful in pastoral care. "Lay members of the Christian faithful can cooperate in the exercise of this same power according to the norm of law."[23] Thus, pastoral care of a parish, a chaplaincy, a rectory, or any Christian community can also be entrusted to a lay administrator. There are also other offices in the church specified by law whereby lay persons are eligible to perform pastoral care.

The Code may sound discriminatory but the emphasis here is neither about the distinction between the clergy and the laity nor about the clergy being the only eligible agents of pastoral care, while the laity being simply the cooperators. When it comes to pastoral care, the Code wishes to highlight the value of accountability in the church especially when it comes to the *cura animarum* of the Christian faithful. Thus in the church, the demise of pastoral care is often accounted to those to whom pastoral care has been entrusted, while its success, the credit goes to the whole ecclesial community.

Being accountable to the *salus animarum* of all Christian faithful, the Holy Father felt the need to issue *Amoris laetitia* as a response to the recently concluded synods on family and to reiterate what the church firmly believes. In this document, the Holy Father urges better pastoral care to ensure the stability of Christian marriage and family especially in a society where "they are given scarce attention in political agendas"[24] and that perceives the church still clinging on to an "old-fashioned and outdated option".[25] He also underscores the pastoral care of those in irregular marital status to be undertaken with "careful discernment and respectful accompaniment".[26] The Holy Father further exhorts every Christian faithful to be a participant of this common endeavor in upholding the ideals of Christian marriage and family. Thus, accountability for the *cura animarum* of the Christian faithful does not belong only to the ordained ministers but to every Christian faithful and ecclesial community. In order to avoid ambiguity in undertaking the responsibility of pastoral care for those concerned Catholics, it is imperative to specify those features in ecclesial life that really make up the *cura animarum* pertaining to Catholics in irregular marriages in the light of *Amoris laetitia*.

5.2 The Features of the Obligation to Pastoral Care for Catholics with Irregular Marital Status

Rereading *Amoris laetitia*, the Holy Father has underscored important features of pastoral care for Catholics in irregular marriages. First, the Holy Father affirms what the Synod Fathers have recommended as pastoral accompaniment for

23 CIC 1983, can. 129 §2.

24 AL 44.

25 AL 53.

26 AL 243.

Catholics with wounded and troubled relationships and restoring them with hope and confidence.[27] This would, of course, involve pastoral visitation, dialogue with them that would bring them to "greater openness to the Gospel".[28] Pastoral experience suggests that it is on this very respect that the longing for the Word of God is ignited. Other events to suffice their longing for the Word will follow through their reintegration into the ecclesial community and participation in the sacred liturgy as well as in catechetical instructions and counseling. To a canonist, their right to the Word corresponds to the teaching function of the church that involves precisely the ministry of the Word. Such ministry is undertaken through homilies, preaching, catechetical instructions, Catholic education, counseling, and other forms of evangelization.[29] Obviously, this feature of pastoral care as an obligation belongs not only to pastors but includes the cooperation of other pastoral workers such as catechists, lay preachers, lay evangelists to name a few and the cooperation of lay movements or associations and the whole ecclesial community.

Second, the Holy Father suggests a process of discernment.[30] This is basically an obligation directed primarily to sacred pastors. Dialogue with these concerned Catholics has to continue. It is on this way that pastors learn the specific situations of each irregularity and discern with them towards regularizing their situation through the reception of the sacrament or through legal procedure and finally leading them towards the reception of the sacraments. If either situations are not possible, at least, through the same process of discernment pastors should lead them still to the sacrament especially to penance and Holy Communion with due regard to the scandal that may incur and to the detriment of the good order of the ecclesial community. Practically the end result of this process is for the sanctifying function of the church to effect also to Catholics in irregular marriages. This sanctifying function includes the celebration of Sacred Liturgy and the administration of the Sacraments and sacramentals.

Finally, the integration into the ecclesial community stands to be the featured direction of pastoral care in *Amoris laetitia* concerning Catholics with irregular marital status. This integration has to take effect only after the process of accompaniment and discernment has been fulfilled. In this way, the misunderstanding that the church might "desist from proposing the full ideal of marriage, God's plan and all its grandeur", [31] and that the faithful and even pastors themselves

---

27 AL 291.

28 AL 293.

29 J.A. CORIDEN: *The Parish in Catholic Tradition: History, Theology and Canon Law*, New York-Mahwah, NJ: Paulist Press, 1997, 94.

30 AL 296-306.

31 AL 307.

might be led into a "kind of relativism"[32] with regard to the church teaching on marriage and the demands of the Gospel are to be avoided. The Holy Father then recalls the behavior of the Good Shepherd to be reckoned with. "Jesus himself is the shepherd of the hundred, not just of the ninety-nine."[33] In this regard, having been entrusted the *cura animarum* of the faithful, every pastor, every pastoral worker, and every ecclesial community is not to judge or condemn anyone as the Gospel demands[34] and not to be arbiters of grace but its facilitators.[35] This feature of pastoral care corresponds well to the governing function of the church. When referring to Catholics with irregular marital status, those entrusted with pastoral care have to know them by visiting their homes and sharing their cares and anxieties.[36] This simple gesture reflects the pastor's administrative skill especially when it comes to pastoral care to those who were isolated due to unfortunate circumstances in life. But then again, integration is more felt when the obligation to pastoral care involves the cooperation of lay pastoral worker, lay movements and associations, and the ecclesial community.

The features pertaining to the obligation to pastoral care demands the church to be more flexible in the *cura animarum* of Catholics in irregular marriages. The church does acknowledge now the various mitigating circumstances that practically made them decide to stay in such irregularity. In the meantime the church needs also to be firm of the ideals of Christian marriage and family which it teaches to be true as one can find in Holy Scriptures and in the tradition of the church. Thus the features as illustrated in this section are not to be taken for granted by those whom pastoral care has been entrusted to ensure sincerity of the church towards those Christian faithful with irregular marital status. Furthermore, to ensure the same sincerity of the church, it seems imperative to illustrate this obligation to pastoral care into the organization or structure especially of the local church which the Code provides.

5.3 Structuring Pastoral Care in the Church in the Light of the Code of Canon Law

It is commendable that in the United States, the United State Conference of Catholic Bishops (USCCB) reported that some bishops were led to establish specific planning committees composed of both laity and clergy as well as those involved in marriage and family life apostolates in response to the challenges of

32 Ibid.

33 AL 309.

34 See AL 308.

35 See AL 310.

36 J.A. CORIDEN: *The Rights of Catholics in the Church*, New York-Mahwah, NJ: Paulist Press, 2007, 59.

Amoris laetitia.[37] Other bishops were also reported to have gone "re-evaluating and changing diocesan office structures in response to Pope Francis' emphasis on ministry to families".[38] These initiatives may perhaps concretize the church's sincerity towards those in irregular marital status but none really would meet the real predicaments of these concerned Catholics than structuring the very pastoral care that directly involves to their cause.

From a canonist perspective, structuring a specific pastoral care for Catholics in irregular marital status means the creation of an office or commission committed to such a noble cause. For the diocesan level, the Code stipulates the importance of the diocesan curia that assists the bishop in the governance of the whole diocese. "The diocesan curia consists of those institutions and persons which assist the bishop in the governance of the whole diocese, especially in guiding pastoral action, in caring for the administration of the diocese, and in exercising judicial power."[39] This norm assumes that the diocesan bishop is in need of assistance to manage the various episcopal tasks in his diocese.[40] Oscar V. Cruz, while he was the archbishop of the Archdiocese of Lingayen-Dagupan, Philippines, made a great deal of observations as to how the local churches in the Philippines set their curia. In his book, *Curia Management*, which was published in 2005, he illustrates several models of managing the curia. Cruz suggests pastoral action, administration, and judiciary, which are explicitly specified in the Code to be the three main sections of the numerous institutions and offices in the diocese.[41] Briefly, the section on pastoral action "consists in planning and implementing, monitoring and coordinating the teaching, sanctifying, and serving ministries/apostolate in the diocese".[42] In the administration section, management of all temporal goods in the diocese are undertaken; and management of formal and or administrative cases through diocesan tribunal and cases or issues undertaken in a permanent or *ad hoc* diocesan Board of Conciliation and Arbitration belong to the judiciary section.[43]

---

37 USCCB: *Report on the Reception and Implementation of* Amoris Laetitia *in the United States*, September 2016, available from www.usccb.orgissues-and-actionmarriage-and-familyuploadReport-on-Reception-and-Implementation-of-Amoris-Laetitia-in-the-United-States.pdf; accessed 01.10.2016.

38 Ibid.

39 CIC 1983, can. 469.

40 O.V. CRUZ: *Curia Management*, Dagupan City, Philippines: ALD Publications, 2005, 11.

41 See ibid., 12. See also B.A. CUSACK: "Title III The Internal Ordering of Particular Churches [cc. 460-572]: Chapter II The Diocesan Curia [cc. 469-494]"; in: J.P. BEAL/J.A. CORIDEN/T.J. GREEN (eds.): *New Commentary on the Code of Canon Law*, 623.

42 O.V. CRUZ: *Curia Management*, 12.

43 Ibid.

Since the area of interest is about pastoral care, the section on pastoral action will be the *locus* where perhaps erecting an office or commission on Catholics with irregular marital status is a possibility. Such an office will concern itself specifically on the apostolate toward those in irregular marital status. This office will be, most likely under an episcopal vicar[44] or a "bishop's delegate"[45] who is to be appointed to undertake the pastoral endeavor on the bishop's behalf with executive power over this specific area of apostolate. Aside from the appointment of an episcopal vicar or bishop's delegate, staff members of a pastoral team composed of lay specialists are also imperative to ensure the cooperation of the laity in pastoral care. In fact, there are a lot of willing lay persons with specialization in social work, psychiatry, counselling, catechesis and etc. who are simply waiting to be discovered and to be invited for such noble apostolate in the church. More importantly, it will be under such commission/office to plan and implement, monitor and coordinate the teaching, sanctifying, and serving ministries/apostolate in the diocese or parish in reference to the canonical situations of Catholics with irregular marital status. In other words, it is the responsibility of this commission/office to finalize any directive to be approved by the diocesan bishop and to be issued to all pastors in the diocese. The purpose of this directive is to guide pastors to be able to elucidate with the concerned persons about the church doctrine on marriage and family, to explain their irregular marital status, and to clarify their canonical status underscoring their rights and obligations in the ecclesial community where they have a domicile or quasi-domicile.

In the parish level, there is no norm suggesting the creation of such office but one can perhaps align the various parochial apostolates with the diocesan structure. After all, most of the pastoral action happens in the parish level where the Christian faithful are visible as either recipients and/or participants of pastoral care. In this regard, a commission for Catholics with irregular marital status maybe created in the parochial level. With the parish priest or his delegated cleric, lay or religious as the chairperson, some members of the ecclesial community might volunteer or be selected to be part of the commission staff. The parish priest has to note also about the importance of some specialists who can be very beneficial in such area of apostolate.

The Holy Father also notes the assistance of association of lay faithful or lay movements in matters pertaining to marriage and family life and perhaps more

---

44 An episcopal vicar is an optional figure in the diocese at the discretion of the diocesan bishop who mandates him to have executive power over a specific territory in the diocese, specific ministry or apostolate, a specific rite or group. See CIC 1983, can. 479 §2.

45 A bishop's delegate is a lay counterpart of an episcopal vicar. See B. LUCAS/P. SLACK/W. D'APRICE: *Church Administration Handbook*, Adelaide: St. Pauls Publications, 2011, 144.

with regard to the pastoral care of those in irregular marital situation.[46] The Couples for Christ and the El Shaddai Communities, both Catholic charismatic movements that originated in the Philippines, can testify to the important role of lay association/movements in parishes. Pastoral experience shows that Catholics with irregular marital status felt more comfortable with such groups as they are welcomed as full members with rights and responsibilities despite their unfortunate status. In this regard it is commendable that parish priests should take notice of the possible collaboration of lay movements and associations in this common endeavor. Again, these possibilities in the parochial level ensure the cooperation of lay faithful in the pastoral care of those in irregular marital situation and consequently confirm that obligation to pastoral care does belong to the whole ecclesial communities.

To conclude, whether on the diocesan or parochial level, the necessity to create such office or commission is imperative. It is through such an commission/office that pastoral care requiring careful discernment and respectful accompaniment for those in irregular marital situation and their families can be more visible in the church.

6 Conclusion

When pastoral care to Catholics with irregular marital status becomes a topic of discourse in the ecclesiastical or even in the public sphere, it seems to imply that pastors have no credibility in undertaking the endeavor or worse they have no idea as to how to do it. There must be truth in it. Many pastors in deciding whether or not to provide pastoral care in cases involving Catholics in irregular marriages simply rely on what the Code and instructions from the Roman Curia have to say, plain and simple. This assumption is not to downplay the importance neither of the Code nor of the Roman Curia. What is simply being emphasized here is that there are situations where the *salus animarum* still stands as the supreme law of the church that the Code or any directives from the hierarchy have to consider. Or in other words, pastoral care is for the *salus animarum* of all Christian faithful whatever situation they may be.

Moreover, with *Amoris laetitia*, perhaps the church is being led to a point where Catholics in irregular marriages are no more an issue but an opportunity for the church to show that there is room for God's mercy to dwell in the hearts of every Christ faithful starting from the pastors, pastoral workers, and the whole ecclesial communities. This assumption, of course, does not mean to undermine the fundamental obligation of the church to be firm in upholding the ideals of

[46] AL 229.

Christian marriages. The church has to teach all Christ's faithful regardless of their situation about these ideals that it firmly believes to be true. Nonetheless pastoral care remains fundamental in realizing this opportunity of God's mercy to be made more visible to every Christian faithful despite someone's unfortunate canonical situation. Indeed, it is an opportunity towards a point of no return.

Via Caritatis – Pastoral Care of the Divorced and Remarried: An Ecumenical Comparison in the Context of *Amoris Laetitia*[1]

Michaela C. Hastetter

All the church's pastoral activity is governed by the command to love our neighbour, and this applies to the pastoral care of the divorced and remarried. Pope Francis has deliberately re-formulated this in *Amoris laetitia* and has expressly invited us to set out on a *via caritatis*.[2] The pastoral care of charity in regard to the divorced and remarried has been given very different emphases in the three major Christian denominations (Protestant, Orthodox, Catholic), and we shall examine and compare them here in a little more detail before broadening our view towards *Amoris laetitia*. We shall start from the hypothesis that the divergent practical forms arise from different theological hermeneutics in the three Christian denominations regarding the biblical ban on divorce. Each of the three, of course, claims to be essentially a *via caritatis* in terms of pastoral practice. In conclusion we shall address the question as to where, ecumenically, we should situate *Amoris laetitia* in regard to the pastoral care of the divorced and remarried.

1 A Comparative View of the Remarriage of Divorced Partners in the Different Denominations

1.1 Protestant

In Protestant teaching marriage has no sacramental character. While its significance cannot be reduced entirely to the level of a "culturally evolved form of co-

---

1 Translation into English by Graham Harrison.

2 FRANCIS: *Post-Synodal Apostolic Letter "Amoris Laetitia" on Love in the Family*, Vatican City: Vatican Press, 2016, 306, in what follows: AL.

habitation",[3] it remains ultimately a "worldly thing" (Martin Luther)[4]. In Protestantism, by contrast with the Catholic understanding, second, third and fourth marriages are permitted practically without restriction, even if, in principle, the indissolubility of marriage is affirmed in virtue of the biblical precept.[5] In the constitutional documents of the *Evangelische Kirche in Deutschland* (EKD) divorce is permitted only in exceptional, proven cases.[6] This means that the collapse and breakdown of shared conjugal life is regarded as a legitimate ground for dissolving the legal bond of marriage, even when, in principle, the parties had entered into it "for life". Marriage may be destroyed by "the power of sin", which is why Reinhard Frieling stresses that "divorce, from the Protestant point of view, is not rejected in cases where the legal continuance of the wrecked marriage would cause more harm than divorce to those concerned".[7] Ultimately it seems that the decision as to whether divorced persons should be allowed to enter a new marriage lies in the hands of the pastor, male or female.

What the EDK documents declared to be an exceptional phenomenon has since assumed dramatic proportions in the Protestant church. Andrea Burgk-Lempart, a Protestant pastor and theologian, is therefore right to raise the question: "Are we really coping adequately with the situation, considering the high numbers of divorces? Divorce is no longer the marginal issue suggested by EDK statements; it can no longer be treated piecemeal, case by case."[8] In the view of this Protestant theologian, both theology and church have "for the most part failed to take account, in their reflections on marriage, of the sudden, rapid rise in di-

---

3 A. BURGK-LEMPART: *Wenn Wege sich trennen: Ehescheidung als theologische und kirchliche Herausforderung*, Stuttgart: Kohlhammer, 2010 (Praktische Theologie heute; 111), 128.

4 M. LUTHER: "Tischreden 777", in: K. ALAND (ed.): *Luther Deutsch: Die Werke Martin Luthers in neuer Auswahl für die Gegenwart*, vol. 9: *Die Tischreden*, Göttingen: Vandenhoeck und Ruprecht, ^{4}1983, 276.

5 Cf. A. BURGK-LEMPART: *Wenn Wege sich trennen*, 103.

6 Cf. EKD (ed.): *Gottes Gabe und persönliche Verantwortung: Zur ethischen Orientierung für das Zusammenleben in Ehe und Familie 1997*, available from http://www.ekd.de/EKD-Texte/zusammenleben_1998_verantwortung4.html; accessed 02.12.2016, here from chapter 4: "The ending of a marriage is an emergency solution, a final way out once the communion between two people is irreparably destroyed. In such cases it should also be accepted in a Christian understanding, because no one can be absolutely pinned down to his failure and guilt; every person should be given the chance of a new start. The decision to end a marriage may be a necessary step on the way to self-respect. Part of such self-respect is the acceptance of one's failure. It cannot be part of the evangelical understanding of marriage to maintain a meaningless obligation, a mere façade." [This and all following translations from the German are by the translator of this article.]

7 R. FRIELING: *Katholisch und Evangelisch: Informationen über den Glauben*, Göttingen: Vandenhoeck und Ruprecht, 2006^{9} (Bensheimer Hefte; 46), 50.

8 Cf. A. BURGK-LEMPART: *Wenn Wege sich trennen*, 104.

vorce numbers in the 1970s and the rapidly changing social context."[9] Not least, this trend can be observed in marriage-sermons, which increasingly appear to be stripped of all theological or dogmatic content: "Increasingly, any talk of marriage being a divine ordinance, or of the lifelong community of the spouses, or of the indissoluble nature of marriage, is dying out as time goes on."[10] In general, as Burgk-Lempart says, there is a certain "poverty of theological utterance"[11] on the Protestant side, which in turn leads to a certain insecurity on the part of pastors (male and female) in their pastoral work.

Provisional summary: in Protestantism, divorce is allowed and remarriage is unrestricted, although originally it was regarded as an emergency measure in cases where a marriage had been destroyed and it seemed no longer possible for the spouses to persevere with a shared conjugal life. Nowadays, from the point of view of pastoral theology, a certain lack of clarity is observable in the theology of marriage, which leads to insecurity of various kinds in pastoral practice.

1.2 Orthodox

In the Orthodox Church there is considerable emphasis on the fundamental indissolubility of marriage. Marriage is held to be a *mysterion*; as in Catholicism, it is a sacrament. "Where man and wife fashion their lives together in the bond of married love, the radiance of God shines forth."[12] The married couple see themselves as an ikon of divine love; according to John Chrysostom they are a kind of theophany, reflecting something, in their community of love, of the divine radiance that was captured in the light from Mount Tabor.[13] In some strict Orthodox traditions, therefore, the bond of marriage endures beyond death – which means that remarriage is out of the question. This does not apply, however, to the whole of Orthodoxy. Whereas in the Catholic rite the couple confer the sacrament on each other, the Orthodox rite is significantly different: the Orthodox couple receive the sacrament of marriage from the church. Here the sacramental marriage comes about only through the priest's uttered pronouncement, in connection with the so-called "coronation", which is interpreted in several ways: it is part of the

9 Here and in what follows ibid. 70.

10 D. PRÖSSDORF: *Die gottesdienstliche Trauansprache: Inhalt und Entwicklung in Theorie und Praxis*, Göttingen: Vandenhoeck und Ruprecht, 1999, 231.

11 A. BURGK-LEMPART: *Wenn Wege sich trennen*, 70. The following observations are also from Burgk-Lempart.

12 T. PFAMMATTER: *Geschiedene und nach Scheidung wiederverheiratete Menschen in der katholischen Kirche: Kriteriologische Fundamente integrierender Praxis*, Freiburg/Schweiz: Universitätsverlag, 2002 (Praktische Theologie im Dialog; 23), 119.

13 Cf. ibid. 119 with reference to J. CHRYSOSTOMOS: "In Epistola I ad Corinthios Homilia XXVI", in: J.-P. MIGNE (ed.): *Patrologiae cursus completus / Patrologia Graeca 61*, Paris: Migne, 1862, 215.

theology of creation (the human being as the crown of creation, and man and wife as king and queen, bound together in love); it is martyrological, where the crown is interpreted as a crown of martyrdom – this is underlined in the coronation by the *troparion* (hymn) in honour of the martyrs; and it is also eschatological, in that the crowned marriage endures beyond death, in which it comes to perfection.[14]

The connection with the mystery of love and the rite of coronation plays an important role, on the Orthodox side, in the discussion about exceptions with regard to marriage indissolubility. Even if marriage is per se indissoluble and divorce is contrary to the divine will, divorce is an issue because of human sinfulness and can be granted as such. In this connection Grigorios Larentzakis points out that separation or divorce is "not a 'normal' development of relations between the marriage partners"; it is "always regarded as a failure, a collapse, a destruction; it is a last resort, an emergency measure that is nonetheless taken legitimately, within the church's pastoral ambit".[15] Anastasios Kallis supports this view, arguing in the context of love as *mysterion*: "When marriage ceases to be a mystical community of love, the Orthodox church does not insist on the continuance of a pseudo-community that is a cruel façade of an ideal."[16] In such a case Kallis regards the sacramental substance of marriage as lost; to continue it would be to prolong a profane reality.[17] Here divorce corresponds to an acknowledgement and formal declaration that a marriage has been destroyed by sin.[18] In the course of

---

14 Cf. I. MOGA: "'Verbinde sie in Eintracht, kröne sie zu einem Fleische… ': Aspekte eines orthodoxen Eheverständnisses", in: *Theologisch-praktische Quartalschrift* 163 (2015), 356-360, here especially 358-359 and the literature to which he refers.

15 G. LARENTZAKIS: "Ehe, Ehescheidung und Wiederverheiratung in der orthodoxen Kirche", in: *Theologisch-praktische Quartalschrift* 125 (1977), 250-261, here 259.

16 A. KALLIS: "Mysterium der Liebe: Ein Beitrag zum orthodoxen Eheverständnis", in: H. ENGELHARDT (ed.): *Die Kirchen und die Ehen*, Frankfurt: Lembeck, 1984 (Ökumenische Rundschau; 46), 44-55, here 54.

17 Cf. T. PFAMMATTER: *Geschiedene,* 142.

18 Cf. ibid. 148. The Catholic Church does not accept the notion that a marriage can die. Joseph Ratzinger sees such a notion as the result of "the dissolution of being and consciousness, which means that only what is present to someone's consciousness is really valid for him. In practice this is a regression to the pre-Christian and Roman theory of consensualism. Once the consent ceases to exist, according to this theory, the marriage has ceased to exist. Theories like this, asserting that a marriage can be dead and hence no longer exist, are forms of phenomenologism that reduce the human being to his consciousness, thereby obscuring that deep dimension in him that faith wishes to open up." (J. RATZINGER: "Zur Frage der Unauflöslichkeit der Ehe: Bemerkungen zum dogmengeschichtlichen Befund und seiner gegenwärtigen Bedeutung", in: G.L. MÜLLER (ed.): *J. Ratzinger Gesammelte Schriften*, vol. 4, Freiburg-Basel-Wien: Herder, 2014, 600-621, hier 616 mit Verweis auf N. VAN DER WAL: "Aspekte der geschichtlichen Entwicklung in Recht und Lehre: Einfluss des profanen Rechts auf die kirchliche Eheauffassung im Osten", in: *Concilium* 6 (1979), 337-339, hier 337, und G. DELLING: "Ehescheidung", in: T. KLAUSER (ed.): *Reallexikon für Antike und Christentum*, vol. 4, Stuttgart: Hiersemann, 1959, 707-719, hier 712-713.

history various catalogues of sin were drawn up which, in addition to adultery, legitimize the death of the marriage, including sexual perversion, wilful neglect of the family, inducing the wife to indecent behaviour, a scandalous way of life, public and unjust accusation of adultery, attempted murder of the spouse and the practice of abortion.[19] Other, non-sinful conditions that justify divorce are: physical impotence; disappearance of a spouse for more than five years; a married priest's nomination for episcopal office with the consent of his wife, who usually enters a convent; entering a religious order; and the Pauline privilege.[20] At the end of the nineteenth century the following causes of divorce were added by the Moscow Patriarchate: apostasy (religious death); grave illness (leprosy, syphilis); incurable mental illness; and life imprisonment (civil death of the marriage). Here we see that in Orthodoxy the collapse of a marriage is traditionally assigned to the context of grave sin, where the church can acknowledge, as it were, the death of such a marriage. Nowadays, however, causes for the collapse of a first marriage are no longer universally investigated in the Orthodox world.[21]

What is the situation with regard to remarriage? Here, historical differences should be noted.[22] Until the ninth century no church blessing was granted for second marriages. In other words, prior to this date there were no second marriages in the Byzantine rite. Patriarch Nikephoros the Confessor († 828) was the first to relax this principle; the second marriage was subject to a two-year period of penance (*epithemia*) during which the reception of holy communion was forbidden. From the eleventh century onward these prescriptions were less and less observed, and a liturgical rite for second marriages was developed. This is shorter than in the case of first marriages, but accompanied by special penitential prayers[23] such as "You who pardoned the unchaste Rahab and accepted the repentance of the Tax-gatherer, remember not our youthful sins of ignorance... Now, O Lord, Who have adopted Your servant N.N. and your handmaid N.N. as Your own, bind them together in love, grant them the conversion of the Tax-gatherer, the tears of the Woman taken in Adultery, the confession of the Thief; so that they who are now whole-heartedly penitent may one day be found worthy of the unity and peace of Your heavenly kingdom."[24] Since, initially, the rite of second marriage also lacked the "coronation", it may have been regarded as non-sacramental, which is still a matter of controversy. Today, as far as the practice of the Russian Orthodox church

19 List drawn from T. PFAMMATTER: *Geschiedene,* 150.

20 Cf. ibid. 151-152.

21 Russian Orthodoxy, for instance, has given up this practice.

22 On the historical background see G. PRINZ: *"Grundsätzlich unauflöslich, aber… ": Das Ehe-, Scheidungs- und Wiederverheiratungsverständnis in der orthodoxen Kirche*, Hamburg: Dr. Kovac, 2016 (THEOS – Studienreihe Theologische Forschungsergebnisse; 127).

23 Cf. T. PFAMMATTER: *Geschiedene*, 156-157.

24 First penitential prayer, quoted ibid. 157.

is concerned, both second and third marriages are solemnized by the church. The rite of second marriage, today, differs from that of the first marriage only by the addition of two penitential prayers. In wide sections of Orthodoxy, the rite of coronation has been re-introduced, which suggests that the second marriage is regarded as sacramentally valid.[25] Nonetheless it is still the case today that, from the point of view of Orthodoxy, every remarriage is only a kind of "emergency measure".[26] The second marriage continues to be regarded as a deviation from the biblical ideal; it is only tolerated, because of human weakness, under condition of penitence.

Provisional summary: In the Orthodox Churches, in general, the theological granting of remarriage for the divorced employs the principle of *oikonomia,* that is, the more flexible application of law on the basis of the divine plan of salvation that takes account of every person in his or her concrete situation. This is a kindness, a forbearance, that distances itself from strict *akribia* (the strict application of law). This does not mean that a remarriage is flooded with bridal radiance from the light of Tabor: only the first marriage is entitled to this.[27] Whether the guilty party may only remarry after the death of the innocent party, or not at all, are matters of considerable debate.[28] In Orthodoxy any second marriage remains problematical, and fundamentally under the sign of penitence. Any remarriage is basically subject to the demands of penitence. The exclusion from holy communion for a lengthy (several year-long) period is largely relaxed on the basis of the principle of *oikonomia.*

1.3 Catholic

The Catholic Church has long held fast strictly to the indissolubility of marriage. In this view, accordingly, sacramental marriage cannot be dissolved: nullity tribunals seek only to establish that the marriage was invalidly concluded or not consummated. In recent years, while the teaching on indissolubility is maintained by the magisterium, voices have been raised in theology calling for relaxation in exceptional cases for pastoral reasons. Such dissenting voices are not only to be found within theological circles. Disunity on this issue existing in the church can also be observed among the laity. Five years before the publication of *Amoris laetitia* Paul M. Zulehner made a supra-denominational study of attitudes vis-à-

---

25 Cf. *Teinstva Braka* [The sacrament of marriage], mit Verweis auf *Trebnik* [=Book of liturgical blessings], chapter 12, available from www.liturgy.ru/tainstrva-braka; accessed 21.11.2016.

26 G. LARENTZAKIS: "Ehe, Ehescheidung und Wiederverheiratung", 259.

27 On the different attitudes on the Orthodox side, cf. T. PFAMMATTER: *Geschiedene*, 159-161.

28 Cf. ibid. 155.

vis the indissolubility of marriage and came to the following conclusion.[29] When asked whether it was good for the church to insist on the indissolubility of marriage, 33% of Catholics agreed, as did 54% of Orthodox, whereas only 16% of Protestants agreed. Among Catholics the percentage of agreement increased with the age of respondents. In the group aged up to 29, a good quarter, that is 26%, agreed with the indissolubility of marriage; among the over 70s the figure was 51%, about half of all respondents.

This shows that dissent regarding the indissolubility of marriage occurs not only at the level of theology and the magisterium but also among the Catholic laity. The empirically demonstrable disunity in the People of God extends to the level of pastoral theology where, in the Catholic community, two basic positions can be distinguished as to the manner of treating failed marriages and the question of remarriage. In contemporary pastoral theology in the German-speaking countries only a few theologians would still put forward the view, regarded as the unquestionable teaching of the Church until Benedict XVI, that a validly concluded marriage is absolutely indissoluble and that remarriage entails exclusion from holy communion.[30] The other approach urges relaxation of the practice of marriage indissolubility. What people are asking for here is a more flexible handling of the biblical teaching on the indissolubility of marriage according to the teaching of Jesus that, what God has joined together, man must not separate (Mk 10,11-12). In this context reference is made to practices of the early church that show that even in apostolic times, in cases of difficulty, exceptional situations were permitted. Examples are the problem of *porneia* (Mt 5,32; 19,9) or the question of separation for the sake of the faith (1 Cor 7,12-16).[31] Reference is also made to the Orthodox practice of *oikonomia* that authorizes second and third marriages for pastoral reasons. There is the question of conscience, which needs to be respected when it veers from the norm; consequently, the church should not insist on external norms, which should be resolved in the *forum internum*.[32] Some also raise the pastoral objection that legal rigorism should not take precedence over pastoral encouragement. It is felt that the law's intransigence, its legalism, is given priority

---

29 Cf. P.M. ZULEHNER: *Verbuntung: Kirchen im weltanschaulichen Pluralismus: Religion im Leben der Menschen 1970-2010,* Ostfildern: Schwabenverlag, 2011, 269.

30 For example A. WOLLBOLD: *Pastoral mit wiederverheirateten Geschiedenen – gordischer Knoten oder ungeahnte Möglichkeiten*, Regensburg: Pustet, 2015; for the foundations of this position, cf. J. RATZINGER: "Zur Frage der Unauflöslichkeit der Ehe", 600-621.

31 Cf. R. SCHNACKENBURG: "Die Ehe nach der Weisung Jesu und dem Verständnis der Urkirche", in: F. HEINRICH/V. EID (ed.): *Ehe und Ehescheidung: Diskussion unter Christen*, München: Kösel, 1972 (Münchener Akademie-Schriften; 59), 11-31.

32 Cf. E. SCHOCKENHOFF: *Chancen zur Versöhnung? Die Kirche und die wiederverheirateten Geschiedenen*, Freiburg-Basel-Wien: Herder 2011, 137-143; Pfammatter: Geschiedene, 368-385.

over human distress in dramatic life-situations. While Jesus brought healing to the sick, the church has turned into the judge "who excludes wounded people from the sacraments and from particular positions in public office".[33] Finally, in more recent times, in the context of the "theology of failure", questions have also been raised about the indissolubility of sacramental marriages.[34] The point of departure here is the reality of human failure, including failure in marriage. These experiences of failure, initially felt as instances of defeat, become transformed into key faith-experiences such as we find in the Bible: the people of Israel, continually failing, but in that failure experiencing God. In the New Testament too, this experience of failure characterizes the people who encounter Jesus. Jesus himself fails on the Cross, but overcomes this human failure in the light of the Resurrection. "The God of salvation, the God of deliverance, who manifests himself in so many ways in the biblical experiences of faith, encounters the weak and powerless human being so that, once he has descended the lowest level, he may raise him up again."[35] By thus reaching out, in particular to failed marriages – so runs the argument – Christianity's credibility can be rediscovered in the modern age. This must not be misused as yet another example of the myth of the eternal victor. Admission to holy communion would give concrete shape to this.

Provisional summary: While, on the Catholic side, the magisterium's theological line does not permit remarriage after divorce, on the other side a widespread alternative view calls for a relaxation of the refusal of holy communion to divorced and remarried persons. Different interpretations of the biblical ban on divorce (a result of differing hermeneutics in the three Christian denominations) have given rise to distinct pastoral consequences; our next step will be to give a brief sketch of their basic structures.

---

33 J. RATZINGER: "Zu einigen Einwänden gegen die kirchliche Lehre über den Kommunionempfang von wiederverheirateten geschiedenen Gläubigen", available from http://www.vatican.va/roman_curia/congregations/cfaith/documents/rc_con_cfaith_doc_19980101_ratzinger-comm-divorced_ge.html; accessed 02.12.2016; on this cf. also T. PFAMMATTER: *Geschiedene*, 332-352.

34 Representatives of this view are D. Sölle, D. Mieth, J. Werbick, G. Fuchs, D. Eckmann; cf. in more detail M.C. HASTETTER: "Between Failure and Jubilation: Contrary Tendencies in the Pastoral Care of Marriage", in: *And God Saw That It Was Very Good: Reinvigorating the Sacrament of Marriage and the Christian Family in Light of the 2014 and 2015 Synods,* Heiligenkreuz bei Wien: Be&Be-Verlag, 2017.

35 E. SCHOCKENHOFF: *Chancen zur Versöhnung?*, 119.

2 Pastoral Measures of Assistance for Failed Marriages and the Divorced and Remarried in the Christian Denominations: Model Approaches

2.1 Protestant: Liturgical Services for People in Divorce Situations, and Other Pastoral Measures

Protestant rejection of the sacramentality of marriage, together with the unlimited permission to remarry, has effectively suppressed the whole pastoral-theological discussion about the admission of the divorced and remarried to communion/the Lord's Supper. However, this does not indicate a lack of pastoral sensitivity or a failure to be open to people in divorce situations. For instance, as a result of her theological research on divorce, Burgk-Lempart states that, while on the one hand wedding anniversaries are celebrated, there is on the Protestant side a lack of rituals dealing with marriage failure. She writes, "a central task for evangelization and the care of souls in the area of separation and divorce would seem to be the opening-up of a space for everything that has remained inchoate (incomplete), including the associated feelings of grief and regret, and for communicating of the certainty that God maintains solidarity with those who have failed, and does not turn his back on them".[36] In the area of *diakonia* and *martyria* [the church's field of service and witness] she suggests practical initiatives such as a dedicated pastoral care for people in situations of separation and divorce, telephone counselling, as well as the church's support for individuals, couples, and single parents [and guardians/educators].[37] In spite of internal controversies in Protestantism, she goes further, urging the need for specific rituals for separation and divorce. She wants to see particular liturgical proposals for a religious service of separation, including the public and official notification of such separation. There is also the idea of including a reference to possible marriage failure even in the marriage service itself, and also in the service of baptism and in preparation for confirmation.[38] These should include themes such as expressions of thanksgiving, grievance (regret), admission of guilt, the offer of forgiveness, and blessing of the separated partners. The aim of these activities would be to guarantee acknowledgement of the status of those living in separation or divorce. In practice however, Burgk-Lempart is aware of the resistance to such initiatives: relatively few people would make use of these provisions, since the very fact of not having kept a marriage promise made before God is felt, fundamentally, as a huge burden of guilt.

The major part of Burgk-Lempart's thesis is taken up with (individually or specially designed) religious services for separated or divorced people. This form

---

36 A. BURGK-LEMPART: *Wenn Wege sich trennen*, 254.

37 Cf. ibid. 120-129, here and in what follows.

38 Cf. ibid. 246-248.

of religious service, originating in Stuttgart at the end of the 1990s,[39] is said to be already established in cities. Her assessment of divorce sermons, thematically classified, shows that experiences of separation are given formal [linguistic] expression, reflected upon methodically, and interpreted biblically.[40] In this way, feelings of isolation are overcome, failure is accepted, separation is not censured by the church, public debate is enriched to include themes of partnership, and the history of divorce in the church is given some objective attention. These would help people to come to terms with themselves, and particularly with the issue of broken marriage-vows, so that God's promise can be extended to them once more and the limitations of human promises can be seen against the background of human finitude. However, Burgk-Lempart envisages making an even earlier start with the process of raising sensitivity to possible marriage failure, by including these issues in the service of baptism and in confirmation preparation. As a way of combating ecclesiastical taboos regarding separation and divorce, she suggests that problems facing the divorced and remarried be fundamentally anchored in the life of the community by means of annual "relationship" Sundays, story-rooms and talk-rooms for youngsters, cooperation with play-schools in cases where children are confronted with their parents' separation, and conferences for church (activity) leaders on the Christian understanding of marriage, to name only the most important.[41]

Provisional summary: On the Protestant side the pastoral care of divorced and remarried persons is profoundly influenced by the Word. This influence is also strongly felt in liturgical practice. The reception of holy communion (participation in the Lord's Supper) does not even come up for discussion in Protestant practical theology. On the other hand, Protestant church life shows a wealth of pastoral projects directed at the divorced and remarried, which might be neglected if the debate were concentrated narrowly on the question of admission to holy communion.

2.2 Orthodox: Pastoral Reticence

On the Orthodox side it is difficult to get hold of literature (at least in German) that could be described as genuinely pastoral on the question of the divorced and remarried. However, there are scattered references to it in the literature on the Orthodox understanding of marriage and on the permission of second and third marriages (seen under the sign of penitence). Basically we can say that in Orthodoxy the pastoral care of marriage is governed by the principle of *oikonomia*. An

39 Ibid. 120.

40 Cf. ibid. 243-244.

41 Cf. ibid. 252-253.

official document tells us that *oikonomia* exercises "the privilege of dispensing with *akribia* in prudence, wisdom and pastoral openness, so that all things may be reconciled in Christ".[42] Translated into western pastoral categories this Orthodox practice would correspond most closely to the "logic of pastoral mercy". Having said this, we must not lose sight of the fact that in Orthodoxy the pastoral care of divorced and remarried persons is applied fundamentally under the sign of penance. In that regard it would in fact come closest to the western practice of penitential liturgy, where the aim is to bring the sinner back to reconciliation with God and his fellow believers. It is significant, in this connection, that in the traditional Orthodox line the divorced and remarried frequent the sacrament of penance during their period of penitence, returning to full participation in the eucharistic assembly once their period of penitence is over. The Orthodox pastoral care of the divorced and remarried is designed, therefore, to maximize the value of the period of penitence for those in second and third marriages. This time lasts for several years and, in the stricter version, the remarried are excluded from the reception of holy communion for its whole duration. This kind of penitential period of several years is a work of penance, understood in the sense of a medicine, a curative treatment or also a restorative tonic.[43] The Orthodox pastoral care of the divorced and remarried, with its penitential character, means that we can assign it to the category of mercy, that is, a therapeutic pastoral care than ultimately aims to bring man back to *theosis,* union with God and the attainment of the kingdom of God. For penance, in Orthodoxy, is generally understood as a soul-therapy, of which the sacrament of penance is the pinnacle. "Its purpose is to help the faithful to loose themselves from the chains of sin and live as 'new human beings' in Christ and in the church. The aim is to awaken habits of conduct that will continue to work against the weaknesses that lead to sin."[44]

Provisional summary: Orthodox pastoral practice in regard to the remarried is not focussed uni-dimensionally on *oikonomia*, understood as the logic of mercy. Rather, it is imbued with a deep sense of penitence, manifested in a therapeutic care of souls that is willing to accept the stress involved in taking the individual believer seriously and adapting itself to him or her. Contemporary debate frequently expresses the demand for the Catholic Church, in its pastoral care of the divorced and remarried, to learn a certain moderation from the Orthodox princi-

42 Cited in G. LARENTZAKIS: "Ehe, Ehescheidung", 258.

43 Cf. T. PFAMMATTER: *Geschiedene*, 170.

44 Ibid. 170 referring to D. STANILOAE: *Erneuerung und Heilung der Gläubigen im Sakrament der Buße nach der Lehre der orthodoxen Kirche*, 1987, 25; cf. on this in more detail concerning the pastoral-theological approach of the celebrated Rumanian Orthodox theologian I. MOGA: "Dumitru Staniloae als Pastoraltheologe: Frühe Ansätze zu einer Erneuerung der orthodoxen Pastoral im 20. Jahrhundert", in: *Studii teologice* 9/2 (2013), 241-261.

ple of *oikonomia;* but this debate largely fails to pay due attention to the other components of the Orthodox tradition, namely, the penitential and the therapeutic aspects of pastoral care.

2.3 Catholic: Divergent Pastoral Directions

The Catholic side presents us with a multi-layered picture of the interaction of pastoral care and the divorced and remarried. If we ask what pastoral consequences follow from the two theological lines indicated, we see that basically two pastoral directions emerge. The first line, following John Paul II (*Familiaris consortio*) and Benedict XVI, aims to forestall marriage-failure as far as possible through marriage preparation and the project of a marriage catechumenate.[45] The exclusion from holy communion of divorced and remarried persons is retained and the practice of spiritual communion is recommended unless the partners agree to live as brother and sister, and provided no public scandal is given by their reception of communion. Nonetheless there has been a growth in sensitivity and an awareness of the need for the pastoral care of the divorced and remarried – for whom the church has a particular responsibility. For instance, even prior to the changes in the canon law of matrimony undertaken by Pope Francis, an important pastoral element was the desire, on the part of nullity tribunals, to declare a previous marriage null and void, thus facilitating canonical acknowledgment of the new conjugal union.

As an example of this first pastoral line we may cite the so-called 5-point plan (2011) of Cardinal Christoph Schönborn of the Archdiocese of Vienna, who initiated sensitive pastoral contacts with divorced and remarried people, inspired by Jesus' option for the poorest of the poor.[46] According to Schönborn the fully worked-out plan is to be understood as a kind of "manual" for "guiding people towards a true conversion, a genuine renewal of the life of faith".[47] On the basis of this approach Cardinal Schönborn, like Pope Benedict, saw the pastoral care of marriage as part of an overall pastoral care of faith,[48] directed to Christ. It examines the following points:

---

45 For reflections on a marriage catechumenate see A. WOLLBOLD: *Pastoral mit wiederverheirateten Geschiedenen*, 231-241; for pastoral approaches in line with Pope Benedict's teaching, cf. M.C. HASTETTER: "Ehe- und Familienpastoral von Benedikt bis Franziskus: Krise oder Kontinuität?", in: *Ambo* 1 (2016), 84-115.

46 Cf. C. SCHÖNBORN: *Die Freude, Priester zu sein*, Freiburg-Basel-Wien: Herder, 2011, 144-157. According to Schönborn this pastoral plan was developed for a diocese in which more than 60% of marriages end in divorce, not counting those who live together without being married, and the number of church weddings is reducing drastically; cf.148.

47 Cf. ibid. 148-149.

48 Cf. M.C. HASTETTER: "Ehe- und Familienpastoral", here especially 99.

1. *Jesus sees the poor and little.* For Schönborn these are not the remarried who are – at a purely human level – taken up into a new partnership, albeit not one envisaged by the church. They are not the real "poor" in the context of divorce and remarriage. The foremost victims of divorce are the children; it follows that it is they who are entitled to the church's whole compassion.[49]
2. *Jesus sees those left alone in the wake of divorce.* Here Schönborn thinks of a second group of the "poor" who need to be "seen", through the church, by Jesus: those, that is, who do not find a new partner in the wake of divorce. Divorce creates loneliness, and many do not immediately find a replacement – which entails serious social consequences for both men and women, from alcoholism to financial ruin.[50] Schönborn sees the church's mercy at work precisely in giving attention to these victims in the complex situation of the divorced and remarried.[51] That is why, for the Cardinal of Vienna, it is so important for there to be a reconciliation with the remaining partner. "What is the point of access to the sacraments if this whole painful situation remains unreconciled, or at least if there is at least no attempt at reconciliation?"[52]
3. *The question of guilt.* Thirdly, Schönborn addresses the fact that, where there is divorce, there is always guilt. There needs to be intervention here; it needs to be established whether the partners have at least made the attempt to forgive each other (even at an initial level) and end divorce hostilities. Accordingly, those in the care of souls are responsible for helping the former marriage-partners to make a step toward each other so that forgiveness may emerge.
4. *The example of faithful marriages.* Fourthly, with regard to the remarried, Schönborn salutes those marriages "that hold together in the face of life's storms because they stand fast by the sacrament. What kind of message do we priests and spiritual guides give *them* if we are always talking about 'poor

---

49 Cf. C. SCHÖNBORN: *Die Freude*, 149: "Where do we hear a lobby for the children of divorced parents? Where can we hear the voice of public opinion saying that the first victims are the children? They have a daddy and a mummy, and then suddenly they've got an 'uncle', an 'aunt', daddy's girlfriend, mummy's boyfriend. How often do the divorced couple put the burden of their married conflict on the backs of their children?"

50 "The Gospel is always on the side of the weakest, the little ones, so we must speak for them, we must become their 'lobby', we must come to the defence of these poor, lonely ones who are left without a partner." (C. SCHÖNBORN: *Die Freude*, 151) In the face of the pain and hopelessness of those left behind after divorce it is difficult to speak of a "new Easter beginning", as Hans-Günther Gruber suggests in his new paradigm of marriage in terms of cross and resurrection. See H.-G. GRUBER: *Christliche Ehe in moderner Gesellschaft: Entwicklung – Chancen – Perspektiven*, Freiburg-Basel-Wien: Herder, 1995[2], 325. For more detail on the problems involved in the pastoral care of marriage and the theology of failure, see M.C. HASTETTER: "Between Failure and Jubilation".

51 Cf. C. SCHÖNBORN: *Die Freude*, 151.

52 Ibid.

divorced and remarried people'?"[53] He urges us to give equal attention to, and gratitude for, faithful marriages at the same time as giving cautious spiritual help to spouses undergoing crises in their marriage.

5. *The divorced and remarried:* with regard to the annulling of marriages and the admission to holy communion of the divorced and remarried, the question, for Schönborn, remains this: How do these individuals live before God with their conscience and in the depth of their soul?[54] At the same time the Cardinal of Vienna knows how difficult it is to make decisions here. His rule is to avoid both extremes, that is, on the one hand making holy communion available to the divorce and remarried without any distinction – which would be a false mercy in the absence of conversion – and on the other hand failing to search for any pastoral solution for the divorced and remarried.[55] Every situation must be examined in detail, but the care of souls is also committed to observe the words of Jesus ("Anyone who divorces his wife and marries another, commits adultery [Lk 16,18; Mk 10,11; Matt 19,9])".[56] For Schönborn, as for Joseph Ratzinger/Pope Benedict XVI, this means that mercy can only be effective in the context of truth. It is important, he says, to try to find out whether there exists a path to a deeper faith.[57] In his 5-point plan, Schönborn ultimately envisages pastoral measures with a martyrological emphasis that would provide a path for conversion and reconciliation – which of course is highly relevant to the church as a whole.

As for the second line: even before the appearance of *Amoris laetitia* there were isolated instances where divorced and remarried couples were admitted to reception of holy communion, as was required by the Freiburg "Memorandum on Admitting Divorced and Remarried Persons to the Sacraments" (2012). At the time

53 Ibid. 152-153.

54 Cf. ibid. 154.

55 Here and in what follows, ibid. 154.

56 Ibid. 155.

57 At this point Schönborn cites the heroic example of a remarried couple who do not receive holy communion, whereas their eight children do. Sometimes the children say, "Mama, today I'm going to communion for you!" The remarried mother has kept her longing for communion, but holds fast to church teaching; to those who tell her that the church has become more liberal and would now allow the remarried to receive communion, she says, "Don't worry about me. Rather, you need to worry about those who could go to holy communion and don't." (C. SCHÖNBORN: *Die Freude*, 155) Schönborn is also aware of others who have not reached an equally deep understanding, and who are looking for a way of reconciliation by appealing to the Orthodox practice of *oikonomia* – which has never been accepted by the Catholic Church. "But she keeps faith with the once-for-all indissolubility of marriage, and that is such a great value for everyone – for the family, the children and for the couple themselves – when she says that one must stand fast and remain true to the words of Jesus: 'What God has joined together, man must not separate.'" (Ibid. 155).

one parish priest gave his view to the press: "We stand by the Archbishop... but there is an urgent problem here. Canon law compels us to engage in pastoral work 'under the counter' by admitting the divorced and remarried to the sacraments."[58] The Freiburg memorandum, published on the Internet, justified its position by pointing out that pastoral activity regarding the divorced and remarried must be guided by mercy: the maxim was *salus animarum suprema lex*.[59] The signatories also referred to the "decisions-in-conscience of the people concerned and the life-situations that have resulted from this"[60], which must be taken into account.

In 2013, almost as a response to the memorandum and as an expression of God's mercy, the Archdiocese of Freiburg was the first German-speaking diocese to publish an instruction regarding liturgical services of blessing for divorced and remarried couples.[61] Pastoral measures foreseen were spiritual guidance interviews and personal discussions, and the exploration of possible grounds for nullity; also pastoral guidance in the case of a personal decision not to receive the sacraments, but, equally in the case where a conscientious decision is made to receive the sacraments.[62] In addition to these areas (that belong more to *diakonia* and *martyrologia*) the central thrust of the instruction is liturgical: envisaged as a conclusion to this process is a final ritual including supportive prayers and a church blessing for the civilly remarried couple. As a sign of this new beginning, as in the case of baptism, a candle is presented to the couple. Here we see that liturgy is at the heart of the Freiburg instruction; this brings it internally closer to the Protestant religious service than to the Orthodox rite for second and third marriages with its strongly marked penitential character, particularly as the latter explicitly intends to avoid any appearance of a "quasi-marriage",[63] though in fact the ecclesiastical blessing *does* impart de facto a quasi-sacramental character to the new marriage.

In the meantime, this "liturgical" line has developed further in different paths in the wake of *Amoris laetitia*. On the homepage of the Archdiocese of Vienna, for instance, we find under the heading "WIGE – the platform for the divorced and remarried in the church" a whole range of liturgical celebrations for the divorced

58 T. NACHBAR: "Pastorale Schwarzarbeit: Gegen das Kirchenrecht reichen Priester Wiederverheirateten die Kommunion", in: *Der Sonntag in Freiburg* (10.06.2012), 1.

59 *Memorandum "Wiederverheiratet Geschiedene in unserer Kirche"*, available from: http://www.memorandum-priester-und-diakone-freiburg.de/?page_id=273; accessed 14.10.2016.

60 Ibid.

61 ERZBISCHÖFLICHES SEELSORGEAMT FREIBURG: *Handreichung für die Seelsorge zur Begleitung von Menschen in Trennung, Scheidung und nach ziviler Wiederverheiratung*, 2013, available from https://www.kfd-bundesverband.de/fileadmin/Bilder/Nachrichten/Wiederverheiratet_broschuere_handreichung_09_2013.pdf; accessed 15.10.2016.

62 Ibid. 9.

63 Ibid. 11.

and remarried: there are three different models of blessings, blessings for people with a broken love-relationship, in addition to two models for a service of thanksgiving for a civil marriage.[64] The literature provided focuses exclusively on the aspect of blessing,[65] which shows, on the Catholic side, a clear shift of emphasis away from the *martyria* of the first marriage-pastoral line with its catechumenal and catechetical thrust, towards *leiturgia* in the second marriage-pastoral line, with its creation of new liturgical forms (services of blessing).

Provisional summary: On the Catholic side, both lines of pastoral care of the divorced and remarried share a claim to be a *via caritatis*. They both adopt the position of *diakonia*. The first line follows Pope Benedict's formula, "the pastoral care of marriage is the pastoral care of faith" and takes the path of *martyria* (supporting faith). In the form of a "root therapy" it begins with faith itself, which "gives the human being the ability to grow and stride forward, based on faithfulness".[66] The second line, with its emphasis on the pastoral and spiritual guiding of the individual's responsible decision-in-conscience, is much more focused on the element of *leiturgia*. Services of blessing for divorced and remarried couples and their admission to holy communion are here seen in their interrelatedness: they belong together like liturgical Siamese twins.

In conclusion, having outlined the Protestant, Orthodox and Catholic ways of approaching the divorced and remarried, we shall examine the pastoral locus of Pope Francis' apostolic exhortation *Amoris laetitia* and indicate any relevant ecumenical connections it may reveal.

3 The Place of *Amoris Laetitia* in the Inter-Confessional Debate on the Pastoral Care of Marriage

In *Amoris laetitia* the question of the pastoral care of divorced and remarried persons extends from chapter 6 (nos. 241-246) under the heading "Accompaniment after breakdown and divorce". The presentation starts from the point of view that

64 Cf. the "building-blocks" under the heading "WIGE – the platform for the divorced and remarried in the church", available from https://www.erzdioezese-wien.at/pages/inst/23674633/segensfeier/bausteine; accessed 15.10.2016.

65 Cf. https://www.erzdioezese-wien.at/pages/inst/23674633/segensfeier/literatur; accessed 15.10.2016, with reference to H. BAUERNFEIND/R. GEIER (eds.): *Leben braucht Segen: Segensfeiern Für alle, die segnen und gesegnet werden wollen*, Freiburg-Basel-Wien: Herder 2001; C. BUNDSCHUH-SCHRAMM (ed.): *Ich will mit dir sein und dich segnen: Segensfeiern und Segensgesten*, Ostfildern: Schwabenverlag, 1999; J. KUHN/D. KUHN: *Hoffnungsworte: 77 Segen und gute Gedanken*, Freiburg-Basel-Wien: Herder, 2010; F. HARANT: "Segen für Liebende", in: *Stadt Gottes* (2/2013), 10-11.

66 J. RATZINGER: "Zur Frage der Unauflöslichkeit der Ehe", 616; for a profile of Joseph Ratzinger's approach to the pastoral care of marriage, cf. M.C. HASTETTER: "Ehe- und Familienpastoral", 110.

there are situations in which a separation, though an extreme measure, is unavoidable.[67] This calls for a particular pastoral sensitivity orientated towards forgiveness and reconciliation.[68] Significantly, it is urged that those concerned should not feel discriminated against by the church, let alone excommunicated.[69] Finally there is reference to the importance of nullity tribunals: they are to be made simpler and used as a pastoral measure in coming to the aid of those in situations of separation.[70] After these rather more general pastoral observations, we come to chapter 8 of *Amoris laetitia*, which centers on "accompanying, discerning and integrating weakness".[71] An introduction confronts the marriage ideal with human weakness and points to the divine mercy,[72] which recalls the Orthodox approach indicated in our introductory remarks. This would also chime in with the *conclusio* of the first paragraphs of chapter 8, which observes that "the Church's task is often like that of a field hospital".[73] The vivid image of the church as a place and an instrument of healing would lead us directly to the therapeutic view of pastoral care that is so clearly apparent in the Orthodox treatment of the divorced and remarried. However, the real thrust of chapter 8 comes out in its renewed reflection on the principle of gradualism in pastoral care, which had also characterized the 1980 Synod of Bishops on Marriage and the Family.[74] According to Pope Francis, pastoral care that is formed by the principle of gradualism manifests itself in "mercy and encouragement" and the "pastoral discernment of the situations of many people for whom [marriage] is no longer a lived reality"[75] in a world where there is a growing number of life-unions that are not marriages. For the Pope, this pastoral decision must always be in the service of evangelization and of promoting human and spiritual growth.[76]

When it comes to distinguishing these irregular unions in all their complexity (and Pope Francis devotes a whole section to this[77]), we become aware of the tension between, on the one hand, drawing lines of exclusion and, on the other hand, the need to re-integrate people. This tension can be traced back ultimately to the balance between rigorism and laxism – a task that has occupied sacramental

67 Cf. AL 241.
68 Cf. ibid. 242.
69 Cf. ibid. 243.
70 Cf. ibid. 244.
71 Cf. ibid. 291-312.
72 Cf. ibid. 291.
73 Ibid. 291.
74 For details on the basis of this idea cf. M.C. HASTETTER: "Between Failure and Jubilation", 2.1.
75 AL 293.
76 Ibid.
77 Here and what follows: ibid. 296.

pastoral care since the time of the early church. What is new, compared with early approaches to sacramental pastoral care, is that here Pope Francis insists that the complexity of the situation be addressed. The line drawn by *Amoris laetitia* clearly includes everyone – which the Pope regards as the only possible conclusion on the basis of the principle of mercy and the "divine pedagogic of grace",[78] in contrast to what he refers to as a "more rigorous" pastoral policy:[79] "the logic of integration is the key to its pastoral procedure".[80] This is why, for Pope Francis, there can be no one solution for all cases; rather, the pastoral task consists in this "accompanying and discernment", encouraging people to act in a responsible and personal way in their own situation, which generally takes place in the *forum internum*.[81] This is why Pope Francis gives such a large scope to personal decisions-in-conscience, even if decisions reached in this way appear initially to conflict with the Church's teaching office – something which has played an important role, in the second Catholic line, in the pastoral care of marriage.[82] This *via caritatis*[83] which Francis sees as the royal road for the pastoral care of divorced and remarried people, is based on what he calls the "logic of pastoral mercy"[84] which he later calls the "primacy of love"[85].

If we attempt cautiously to sum up the results of this investigation, we shall see that *Amoris laetitia* stands at the intersection, so to speak, of the various pastoral approaches with their particular confessional views. Here, it seems, a new supra-confessional synthesis is emerging, embracing the claim of God's solidarity with those experiencing failure (Protestant tradition), the Orthodox principle of *oikonomia* with its twin sources in penitential practice and therapeutic care of souls, and the two Catholic lines. Of the latter, the first emphasizes preparation for marriage and the establishment of marriage sacramentality; and the second focuses on the personal decision-in-conscience and an intensive, accompanying pastoral presence. Generally speaking, the first Catholic line, the martyrological approach (the pastoral care of marriage understood as the pastoral care of faith) with its "root-therapy" (*Wurzeltherapie*) has been downplayed in chapter 8 of *Amoris laetitia* in the context of the divorced and remarried. The emphasis on strengthening faith, which has such an important place in other parts of the document, and in particular in the context of passing on the faith to children, has lost a certain focus. Conversely the principle of gradualism, that is, the pastoral accom-

78 Ibid. 297.

79 Ibid. 308.

80 Ibid. 299.

81 Cf. ibid. 300-301.

82 Cf. ibid. 301-306.

83 Ibid. 306.

84 See the heading for this section: ibid. 307 ff.

85 Ibid. 311.

panying of a process of growth and understanding, which requires the pastoral guide or minister to show patience and the ability to listen, has been significantly strengthened. As regards new liturgical forms – where the Protestant position has come close to the second Catholic line – *Amoris laetitia* seems at first glance to have contributed no specific impulses. It contains, for instance, no encouragement of blessings for divorced and remarried people. Where the document speaks positively about new forms and how to promote them, this occurs expressly outside of chapter 8. Such forms refer to people with handicaps, with the development of new gestures, languages and structures,[86] new ways of fruitfulness,[87] new forms of marriage preparation with the help of families who have a sense of active mission,[88] new forms of spiritual guidance for married couples after the wedding ceremony[89] and the development of new forms of mutual respect in the family.[90] With regard to news forms and the pastoral integration of the divorced and remarried, chapter 8 is strikingly negative in tone: discernment is necessary as to "which of the various forms of exclusion currently practised in the liturgical, pastoral, educational and institutional framework, can be surmounted".[91]

Does this suggest indirectly that, in the future, new liturgical forms are to be drawn up that may perhaps include the twofold provision of services of blessing for divorced and remarried and their admission to holy communion? Such an interpretation can be envisaged – particularly as the Pope goes on to insist that any feeling of having been excommunicated must be avoided: "They should be able to live and mature as living members of the church, experiencing the church as a mother who is always there to lift them up, who cares for them in love and encourages them on the path of life and of the Gospel."[92] This could be seen as a pastoral and liturgical response to the controversial reception of the papal document concerning the possible granting of communion to divorced and remarried persons – a controversy that was stirred up by the inflammatory footnote 351 of chapter 8.[93]

86 Cf. ibid. 47.

87 Cf. ibid. 181.

88 Ibid. 208.

89 Ibid. 230.

90 Cf. ibid. 276.

91 Ibid. 299.

92 Ibid. 299.

93 "Because of existing conditions or mitigating factors it is possible for someone to be living in the grace of God in an objective situation of sin – which is not subjectively sinful or at least not fully so – and be practising love and growing in grace and in love, provided that this person receives the church's help." (AL 305) The contentious footnote says, "In certain cases this help could take the shape of reception of the sacraments. Therefore I remind them [priests] that the confessional is not meant to be a torture-chamber but a place of the Lord's mercy. (Pope Francis: Apostolic Exhortation *Evangelii Gaudium* [14 November 2013], 44: *AAS* 105 [2013], 1038). Similarly I emphasize that the Eucharist is not a reward for the perfect, but a generous

Amoris laetitia has managed to bridge a huge gap. As a papal pronouncement it endeavours to reconcile the "second" Catholic line – which has long been critical of Rome – with elements of the "first" Catholic line; it has also integrated essential aspects of the Protestant and Orthodox traditions in the pastoral care of marriage within a larger totality. Has it thereby replaced the "first" Catholic pastoral line that up to now was closely dependent on the teaching of John Paul II and Benedict XVI? No, not in all elements. But the openness to new liturgical forms could mean that, in the future, with the liturgical "Siamese twins" (services of blessing for the divorced and remarried, and their admission to holy communion), the Catholic Church could draw closer to the Protestant individual liturgical services (*Kasualgottesdienste*) and the Orthodox practice of official solemnization of second and third marriages. As reception of *Amoris laetitia* widens with the passage of time, this convergence could become more prominent than heretofore. On one occasion, observing this tendency in Orthodoxy, Ratzinger interpreted it as an assimilation to secular law which, in the Byzantine Empire, caused a weakening of "what is specific to the life of faith"[94], but which also revealed the limits of the Lord's word – limits which would require further pastoral clarification.[95]

Such pastoral clarification remains the church's task even after *Amoris laetitia* if she wishes to be present at Jacob's Well with Jesus, speaking to men and women about true love, and if she wants to liberate people from all that darkens their lives, bringing them to the fulfilled joy of the Gospel.[96] This is a task that unites all churches and Christian communities.

medicine and nourishment for the weak. (*ibid.*, 47: 1039)." (AL, note 351).

94 J. RATZINGER: "Zur Frage der Unauflöslichkeit der Ehe", 617.

95 On this whole line of argument cf. ibid. 617-621, which gives a series of concrete examples.

96 This idea and part of its formulation is taken from AL 294.

"Nourishment for the Journey, not a Prize for the Perfect": Reflecting with *Amoris Laetitia* on Eucharistic Sharing in Interchurch Marriages

Corinne Bernhard-Bitaud & Thomas Knieps-Port le Roi

In his letter to the bishops of the Buenos Aires pastoral region of September 2016, Pope Francis explicitly confirmed an interpretation of *Amoris laetitia* according to which the church opens a path of personal and pastoral discernment offering divorced and remarried Catholics the possibility of having access to the sacraments of Reconciliation and the Eucharist.[1] The pope has thus unmistakably changed the church's discipline with regard to the divorced and remarried and revised the theological vision that had undergirded the previous practice.[2] While this is certainly good news for Catholics in second marriages and their families, others who are also living in what the Catholic Church regards as "irregular or complex marital situations" may not be equally pleased with the Post-Synodal Exhortation. Interchurch families,[3] for instance, had asked the 2015 Bishops' Synod for an explicit statement that spouses "who express a real need and desire for Eucharistic

[1] For an English translation of the guidelines issued by the bishops of the Buenos Aires pastoral region for implementation of chapter VIII of *Amoris Laetitia*, and Pope Francis's response to those guidelines, see https://cruxnow.com/global-church/2016/09/18/guidelines-buenos-aires-bishops-divorcedremarried/; accessed 15.01.2017.

[2] For a detailed analysis of the theological and practical shift from previous church teaching to *Amoris laetitia*, see E.-M. FABER/M.M. LINTNER: "Theologische Entwicklungen in *Amoris laetitia* hinsichtlich der Frage der wiederverheirateten Geschiedenen", in: S. GOERTZ/C. WITTING (eds.): *Amoris laetitia – Wendepunkt für die Moraltheologie?* (Katholizismus im Umbruch; 4), Freiburg-Basel-Wien: Herder, 2016, 279-320; also B. PETRÀ: "From *Familiaris Consortio* to *Amoris Laetitia*: Continuity of the Pastoral Attitude and a Step Forward", in: *INTAMS Review* 22/2 (2016), 202-2016.

[3] We refer in this paper to "interchurch family" in terms of a family that "includes a husband and wife who come from two different church traditions (often a Roman Catholic married to a Christian of another communion). Both of them retain their original church membership, but so far as they are able they are committed to live, worship, and participate in their spouse's church also. If they have children, as parents they exercise a joint responsibility under God for their religious and spiritual upbringing, and they teach them by word and example to appreciate both their Christian traditions", a definition given in: *Interchurch Families and Christian*

sharing, and who fulfil the criteria for admission, can be allowed to receive communion alongside their Catholic partners on an on-going basis, whenever they are at mass together."[4] *Amoris laetitia*, however, which dedicates only one paragraph to interchurch families,[5] simply refers to the 1993 *Directory for the Application of Principles and Norms on Ecumenism*, stipulating that admission to Eucharistic communion for the non-Catholic spouse can only be granted in exceptional cases.[6]

In this paper we will explore whether or not *Amoris laetitia* also has a positive message for interchurch families. In a first step, Corinne Bernhard-Bitaud reads the document from the perspective of an interchurch family that experiences the pain of being united in the domestic church of the family day by day and yet separated at the Lord's Table on Sunday. She regrets that *Amoris laetitia* does not recognize more explicitly the existential need of these families to be offered Eucharistic hospitality. Sharing her concerns, Thomas Knieps-Port le Roi pushes the reading of *Amoris laetitia* a step further beyond what it explicitly states. Looking at how the exhortation deals with the admission to communion of remarried divorcees, he argues that, seen in its entire theological and pastoral orientation, Pope Francis implicitly entitles and encourages interchurch couples to embark on a path of personal and pastoral discernment which may include Eucharistic sharing not only for exceptional occasions but on an ongoing basis.

1 Reading *Amoris Laetitia* from the Lived Experience of Interchurch Families

The apostolic exhortation *Amoris laetitia* offers general concerns about Christian families (AL 292) which do not specifically focus on interchurch families but do not exclude them either (AL 297: "Here I am speaking not only of the divorced and remarried, but of everyone, in whatever situation they find themselves.") In the title itself, this exhortation is addressed to "Christian married couples", and

Unity, Rome, 2003, available from http://interchurchfamilies.org/confer/rome2003/documents/roma2003_en.pdf; accessed 15.01.2017.

4 *Response to the 2015 Synod on the Family from the Interchurch Families International Network*, 6 April 2015, 12, available from http://interchurchfamilies.org/ifin/IFIN_Response_to_Synod 2015.pdf; accessed 15.01.2017.

5 FRANCIS: *Post-Synodal Apostolic Exhortation* Amoris Laetitia, 2016, 247 (henceforward abbreviated as AL), available from https://w2.vatican.va/content/dam/francesco/pdf/apost_exhortations/documents/papa-francesco_esortazione-ap_20160319_amoris-laetitia_en.pdf; accessed 15.01.2017.

6 See PONTIFICAL COUNCIL FOR PROMOTING CHRISTIAN UNITY: *Directory for the Application of Principles and Norms on Ecumenism*, 160, available from http://www.vatican.va/roman_curia/pontifical_councils/chrstuni/documents/rc_pc_chrstuni_doc_25031993_principles-and-norms-on-ecumenism_en.html; accessed 15.01.2017, hereafter referred to by its common short name, the *Ecumenical Directory*.

not only to Catholic married couples. I am the Protestant spouse in an interchurch family, and I was myself a child in an interchurch family, so that I have been living daily ecumenism for almost 50 years. That is the reason why, from this specific point of view, I want to give an account of of how I received the elements of this text related to the admission of Christian spouses to the Eucharist and its spiritual function for couples.

1.1 The Domestic Church – Disunited at the Lord's Table

Pope Francis recalls that Christian marriage is a "domestic church" (AL 292) in reference to St John Chrysostom: "Make your house a church. Indeed, you are also responsible for the salvation of your sons and your servants."[7] The Second Vatican Council had taken up and developed this term, stating that it means that the family should be a place where the baptized live their Christian vocation: "For where Christianity pervades the entire mode of family life, and gradually transforms it, one will find there both the practice and an excellent school of the lay apostolate. In such a home husbands and wives find their proper vocation in being witnesses of the faith and love of Christ to one another and to their children."[8]

Interchurch families from all countries recognize themselves completely in this formulation, which they used themselves during their Second World Gathering in Rome in 2003: "Like every other Christian family, an interchurch family represents the Body of Christ in the home, and can, therefore, be described as a domestic church."[9]

What we want to bear witness to on this subject has already been described in theological research:[10] we are a domestic church, we are experiencing, in our couples, a *united* church, in full communion, even if we are not in the classical ecclesiological patterns of unity. Indeed, as is highlighted by the papal document: "If a family is centred on Christ, He will unify and illumine its entire life" (AL 317). So we are living witnesses, and we will not remain silent that the most complete unity is really possible even while respecting our diversity. If this is possible for the "cellular" level that the family is, why should it not be possible at higher levels?

Nevertheless, referring to the *Ecumenical Directory*, the pope reminds us that the Roman Catholic Church's general rule for the Protestant spouse in an interchurch family is "Eucharistic inhospitality". Restricting admission to the Eucharist to exceptional circumstances (AL 247) and forbidding Catholic believers

---

7 JOHN CHRYSOSTOM: *In Genesim*, Sermo 7 (PG 54, 607).

8 *Dogmatic Constitution on the Church* Lumen Gentium, 35 (henceforward abbreviated as LG).

9 *Interchurch Families and Christian Unity*, 3.

10 See e.g. T. KNIEPS-PORT LE ROI/R. TEMMERMAN (eds.): *Being One at Home: Interchurch Families as Domestic Churches*, Münster: LIT-Verlag, 2015.

from participating in the Protestant Last Supper (formally restated in 2003[11]) leads interchurch couples to have to disunite themselves *each Sunday* before the Lord's Table. It is really necessary to underline here that this is not just a question of experiencing the scandal of division once a year, during the Week of Prayer for Christian Unity, or from time to time during ecumenical assemblies, as is for example the case for most of our ministers, but of experiencing this scandal each week. Month after month. For our whole lives. We are united domestic churches during the whole week, except on Sunday before the Lord's Table.

Along with the Synod Fathers, Pope Francis underlines that remarried divorcees "are baptized; they are brothers and sisters; the Holy Spirit pours into their hearts gifts and talents for the good of all" (AL 299). The Protestant spouses in interchurch families would be delighted to be described in the same manner. For the moment, in the current state of the Roman Catholic Church's practice, I no longer feel fully accepted as a baptized sister, even though I grew up in this church almost as much as in the one I chose.

The real pain that results does not give testimony to God's unconditional love. Yet, the apostolic exhortation tells us that this unconditional love is related to "the highest and most central values of the Gospel", and suggests that these values could be superior to the (Catholic) church's moral teaching (AL 311). All Christians can feel the pain coming from division. As families, this division hurts us in our flesh because it concerns not only our life partner, our spouse, but also our children. Academic theological debate is not within the expertise of interchurch families, even though we make efforts to understand it and to benefit from it. But in contrast, we can recount what is perhaps the main contribution from interchurch families to ecumenical debates: the testimony of what we live, of what happens inside our domestic church.

When, years ago, one of my sons asked to receive his First Communion in the Catholic Church, as a Protestant mother, I welcomed this request and I thanked the Lord for it, without the shadow of a partisan ulterior motive, because this is not at all the issue. I met the priest who was accompanying the children, I explained our family situation, and I asked permission to receive the Eucharist with my son on this day of celebration. As a matter of fact, even if I do not share the ecclesiological reasons for stipulating discriminative conditions for the admission to the Lord's Table, I respect the Catholic Church's rule. The priest (I have to say that he had reached a certain age) gave me the authorisation with a big smile and a most fraternal "yes, of course". Two years later, another of my sons made the same request. I asked the same question to the new parish priest – he was younger – but he answered that it was not possible at all. He added, as an explanation, that Catholic

[11] See JOHN PAUL II: *Encyclical Letter* Ecclesia de Eucharistia, 2003, 30.

and Orthodox Churches had needed eight centuries to become reconciled, and Protestants and Catholics have "only" been divided for five centuries. And, after that, he ended our discussion. Not a fraternal word. No questions about my Eucharistic faith. No opportunity for dialogue. So, I did not receive the Eucharist with my little boy on the day on which he received this sacrament for the first time. During the entire celebration, I have to say that I was really angry. A painful anger, deep inside of me, obviously unable to consider any ecclesiological reason. An anger which totally prevented me from giving thanks on this day. Of course I did it later; interchurch families are resilient, and they move forward. But this division felt in the flesh was for me an existential experience of the spiritual violence of our separation. What can justify forbidding a baptized mother, believer, and activist for Christ, from receiving the Eucharist with her own children?

It is probably true that this priest was clumsy; it is certainly true that all priests do not react like he did. But the Catholic Church, for the moment, agrees with him on this issue, even if not on the form of his answer. Moreover, interchurch families testify that they are more and more often facing such refusals, even in "exceptional circumstances", in particular from priests who didn't experience the ecumenical momentum of the Second Vatican Council. And these priests are, of course, more and more numerous in the church. All the possible sociological thoughts on this situation cannot take away the reality that it induces and that we live in.

The Eucharistic fast can be a solution, or even a powerful act from ministers of our churches on the occasional situations of ecumenical celebrations. But I want to emphasize that it is inconceivable to fast each Sunday throughout our life as an interchurch couple. We would starve. So, let's listen again to the pope: "At times we find it hard to make room for God's unconditional love in our pastoral activity. We put so many conditions on mercy that we empty it of its concrete meaning and real significance. That is the worst way of watering down the Gospel." (AL 311) We can ask ourselves if this could not be true for ecclesiological considerations as it is for moral considerations.

1.2 What Kind of Example for our Children?

Concerning the children of divorced couples, the apostolic exhortation quotes a question from the pope's catechesis of August 5th 2015: "How can we encourage those parents to do everything possible to raise their children in the Christian life, to give them an example of committed and practical faith, if we keep them at arm's length from the life of the community, as if they were somehow excommunicated?" (AL 246) This question can also be asked concerning interchurch families. We make efforts to give a Christian education to our children; we teach them the words of our Lord: "Therefore, if you are offering your gift at the altar and there remember that your brother or sister has something against you, leave your gift there in front of the altar. First go and be reconciled to them; then come and offer your gift" (Mt 5,23-24). Unfortunately, they can observe, Sunday after Sunday, that we have now believed for five centuries that we are not reconciled enough to share together the bread of our Lord. What can be their thoughts when they observe the gap between announcing the primacy of God's powerful love and the fruits of sorrow that arise from the practical rule of the church? Moreover, when they ask to be confirmed, if they want to bear witness to their dual background – which is entirely different from a supposed third church –, they are told that it is impossible, and they can feel themselves condemned for what they are. This unity that they have lived inside of the domestic church of their family is to be shattered when they become adult persons in faith. What kind of example do we give with such a rule?

My personal experience is that at the beginning of our life as an interchurch couple, we alternated going to both churches. But for some years now, because of explicit refusals from ministers or magisterial messages unfavourable to Eucharistic hospitality, we have anchored our spiritual life in a Protestant harbour. So our children grew up as teenagers more in Protestantism than in Catholicism, although this was not our initial choice. It was not our life project. We really wanted to offer them the wealth of our spiritual diversity. But the attitude of the Roman Catholic Church, despite the work of some of its theologians,[12] has made this project so difficult that we eventually gave it up.

The paper adopted by the Second World Gathering of Interchurch Families, Rome 2003, quoted interchurch teenagers as declaring: "It is not we who are confused in refusing to choose one Church or the other. It is you of former generations who have been confused in accepting and perpetuating the divisions of the churches. Christ willed only one church."

"Let the little children come to me, and do not hinder them, for the kingdom of God belongs to such as these" (Lk 18,16).

1.3 A Reading of John 6

Facing all these questions, here is my reading of John 6. Five thousand men are there, and the women and the children. All are going to share, without any discrimination, the bread and fish. Judas Iscariot is there, too! All these people are the guests of our Lord. No entry ticket. Many of them are there simply out of curiosity, expecting a miracle. John is clear on that point: "a great crowd of people followed him because they saw the signs he had performed by healing the sick."

---

12 See e.g. CENTRE D'ETUDES ŒCUMÉNIQUES (STRASBOURG)/INSTITUT DE RECHERCHES ŒCUMÉNIQUES (TÜBINGEN)/INSTITUT DE RECHERCHES CONFESSIONNELLES (BENSHEIM): *Le partage eucharistique entre les Eglises est possible: Thèses sur l'hospitalité eucharistique*, Strasbourg: Academic Press, 2005.

Jesus himself says, later: "Very truly I tell you, you are looking for me, not because you saw the signs I performed but because you ate the loaves and had your fill." This is not even linked to curiosity, even less an issue of understanding what happens or what is the meaning of these signs. If those people are there, it is only because of the call of their bellies. They are here like beggars standing outside the door of a church. Even so, Jesus welcomes all of them, and he feeds them, himself. He does not say that their curiosity, or appetite, are not enough in order to be able to receive a part of this bread of life, or that it is necessary to fully understand everything, or have a pure doctrine before being able to ask and receive. He simply acts. He shares the bread and gives it to all these men, women, and children. Without any consideration of social background, age, intellect, moral value, or religious purity. It is enough to be there, to have followed the Master on this road, on this day. He does not ask for any baptismal certificate, nor promise of a commitment. Only later, will they understand. And, even then, they will not understand quickly. Even the apostles will become aware of the real signification of that sign only after the Resurrection. And probably some of those people will not understand at all. John tells us that many disciples will not accept Jesus's explanation of this sign, and will leave the community. But this was their choice, nobody had excluded them from the sharing of the bread and the Word. Jesus gave them first, without any condition, this possibility to understand the Eucharistic sharing by living (or experiencing) it.

I believe in a God who became human, who really experienced our lives, and whose Body was given for us, for all of us, without any discrimination, without any conditions for access. I do not believe that He rejoices when we stand divided when we are to remember or to make present the sacrifice, never mind *in reality* how we name it. An eminent educator of the beginning of the 20th century promoted the basic principle of "learning by doing" (Lord Robert Baden-Powell). I believe that this is what is at stake in Eucharistic hospitality. I believe that the strength given by the sacrament of unity is the ability to walk towards unity. This means learning unity by living it, by being confident in our God's power, by letting go of our intellectual – and so very human – certainties.

As interchurch families, we want to testify that each time we can receive the Eucharist together, we do not live this transgression of the rule as a transgression of the divine commandment (Lk 22,19; 1 Cor 11,25-26). On the contrary, it produces in our family life many spiritual fruits of joy, revival, encouragement, and strength, exactly the same as for other Christian families. Hence we share with the pope the belief that "[t]he family's communal journey of prayer culminates by sharing together in the Eucharist, especially in the context of the Sunday rest... For the food of the Eucharist offers the spouses the strength and incentive needed to live the marriage covenant each day as a 'domestic church'" (AL 318).

Then, why should we be eternally deprived of a "regular" access to this divine grace – "regular" having the dual meaning of "constant" and "in line with the rules" (see AL 316, 296)?

2 Reading *Amoris Laetitia* from the Perspective of a Theology of Interchurch Families

When interchurch families show themselves disappointed with the outcome of the 2014/2015 bishops' synods and the Post-Synodal Exhortation, their reaction may be understandable on a human level. But it is also perfectly justifiable from a theological point of view. I will first briefly summarize in what way contemporary church teaching and theological scholarship deal with interchurch marriage and the question of Eucharistic sharing. It will become clear that calling for the admission to communion of the entire interchurch family on a regular basis is not an exaggerated claim by those concerned but theologically sound and legitimate. I will then analyse what *Amoris laetitia* explicitly has to say about interchurch families and Eucharistic communion. In a third and final move I will try to infer what implications the overall theological and pastoral orientation of Pope Francis's exhortation may have for spouses and families who share their lives across denominational borders. The pope's message for them may then in the end be more hopeful than first thought.

2.1 Contemporary Church Teaching and Theology on Interchurch Families and Eucharist Sharing

Catholic teaching and theology refer to the Eucharist as "the fount and apex of the whole Christian life" (LG 11) by which the Christian faithful share in the life of the Triune God and the unity of the People of God is brought about. The Second Vatican Council regards the Eucharist as both *sign* and *source* of ecclesial unity. The Decree on Ecumenism states that Christ instituted "the wonderful sacrament of the Eucharist by which the unity of His Church is both signified and made a reality".[13] It goes on to say that common worship, including sharing the Eucharist, should bear witness to the unity of the church and provide a sharing in the means of grace to further perfect such ecclesial union. Where such unity is lacking or is imperfect, the Eucharist should as a rule not be shared unless it can serve in special circumstances as a means of grace to help restore lost or deficient ecclesial unity (see UR, 8). Seen from an ecclesiological point of view, there is thus not much to recommend Eucharistic sharing in the interchurch family on a regular basis. But

13 *Decree on Ecumenism* Unitatis Redintegratio, 2 (henceforward abbreviated as UR).

ecclesiology is only one aspect to be considered here; another and complementary one is the theology of marriage.

In the very same article of the Constitution on the Church mentioned above, the council refers to the sacrament of matrimony by which Christian spouses are said to "signify and partake of the mystery of that unity and fruitful love which exists between Christ and His Church" (LG 11). By virtue of the marital sacrament they not only "help each other to attain to holiness in their married life and in the rearing and education of their children" but have a special position and role within the church. The marriage of Christians gives rise to the family "in which new citizens of human society are born, who by the grace of the Holy Spirit received in baptism are made children of God, thus perpetuating the people of God through the centuries". It is here that the council refers to the family as a "domestic church", a realization of the church in its smallest unit.[14] This has massive implications for interchurch couples whose marriages the Catholic Church regards as sacramental[15] and whose families can then truly be called domestic churches as well.[16] Moreover, signifying and sharing the mystery of Christ's union with the church in their interpersonal conjugal union, interchurch spouses, just like Catholic same-church couples, bring about that ecclesial unity which finds its expression in and through the Eucharist. The close link between marriage and the Eucharist, which post-conciliar teaching consistently emphasizes, must therefore also be asserted for interchurch marriages and their families. There is no reason at all why interchurch families should not feel equally addressed when Pope Francis writes in *Amoris laetitia* that the family, which is entitled to "become a communion of persons in the image of the union of the Father, the Son and the Holy Spirit", is called "to join in daily prayer, to read the word of God and to share in Eucharistic communion, and thus to grow in love and become ever more fully a temple in which the Spirit dwells" (AL 29). It may then be that ecclesiological considerations advise against Eucharistic sharing in the domestic churches that are interchurch families as long as the church communities to which they belong are not in communion with one another – the theology of marriage in any case commends it despite the lack of full ecclesial unity. And that is why interchurch families cannot and should not turn a deaf ear to Pope Francis when he proclaims that "the family's communal journey of prayer culminates by sharing together in

---

[14] On the concept of domestic church see T. KNIEPS-PORT LE ROI/G. MANNION/P. DE MEY (eds.):*The Household of God and Local Households: Revisiting the Domestic Church* (BETL; 254), Leuven: Peeters Publishers, 2013.

[15] CIC 1983, can. 1055 §1 stipulates that every marriage between the baptized "has been raised by Christ the Lord to the dignity of a sacrament".

[16] The idea of interchurch families being domestic churches is developed in detail in T. KNIEPS-PORT LE ROI/R. TEMMERMAN (eds.): *Being One at Home*.

the Eucharist, especially in the context of the Sunday rest", and that "the food of the Eucharist offers the spouses the strength and incentive needed to live the marriage covenant each day as a 'domestic church'" (AL 318).

Contemporary theology has further developed these lines set out in Vatican II ecclesiology, sacramentology, and theology of marriage, arguing that the interchurch family is an ecclesial community which, on the basis of baptism and sacramental marriage, is entitled to share Eucharistic communion together.[17] Also, post-conciliar church teaching and discipline have come to acknowledge that interchurch spouses find themselves in a particular situation which differs from that of any other ecumenical grouping because of "the reception of the sacrament of Christian marriage by two baptized Christians".[18] The *Ecumenical Directory* thus admits the non-Catholic spouse in an interchurch marriage to Eucharistic communion but further stipulates that this admission "can only be exceptional" and that "in each case" the ecclesial norms concerning intercommunion must be observed.[19] What justifies such exceptional admission – in the case of interchurch marriages but also more broadly – are, according to the 1983 Code of Canon Law and the 1993 *Ecumenical Directory*, "situations of grave and pressing need".[20]

---

[17] See e.g. P. NEUNER: *Geeint im Leben – getrennt im Bekenntnis? Die konfessionsverschiedene Ehe: Lehre – Probleme – Chancen*, Düsseldorf: Patmos, 1989, 110f.; ID.: "Ein katholischer Vorschlag zur Eucharistiegemeinschaft", in: *Stimmen der Zeit* 211 (1993), 443-450; G. HINTZEN/P. NEUNER: "Eucharistiegemeinschaft für konfessionsverschiedene Ehen?", in: *Stimmen der Zeit* 211 (1993), 831-840; E. FALARDEAU: "The Church, the Eucharist and the Family", in: *One in Christ* 33 (1997), 20-30; B. PRUSAK: "The Ecumenical Household as Domestic Church: Ecclesial Threat of Pastoral Challenge and Even Resource?", in: T. KNIEPS-PORT LE ROI/R. TEMMERMAN (eds.): *Being One at Home*, 155-173; E. FALARDEAU: "Eucharistic Hunger in the Domestic Church: A View from Interchurch Families", in: T. KNIEPS-PORT LE ROI/R. TEMMERMAN (eds.): *Being One at Home*, 175-187.

[18] PONTIFICAL COUNCIL FOR PROMOTING CHRISTIAN UNITY: *Directory for the Application of Principles and Norms on Ecumenism*, 159.

[19] "Although the spouses in a mixed marriage share the sacraments of baptism and marriage, Eucharistic sharing can only be exceptional and in each case the norms stated above concerning the admission of a non-Catholic Christian to Eucharistic communion, [...] as well as those concerning the participation of a Catholic in Eucharistic communion in another Church, [...] must be observed." (Ibid. 160)

[20] See ibid. 130. The CIC 1983 in its can. 844 §4 stipulates the case and conditions of exceptional admission to the sacraments (of Penance, Eucharist and Anointing of the Sick) in the following way: "If the danger of death is present or if, in the judgment of the diocesan bishop or conference of bishops, *some other grave necessity* urges it, Catholic ministers administer these same sacraments licitly also to other Christians not having full communion with the Catholic Church, who cannot approach a minister of their own community and who seek such on their own accord, provided that they manifest Catholic faith in respect to these sacraments and are properly disposed" (emphasis added). It is obvious that while the Code primarily refers to objective circumstances (the absence of the non-Catholic minister and similar cases of "grave necessity") which may justify the admission of non-Catholics to the Eucharist, the *Ecumenical Directory*

Various bishops and bishops' conferences have since then specified that interchurch couples may indeed experience a "serious spiritual need" for sharing the Eucharist together which springs from the very nature of their marital commitment.[21] To accommodate this spiritual need, the concrete regulations in the respective pastoral guidelines of the local churches vary. Some restrict the admission of the non-Catholic spouse to a one-off event at unique occasions such as the nuptial mass or the funeral of the Catholic partner, others extend it to occasions of ecclesial or familial significance (such as ecclesial feast days or the celebration of first communion, confirmation, or the wedding of a child), while still others see a spiritual need arise every time an interchurch couple attends mass together. If indeed one follows the central theological argument that in the Eucharist "Christian spouses encounter the source from which their own marriage covenant flows, is interiorly structured, and continuously renewed",[22] it seems perfectly plausible to situate the spiritual need of interchurch spouses in the uniqueness of their situation as such rather than restricting it to unique occasions. For if marriage requires a continuous commitment of the spouses to realize conjugal and ecclesial unity in the domestic church, it also needs to be sustained on an ongoing basis.[23] The Interchurch Families International Network (IFIN) has therefore pointed out in its "Response to the 2015 Synod on the Family" that "Christian marriage is not a series of special occasions, but an on-going daily commitment to becoming ever more fully an intimate community of life and love, a domestic church. Exceptional Eucharistic sharing is needed throughout an interchurch marriage to sustain this communion in Christ, to express and to deepen it." Hence, it made the request to the Synod "that interchurch spouses who express a real need and desire for Eucharistic sharing, and who fulfil the criteria for admission, can be allowed to receive communion alongside their Catholic partners on an on-going basis, whenever they are at mass together."[24] Neither the Final Report of the 2015 synod nor the pope's Post-Synodal Exhortation, however, responded positively to this request.

also reckons with subjective "needs" on the part of the persons involved.

21 For an overview of such pastoral guidelines see B. PRUSAK: "The Ecumenical Household as Domestic Church", 161-171.

22 JOHN PAUL II: *Apostolic Exhortation* Familiaris *Consortio*, 1981, 57 (henceforward abbreviated as FC.

23 See R. REARDON: "One Bread One Body: A Commentary from an Interchurch Family Point of View", in: *One in Christ* 35 (1999), 109-130.

24 See *Response to the 2015 Synod on the Family from the Interchurch Families International Network*, 12.

2.2 *What* Amoris Laetitia *Says on Interchurch Marriage and Eucharistic Sharing*[25]

We have already indicated that *Amoris laetitia* as a whole does not pay excessive attention to interchurch families and their particular situation. The only paragraph dedicated to this issue (AL 247) simply repeats what the *Relatio synodi* of the 2015 synod had to say in its no. 72.[26] It states first that "marriages between Catholics and other baptized persons" have an intrinsic value and can make a contribution to the ecumenical movement. With a quotation from *Familiaris consortio* (no. 78), it is then urged that "an effort should be made to establish cordial cooperation between the Catholic and the non-Catholic ministers from the time that preparations begin for the marriage and the wedding ceremony". The remaining half of the paragraph is finally dedicated to Eucharistic sharing but it simply quotes what is said in nos. 159-160 of the *Ecumenical Directory*: a decision as to whether the non-Catholic party may be admitted to communion is to be made in keeping with the general norms, taking into account the particular situation of the reception of the sacrament of matrimony by two baptized Christians; although the spouses share the sacraments of baptism and matrimony, Eucharistic sharing can only be exceptional and in each case according to the stated norms.

Ruth Reardon has argued that although interchurch families had hoped for more, the exhortation's reference to the *Ecumenical Directory* has to be welcomed nonetheless. This is because the Directory's specific regulations with regard to interchurch marriages are not well known among many priests and even bishops who still tell non-Catholic spouses that they may not receive the Eucharist. "The general norms on Eucharistic sharing (*Directory* 129-131) are often quoted as though there were no specific reference to the particular situation of those who 'share the sacraments of baptism and marriage' later in the document", namely in its nos. 159-160.[27] In this way, the *Relatio synodi* 2015, and the Post-Synodal Exhortation which quotes from that final report, have corrected the false impression still given by the *Instrumentum laboris* 2015 which suggested that the non-Catholic spouse in an interchurch marriage may receive the Eucharist only if his or her pastor is not available, without referring to any spiritual need.[28] By quoting

25 This section draws on R. REARDON: "*Amoris Laetitia*: Comments from an Interchurch Family Perspective", in: *One in Christ* 50 (2016), 66-86.

26 See *The Final Report of the Synod of Bishops to the Holy Father, Pope Francis*, 24 October 2015, available from http://www.vatican.va/roman_curia/synod/documents/rc_synod_doc_20151026_relazione-finale-xiv-assemblea_en.html; accessed 15.01.2017.

27 R. REARDON: "*Amoris Laetitia*: Comments from an Interchurch Family Perspective", 67.

28 The *Instrumentum laboris* 2015 had formulated in its no. 128: "Some suggest that mixed marriages might be considered as cases of 'grave necessity,' in which it is possible that a baptized person who is not in full communion with the Catholic Church, yet shares the Church's faith

nos. 159-160 of the Directory, Pope Francis clearly confirms the special needs interchurch couples may have with regard to Eucharistic communion and, according to Reardon, implicitly warrants the pastoral option of exceptional Eucharistic sharing on an *ongoing* basis for those who wish to adopt it.

When the Catholic Bishops' Conference of England and Wales, Ireland, and Scotland issued *One Bread, One Body: A Teaching Document on the Eucharist in the Life of the Church, and the Establishment of General Norms on Sacramental Sharing* in 1998, Reardon had compellingly shown in her "Commentary from an Interchurch Family Point of View" that the bishops' had opted for a restrictive interpretation of the *Ecumenical Directory* when they read "exceptional" in the sense of "occasional" admission and finally reduced the possibility of Eucharistic sharing to "unique occasions". She continues that

> [t]he Directory itself never refers to occasions, nor to occasional Eucharistic sharing. It speaks of admission to Eucharistic communion as being permitted, or even commended, "in certain circumstances, by way of exception, and under certain conditions" (129). It is at the very least a legitimate reading of the text in n. 160 to refer the "exceptional" to the "cases" which follow, when it would mean that Eucharistic sharing for spouses in a mixed marriage is possible in exceptional cases where the conditions for admission are fulfilled. Here "cases" is taken to refer to couples, that is, to persons and not to "occasions".[29]

One could find a late proof that Reardon's reading is indeed legitimate when cross-checking it with a sequence in *Amoris laetitia* which deals with the admission to the Eucharist of divorced and remarried spouses. In AL 305 Francis maintains that "it is possible that in an objective situation of sin... a person can be living in God's grace, can love and can also grow in the life of grace and charity, while receiving the Church's help to this end", and then adds in footnote 351 that "[i]n certain cases, this can include the help of the sacraments". This is a rather convoluted way of saying that in particular cases and under certain conditions divorced and remarried Catholics can be admitted to the sacraments of Penance and the Eucharist. But nobody would ever doubt that the wording "in certain cases" (in Italian: *in certi casi*) does indeed directly refer to a category of *persons* being exceptionally admitted to the sacraments rather than to specific or unique *occasions* in the life of these persons. What the pope wants to express here is that they may receive the communion whenever they wish to do so, supposing that the conditions for ad-

---

in the Eucharist, be allowed to receive the Eucharist, when their pastors are not available and taking into account the criteria of the ecclesial community to which they belong (cf. [*Ecclesia de Eucharistia*], 45-46; Pontifical Council for Promoting Christian Unity, *Directory for the Application of Principles and Norms on Ecumenism*, 25 March 1993, 122-128)."

29 See R. REARDON: "One Bread One Body: A Commentary from an Interchurch Family Point of View".

mission are fulfilled. Analogously, when the Directory stipulates that Eucharistic sharing of the non-Catholic spouse in an interchurch marriage "can only be exceptional" and that "in each case" the existing norms have to be observed (no. 160), this can be taken to mean that in particular cases an interchurch couple may be allowed to receive communion whenever they attend Mass together and desire to do so.

We do not have to prove here, however, whether or not ongoing Eucharistic sharing in interchurch marriages is possible on the basis of the stipulations of the Ecumenical Directory. It seems in any case very likely that it is, since some local bishops and bishops' conferences have interpreted the Directory precisely in this way.[30] Likewise, there is no indication whatsoever that Pope Francis would want to negate this possibility. But has *Amoris laetitia* then no other message for interchurch families than that everything remains as it was before?

2.3 The Implicit Logic of Eucharistic Sharing in Amoris Laetitia

It is obvious that Pope Francis does not see the need to change doctrine or canon law. "...not all discussions of doctrinal, moral or pastoral issues need to be settled by interventions of the magisterium", he writes in the introduction to *Amoris laetitia* (3), and later explains that because of the "immense variety of situations" families are living in today, "neither the Synod nor this Exhortation could be expected to provide a new set of general rules, canonical in nature and applicable to all cases" (AL 300). When it comes to marriage and family, his aversion to doctrinal and canonical "one-size-fits-all" solutions has a self-critical note: "We have long thought that simply by stressing doctrinal, bioethical, and moral issues, without encouraging openness to grace, we were providing sufficient support to families, strengthening the marriage bond, and giving meaning to marital life." (AL 37) A mainly normative discourse, Francis seems to argue, has obscured the church's primary task of helping couples and families "better to respond to the grace that God offers them" (AL 35). The theme of God's grace being present in the lives of families and waiting to be discovered and responded to is indeed a frequently recurring, and probably the most central, concern of the pope in *Amoris laetitia*. He is also aware of the fact that many "appreciate the Church's efforts to offer guidance and counselling in areas related to growth in love, overcoming conflict and raising children" and are therefore "touched by the power of grace experienced in sacramental Reconciliation and in the Eucharist, grace that helps them face the challenges of marriage and the family" (AL 38). That this powerful source of support may flow more abundantly and reach families in their concrete living conditions is Francis's strongest desire, which finally makes him put all

[30] See ibid. 118f.

norms and rules, whether moral or ecclesiastical, in their place as the two by now famous footnotes 340 and 351 clearly demonstrate. Even a person who lives in an objective situation of sin "can be living in God's grace, can love and can also grow in the life of grace and charity, while receiving the Church's help to this end" which, as the footnote explains, "can include the help of the sacraments" (AL 305, footnote 351). Likewise, "the consequences or effects of a rule need not necessarily always be the same" which, as footnote 336 expounds, "is also the case with regard to sacramental discipline" (AL 300), if only the degree of responsibility of a person is taken into account. Both are clear indications that the power of divine grace and, even more so, a person's need of such grace, can definitely trump laws and rules, in this case ecclesiastical rules governing the dispensation of the sacraments.

It is not always so clear whether the pope refers to moral or ecclesiastical laws which both may be imposed to curtail the working of God's grace. When referring to divorced and remarried persons, his focus is primarily on the moral law, since living in a second union while the previous marriage is still valid is regarded by the church as living in adultery. But because, as we have already seen, "it is possible that in an objective situation of sin – which may not be subjectively culpable, or fully such – a person can be living in God's grace" (AL 305), it would be "reductive simply to consider whether or not an individual's actions correspond to a general law or rule, because that is not enough to discern and ensure full fidelity to God in the concrete life of a human being" (AL 304). It can therefore be that a person who has good reasons to stay in the second union[31] can recognize in his/her conscience "with sincerity and honesty what for now is the most generous response which can be given to God, and come to see with a certain moral security that it is what God himself is asking amid the concrete complexity of one's limits, while yet not fully the objective ideal" (AL 303). The moral law which prohibits adultery does thus not necessarily allow a judgment on the behaviour of a person which objectively contradicts the law but may subjectively be justified. To substantiate his claim, Francis recalls both a classical moral insight which says that general moral principles fail when it comes to matters of detail[32] and the understanding of the natural law which should not be regarded "as an already established set of rules that impose themselves a priori on the moral subject" but rather as "a source of objective inspiration for the deeply personal process of mak-

[31] Some of these reason are listed in AL 298.

[32] See AL 304. While referring to Thomas Aquinas, the pope in fact recalls the principle of *epikeia* which goes back to Plato and Aristotle. See G. VIRT: "Moral Norms and the Forgotten Virtue of Epikeia in the Pastoral Care of the Divorced and Remarried", in: *Melita theologica* 63/1 (2013), 17-35.

ing decisions"[33]. Moral decisions have thus to be taken in a personal process of prudent discernment for which general moral principles serve as sources of orientation and inspiration but as such do not determine a person's moral responsibility once the decision has been made nor do they give any indication of the state of grace this person at this point is in.[34]

If moral laws ought not cut off people from the inexhaustible source of divine grace, ecclesiastical rules should do so still less. This is the pope's second concern with regard to the discipline of the sacraments, which makes him call for the possibility of divorced and remarried persons to receive the sacraments of Reconciliation and the Eucharist. He thereby recalls what he had expressed already in *Evangelii gaudium*,[35] namely that "the confessional must not be a torture chamber, but rather an encounter with the Lord's mercy" (EG 44) and the Eucharist be "not a prize for the perfect, but a powerful medicine and nourishment for the weak" (EG 47).[36] In fact, the same conditions that are applicable to personal moral decision-making also apply here to canonical decisions with regard to the admission to the sacraments: "general rules set forth a good which can never be disregarded or neglected, but in their formulation [...] cannot provide absolutely for all particular situations" (AL 304); and "the consequences or effects of a rule need not necessarily always be the same" (AL 300). The only additional requirement here is that the process of personal discernment has to be accompanied and supported by a pastoral discernment, i.e. a "[c]onversation with the priest, in the internal forum, [which] contributes to the formation of a correct judgment on what hinders the possibility of a fuller participation in the life of the Church and on what steps can foster it and make it grow" (AL 300).

If we try to draw any conclusions from the perspectives *Amoris laetitia* opens for the admission to communion of remarried divorcees for the Eucharistic practice in interchurch families, we should start from the pope's genuine concern that God's grace may not be hindered to help couples face the challenges of married and family life. Having unmistakably pointed out that the grace of God works

33 AL 305 quotes here from a document of the INTERNATIONAL THEOLOGICAL COMMISSION: *In Search of a Universal Ethic: A New Look at Natural Law*, 2009, 59, available from http://www.vatican.va/roman_curia/congregations/cfaith/cti_documents/rc_con_cfaith_doc_20090520_legge-naturale_en.html; accessed 15.01.2017.

34 AL 301 expresses clearly that "it is can no longer simply be said that all those in any 'irregular' situation are living in a state of mortal sin and are deprived of sanctifying grace".

35 FRANCIS: *Apostolic Exhortation* Evangelii Gaudium, 2013 (henceforward abbreviated as EG).

36 AL 305, footnote 351. With regard to the Eucharist, Francis clearly opts here for the second of two principles which the Decree on Ecumenism of Vatican II had formulated for practicing common worship with separated churches: "first, the bearing witness to the unity of the Church, and second, the sharing in the means of grace. Witness to the unity of the Church very generally forbids common worship to Christians, but the grace to be had from it sometimes commends this practice." (UR 8)

in their lives as well [i.e. of those who participate in the Church's life in an incomplete manner] by giving them the courage to do good, to care for one another in love and to be of service to the community in which they live and work" (AL 291), Francis has broken new ground in theology which finally makes him demand that the flow of grace should not be hindered by any moral or church law. But it is here already that interchurch families would reject, and rightly so, any attempt to put their situation on equal footing with what *Amoris laetitia*, although respectfully, refers to as "irregular marital situations".[37] When falling into love with and marrying someone from a different church or church community, interchurch spouses do not go against any moral ideal of the Catholic Church. We have shown above how contemporary church teaching and theology recognize the value of interchurch marriage on the basis of common baptism and the shared sacrament of marriage. And also *Amoris laetitia* talks about the "intrinsic value" of interchurch marriage (247). The exclusion of the non-Catholic spouse from sharing the Eucharist is thus not caused by any moral failure as in the case of divorced and remarried spouses whose state and condition of life, at least in previous church teaching, was said to "objectively contradict that union of love between Christ and the Church which is signified and effected by the Eucharist" (FC 84). What impedes the union between Christ and the church to be symbolized in the Eucharistic sharing of the interchurch marriage is the lack of full "unity in faith, worship and community life" between the churches to which the spouses (and their families) belong[38] a fact that the spouses are not responsible for nor can do anything about. If one follows the logic of *Amoris laetitia*, it is unthinkable that interchurch families should remain deprived of "the food of the Eucharist [which] offers the spouses the strength and incentive needed to live the marriage covenant each day as a 'domestic church'" (AL 318), only because official church bodies refuse – or do not succeed in realizing – the full unity of and in the Body of Christ.[39] When visiting the Lutheran church in Rome in November 2015 and

---

37 *Amoris laetitia* puts "irregular situations" continuously in inverted commas. – In the *Relatio synodi* of 2014, interchurch or, in ecclesiastical parlance, "mixed marriages" were still dealt with under the heading of "Caring for Wounded Families"; see *Relatio synodi*, 2014, 54, available from http://www.vatican.va/roman_curia/synod/documents/rc_synod_doc_20141018_relatio-synodi-familia_en.html; accessed 15.01.2017. AL 247 lists them in a section entitled "Certain complex situations".

38 See *Ecumenical Directory*, 129.

39 It is true that Pope Francis knows of situations in which, following St Paul's admonition in 1 Cor 11,17-34, the unity of the Body of Christ is indeed wounded and the Eucharist should not be received (see AL 185-186). This is the case when "scandalous distinctions and divisions among its members" are being created (AL 186). Francis reads the Pauline text as "a serious warning to those families who withdraw into their own comfort zone and close themselves off, in particular, however, for families who remain indifferent vis-à-vis the suffering of poor and most needy families" (AL 186; the English translation leaves out this sentence which in the

being asked by the Lutheran wife married to a Roman-Catholic about Eucharistic communion in the interchurch family, Pope Francis gave an answer completely in line with this theological logic:

> I respond to your question only with a question: how can I participate with my husband, so that the Lord's Supper may accompany me on my path? It is a problem to which each person must respond. A pastor friend of mine said to me: "We believe that the Lord is present there. He is present. You believe that the Lord is present. So what is the difference?" – "Well, there are explanations, interpretations… ". Life is greater than explanations and interpretations. Always refer to Baptism: "One faith, one baptism, one Lord", as Paul tells us, and take the outcome from there. I would never dare give permission to do this because I do not have the authority. One Baptism, one Lord, one faith. Speak with the Lord and go forward. I do not dare say more.[40]

One may indeed complain – and some have done so with regard to the somewhat cryptic admission of divorced and remarried spouses to the sacraments contained in the two footnotes[41] – that *Amoris laetitia* does not draw out more explicitly the implications of its theology for the issue of Eucharistic sharing in interchurch families. Pope Francis, however, seems convinced that a change of attitude is more important than, and must be prior to, changing the rules and regulations. Reardon has therefore well captured what might be the answer to the question of so many interchurch families: "Does this leave interchurch families where we were before? Does *Amoris Laetitia* leave the Church where we were before? There has been no change in legislation. But the entirely new insistence on discernment by couples and families and their pastoral accompaniment by parishes, priests, and bishops may in time create an entirely new climate of pastoral understanding that will lead to a new flourishing of the domestic churches that contribute to as well as receive from the life of the Church."[42] It is this new climate of pastoral understanding, supported by a renewed theology of marriage, grace and Eucharistic unity, that interchurch families may put their hope in.

Italian original runs as follows: "Questo testo biblico è un serio avvertimento per le famiglie che si richiudono nella loro propria comodità e si isolano, ma più specificamente per le famiglie che restano indifferenti davanti alle sofferenze delle famiglie povere e più bisognose"). This warning, however, includes interchurch as much as same-church families.

40 Quoted in R. REARDON: "*Amoris Laetitia*: Comments from an Interchurch Family Perspective", 86.

41 See e.g. N. LÜDECKE: *Déjà vu 2.0*, 18 July 2016, available from http://theosalon.blogspot.be/2016/07/deja-vu-20.html; accessed 15.01.2017.

42 R. REARDON: "*Amoris Laetitia*: Comments from an Interchurch Family Perspective", 86.

Part III

PASTORAL MINISTRY TO THE DIVORCED AND REMARRIED AFTER *AMORIS LAETITIA* – VOICES FROM THE PRACTICE

Divorced-Remarried Catholics: Pastoral Care in England and Wales

Elizabeth Davies

When I was invited to describe new perspectives and possibilities in pastoral care for divorced-remarried persons in England and Wales, in the light of *Amoris laetitia*, I will admit that my heart sank a little. After all, we are still in the very earliest days of reflecting on Pope Francis' exhortation. Our bishops were due to convene in plenary session shortly after *The Joy of Family* was published, and were therefore able to issue an immediate positive reaction. But the concrete, practical implications of this innovative document will take longer to be thought through and implemented. So, in England and Wales, we remain, for the present, only on the threshold of new possibilities.

Since I have also been asked to describe current provision for divorced-remarried Catholic-Christians, this will be the main focus of this article, prefaced by historical context covering the last thirty years or so. I will then turn to some current challenges and implications of *Amoris laetitia* as noted by a group of diocesan clergy, before concluding with my own thoughts on the practical challenges of the journey on which we are all now embarking.

1 Historical Context

Concern for the divorced-remarried has been a constant theme of pastoral care in England and Wales for many years, evidenced in both public and private documents. In 1980 our National Pastoral Congress noted that:

> While the problem of divorce is daunting enough, the questions posed by Catholics who enter a second irregular marriage are even more searching. Can they ever be admitted again to Holy Communion? May they ever have their second marriage blessed by the Church?[1]

---

1 CATHOLIC BISHOPS OF ENGLAND AND WALES: *The Easter People: A Message from the Roman Catholic Bishops of England and Wales in the Light of the National Pastoral Congress, , Liverpool, 1980*, Slough: St. Paul Publications, 1980, 109.

Stimulated by the findings of the Pastoral Congress, Archbishop Derek Warlock used his intervention at the 1980 Synod of Bishops on the family to highlight this great concern:

> Nor can the Church neglect those Catholics whose first marriage has perished and who now find themselves in a second more stable and perhaps more mature union which have many of the desirable qualities of the Christian family... The number of such members of the Church is growing daily and very many long for full Eucharistic communion with the Church and its Lord... many pastors and many theologians are of the view that such Catholics may be admitted to Holy Communion... many married laity, moved by pastoral compassion, are of the same opinion and do not fear that Christian marriage will be destroyed by such a practice.[2]

In 1981 a lay-led Association for Separated and Divorced Catholics was launched in the diocese of Salford. This group offered peer-support around the country, though possibly not for the divorced-remarried. A similar network of support groups developed in the Archdiocese of Liverpool, known as Rainbow Groups. For a number of years these groups have been the main referral route for diocesan coordinators when approached for support by separated or divorced Catholics.

In 1989 the Bishops' Committee for Marriage and Family Life commissioned an inter-disciplinary study of the various situations of people whose marriages "have broken down or who are in second or invalid marriages".[3] Fr Timothy Buckley, a Redemptorist priest, reported the findings of this research to the Bishops in 1994, after which they issued a statement expressing regret for the failings of the Catholic community in this area of pastoral ministry. It was accepted that many separated, divorced and divorced-remarried Catholics felt alienated or ostracised.

One of Buckley's objectives was to suggest a "coherent pastoral policy based on a sound theology of sacrament and Church".[4] In his book *What Binds Marriage?* Buckley highlighted the fundamental challenges of devising a "coherent pastoral policy". He examined the possibilities in the Orthodox tradition and in the work of the German bishops before concluding that the church remained at something of an impasse. In his view the theology underpinning the ontological bond would need to be revisited before a way through this impasse could be found.

Stimulated by Buckley's findings, the Committee for Marriage and Family Life developed a number of recommendations regarding pastoral care of separated, divorced and divorced-remarried Catholics, which were accepted as guide-

2 C. LONGLEY: *The Warlock Archive*, London: Geoffrey Chapman, 2000, 290.

3 T. BUCKLEY: *What Binds Marriage? Roman Catholic Theology in Practice*, London: Geoffrey Chapman, 2002, 1.

4 Ibid. 2.

lines by the bishops in 1996.[5] These recommendations included setting up support groups, providing counselling, skills training for listening to and supporting those in irregular situations, continued ministerial formation to help clergy respond, improved processes in diocesan tribunals and the need for sensitive language in describing these situations.

Ten years later, in 2006, the Bishops' Conference returned to the question of pastoral care for the divorced and remarried following the national family consultation Listening 2004. The report on Listening 2004 notes that:

> We repeatedly heard requests that the practice of excluding divorced-remarried people from the Eucharist be reconsidered.
>
> *"There's not enough understanding on behalf of our Catholic Church. Bashing people instead of a supportive ear. Can't receive sacraments at people's lowest hour. Life is very difficult for most people all the time. Listen to people's point of view & try to learn." (East Anglia)*
>
> *"To tell people who are not 'in good standing' to stay away from Communion is like telling people who are cold to stay away from the fire." (Menevia)*
>
> These requests did not come only from those personally affected but from a significant proportion of the participants in Listening 2004. Many families had at least indirect experience of divorce and remarriage and the practice was most often interpreted as representing a lack of forgiveness and mercy on the part of Christ's church.[6]

A leaflet, endorsed by the bishops, was developed for the national project *Everybody's Welcome*. This had the rather long title: *What is Life Like if You or Someone in Your Family is Divorced and Remarried and what Can Your Parish Family Do to Make a Difference?*[7] Aimed at parish pastoral councils its simple structure included a glimpse of what life is like for divorced-remarried Catholics, the questions this raises for the parish, some possible resources with which to respond, ideas for involving these Catholics in the liturgical and ministerial life of the parish and some prayers, particularly a prayer for a spiritual communion. (I remember the search for a suitable prayer and being surprised how few there were to choose from. We created our own in the end.)

So, that's the history, and it's a history of continued concern and some practical action. So where are we now?

---

5 Available from www.catholicfamily.org.uk/what-we-do/marriage/divorced-and-separated-catholics; accessed 29.12.2017.

6 CATHOLIC BISHOPS' CONFERENCE OF ENGLAND AND WALES: *"Not Easy But Full of Meaning": Catholic Family Life in 2004*, Chawton, Hants: Redemptorist Publications, 2005, 177-178.

7 Available from www.catholicfamily.org.uk/what-we-do/marriage/divorced-and-separated-catholics; accessed 29.12.2016.

2 Current Challenges

The pre-Extraordinary Synod consultations showed that concerns for the divorced-remarried remain a priority for both priests and people in England and Wales. This issue was highlighted across all diocesan reports. Exclusion of the divorced-remarried from the Eucharist was seen as an unnecessary lack of love by the church. Although we had no statistics about the numbers of divorced-remarried Catholics, diocesan coordinators of family ministry felt that in this respect the Catholic community was no different from the rest of society. In 2013 33% of marriages in England and Wales were remarriages for one or both partners.[8]

I want to briefly share just one story from our pre-Synod consultation – you will have your own I know, but testimonies are important in an arena such as this. This is a glimpse of the experience of a young divorced-remarried mother writing after having been received into the church with all her children from her first marriage. She had chosen to live as brother and sister with her second husband who was not a Catholic, rather than forego becoming Catholic. She wrote:

> Sometimes when we turn to faith, life can be turned upon its head and become utterly crucifying. I am living through such a moral dilemma. I have felt that any which way I turn I morally fail someone, whether my husband, the church, my children, or myself. My husband and I have had to learn to be with each other in a new way, and to succeed in this at times makes life even harder. It would be easier to walk away. We are just barely companions, any form of emotional togetherness or intimate truth is ruined... I am still a young woman at 43, to have the intimacy removed is crucifying, because all emotional intimacy was withdrawn from me. We cannot afford to live in two houses. We have children who have been witness to the visible strain.

Given the continuing need for pastoral care for divorced-remarried Catholics, it was therefore disconcerting to learn in 2015 that the Association of Divorced and Separated Catholics had decided to cease activities due to a decline in membership. This prompted an enquiry with dioceses which revealed few other available resources. This feedback comes from Diocesan Coordinators of Family Ministry:

> Books and websites are useful for information and sign-posting... However, those who live with the pastoral difficulties involved with Divorce & Remarriage need and fully deserve the sensitive & loving support of the entire community of faith.
>
> 1. The network of family, friends & parish community are the most vital resource.

8 See www.ons.gov.uk/peoplepopulationandcommunity/birthsdeathsandmarriages/marriagecohabitationandcivilpartnerships/bulletins/marriagesinenglandandwalesprovisional/2013; accessed 29.12.2016.

> 2. The understanding & support from our priests is a "post-code lottery". Some priests are not aware of the changing language and sensitivity of pastoral outreach that they are called to offer. They are not always aware of the "paths of discernment" and the appropriate use of the "internal forum".

It appears that most of our available resources are relational, that is, putting people in touch with one another, matching need with service and especially putting divorced-remarried Catholics in touch with sensitive clergy. One Coordinator wrote:

> I see myself as a facilitator, go-between, bridge-builder and point-of-reference for both clergy and laity.

The enquiry also revealed that many of the challenges that our bishops' 1996 Guidelines for Pastoral Care sought to address remain unresolved. Another of our Coordinators identified:

> ...an urgent need to educate our Clergy concerning: The appropriate sensitivity of language. The developing pastoral responses available, including Revised process for annulments ie Paths of discernment, Internal Forum to enable them to generously respond with the tenderness, mercy & compassion of Christ. There is then a need to increase the awareness of the Lay Faithful so that they can feel confident in approaching their clergy – especially in this Jubilee Year of Mercy.

3 Reception of *Amoris Laetitia*

Amoris laetitia has received mostly a very positive response, especially among the laity, though a few not so positive, frustrated, responses can be read in the online media. Here I want to draw on feedback from a group of clergy from a large, rural diocese with whom I worked recently. Together we took a "birds-eye-view" at the document and identified some of its implications. A good portion of time was set aside for their own conversations and feedback, to "feel for the pulse" of their reaction. This can be summed up in three words: good, affirming and confusing.

Good because:

> It opens up the way to discernment, and the emphasis is on the bishop and his representatives – that's a good thing because of all the cultural differences in the church.

Affirming because:

> What we've been doing for years very much reflects the approach in Amoris laetitia – so it feels like vindication.

Confusing because:

> Parishioners thought that Holy Communion would be allowed. Some won't bother [to read it], some will read bits but most will use what they hear from others. There is also confusion among the clergy. Our worries lie with the ambiguities, which are confusing and unclear.

This word *confusing* has recurred in other conversations I've heard about *Amoris laetitia.* In my view it is simply indicative of the complexity highlighted in *Amoris laetitia* that emerges when walking alongside individuals in seeking what God asks of us. The diocesan clergy also used this term:

> There is complexity in *Amoris laetitia* because it is so conscious that doctrine cannot be applicable in every respect, therefore pastoral discernment is essential. It doesn't answer a lot of questions that arise, but it calls us to reach out to everyone, to take people where they are and not where they should be.

Happily, a good number of them expressed a willingness to work through this complexity with their parishioners.

4 Concluding Thoughts

I'd like to conclude with my own thoughts on the practical implications of accompanying, discerning and integrating our neighbour, as envisaged in *Amoris laetitia*:

1. Accompaniment invites us not to avoid the issues, but to walk alongside each other with honesty and transparency. A key role in accompaniment is taken by family and friends. Ideally they will appreciate that the church is also a companion for them on the journey and can support them in their inalienable role. However, our experience in family ministry shows us that it is sensitive work for which not all in the church are necessarily equipped or inclined. More thought must be given to how best to prepare the whole community for walking alongside the divorced-remarried and others in difficult situations in a steadfast, non-judgmental, caring way.

2. Regarding discernment, there are clearly challenges for the local magisterium in determining how they would prefer this to unfold practically: which path to take when the road ahead appears to diverge, how to express uniformity and unity within diversity. Everyone is concerned for unity and to avoid conflicting approaches in different parishes and dioceses. For busy priests there are also time implications in accompanying those in difficult situations over a sustained period: "We may not have time to be present to parishioners – we need to form more people to do this."

3. Integrating those who have felt excluded is undoubtedly a welcome re-emphasis for the future, particularly with greater clarity about the possibilities of

participating in the liturgical and ministerial life of the church. Expectations in this regard will, I think, be just as high as expectations of receiving the Eucharist. One of the greatest gifts of this exhortation is that it tells families and the church that families no longer need to be perfect and that they can expect the church to bend over backwards to care for them – just as we parents often find ourselves going to great lengths to accommodate our children.

In conclusion, I believe that the possibilities envisaged in *Amoris laetitia* are liberating but labour-intensive, challenging but necessary. I am not convinced that this calls for new resources (barring the Bishops' Conference guidance on discernment requested by the clergy) but rather for better information and formation and for us all to have much bigger hearts. Community-building initiatives within the parish are especially essential if families in challenging situations are to experience the love and care of the Christian community.

Existing Practices and New Initiatives for the Divorced and Remarried in France

Monique Baujard

It is rather difficult to give an overview of the new perspectives and possible changes after *Amoris laetitia*. It is too early to have a realistic view on what this text will yield. As different voices have pointed out already, Pope Francis does not change canon law but he makes room for discernment and conscience. And even for this, he does not give concrete guidelines.

1 Discovering the Text of *Amoris Laetitia*

What can be concretely observed until now in France, is that many dioceses take their time. Often a first step is the organization of study-days, talks, and meetings to bring priests and lay people in contact with the text. A certain number of dioceses organized their autumn session around *Amoris laetitia* and found it important that priests and lay people work on the text together. An important academic study-day took also place at the *Institut Catholique de Paris* on the 17th of October 2016.

The text is long and many people won't read it unless they are guided. To promote widespread reading, the French Bishops' Conference issued a reading guide[1], with introductions for each chapter, questions to go beyond the text, a glossary, etc. The idea is to bring as many people as possible in direct contact with the text, to enter the spirit of conversion Pope Francis is speaking about. Small reading groups are set up in different places, the diocese of Metz registered an audio version of the text, the diocese of Versailles proposed to live Lent with *Amoris laetitia*, etc. But again, it will take time to spread the message of *Amoris laetitia*.

1 FRANÇOIS: *La joie de l'amour*, édition présentée et annotée sous la direction du Service national Famille et Société de la Conférence des évêques de France et de la Faculté de théologie du Centre Sèvres, Paris: Fidélité-Namur: Lessius, 2016.

2 New Initiatives and Guidelines to Come

Amoris laetitia was also on the agenda of the plenary session of the French bishops in Lourdes early November. But there is no project for national guidelines.

The Archbishop of Rouen was the first to launch a concrete project within the framework of the Holy Year of Mercy. He wrote a letter inviting divorced, separated and/or remarried persons to come to the cathedral on the 1st of November, to pass the threshold of the Holy Door with him, pray Vespers together and receive his benediction/blessing before starting a period of discernment. His letter is published on the website of the diocese, but was also handed out to Catholics in person.[2] In his letter he asks them several times for forgiveness: forgiveness if the attitude of the church hurt them, forgiveness if they experience the law as a burden or as stones cast on their lives, and forgiveness if they suffer from their exclusion from the sacraments. He has entrusted seven priests with the mission to become "missionaries of mercy": they are to listen to anyone who is in a difficult situation with regard to marriage and family and who wants to think about his or her place in the church. The process of discernment goes through two stages: firstly, in an inner sanctum as it were, between the person or couple and the "missionary of mercy", and only later within the wider circle of community, with the parish and its priest. The possibility of access to the sacraments is mentioned, but it is clear that it is not automatic. The document points out the diversity of situations and repeats that *Amoris laetitia* asks for a case-by-case approach and not for general rules.

The Bishop of Le Havre, who is also the president of the Council for Family and Society in the French bishops' Conference, launched his pastoral orientations by the end of 2016. He insists on the personal and pastoral discernment and the role of the parish. In his diocese, lay people as well as priests can accompany those who want to start this process of discernment. For him, it is clearly an open and ongoing process in which each person will have to find out in conscience, and with the help of others, how he or she can best be integrated in the church. Other bishops will probably issue documents during 2017. Some already have projects in the books but want to listen to the needs of their diocese and are taking advice from different stakeholders. Several questions came up in these informal discussions: what is the place of the bishop? Is it at the start of the process, to launch it and encourage participation, or at the end of it, to approve the outcome and potentially grant access to sacraments? What is the finality of this discernment

---

2 *Lettre et invitation de Mgr Dominique Lebrun, aux personnes séparées, divorcées, divorcées remariées, membres de l'Église catholique*, 8.9.2016; available from http://www.la-croix.com/Religion/France/Lettre-invitation-Mgr-Dominique-Lebrun-personnes-separees-divorcees-divorcees-remariees-membres-lEglise-catholique-2016-11-02-1200800269; accessed 12.01.2017.

process? Integrating a community means more than blessing a second union. And what is the place of the community? Should the community be informed of the outcome of the process of discernment of one of its members? How will "inward" and "outward" discernment be articulated? What if a conflict arises? It is expected that a certain number of questions will be resolved in practice as things will go along.

Another interesting initiative is fostered by *SeDiRe – Séparés, Divorcés, Remariés*, an organization gathering lay people and priests. The project is called "Bartimée" and aims to (re)integrate persons into the community. It offers personal and pastoral discernment within a parish for divorced and remarried people. The project has been taken up by a parish nearby Lyon and for the moment there has only be one meeting to inform people about this new project, but it shows that spontaneous, local initiatives are also to be expected.

While there is a lot of activity and reflection around *Amoris laetitia*, this does not mean that all bishops, priests and lay people are convinced. There still is a lot of resistance. An article published in *La Croix*, France's largest Catholic daily, on October 17th 2016, spoke about "those Catholics whom Pope Francis disturbs". It will take time and a lot of perseverance to get changes into practice.

3 Existing Practices and Documents

It is perhaps a little deceiving to focus only on initiatives following the publication of *Amoris laetitia.* This overview should not hide the great number of already existing practices and documents that find themselves strengthened and encouraged by *Amoris laetitia.* In a great number of parishes, it's been years since informal groups of divorced and remarried people gather to pray, read Scripture and share their experiences. These groups will certainly take up *Amoris laetitia*, but their feedback is yet to come.

There are also established organisations in France that specifically take care of divorced and remarried people: *Miséricorde et Vérité*; *Cana Samarie*, part of the charismatic *Chemin Neuf*; *Amour et Vérité*, part of the *Communauté de l'Emmanuel*; *Equipes reliance*: part of *Equipes Notre-Dame*; *Chrétiens divorcés chemin d'espérance*, with more than 50 groups in France, having actively promoted access to sacraments after discernment since a long time; *SeDiRe*, a group a lay people and priests who offer a prayer to celebrate a civil marriage after a divorce.

These groups are not at all on the same wavelength. For some, *Amoris laetitia* clearly grants access to the sacraments, while for others nothing changed and *Amoris laetitia* just asks for taking more patience and more time to explain to divorcees and remarried people why they can't access sacraments! But all are working on *Amoris laetitia.*

One also notices that other organisations are starting to take greater notice of remarried divorcees. For instance, the Jesuit Centre *Manrèse* organizes sessions every year for couples and also for divorced or separated couples. For the first time now, they have planned a weekend specially devoted to divorced and remarried people.

In several dioceses too there were existing documents on the pastoral care of remarried divorcees, which had remained very confidential until now. At least two dioceses where such documents existed took them up again with a variety of people (priests, lay people, remarried divorcees etc.). Here again we are waiting for the outcome.

The French Bishops' Conference sent out an inquiry to all dioceses to get a better overview of existing practices and new initiatives. The outcome showed a large variety of situations across France. The national meeting of diocesan delegates for family at the end of January 2017 was dedicated to the question of accompaniment and discernment and pointed out a huge need of training for pastoral care of families. This brought both the Catholic Universities of Paris and Lyon to start in autumn 2017 specific trainings for those who are active in this field.

Finally, quite frequently, priests were already practising discernment on access to sacraments. As a rule these cases remained confidential. When remarried couples were authorized to access the sacraments, publicity was avoided. Sometimes they were asked to do so outside of their usual parish. Consequently, some priests say that *Amoris laetitia* is only formalizing existing practices.

4 Changes to Come

In France, as elsewhere, the question of what *Amoris laetitia* really changes is still open. We have a conservative stream within the Catholic Church, not very important in numbers, but quite active in social media. For the conservatives, as the law does not change, nothing changes at all. Of course, we also have a more progressive stream, which was hoping for a quick and radical change. They are screening the text and see many possibilities for change but do not quite know how far they can go. And as it takes time to put things into practice, they are afraid that finally nothing will change.

A close reading of *Amoris laetitia* reveals an unexpected answer: Pope Francis does not change the rules but asks *us* to change. He asks us to change our outlook on the world and the way we view each person. He asks us to see how the love of God is already at work in each and every one of us, regardless of matrimonial situations. And, starting from this point, he asks us to find out how to best accompany a person on his or her way to God. But there will be no change as long as Catholics don't accept to change themselves.

Alongside this first personal change the Pope is calling for, *Amoris laetitia* also induces important institutional changes inside the church itself. Discernment and conscience ask for a more individual approach and for specific treatment in each case. This means that in two apparently similar cases, the concrete outcome of the process of discernment can be different: some divorced and remarried people will have access to the sacraments, others will not. Bishops and priests will have to explain this to the faithful and seem anxious that this might become a contentious issue within Catholic communities. To accept that we are no longer in a uniform or monolithic church, but in a polyhedral church, is a second big change.

In creating space for conscience and discernment, Pope Francis decentralizes the church and puts each and every bishop, priest and lay Catholic in front of his or her own responsibility. Here lies a third important change *Amoris laetitia* can foster: teaching Catholics to think and decide by themselves. That is not in our catholic culture. Too often lay people are used to obey a priest, priests to listen to their bishop and bishops to wait for instructions from Rome. *Amoris laetitia* does not say we can all do whatever we want. Instead, *Amoris laetitia* speaks about personal and pastoral discernment, a discernment that takes place in a dialogue. Lay people still have to listen to priests, and priests to bishops and bishops to Rome, but the listening needs also to be done the other way round. Thus while it undermines the top-down culture which has prevailed in the Church until now, *Amoris laetitia* preserves and perhaps even strengthens a sense of community and communion.

To conclude, implementing *Amoris laetitia* requires continuing the process initiated by the Synod on family. Pope Francis is calling for a synodal church, a church where we all have to learn from each other and where each individual accepts to serve the others. *Amoris laetitia* is a milestone on the way to this synodal church. It certainly marks a point of no return, but it is too early to know to what extent. Speaking in rugby terms: Pope Francis scored a try, it is now up to local churches to convert it.

Pastoral Care of Divorced People in the Catholic Church in Flanders

Hilde Pex

In this presentation I will briefly discuss pastoral care of divorced and separated people in the Flemish dioceses of the Catholic Church. First, I will give some numeric data on the current situation and discuss some current initiatives for divorced people in our Flemish dioceses. Then I will present the opinions and considerations of people involved in and responsible for the pastoral care of divorced people in the dioceses, as collected almost eight years ago. We consulted them on the situation of divorced people in their relation with and to the church. These considerations will be shown to be very much in line with what the broader community of the faithful answered in a questionnaire sent by the Belgian Bishops at the end of 2013, in preparation of the first Bishops' Synod on the family. Finally, I will briefly recall some specific aspects in *Amoris laetitia* which address some of the concerns raised previously. But some issues remain.

1 Divorce Trends in Belgium

According to official Belgian statistics,[1] until 2007 the number of yearly divorces is quite stable at 30.000 per year. In 2008 there is a sudden increase to more than 35.000 divorces, but this is likely due to a new law that was put in force in Belgium to simplify the procedure to divorce. In particular, it became much easier to divorce in cases of mutual agreement. It is likely that some couples waited for this law to decide on the future of their marriage. But since 2009 the number of divorces consistently diminishes from year to year, from more than 32.000 in 2009 to around 24.000 in 2015, and seems to stabilize in the last three years.

It seems relevant to make some observations about this decreasing tendency: 1) The number of civil marriages varied slightly in this period, and averages around 42.000. It was much higher though in the period before, systematically

[1] Source: http://statbel.fgov.be/nl/statistieken/cijfers/bevolking/huwelijken_echtscheidingen_samenwoning/; accessed 14.10.2016.

coming down from 64.000 marriages in 1990. The number of people that cohabit with a registered contract increased to about 80.000, with half as many contracts ended yearly. 2) Marriages that end in divorce, have lasted on average 15 years in Belgium. This number is more or less constant since 2000. 3) Despite the decreasing number of divorces, the number of marriages that do not survive remains very high. More than 24.000 divorces a year is quite a lot. Not only are almost 50.000 partners involved, but we should also consider their children, family and friends. Many people suffer from a divorce, many people feel the pain. 4) The fact that the Belgian civil law simplified divorce, obviously does not imply that the personal story has become easier too. A divorce or a separation is never a trivial affair. For the majority of the people involved, a separation is a traumatic experience.

So, evidently, quite a lot of people in our society are involved in family breakdown, in separation and divorce. We meet them in our local Christian communities, for instance when their children prepare for sacraments, for their first Holy Communion or Confirmation. We also meet them in the liturgy, in social activities and so on.

2 Current Pastoral Programs for Divorced People in Flanders

I will discuss now some current initiatives in some of our Flemish dioceses. Some dioceses set up support groups, where divorced people meet six or eight times in a closed group of about ten to fifteen people, together with an experienced facilitator. These groups are a kind of safe haven, where divorced people can share experiences and personal stories with each other, where they are listened to, where they can find some peace and quiet in stormy days. These support groups do not offer any therapeutic treatment, but they are often considered as complementary to therapy, particularly with regard to a new network that can support people. There is a common way of dealing with the personal stories, namely the link with faith and church.

With regard to faith and church we notice an evolution: about twenty years ago divorced people participated in the support groups because they experienced tensions with their faith or with their position as divorced in the church. Nowadays faith does not play that important role anymore. Divorced people nowadays participate in the support groups because they are listened to, because they can share their stories and can get new insights in their situation, because they feel accepted and recognized. Such groups can be an ecclesial place for people who feel excluded from their local community.

Participating in support groups is cheap, there are no waiting lists and one can participate quite anonymously in these diocesan groups. The chance is rather small that one meets someone from their own parish there. These support groups used to be set up in all the dioceses ten to twenty years ago, but this has changed over the last few years. Some dioceses set up two groups a year, some only one group every two years. This means that these initiatives are very small.

Some dioceses set up monthly meetings for separated and divorced people. These meetings are open to everybody who wants to join: people can participate when they take interest in the theme of the meeting. Themes can be for example: how to deal with the former family-in-law? How to get through lonely days? My ex and me: we share a common past... Sometimes a speaker is asked to introduce the theme, with discussion afterwards.

One diocese sets up a weekend in an abbey, another diocese organizes more relaxing activities such as a sightseeing trip, a walk or a meal. The people that the church reaches with these activities do not always have a close bond with the church, but they appreciate these initiatives.

We have to acknowledge that these pastoral initiatives are rather small and that they reach only a very small number of people. The facilitators of the support groups think that this is due to the following reasons: 1) For a lot of people it is not important anymore what the church thinks or says about divorce. People are alienated from the church. 2) A lot of priests do not have the habit of informing the divorced about the diocesan groups and initiatives. Sometimes they do not even know that these initiatives exist, sometimes they refuse to provide information about it. 3) There are also initiatives for separated and divorced people outside the church.

The last few years there is a tendency to focus on the integration of the divorced people in other diocesan pastoral initiatives and to no longer provide a separate program for them. For instance, single parent families are welcome on family holidays, organized by the dioceses.

3 Results of the IDGP Survey of 2009

The Interdiocesan Council for Family Ministry (*Interdiocesane Dienst voor Gezinspastoraal*, IDGP) itself does not organize any programs for divorced people, but supports the diocesan initiatives by promoting them with a digital newsletter sent to about 3.000 email addresses (including clergy and pastoral workers) and by gathering the facilitators of diocesan support groups once a year to discuss common points of interest and to provide formation on specific topics.

Almost eight years ago we extensively talked with them about their perspective on the situation of divorced people in the church: how do the divorced people they meet in their activities, feel in and about the church? What kind of difficulties do they have to cope with their situation, what could be done better, and so on. Thus, six years before the questionnaire of pope Francis in preparation of the first

Synod, we collected information and remarks from these facilitators and responsible people about the feelings of divorced people in relation to the Catholic Church in Flanders.

They told us that the mourning induced by a divorce is not appropriately recognized and acknowledged. A divorce has great impact on people's lives, and this is often not paid attention to appropriately. When someone dies, neighbors, family and friends, colleagues offer condolences and support. There are well established traditions, formulations and rituals for this. But, when a couple separates, the pain and mourning are often not seen. And if they are, it seems to be more difficult to address them. Even worse, there might even be gossiping. The divorced people themselves experience loss: loss of a partner, loss of self-esteem, and also loss of friends. Their social network is almost always drastically reduced. Onc experiences loneliness in dealing with the pain, all the more when one has taken the initiative to leave the partner.

After divorce, people experience clumsily formulated expressions of consolation, for instance: "You're still young, and you'll easily find someone else." These remarks, even when said with the best intentions, do not address the mourning and spiritual pain.

People who have to cope with a divorce need a listening, supportive ear, understanding and support. They do not need condemnation and exclusion. I will give some specific examples. Bad things happen, fortunately not everywhere, and not always, but they do happen in parishes and Christian communities.

A person who remarried was no longer permitted to read during Mass. Someone was asked to leave the parish team. Someone noticed she was no longer asked to participate in activities she had always happily volunteered for. There were stories about people being refused access to the Eucharist, even when they had not entered a new union. Some priests failed to refer people to the appropriate diocesan support initiatives, on the pretense that "the church has nothing to offer in these conditions". The generic discourse of the church about divorce in terms of "sin" and "irregular situations" was in many cases considered offensive and painful.

These examples clearly show that some people feel they are rejected by, and excluded from what they always had considered to be "their church". They no longer felt welcome in their community. People and institutions they considered important in their lives, failed them, exactly in times when they needed them so badly. A significant livelong traveling companion, their church, failed to provide support in times of need.

Clearly, there were also many positive experiences. There were moving stories by divorced people about the support they did get from their priest and the local community. Good relationships with the priest were experienced as healing and redemptive. In several communities, people were allowed and encouraged to continue their volunteering engagements.

A general conclusion was that a lot depended on local conditions and people, that the local priest had an important role in it, and that the official doctrine of the church was often considered inappropriate.

Last but not least two areas of concern were also discussed eight years ago: the desire for a blessing of a new relationship or a second marriage and the hope that the church will grant the remarried divorced access to Holy Communion.

4 The 2014 Questionnaire in Preparation of the Bishops' Synod on the Family

Five years later, in 2014, the Belgian Conference of Bishops had held a large scale questionnaire among the faithful, and submitted a summary report[2] to the Vatican, in preparation of the first Synod. The following issues of the respondents were mentioned in this report. The respondents pointed to the numeric relevance of divorced people in our society. Also inside the church, divorce is not exceptional, and the church has to be aware of it. A lot of respondents asked to consider the possibility of giving the divorced and remarried access to the Sacrament of the Eucharist but respondents also asked the church not to focus exclusively on this aspect. The majority of the respondents asked that the church no longer distinguishes between "broken families" and so called "normal families". Failure does happen. The respondents also stipulated that words such as "irregular situation" are offensive. Most of the divorced people do not consider themselves as living "in an irregular situation", either because they do not know the exact doctrine of the church or they do not agree with it. Respondents considered it important that a new relation after a divorce could take place in the best possible circumstances. Some asked the church to examine the possibility of a kind of blessing for divorced who enter a new union. Some referred to the practice in the Orthodox Church, which has a notion of a second, non-sacramental marriage. Some respondents asked that the church should recognize a kind of "psychological death of the marriage", apart from annulment. Respondents also valued the initiatives for divorced people in the dioceses.

So, the results of the Vatican questionnaire were largely consistent with what we had gathered previously from facilitators of supporting groups in the church.

2 Available from http://www.gezinspastoraal.be/cms2/uploads/idgp/file/idgp/14%2002%2005%20Synthese%20rapport%20vragenlijst%20synode%202014.pdf; accessed 14.10.2016.

5 Does *Amoris Laetitia* Address the Concerns of the Flemish Catholics Regarding Divorce?

If we now look into *Amoris laetitia*,[3] what can we say about the way it addresses these concerns of the Flemish or Belgian Catholics? One can argue that it effectively deals with the majority of the raised issues, and moreover, that especially on style, attitude and language answers are largely positive.

Let us consider some points in more detail. AL 243 stipulates that remarried divorced people do remain part of the ecclesial community. Language or conduct that might lead them to feel discriminated against should be avoided, and they should be encouraged to participate in the life of the community.

In AL 297 Pope Francis says that no one can be condemned for ever, because that is not the logic of the Gospel. And Pope Francis continues in AL 299 that the baptized who are divorced and civilly remarried need to be more fully integrated into Christian communities in a variety of ways possible. Pope Francis stipulates that the logic of integration is the key to their pastoral care, a care which would allow them not only to realize that they belong to the church as the body of Christ, but also to know that they can have a joyful and fruitful experience in it. They are baptized, they are brothers and sisters, the Holy Spirit pours into their hearts gifts and talents for the good of all.

Under the same no. 299 Pope Francis insists on discerning which of the various forms of exclusion currently practiced in the liturgical, pastoral, educational and institutional framework, can be surmounted. And he repeats that such persons need to feel not as excommunicated members of the church, but instead as living members, able to live and grow in the church and experience her as a mother who welcomes them always, who takes care of them with affection and encourages them along the path of life and the Gospel. Pope Francis adds that this integration is also needed in the care and Christian upbringing of their children, who ought to be considered most important.

This is precisely what divorced people in the Flemish dioceses expected: to be respected as active members who contribute to the church, just by being who they are, and by doing what they do as lectors, as catechists, as volunteers in the local parish life, in fact, as children of God.

I think that the fact that these things are so clearly pointed out in *Amoris laetitia*, will lead over time to more uniformity in the attitudes towards divorced people, and will – hopefully – eliminate bad practices of exclusion in some of our local communities.

---

3 Available from http://w2.vatican.va/content/dam/francesco/pdf/apost_exhortations/documents/papa-francesco_esortazione-ap_20160319_amoris-laetitia_en.pdf; accessed 14.10.2016.

And although *Amoris laetitia* does not give a clear answer on some other topics mentioned in the summary report, such as a blessing of a second union and the access to the Eucharist, it does at least open a door for further reflection, distinction and discernment.

I come to my conclusion:

1. What the faithful answered in the questionnaire in preparation of the first Synod is in line with the information that we collected almost eight years ago in the support groups.
2. *Amoris laetitia* effectively deals with the majority of the raised issues, especially with the topics on style, attitude and language towards divorced people, and with their concerns for better integration in the Church.
3. The Flemish Catholic Church reaches only a few people with their pastoral initiatives for divorced people, but we do not know anything about the number of one-to-one pastoral counseling by priests and pastors.

In a Second Marriage before God and before Others: New Paths of the Church and in the Church in Austria

Franz Harant

Preliminary Remark

I have been asked to speak at this international Symposium with an "input from the pastoral care of relationships, marriage, and the family". I have chosen a topic that obviously was not discussed in a decisive manner at the two Synods in 2014 and 2015, and that therefore is not mentioned explicitly in *Amoris laetitia.* But this topic belongs to the spectrum of the "pastoral care of divorced persons", which focuses both on "divorced persons" and on "divorced and remarried persons". I prefer to speak of "persons in a second (civil) marriage" since this is their basic condition – namely, that they are in a second or third marriage. Their self-understanding is that they are living a marriage, without denying the fact of a previous marriage and its civil divorce.

Beginning Afresh in a Second Marriage

Persons who have been divorced, and who rediscover trust in a new relationship, who find the courage to make a new beginning, and who intend to get married, enter a new union that is institutionalized by the law of the state. They bring to this new union the intention of life-long fidelity, the unconditional acceptance of their partner, and the willingness to lead a comprehensive personal life together and to assume responsibility for children.

People wish for God's blessing

Many women and men bring this second civil marriage, which is not sacramental as canon law understands this term, into a relationship with faith and with the Church (as they did with their first marriage), because they want to live out of the groundwater of the divine love. Increasing numbers of couples want to be accompanied ritually by prayer and blessing.

A Salutary Accompaniment in a Process of Reconciliation with Life

The Gospel lays on those engaged in pastoral work the obligation of actively accompanying people in their broken situation on the path to new hope. And this essentially involves a process of reconciliation. Nothing that has happened can be undone. But it is necessary to take bid farewell, in a positive evaluation, to the earlier marriage, which continues to exist in canon law. The Church, as a community of reconciliation, can offer a "service of peace" here. It is salutary to bring one's life to God as it was and as it is, to give both joy and grief their place in the community, and to celebrate them. The biblically oriented Christian faith is, in a very profound sense, a religion of remembrance and reconciliation for the sake of the future. Where the past is allowed to exist in its own right, the future has a chance.

Living out of Faith for Those Divorced and Remarried in a Civil Second Marriage

In the endeavor to cultivate a positive pastoral care of divorced persons who contract (or have contracted) a second civil marriage, the diocese of Linz went through two fundamental processes of development – from 1985 to 1986, and from 1997 to 1999 – in the aftermath of the Synod on the family (September 16 to October 25, 1980) and of the Apostolic Exhortation *Familiaris consortio,* which was published on November 22, 1981. This led to the development of a praxis that has stood the test of time down to the present day. I shall give an account of this well-tried praxis and link it to affirmations by Pope Francis in *Amoris laetitia.* In April 1986, the results of the first process were published by the Pastoral Council, the Priests' Council, and the Conference of Deans as "Orientations for Pastoral Care in the Diocese of Linz".[1] The introduction indicates both "the clear line of the truth about marriage as a permanent bond" and the necessity, in view of the fact that marriages break down, "to complement" this clear line with "an attitude of respectful mercy, so that justice is done fully to both of these realities." This leads into a discussion of the situation of divorced and remarried persons and of the developments in the Church. The "Orientations for Pastoral Care" are concerned first of all with prophylactic measures on behalf of marriage, with how one should behave in crises, and with the integration of divorced and remarried persons into the community. Pope Francis too is concerned about "the logic of pas-

1 PASTORALRAT DER DIÖZESE LINZ (ed.): "Pastoral an wiederverheirateten Geschiedenen: Orientierung für die Seelsorger in der Diözese Linz", in: *Herder Korrespondenz* 40 (1986), 420-424.

toral mercy",[2] "discernment",[3] and "integration". He invites us "to mercy and the pastoral discernment of those situations that fall short of what the Lord demands of us".[4] This is why he introduces a new "pastoral culture" with a "far-reaching change of perspective."[5]

Accompanying People in a Pastoral Conversation, with Respect for the Judgment That Is Made by the Conscience of Those Concerned

The core of these orientations, which have been put into practice and have proved their worth in the diocese of Linz for thirty years now (1986 to 2016), is the pastoral conversation. This was already suggested by Pope John Paul II in *Familiaris consortio*[6] and now Pope Francis recommends it in *Amoris laetitia* as a pastoral

---

2 The title of AL 307-312.

3 AL 300: "What we are speaking of is a process of accompaniment and discernment which 'guides the faithful to an awareness of their situation before God. Conversation with the priest, in the internal forum, contributes to the formation of a correct judgment on what hinders the possibility of a fuller participation in the life of the Church and on what steps can foster it and make it grow'."

4 AL 6; see AL 308: "... from our awareness of the weight of mitigating circumstances – psychological, historical and even biological – it follows that 'without detracting from the evangelical ideal, there is a need to accompany with mercy and patience the eventual stages of personal growth as these progressively appear,' making room for 'the Lord's mercy, which spurs us on to do our best'. [...] I understand those who prefer a more rigorous pastoral care which leaves no room for confusion. But I sincerely believe that Jesus wants a Church attentive to the goodness which the Holy Spirit sows in the midst of human weakness, a Mother who, while clearly expressing her objective teaching, 'always does what good she can, even if in the process, her shoes get soiled by the mud of the street.' [...] The Church's pastors, in proposing to the faithful the full ideal of the Gospel and the Church's teaching, must help them to treat the weak with compassion, avoiding aggravation or unduly harsh or hasty judgments. The Gospel itself tells us not to judge or condemn (cf. Mt 7:1; Lk 6:37). Jesus 'expects us to stop looking for those personal or communal niches which shelter us from the maelstrom of human misfortune, and instead to enter into the reality of other people's lives and to know the power of tenderness. Whenever we do so, our lives become wonderfully complicated' [...]."

5 PAUL M. ZULEHNER: *Vom Gesetz zum Gesicht: Ein neuer Ton in der Kirche; Papst Franziskus zu Ehe und Familie*, Ostfildern: Patmos, 2016.

6 FC 84: "Daily experience unfortunately shows that people who have obtained a divorce usually intend to enter into a new union, obviously not with a Catholic religious ceremony. Since this is an evil that, like the others, is affecting more and more Catholics as well, the problem must be faced with resolution and without delay. The Synod Fathers studied it expressly. The Church, which was set up to lead to salvation all people and especially the baptized, cannot abandon to their own devices those who have been previously bound by sacramental marriage and who have attempted a second marriage. The Church will therefore make untiring efforts to put at their disposal her means of salvation. Pastors must know that, for the sake of truth, they are obliged to exercise careful discernment of situations. There is in fact a difference between those who have sincerely tried to save their first marriage and have been unjustly abandoned, and

approach.[7] Men and women who are involved in pastoral work are instructed to be willing to have detailed conversations, always entering into the special situation of the couple. They must first of all examine whether "the situation of conflict" can be "cleared up on a legal path". If the return to the first partner is objectively and subjectively ... no longer possible, it must be established whether "there is a willingness to acknowledge the guilt that may under certain circumstances be linked to the breakdown of the sacramental marriage and to the remarriage, and to do one's best to fulfill existing obligations (towards the first partner and the children)." It must also be established whether "the new union is based upon the mutually declared intention to enter into a marriage and the willingness to lead a Christian life together that corresponds to this, and to give the children a Christian education." It must also be borne in mind whether a "public reception of the sacraments is justifiable, [and whether] the desire for the sacraments comes from pure motives."[8] In the diocese of Linz – and later in other Austrian dioceses too – pastoral agents were trained to conduct these highly differentiated conversations, and the parish communities were urged to treat divorced and remarried persons with sensitivity. The goal of this pastoral accompaniment is that couples should make their own independent judgment in conscience with regard to the reception of communion – in an orientation to the teaching of the Church, and bearing in mind their concrete personal situation. The pastoral agent can accompany them to this destination and confirm the honesty of the path that has been taken and of the personal judgment of conscience; if necessary, he or she can also attest it vis-à-vis the parish community. "The assessment of their existential situation, taking all the relevant circumstances into account, can be carried out only by the persons concerned, in their conscience."[9] This means that "permitting" and "prohibiting"

---

those who through their own grave fault have destroyed a canonically valid marriage. Finally, there are those who have entered into a second union for the sake of the children's upbringing, and who are sometimes subjectively certain in conscience that their previous and irreparably destroyed marriage had never been valid."

7 AL 312: "I encourage the faithful who find themselves in complicated situations to speak confidently with their pastors or with other lay people whose lives are committed to the Lord. They may not always encounter in them a confirmation of their own ideas or desires, but they will surely receive some light to help them better understand their situation and discover a path to personal growth. I also encourage the Church's pastors to listen to them with sensitivity and serenity, with a sincere desire to understand their plight and their point of view, in order to help them live better lives and to recognize their proper place in the Church."

8 These criteria were adopted by the advisory council of the Conference of German-speaking Pastoral Theologians.

9 E. SCHOCKENHOFF: *Kirche als Versöhnungsgemeinschaft: Für die Zulassung wiederverheirateter Geschiedener zum Kommunionempfang*, unpublished manuscript at the conference "Chancen zur Versöhnung? Die Kirche und die wiederverheiratet Geschiedenen," February 1, 2012, in St. Virgil, Salzburg (organizers: Katholische Aktion Österreich. Forum Beziehung, Ehe

are inappropriate categories. Pope Francis also proposes this pastoral path of the formation of the conscience as basis for a decision.[10]

Prayer and Blessing for Couples in a Second Civil Marriage

The second process of developing a careful pastoral ministry to divorced persons bore important fruit in the "Orientations for the Pastoral Accompaniment of Divorced Persons II." The title was the same as in the 1986 "Orientations"; the Roman numeral "II" indicated that the new text was building on the earlier one. The Priests' Council announced it on March 11, 1999 as an aid that was to be used with pastoral prudence. The point of departure was the increasing desire on the part of couples to pray publicly and to receive an "ecclesiastical" blessing when they entered a second civil marriage. It was also intended to curb pastoral and liturgical abuses. Although *Familiaris consortio* is unambiguous on this point,[11] the great pastoral concern of the Council of Priests of the diocese of Linz, as well as the great distress experienced by couples, led the Council of Priests in March 1997 to ask the Department for Marriage and Family in the Diocesan Pastoral Office to do further work on what the 1986 paper on the pastoral care of divorced persons had

---

und Familie; Arbeitsgemeinschaft der österreichischen Pastoral- und Seelsorgsämter).

10 AL 37: "We have long thought that simply by stressing doctrinal, bioethical and moral issues, without encouraging openness to grace, we were providing sufficient support to families, strengthening the marriage bond and giving meaning to marital life. We find it difficult to present marriage more as a dynamic path to personal development and fulfilment than as a lifelong burden. We also find it hard to make room for the consciences of the faithful, who very often respond as best they can to the Gospel amid their limitations, and are capable of carrying out their own discernment in complex situations. We have been called to form consciences, not to replace them." AL 303: "Recognizing the influence of such concrete factors, we can add that individual conscience needs to be better incorporated into the Church's praxis in certain situations which do not objectively embody our understanding of marriage. Naturally, every effort should be made to encourage the development of an enlightened conscience, formed and guided by the responsible and serious discernment of one's pastor, and to encourage an ever greater trust in God's grace. Yet conscience can do more than recognize that a given situation does not correspond objectively to the overall demands of the Gospel. It can also recognize with sincerity and honesty what for now is the most generous response which can be given to God, and come to see with a certain moral security that it is what God himself is asking amid the concrete complexity of one's limits, while yet not fully the objective ideal. In any event, let us recall that this discernment is dynamic; it must remain ever open to new stages of growth and to new decisions which can enable the ideal to be more fully realized."

11 FC 84: "The respect due to the sacrament of Matrimony, to the couples themselves and their families, and also to the community of the faithful, forbids any pastor, for whatever reason or pretext even of a pastoral nature, to perform ceremonies of any kind for divorced people who remarry. Such ceremonies would give the impression of a new sacramentally valid marriage, and would thus lead people into error concerning the indissolubility of a validly contracted marriage."

said about liturgical accompaniment. Looking beyond the diocesan boundaries, I led an interdiocesan working group that elaborated a goal. The basic aim of the working group was to do justice to what Pope John Paul II had urged on pastoral agents in *Familiaris consortio*. On the one hand, the Church should "help the divorced, and with solicitous care make sure that they do not consider themselves as separated from the Church". On the other hand, the liturgical ceremony must not "give the impression of the celebration of a new sacramentally valid marriage, and would thus lead people into error concerning the indissolubility of a validly contracted marriage".[12] The path of (only) taking into consideration everything that had to be avoided led to a dead end. Finally, in a new approach, the most important element was the way in which the couple themselves viewed the past and the future. These "Orientations II" are characterized by two things: first, the obligation, which derives from the Gospel, to accompany people actively in their broken situation on the road to new hope. And secondly, this accompaniment must give the persons concerned the courage to live before God with their fragmentary history, and to base their longing for a successful relationship on the foundation of a reconciliation with the past. Pope Francis too points out the particular urgency of reconciliation for "those whose marital relationship has broken down".[13]

The Integration of the Past in a Process of Reconciliation with Life

This is not a question of becoming reconciled to the fact that what has happened in our shared history cannot be undone, since it remains true that the first marriage created a personal bond that was marked by dignity and creative power. It must be acknowledged that the first sacramental marriage continues to exist, because it cannot be dissolved. Many couples acknowledge this indissolubility, although the relationship came unstuck. This led to a caesura in their lives and to divorce, because the personal lived community of the marriage partners could no longer be sustained; it is this personal community of life that no longer exists. In general, couples who ask for prayer and blessing for their second marriage acknowledge

12 Ibid.

13 AL 238: "While realizing that reconciliation is a possibility, we also see that 'what is urgently needed today is a ministry to care for those whose marital relationship has broken down'. [...]" AL 243: "It is important that the divorced who have entered a new union should be made to feel part of the Church. 'They are not excommunicated' and they should not be treated as such, since they remain part of the ecclesial community. [...] These situations 'require careful discernment and respectful accompaniment. Language or conduct that might lead them to feel discriminated against should be avoided, and they should be encouraged to participate in the life of the community. The Christian community's care of such persons is not to be considered a weakening of its faith and testimony to the indissolubility of marriage; rather, such care is a particular expression of its charity'. [...]"

that their previous partners are very important in their lives and are still a part of their life history. They accept that they have a continuing obligation to children of the first marriage. It is necessary to bid farewell, in a positive evaluation, to the earlier marriage, which continues to exist in canon law – and it is even more necessary to bid a positive farewell to one's partner in this earlier marriage. The Church, as a community of reconciliation, can provide a "service of peace" here. Where the past is allowed to exist in its own right, the present can flourish, and the future has a chance. This process gives people the courage to shape the future responsibly. Repentance does not mean returning to the past – that is to say, returning to the earlier partner, with whom it is no longer possible to live. Repentance can also mean turning to new possibilities of living, after the integration into one's life history of all that has gone before. Preparatory conversations center on clarifying the meaning of reconciliation with the past relationship and with all those who played an important role in it. Partners who are reconciled to the past and with those who were involved in it can be accompanied honestly with prayer and blessing. If both partners recognize and acknowledge their past, with all the bonds and ruptures, with pain and grief, and with the personal obligations that continue to exist, and if they are reconciled to their past and are able to let history be history, then we can assume that they are ready to receive God's blessing for something new.

Beginning Afresh in a Second Marriage

After the breakdown of the first, sacramental marriage, trust and a firm desire to get married often arise in a new union. As a Church, we must take respectful note of this fact. And we must also appreciate it and approve of it. Some couples bring their second union, which has been institutionalized by the state, into a relationship with faith and with the Church, because they want to live out of the groundwater of the divine love. It must be acknowledged that although the second civil marriage – which often is a second marriage for only one of the partners – is invalid in canon law, it can nevertheless display all those elements that are constitutive of a marriage: the intention of life-long fidelity, the unconditional acceptance of their partner, and the willingness to lead a comprehensive personal life together and to assume responsibility for children.

Preconditions for Public Prayer and Blessing

If, therefore, a marriage breaks down, and new trust and a firm desire to get married are found in a new relationship, in addition to an explicit wish for public prayer and a church blessing – which, ultimately, is always a divine blessing – for the new path in life, such couples are entitled to expect a pastoral and liturgical accompaniment. This is to be given in accordance with the biblical commission to exercise pastoral care. Pastoral agents find their orientation here in the truth taught by Jesus, that is to say, in the mercy of the God who forgives, the mercy that is presented in the Gospels as a fundamental attitude and mood, the mercy that Pope Francis has located in a special way in the center of the Church's action. Since there is no second church wedding for Catholics (as there is in the Orthodox and Oriental Orthodox Churches), one must be careful lest a service of prayer with a blessing for the couple might give the impression that a wedding is being celebrated. Nevertheless, the pastoral accompaniment must give the partners the feeling that they are at home in the Church, since "[t]he joy and hope, the grief and fear of people today, especially of the poor and those who are oppressed in any way, are also the joy and hope, the grief and fear of the disciples of Christ" (that is, of the Church).[14] "When the request for a service of blessing is made, one's 'yes' should have the corresponding quality."[15] "People with painful experiences that led to ruptures in the course of their lives are very receptive to kind words. It is a pastoral act to utter the good word – and the blessing of God is [always and everywhere] a good word. It should not be left dangling in mid-air."[16] One question that must be cleared up in a dialogue with the couple is whether the one who is entering a second marriage is able to speak with a reconciled serenity about the first marriage. If there are children from the first marriage, have the custody and the visiting rights been regulated? It is also essential to clarify in these conversations, which are an indispensable preliminary, whether the person who is getting married for the first time respects the previous marriage of his or her partner as a part of this person's biography.

A Liturgical Celebration with a Profile of its Own

What then should we do if a couple expresses the wish for a church ceremony, the wish for prayer and blessing, on the occasion of a second civil marriage? First of all, this wish should be welcomed with gratitude and joy. Although the celebration of God's blessing must not be made dependent on fulfilling particular conditions, the public prayer that requests a blessing does have certain presuppositions. One should consider generously – with sound judgment, caution, and also clarity – what is possible under the individual circumstances, and what requires

---

14 *Gaudium et spes*, 1.

15 F. HARANT: "In zweiter Ehe neu beginnen: Segensfeier bei Wiederheirat", in: *Diakonia* 33/1 (2002), 31-37.

16 F. HARANT: "Umgang mit Menschen in Beziehungen 'außer der Norm'", in: W. KRIEGER/B. SIEBERER (eds.): *Beziehung zwischen Ideal und Wirklichkeit*, Linz: Wagner-Verlag, 2010.

special attention. In order to avoid arbitrariness and abuses from getting the upper hand, clarifications and concrete agreements can be a help from the very outset, or else in the course of the dialogue process, so that the liturgical action is pastorally responsible. We should arrive at an independent, simple, and humane form of celebration that takes account of the importance and the emotional impact of signs. The usual framework for such a ceremony of blessing is a Liturgy of the Word. In the long term, it will thus be possible to elaborate and put into practice a rite that is also celebrated by laypersons involved in parish work (in the diocese of Linz, these are called "pastoral assistants" and "parish assistants") who have received an appropriate training; this rite need not be reserved to ordained priests or deacons. One must also underline the independence and the specific value of such a celebration of prayer and blessing.[17] We must discuss whether both partners accept that the previous history should be mentioned in an act of worship, with caution but without ambiguity. Both partners must understand that a new beginning can succeed only when reconciliation with the ruptures of the past has taken place. There must be agreement that everything that simulates a church wedding must be avoided; the same applies to everything that resembles a wedding either in principle or in accordance with local customs. This is why the wedding vows are not exchanged – that takes place in the registry office. Nor is there a blessing and an exchange of rings. The way in which they enter the church, the place where the couple sit, and similar matters must not be the same as in a church wedding. The blessing of signs, such as a candle, a cross, or a Bible, could be one prominent point in the ceremony. But the priority belongs to the blessing of the couple, expressing the wish that they may be a blessing for each other in their life together. This has acquired a firm place as the central point of the celebration. The solemn prayer of blessing for the couple, perhaps with outstretched hands as a gesture of blessing, thus lends this liturgy a special accent. It is decisively important that the pastoral agent is clear about how he or she can accompany the pair pastorally and liturgically with a clear conscience. It is best to take no shortcuts. Honesty requires us to have detailed discussions, involving processes of reconciliation, as the necessary preliminary to a public celebration of prayer and blessing. It is necessary to state clearly that this path costs time and energy for all who are involved, both for the couple and for the pastoral agent. They must be aware of this, and they must give their explicit consent to it, if they want to attain the goal. I myself take sufficient time for each couple – from four to twelve hours – for a conversation about the history or histories of their lives and relationships and about their integration. We clarify the motivation, the formulation of the agreements we will make, and

[17] See F. HARANT: "In zweiter Ehe neu beginnen".

the preparation of the celebration of prayer and blessing. This investment is well worthwhile, because it allows the celebration to take a fully appropriate form.

A Home for Everyone: Pastoral Experiences with the Divorced and Remarried in Italy

Teresa Ventimiglia & Giordano Barioni

1 The Presentation of the Exhortation by the Italian Bishops' Conference

In presenting the Post-Synodal Exhortation of Pope Francis, *Amoris laetitia* (AL), Fr. Paolo Gentili, director of the National Office for Family Ministry writes about a "multi-faceted gem" (see AL 4) of 325 sections, born out of listing to, confronting, and gazing on Christ in the horizon of collegiality.[1] Emphasizing that *Amoris laetitia* is the result of the Church's more than two-year reflection, the office invited dioceses to "create moments in which the text of the Holy Father can be reflected on together in presbyterial gatherings, in more formal clerical assemblies, in parish and diocesan committees, as well as in associations, movements, and new communities. The motive was to promote community life that lives a "culture of encounter" and makes present "the secret of Nazareth, exuding the beauty of family life" (AL 65).

In the communication to the dioceses, Fr. Gentili stressed the importance of following Pope Francis's call to avoid jumping to quick solutions: "Since 'time is greater than space', I would make it clear that not all discussions of doctrinal, moral or pastoral issues need to be settled by interventions of the magisterium" (AL 3). The local churches were asked to imagine new ways to spread the gospel of the family and make it truly take root in the contemporary situation; as Francis wrote, "we have been called to form consciences, not to replace them" (AL 37).

Along with these pastoral directives, there has been another equally significant initiative by this office: the promotion of two symposia of professors of theology in the city of Monteporzio Catone, near Rome, dedicated to reflection on and dialogue about *Amoris laetitia*, one in May and the other in October of 2016.

1 The presentation document can be found at https://docs.google.com/document/d/1H0o8cee2BEf182mkwgm-7YcMvsvo5Rh9DkSr-ay_zU0/edit; accessed 20.01.2017. This section is for the most part a word-for-word representation of that document.

1.1 A Special Interpretive Approach: "The Lens of Mercy"

Referring to the words of Pope Francis at the conclusion of the Synod (24 October 2015), Fr. Gentili pointed to the key for understanding *Amoris laetitia*: "The Synod experience also made us better realize that the true defenders of doctrine are not those who uphold its letter, but its spirit; not ideas but people; not formulae but the gratuitousness of God's love and forgiveness."[2] Thus *mercy* – the theme of the special Jubilee Year – is proposed as the method of interpretation, a lens for this new way of looking, encouraging the Church to open its heart wider to the situations in which family life is not lived perfectly (cf. AL 5).

The exhortation is presented as a document to apply according to the needs of the moment by those who need it (cf. AL 7): spouses, entire families, pastoral workers, presbyterial councils, parish and diocesan committees. The aim is to make it the common reference for ministry to families, a process that requires time and effort. The new language of AL takes up the freshness and the different emphases reflected in the *Final Report of the Synod of Bishops* in 2015. It is a language of concreteness, full of pastoral sensibility, that departs from the usual approaches and requires a true change of attitude for the entire Christian community, asking families to help families, as when it points to the risk involved when couples no longer take part in community life after the wedding. As the exhortation says, "Nowadays, pastoral care for families has to be fundamentally missionary, going out to where people are. We can no longer be like a factory, churning out courses that for the most part are poorly attended." (AL 230)

1.2 Accompany, Discern, and Integrate Fragile Love

An approach that recognizes the fragility of love is free of condemnation and takes as its guide the "law of graduality" that St. John Paul II speaks of in *Familiaris Consortio*, 34. To *accompany* implies to "walk alongside" in the style of Jesus and the disciples on the way to Emmaus (Lk 24,13-35) so that the face of Christ can be discovered in one's own life (Lk 24,18-19). To *discern* means seeking the light of the Spirit to be able to be illuminated by the Word and become capable of finding the way ahead in these concrete situations. To *integrate* is to bring from the outskirts to the center. Such an approach is also that of the parables of mercy. Only those who are themselves being converted can guide others to a change of heart; otherwise, it is a case of the blind leading the blind (Mt 15,14); "we are

---

2 FRANCIS: "Conclusion of the Synod of Bishops, Address of His Holiness Pope Francis", 24 October 2015, available from http://w2.vatican.va/content/francesco/en/speeches/2015/october/documents/papa-francesco_20151024_sinodo-conclusione-lavori.html, accessed 20.01.2017.

called to show mercy because mercy has first been shown to us".[3] There is still too much loneliness in the wake of many failed marriages, and it is evident that those who find themselves in the midst of human and ecclesial relationships are better able to make it through the crisis. The task given to each of us is that of the "common home" to construct together for the families of the world, in the realization that the family is a "workshop of hope"[4].

2 The Italian Situation

Studies on marriage and divorce from the Italian government's institute for statistics (ISTAT) indicate a trend whereby a drastic fall in secular and religious marriages is simultaneous with an increase in divorce and new partnerships. This seems to indicate quite clearly a crisis in the institution of the family and its credibility. This is the reality that vigorously claims the attention of a pastoral ministry that has sought for some time to meet the challenges of the modern day. At the same time, the National Consultation on Family Ministry has gathered data relative to the formation and spiritual programs offered from 1994 to 2003 to wounded families and shows a progressive increase in these initiatives and the predominance of diocesan programs over other programs.

2.1 The Pastoral Response

The Italian Church has for a while tried to offer a concrete outreach to the remarried divorced faithful. The proposals for pastoral accompaniment have also seen a gradual modification of the language used (moving from a focus on addressing the so-called irregularity of the situations of remarried divorced couples to dealing with the reality of "wounded families") that in some way has also indicated a change of pastoral approach. The increase in the number of such pastoral approaches is certainly due not only to the objective increase in these family problems but also to the work of formation by the bishops' office.

The office has organized different formation events on these themes, beginning with the third national meeting of diocesan officers and of the Family Ministry Consultation on the theme "Marriages in Difficulty: What Kind of Welcoming and Pastoral Care?" in 1998 in Rome. In 2006, it organized the week of for-

[3] FRANCIS: *Misericordiae Vultus: Bull of Indiction of the Extraordinary Jubilee of Mercy*, 11 April 2015, 9, available from https://w2.vatican.va/content/francesco/en/apost_letters/documents/papa-francesco_bolla_20150411_misericordiae-vultus.html; accessed 20.01.2017. See also AL 310.

[4] FRANCIS: "Prayer Vigil for the Festival of Families: Address of the Holy Father", 26 September 2015, available from https://w2.vatican.va/content/francesco/en/speeches/2015/september/documents/papa-francesco_20150926_usa-festa-famiglie.html; accessed 20.01.2017.

mation "I Will Give You a New Heart (Ez 36:26): Difficulties and Crises for Couples, Failure or New Hope?" in Paestum in collaboration with the Confederation of Clinics (religious and secular). The last conference was in Salsomaggiore, near Parma, entitled "Light of Hope for the Wounded Family: Separated, Married and Divorced Persons in the Christian Community", which was particularly addressed to family ministry workers.

As the introduction to the week of formation in Paestum says, in these moments of reflection and discussion, the motivations and objectives of pastoral reflection take into consideration that "marital failure no longer affects only those couples that seemed to be 'at risk' from the beginning because of an evident lack of maturity and the necessary requisites to enter into marriage or who lacked real motivation to live a Christian marriage or lacked faith. Today, failure affects couples of every age, even those who seemed to be able to confront any difficulty, couples that completed detailed and robust preparation programs, and couples involved in the life of the Church."[5] There has emerged – beyond the rigidity of the norms that define the category of divorced and remarried – the need for a spiritual accompaniment of those faithful in conditions of imperfect communion with the Church. The experience of pastoral workers has shown the gradual development of such attention in the varied situations across Italy.

There have emerged specific instruments of formation using methods of spiritual accompaniment. They are based on proposals drawn from various experiences such that diocesan offices can be as effective as other programs that are trying to meet the current need.[6] The local churches are thus committed to programs that give attention and pastoral care to the remarried divorced faithful. Many dioceses have chosen to develop specific programs for these people, "a tactic that is at times controversial, but nonetheless one that is often employed".[7] Ecclesial structures that have the responsibility to care for this portion of the faithful have increased in number. They are established in order to move beyond a logic of judgment and take up one of welcoming (the Church sees these relationships as irregular; the partners see the Church as a harsh judge), in which the ecclesial community often

5 S. NICOLLI: "Introduction to the summer formation week I Will Give You a New Heart (Ez 36:26): Difficulties and Crises for Couples, Failure or New Hope?", 25-29 June 2006; discourse available from http://banchedati.chiesacattolica.it/pls/cci_new/BD_EDIT_DOC_TXT.edit_documento?p_id=12090&id_sessione=&pwd_sessione=, accessed 20.01.2017.

6 P. PASQUINI: *Vita da ex: Famiglie, divise e ricostruite*, Cinisello Balsamo: Edizioni San Paolo, 2005, 6.

7 B. PETRÀ: *Divorziati e risposati e seconde nozze nella Chiesa: Una via di Soluzione*, Assisi: Cittadella Editrice, 2012, 41. See also S. CACCIA (ed.): *La sfida di speranza oltre i fallimenti: L'attenzione pastorale alle famiglie in situazioni difficili e irregolari*, Atti della Scuola Diocesana per Operatori di Pastorale, Milano, febbraio-marzo 2003, Milan: Centro Ambrosiano, 2005.

manages to offer a fruitful environment where conversion and growth can happen. It becomes a community in pilgrimage, united by a profound solidarity, a reality at times experienced by the remarried divorced couples themselves.[8] Without this, they often experience loneliness and distance from the community, where they must confront pain, exhaustion, and difficulties alone.

It seems important to underline what kind of help those who work in family pastoral care are meant to give, remembering that "the word *pastoral*, before indicating *what to do*, suggests an attitude and a *way of being* within the social ecclesial context"[9] without hypocrisy and without superficiality. It is in this pastoral context, that sees attention to the person as the point of departure, that the new approach of *Amoris laetitia* is particularly relevant. We find in these experiences the face of a Church as a "field hospital" capable of embracing the existential margins of our time, capable of applying the balm of mercy to the wounds of the family, capable of opening new pathways and processes in order to accompany and integrate fragility as a common path where time plays an essential role.

Honoring the different levels of experience that are not definable in terms of objective law (which remains as a reference) means to involve the conscience, the real person. This involvement requires accompaniment, discernment, integration. One can say that accompaniment becomes in these journeys the condition of possibility to be able to discern and that discernment becomes the condition of possibility for integration into the ecclesial fabric. In some cases, the presence of divorced and remarried couples in diocesan pastoral structures has become an important sign of the need to work together, a reality that only a few years ago was unimaginable.

The Diocese of Bergamo offers an example where a center within diocesan territory has been established that can offer spiritual accompaniment and canonical advice for separated, divorced, and remarried faithful.[10] It shows that there were already in place for some time certain of the recommendations present in *Amoris laetitia*. Of course, a reality of this type can also be developed in a different way even within the same territory. It would not be a matter of creating closed groups

---

[8] See, for example E. ZANETTI (ed.): *Dopo l'inverno: Testimonianze, domande e messaggi di separati, divorziati o risposati che vivono nella Chiesa*, Milan: Ancora, 2005, and ID. (ed.): *Porte aperte: Accompagnare, discernere, integrare vissuti di separazione, divorzio, o nuova unione alla luce di Amoris Laetitia*, Milan: Ancora, 2016.

[9] G. GRANDIS/L. TOSONI: *Coniugi in crisi matrimoni in difficoltà: Teologia, magistero e pastorale si confrontano*, Cantalupa: Effatà, 2003, 100.

[10] The example of "La Casa" of the diocese of Bergamo is very interesting in that it now has been in existence for over twenty years and is integrated into the pastoral outreach of the diocese and of the region. It is an experience that has been reflected on and shared by all of those involved. The two books that reread and reflect on this journey shows how such an experience can be especially enriching as fertile ground for receiving the recommendations of *Amoris laetitia*.

but of developing experiences that are integrated into the family pastoral care of the diocese so that divorced and remarried couples can find in their own parish communities the possibility to live their Christian life in its fullness, seeking at the same time to help the community develop the right spirit and attention. To respond to these persons requires listening to them in their own situations without judgment, without marginalizing them, and making them feel a part of the community while at the same time keeping in mind that they find themselves in complex and at times problematic situations. A listening attitude puts priority on the needs of the faithful, seeing their needs and suggestions in the light of the Word of God and of the Church.

2.2 Accompany

2.2.1 Prayer

A pastoral outreach centered on prayer, moments of encounter with the Word of God, and with the invocation of its help are times of intense spirituality and interior revitalization in which all involved – priests, pastoral ministers, and the remarried divorced couples – can find a profound spiritual sharing. It offers a pathway of spirituality that invites even the priests of the area to participate. This offer of help becomes a reciprocal occasion of reception to the degree that each puts themselves at the service of the other. Those who live the reality of a reconstituted family with the satisfaction of a successful resolution also often have many questions regarding their proper position within the Church and before God. The challenge of letting oneself be illuminated by the Word together, going beyond attitudes of marginalization and recrimination, helps to allow the seeds of the good that are found already in the family life of these friends to mature. As the Synod Fathers wrote, and Pope Francis repeated, the "discernment of the presence of 'seeds of the Word' in other cultures (cf. *Ad Gentes* 11) can also apply to the reality of marriage and the family" (AL 77).

A powerful first form of accompaniment is thus that of prayer and meditation on the Word of God. Attention to how the people are welcomed is essential. It is the first open door in which the first steps of pastoral accompaniment take place. Whether a remarried divorced couple decides to enroll in a process offered by the local church depends to a great extent on the way in which they are welcomed by the church and the relationships that are established there. To be looked at, welcomed, and accompanied with love produces faith and hope and restores the dignity of these fragile ones who are always loved by the Father. It is important that these couples encounter in the pastoral workers the gaze of the Father that is far from that of a hooded judge but one that penetrates the heart with a love that establishes the possibility to find answers to questions. It is a gaze that meets the need to be loved that is especially important for those who feel themselves "far" from God. The goal is to offer places in which the couples can find a home so that their continuing journey of faith can allow them to discover little by little the will of God for them. Personal conscience is the place where the dialogue with God happens on this journey in the midst of questions and listening. These are essential steps for the maturing of the Christian conscience that can offer occasions of conversion and growth, a reconciliation with the couple's own history so that they can find pardon. They are given new eyes and new hearts that help them to better consider the choices before them so that they can better shape their own familial development.

2.2.2 Formation and Dialogue: The Process of Sharing

In addition to spiritual opportunities, it is important to offer a time for the narration of oneself and of one's own history, giving voice to one's own experience that is often characterized by suffering and disorientation. To look one's own reality in the face and re-describe what happened in one's own history helps the person to recover a confidence in oneself that is authentically Christian, based on one's own value in the eyes of God. It is important to create and cultivate a familial atmosphere and an assurance of confidentiality so that people can feel themselves taken care of. This requires time so that the roots of pain and existential fatigue can be brought to light. A healthy group atmosphere helps the experience of friendship and trust to develop.

A welcoming space that is friendly, attentive, and open in which couples share the experience of failed marriages and reconstituted families is indispensable in the process of rereading the couples' own lives in the light of the faith with others (pastoral workers) who wish to journey together with them for a serious re-elaboration of their own lived reality, past, present, and future. Listening enables dialogue in which one can be challenged and communicate one's opinions in love and truth. From this a real sharing emerges where one is engaged in and takes on the life of the other (a com-passion of joys and pains, of failures and hopes). One can then continue on the journey with the knowledge of one's own relational strengths and weaknesses, of wounds given and received, which can then help one to take charge of one's own life in this opportune time of accompaniment and discernment. To speak and to let oneself be spoken in a group helps the person regain balance in life. To be more aware of the present and one's own journey allows individual paths of healing to emerge, identifying what is essential to learning and overcoming that specific aspect of one's life.

The task of accompaniment is to move from crisis (an existential problem) to action (the spiritual/religious dimension), always keeping in mind not only two elements in tension – the capacity of the subject and the problematics of the situation – but also a third element: the revelation of God (the meaning of what it is to live in the logic of trust in God), retelling one's own story in another perspective and in the group context.

The task is to cultivate and develop within one's lived reality the desire to live one's life as promise of goodness and happiness, moving towards a completion that is made possible by the infinite Mystery that humans, finite creatures, can do nothing more than receive. The salvation that the Lord is making present emerges with more urgency and evidence when one experiences the dissolution of one's life project and has to rethink and relive life in a new family context. The goal is an accompaniment that seeks to listen, understand, and support in the midst of these existential problems, that at the same time holds to a deep sense of transcendence and hope that grace will transform lives through the various means the Lord has placed in the hands of the Church as instruments and places of growth. The Spirit asks that these means of grace be made available to these couples with intelligence and creativity so that they can experience a true encounter with the Lord, the only thing that can give back to them the hope and salvation that everyone seeks.

The first step is that of reconciliation and pardon with oneself and with others – the former spouse for example – and above all with God, from whom the person may feel distanced or completely alienated. Reconciliation is to be understood as a process of unmasking illusions, rationalized repressions, false concord, and self-defensive protections due to rigidity, pretense, and justified or unjustified reasons. This process produces unexpected fruits in the journey of faith and gives to the persons the possibility of development of new opportunities of seeing their life in a new way. Each person will emerge with different results according to their own stage in the journey.

2.3 Discern

Some decide to take up a process of discernment in order to understand their situation in an ecclesial and religious perspective (AL 300). Perhaps they have been advised by someone – a priest, a friend – or perhaps they have received informational material. In any case, they are moved by a desire, vague and confused at this point, to see their situation from an ecclesial point of view. Taking this first step is not easy and not everyone can do it. Each component is difficult: breaking the ice of one's own isolation, trusting someone when perhaps one feels marginalized and judged, overcoming a situation of resentment because the marital breakdown was an experience of abandonment, risking the judgment of others that the second union is "irregular".

Individual encounters are the first steps in discernment, and the central theme of the exhortation is that these initial encounters should be made in a climate of warm welcoming. The spiritual benefits of a warm welcome that makes one feel at home are felt by both the ones welcomed and the ones welcoming.

Usually, the initial reason for an appointment with church officials is to discuss the annulment of the first marriage. This requires a priest that is competent both relationally and canonically. The Church needs to offer this service in an efficient manner where investigations into the nullity of a previous union are integrated into the wider pastoral care dedicated to those who are separated, divorced, or remarried (see *Mitis Iudex*, 2-3, cited in AL 244). It is in any case necessary to recognize that the complexity of the existential issues cannot be resolved instantaneously by a case for nullity. The development of the proper human response to the separation and its relational consequences is a complex question that involves both this important step and a more extended process where time for healing is given so as not to repeat in the new union the same problems that arose in the previous one. Thus, the canonical evaluation becomes only one step, an important one, in the broader process of rethinking and reimagining one's own matrimonial existence. It is certainly not easy to separate the various dimensions within the complexity of the situation, whether they be existential, moral, spiritual, ecclesial, psychological, or canonical. For this reason, couples need to find themselves guided by persons that are both understanding and truly competent.

If the canonical evaluation results in a negative judgement, it is important that this is not the end of the church's engagement. The journey of growth and maturity is still necessary, and for this reason canonical instruments cannot be in any way detached from the broader pastoral care. It is a beginning in which knots that need to be untied emerge along with dissolutions that need to be confronted. What is needed is a discernment over time, with different means, different paths, accompanied by competent guides attentive to the individual and to their place in the community. Both individual and group processes are involved. The first steps with a spiritual guide supported by specialists (psychologists, counsellors) help to unfold the life context of the person in what they have accomplished and what remains to be done. Here recourse needs to be had to the spiritual aids necessary and possible (including sacramental ones), including accompaniment in the internal forum (cf. AL 300). The diocesan bishop is called upon in this sense to facilitate those who need to make use of this, providing contact with the appropriate persons so that such accompaniment can take place. This personal development should also be supported by group encounters in order to give further occasions for reflection, stimulate development, and offer steps that can be of use both spiritually and existentially. A positive interweaving of the personal and the group can enhance the process of discernment so that the possible good of each stage of growth by the person and by the couple can be promoted (cf. AL 308).

The situation of remarried divorced persons gives rise to particular pastoral needs, both in regard to the process itself and in regard to the discovery of how the couple can be inserted into the Christian community. The request of access to the sacraments often hides the need for a full acceptance of the couple's presence by the community and the request that the new love be affirmed and recognized. It is important to propose a dedicated but limited time for the process that can help the couples to take up a style of Christian life in and with their own parish community. Specific pastoral proposals should be "bridge experiences" towards a fruitful insertion into the local parish community.

Attention and welcoming define a style of familial relationship that responds to the deep desire to be accepted, to be in some way recognized as a couple (often the couples feel that their second union is the real matrimony). A new trust has been made in the possibility of love, a trust despite previous sufferings in the previous marriage. There is in them a renewed faith in the good and in happiness in a relationship that seriously opens itself to a life together in a new life project and that hopes for an ever-greater fullness. This is a love that lets itself be nourished by divine mercy, and a wise accompaniment by the Church can enrich the Christian community. In this pathway towards communion, the help of the sacraments as support and nourishment in situations of fragility and imperfection (cf. AL 305, note 351) seems to be the most promising context in which the local churches are called to identify concrete pastoral recommendations towards the promotion of these faith journeys for a full ecclesial integration.

2.4 Integrate

The logic of integration is the key to a pastoral accompaniment that is a joyful and fruitful ecclesial experience (cf. AL 299). The recommendations described above should be considered steps towards integration and should involve the parish community as a whole. All those in the parish are called to accompany the process of personal development by the couple. The local churches can take up these recommendations only if all those involved in the pastoral care of families are involved in an effort to form and inform parishes through meetings with pastoral councils, pastors, the distribution of informative materials, the publishing of articles in parish bulletins, and through involvement in the Sunday liturgies.

At the same time, the establishment of a service of welcoming and of information is essential to those who need to be listened to and encouraged. This is not a matter of providing a professional service. It is, rather, the case of giving essential responses and useful indications; such a service can be given by separated or divorced persons who give of their time for the Church. In this way, the divorced and remarried are also given value as ministers. Their "experience, language, way of approaching the situations and the individuals" become a valued resource for the welcoming of these "difficult family situations". They are, in a certain sense, "'wounded healers', who do not lose the memory of their experience of suffering but, rather, put it at the service of brothers and sisters in difficulty"[11]. This initial service should also be given by groups made up of people with different situations, and these should be put into contact with other regional entities present in the diocese, such as family counsellors.

The Jubilee Year of Mercy provided the opportunity of a process linked to the liturgical year in which discernment, integration, and reconciliation were linked with the theme of mercy in afternoon celebrations of listening to and reflection on the Word of God with opportunities for spiritual conversations with priests. This was an opportunity that allowed the participants to live the grace of the Jubilee by feeling themselves integrated into the ecclesial journey of mercy and conversion, a journey that continues for everyone.

3 Travelling Companions and Witnesses to the Love of God

Those who decide to take on this specific pastoral situation – at the diocesan level or in the individual parishes – should be evaluated in terms of their capabilities and their energy. The decision to involve oneself and enter into the sufferings of another springs from a generous heart, but if this is not supported by preparation, it does no good to anyone. At the same time, even though to help is difficult, the Church cannot delegate action only to the professionals and experts. Everyone can help according to their own interests and capacities. What is needed is that each person ask themselves at what level they can assist according to their own capabilities and preparation, and to focus on this. It is important to evaluate one's own professional qualifications on the one hand and on the other to assess the human qualities necessary to give help (it takes time to develop the capability to be present to another and be in relationship with them). It is important to have ample time for formation and for action in order to cultivate properly the relationship between knowledge, assessment, and action. A patient and constant work is thus necessary so that the person can be formed in the proper abilities to bring about the true change in the community such that it becomes the face of a mercy that is received and given.

---

[11] I. SIVIGLIA: "Da esistenze in frantumi a germogli per una vita buona", the conclusion of an address given at the above-mentioned conference in 2011 in Salsomaggiore: "Light of Hope for the Wounded Family: Separated, Married and Divorced Persons in the Christian Community", available from http://www.cpm-italia.it/index.php/famiglia-domani/articoli/124-giovani/478-da-esistenze-in-frantumi-a-germogli-per-una-vita-buona-ina-siviglia; accessed 20.01.2017. The quote references H.J. NOUWEN: *The Wounded Healer: Ministry in Contemporary Society*, New York: Doubleday, 1972.

Contributors

Monique Baujard was the Director of the Family and Society Service of the French Bishops' Conference from 2009-2015 and is currently a PhD student at Catholic University of Leuven.

Corinne Bernhard-Bitaud is president of the *Association Français des Foyers Mixtes Interconfessionnels Chrétiens* (Affmic) and the Protestant spouse in an interchurch marriage.

Elizabeth Davies was until December 2016 Marriage & Family Life Project Officer at the Catholic Bishops' Conference of England and Wales. Since January 2017 she works for the relationship education and counselling charity Catholic Marriage Care Ltd as Director of Volunteer Recruitment, Training and Formation.

Nadia Delicata is Lecturer in Fundamental Moral Theology and Christianity and Culture in the Department of Moral and Spiritual Theology, Faculty of Theology, University of Malta.

Christine Galea is a pastoral worker in the field of marriage and family ministry and a part-time Lecturer in Theology of Marriage and the Family at the Institute of Pastoral Formation of the Malta diocese.

Paul Galea is Associate Professor and Head of Department of Pastoral Theology at the Faculty of Theology of the University of Malta. He is a licensed clinical psychologist and ordained priest of the Archdiocese of Malta.

Arnaud Join-Lambert is Professor of Pastoral Theology and Liturgy at the *Université Catholique de Louvain*, Belgium.

Franz Harant is a parish priest and consultant in marriage, family, and life issues in the Diocese of Linz, Austria.

Michaela C. Hastetter is a Lecturer in Pastoral Theology at the International Theological Institute, Trumau, Austria, Visiting Professor at the *Philosophisch-Theologische Hochschule Benedikt XVI.*, Heiligenkreuz, Austria, and a Lecturer at the Albert-Ludwigs-Universität, Freiburg i. Br., Germany.

Stephanie Höllinger is a PhD student at the Department of Systematic Theology and Theological Ethics of the Catholic-Theological Faculty, University of Vienna, Austria. She is preparing a doctoral dissertation focusing on successful interactions in marriages and relationships with particular regard to excessively high expectations.

Peter Hünermann was Professor of Dogmatic Theology at the Catholic Theological Faculty of the University of Tübingen, Germany, until his retirement in 1997. He was the Founding President of the European Society for Catholic Theology and has been its Honorary President since 1995.

Thomas Knieps-Port le Roi holds the INTAMS Chair for the Study of Marriage & Spirituality at the Faculty of Theology and Religious Studies of the Catholic University of Leuven, Belgium.

Branislav Kuljovsky is a PhD student at the Faculty of Theology and Religious Studies, Catholic University of Leuven, preparing a doctoral dissertation on Joseph Ratzinger's conceptualization of the relationship between faith and culture.

Michael G. Lawler is the Amelia and Emil Graff Professor Emeritus of Catholic Theology at Creighton University.

Martin M. Lintner, OSM, is Professor for Moral Theology and Spiritual Theology at the *Philosophisch-Theologische Hochschule* in Brixen/Bressanone and Lecturer for Ethics at the Free University of Bozen-Bolzano (South Tyrol, Italy).

Reinhard Cardinal Marx is the Archbishop of Munich and Freising (Germany) and President of the German Bishops' Conference. Since 2012, he is President of COMECE and since 2013 a member of Pope Francis's Council of Cardinal Advisors.

Hilde Pex is coordinator of the Interdiocesan Council for Family Ministry in Flanders, and member of the steering group "Formation for permanent deacons" and "Training for pastoral workers" in the Archdiocese of Mechelen-Brussel.

Timothy Radcliffe, OP, is a friar of the English Province of the Order of Preachers. He was Master of the Dominican Order from 1992 to 2001.

Vincent Mynem C. Sagandoy is a diocesan priest of the Apostolic Vicariate of Bontoc-Lagawe, Philippines, and currently a PhD student in Canon Law at the Catholic University of Leuven.

Todd A. Salzman is the Amelia and Emil Graff Professor of Catholic Theology at Creighton University, Omaha, NE, USA.

Teresa Ventimiglia & Giordano Barioni are Coordinators of the National Service for Family Ministry of the Italian Bishops Conference.

George S. Worgul is Professor at the Department of Theology of Duquesne University, Pittsburgh, PA, USA.